The Armenians of Aintab

The Armenians *of* Aintab

The Economics of Genocide in an Ottoman Province

Ümit Kurt

Harvard University Press
Cambridge, Massachusetts
London, England
2021

Second printing

Library of Congress Cataloging-in-Publication Data

Names: Kurt, Ümit, author.
Title: The Armenians of Aintab : the economics of genocide in an Ottoman province / Ümit Kurt.
Description: Cambridge, Massachusetts : Harvard University Press, 2021. | Includes bibliographical references and index.
Identifiers: LCCN 2020044139 | ISBN 9780674247949 (cloth)
Subjects: LCSH: Armenians—Turkey—Gaziantep—History. | Armenian massacres, 1894–1896. | Abandonment of property—Turkey—Gaziantep. | Deportation—Turkey—Gaziantep—Citizen participation. | Gaziantep (Turkey)—Economic conditions. | Gaziantep (Turkey)—Politics and government.
Classification: LCC DR435.A7 K873 2021 | DDC 956.6/20154— dc23
LC record available at https://lccn.loc.gov/2020044139

To Hasan and Hanım

Contents

Tables

Preface

Following my graduation from Middle East Technical University in Ankara, I found myself again at my parents' house in my hometown of Gaziantep, formerly known as Aintab, where I escaped the stifling heat and passed the days dozing on the sofa. One day I was jarred from my nap by a call from an old friend: "Ümit, where have you been? It's been ages! I know a great place in Kayacık where we can catch up." Though I was born and raised in Aintab and hadn't left the city until college, the word "Kayacık" did not mean anything to me. It was just another district in the city, a neighborhood I had never visited, of which I knew nothing.

She said she would wait for me at Papirüs Café and gave me directions. I took a bus to the Kayacık neighborhood, and upon arrival found myself dazed by the charming atmosphere, letting myself get lost in the side streets, and leaving my poor friend waiting some more.

Embarrassed by my obliviousness, I found myself asking, "*Where am I? What is this place?*"

I was on a narrow street with beautifully constructed stone houses lining each side, taking me back to a simpler, though slightly mysterious, time. Tucked away between the high-rise concrete apartment buildings of "modernized" Gaziantep, this neighborhood was like an architectural mirage. I felt nostalgic for a past that was never mine.

Finally, I found Papirüs Café, which turned out to be located in one of those exotic houses. Like most of the houses on the street, it had been converted into a café as part of the process of "restoring" the city. Upon entering, a few letters carved at the top of the majestic gate caught my eye. Not recognizing the script, I simply assumed these were Ottoman characters.

Inside, I was once more left speechless. A spacious courtyard with staircases on either side leading up to two large rooms welcomed me. The rooms were filled with antique furnishings, and the high ceilings were adorned with frescos and engravings similar to Florentine cathedrals. The experience was a kind of historical voyeurism, like stepping into a living museum.

Feeling a surge of pride in my hometown and ancestors, I decided to talk to the owner to try to glean some information about the history of the house. I approached him, intending only to compliment his establishment, but before I could stop myself, I asked, "I was just wondering, from whom did you get this place? Who was here before you?"

He wearily explained that he inherited this place from his grandfather. It must have been especially strong coffee they were serving that day, as I was emboldened to press further. "And how about your grandfather? From whom did he buy this place?" The man paused hesitantly before responding. And then after a few moments, he softly murmured to the ground beneath him, "There were Armenians here." I asked, "What Armenians? What are you talking about? Were there Armenians in Gaziantep?" He nodded. I was getting annoyed with the opacity of his answers. "So, what happened to them? Where did they go?" He retorted indifferently: "They left."

As I rode the bus back home, I pondered why the Armenians—why anyone—would just leave and hand over such an exquisite property to someone. I was a naïve-to-the-point-of-ignorant twenty-two-year-old university graduate, unaware of the existence of Armenians in my hometown. A few years later, I would find out that the house belonged to Nazar Nazaretian, honorary consulate to Iran, who was a member of Aintab's wealthiest and most prominent family, and that he, his children, and his grandchildren used to live in this house. Those letters above the gate were not Ottoman but Armenian, spelling out the surname of Kara

Nazar Agha, who built the house. Years later, I would also have the chance to meet the youngest member of the family, Shusan, whose grandmother was deported at the age of one during the 1915 Armenian genocide. Shusan kindly spoke Turkish to me in Aintab dialect.

That building is no longer Papirüs Café for me. For me, it is the house of Kara Nazar Agha, the Nazaretians' home, the house where the grandmother of Shusan was born. Hence, for me, the houses in Kayacık are the homes of the Barsumians, Pirenians, Ashjians, Krajians, Leylekians, Jebejians, and Karamanougians.

In Turkish, there is a saying: "Mal sahibi, mülk sahibi, hani bunun ilk sahibi?" Roughly translated, it reads, "Landlord, property owner, where is the original owner?" This book is the story of the Aintab Armenians, who were torn away from their homes, neighborhoods, and the city where they were born and raised. This is the account of how their material and spatial wealth changed hands and was transformed. This is the historical record of their persecution and subsequent erasure.

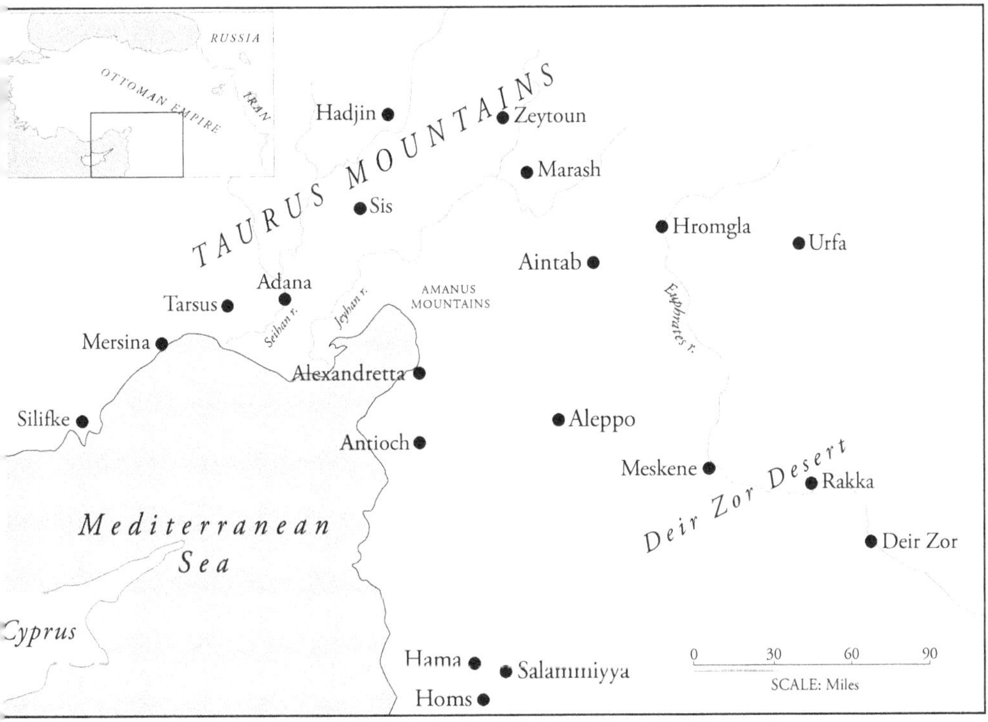

MAP 1 Cilicia region of the Late Ottoman Empire. © Ümit Kurt.

Original owner	*Present-day owner*
1. Otacı (eye-healer) Iskender's house	Kasım Ergül and Emine Türkhan
2. House of Armenian priest	Agricultural Bank
3. House of Leylekian family	Dündar Gürbüz, Esen Lütfiye Güç
4. Armenian house	Mehmet Hayri and Kifayet Sıvakcıgil
5. Armenian house	Osman Morcalı
6. Armenian house	Ökkeş Erkut
7. Barsumian house	Gaziantep Metropolitan Municipality
8. Armenian house	Gaziantep Provincial Special Administration
9. Armenian house	Gaziantep Provincial Special Administration
10. Avedis Jebejian house	Atatürk Culture Center
11. Garuj Karamanougian house	Hasan Süzer Ethnography Museum
12. Najarian house	Mehmet Yılmaz
13. House of Barsumian family	Yanç Family
14. Garuj Kurkchuian house	Ministry of Culture and Tourism
15. House of Jebejian family	Gaziantep Metropolitan Municipality
16. House of Barsumian family	Fazilet Çoruh and Fatma Ayberk
17. Sarkis Krajian house	İhsan Dai
18. House of Krajian family	İhsan Dai
19. House of Krajian family	İhsan Dai
20. House of Krajian family	Fatma Hilal
21. House of Krajian family	Sultan Çelik
22. House of Krajian family	İhsan Dai
23. House of Krajian family	Fatma Hilal
24. House of Krajian family	Serdar Doğu
25. House of Krajian family	Serdar Doğu
26. House of Krajian family	Serdar Doğu
27. Hadidian house	Cevdet Uyanık
28. Bulbulian house	Ali İhsan Ertütüncü
29. Armenian house	Mehmet and Ramazan Kar
30. Pirenian house	Ahmet Hurşit Dai
31. Pirenian house	Şaşmaz Family
32. Pirenian house	Ersoy Barak
33. Armenian house	Cuma Öztürkmen
34. Armenian house	Büyükbeşe Family
35. Nazaretian house	Doğan and Özdemir Families
36. Nazaretian house	Necati Gültekin
37. Nazaretian house	Kimya Family
38. Nazaretian house	Konukoğlu Foundation
39. Demirdjian house	Abdülkadir and Ali Şaşmaz
40. Armenian house	Abdullah Bakkaloğlu
41. Armenian house	Sait Kurt
42. Bedros Ashjian house	Yetkin Family
43. Armenian house	Mehmet Doğan Özgen
44. Armenian house	Durdu Kılıç
45. Armenian house	Çoşkun Uğurlu

CITY OF AINTAB

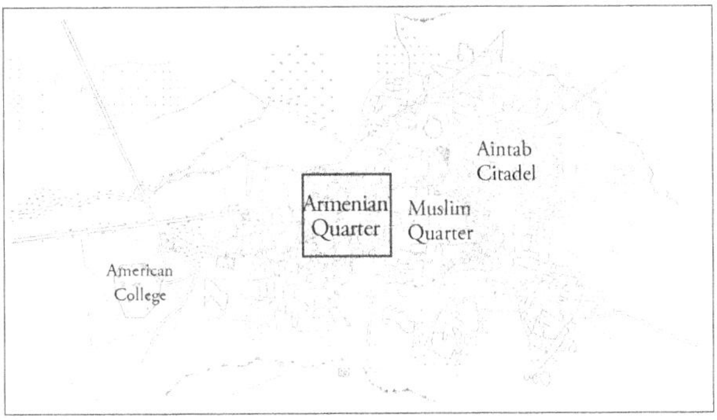

MAP 2 Sites and owners of confiscated Armenian properties in Gaziantep. © Ümit Kurt.

The Armenians of Aintab

Introduction

In his 1944 book *Axis Rule in Occupied Europe,* Raphaël Lemkin says that "genocide is composite and manifold, and that it signifies a coordinated plan of different actions aiming at the destruction of the essential foundations of life of a [specific] group."[1] Collective dispossession, including plunder and spoliation, is only one of the many crimes that accompany and even fortify genocidal policies—or perhaps better said, expropriation and pillaging are important aspects of the political economy of genocide. As Martin Dean, an authority on Nazi looting and plundering of Jewish property, remarkably underlines, "ethnic cleansing" and genocide usually have a "powerful materialist component: seizure of property, looting of the victims, and their economic displacement are intertwined with other motives for racial and interethnic violence and intensify their devastating effects."[2] In the case of the Armenian genocide, the state-orchestrated plunder of Armenian property immediately impoverished its victims; therefore, it was simultaneously a condition for and a consequence of the genocide.

The Armenians of the Ottoman Empire experienced calamity of the greatest degree during World War I. Many males, including youth, were executed outright, while the rest—men, women, children, and the elderly—were deported to barren lands in Iraq and Syria. Those deported were subjected to every manner of misery—kidnapping, rape, torture, murder, and death from exposure, starvation, and thirst—by every possible adversary—Ottoman gendarmes, Turkish and Kurdish irregulars, tribespeople, and the army. As Donald Bloxham emphasizes, those who escaped deportation, primarily women and children, were forced to convert to Islam, as Muslim identity was considered a cornerstone of the new nation-state, Turkey.[3] Principally perpetrated by the "Committee of Union and Progress" (*İttihad ve Terakki Cemiyeti;* hereafter CUP) elite, who largely controlled the Ottoman government at the time, these events constitute what we now know as the Armenian genocide. Cloaked under the guise of war, this violence surpassed the war crimes of Russia, Germany, and Austria-Hungary.[4] Through these policies and their mechanisms, the CUP achieved its goal of eliminating the "Armenian question" and establishing Anatolia as a "purified" homeland for those whom the CUP elite deemed the true Turkish peoples.[5]

The Ottoman Empire's participation in World War I included a major campaign aimed at eliminating certain minorities—first and foremost Armenians—depicted by the CUP regime and Muslim society as dangerous and treacherous domestic enemies. This campaign led Armenians to be subjected to wartime mass deportation, internment, total extermination, and expropriation. However, the Ottoman Empire was by no means the only state to take measures against its own citizens. Both Central and Allied Powers carried out brutal policies against domestic political suspects and enemy aliens during the years 1914–1918.[6] For example, Russia's campaign against its enemy citizens quickly widened in scope to include "the empire's large population of ethnic Germans to Russian-subject Jews, Muslims, and others."[7] Only in one state, according to Matthew Stippe, the Ottoman Empire, did this "'dynamic of destruction' get pushed as far as *genocide.* In others, including Austria-Hungary, the quest for military security had murderous, rather than genocidal consequences" (italics added).[8] Pursuing this global dynamic of violence during the Great War, the CUP campaign resulted in the forced displacement of more than a million civilians, the nationalization of a substantial portion of the imperial economy, and the transfer of extensive lands, assets, and properties from the targeted minorities (Armenians, Greeks, and Assyrians) to favored groups.

Historically, few governments formally took measures in times of war against their own subjects.[9] However, as Eric Lohr underscores, World

War I introduced systematic and brutal measures against enemy citizens and other civilians, measures that proliferated both during and after World War II.[10] One cornerstone of the wartime campaign against Armenians in the Ottoman Empire was the confiscation of their properties and wealth, which were subsequently transferred to Muslim elites and used in reshaping the domestic economy as well as covering wartime expenses. These were among the radical practices of the CUP regime aimed at nationalizing the economy. First, many businesses and properties were transferred to state institutions. Second, a lesser but substantial number of firms were transferred to "reliable" Muslim individuals and social institutions. More significant than the transfers themselves was the fact that these extraordinary measures belonged to a set of laws, regulations, rules, and decrees that created a legal basis for a more systematic campaign against the movable and immovable properties of Armenians.[11] In this capital transfer, we see that genocide also created the circumstances to enable "the complete fulfilment of the established policy of ethnic domination through expropriation."[12]

Economic dispossession was far from a process carried out "from above" by means of the simple execution of CUP orders. If the process of the economic exclusion of Armenians is to be described fully, a regional historical analysis is necessary. Not only will the fundamental features of regional anti-Armenian policy be examined, but decision-makers, local actors, provincial notables, and ordinary Muslims will be scrutinized in detail. In that sense, as Bloxham and Dirk Moses have suggested, "the matter of location tells us much about the political calculus underpinning genocide."[13]

In fact, to grasp the full implications of state-sponsored genocide, we must look at local atrocities and their long-term outcomes. I employ evidence and materials provided by "local protagonists, in the form of diaries, letters, eyewitness accounts, testimonies, interviews, and memoirs." As Omer Bartov and Eric Weitz have contended, "Only in this manner, the combination of standard state documentation with locally generated sources, can historians reconstruct local events in all their complexity and thereby gain more insight into the socio-psychological makeup of interethnic violence, its motivations, rationalizations, dynamics of perpetration, and subsequent narratives."[14]

Drawing upon primary sources from Armenian, Ottoman-Turkish, British, and French archives, as well as memoirs, personal papers, local newspapers, periodicals, testimonials, and oral accounts, this book explores how the process of genocide and deportation directed at the Armenians of Aintab—present-day Gaziantep, thirty-five miles west of the Euphrates and twenty-eight miles north of today's Turkish-Syrian border—was implemented. Shifting focus from state to society, thereby prioritizing the local roots of a genocide in the making, this work highlights the crucial role played by local elites and provincial notables, actors who prospered in the new social stratum through the acquisition of Armenian property and wealth. In this respect, I argue that the CUP genocide and deportation decision had a degree of social support through the practice of effective power and control mechanisms at the local level.

Influenced by renowned Holocaust scholar Frank Bajohr's *"Aryanization" in Hamburg* and Martin Dean's *Robbing the Jews,* this book treats Aintab as a microcosm to elucidate the confiscation and transfer of Armenian properties. This process was an essential component of the genocidal policy, and plunder was an influential incentive behind the support and involvement of local elites in the Armenian genocide.[15]

The sheer scale of actions constituting genocide could not be carried out by a single order from the central government. Therefore, local dynamics played an extremely important role in this destruction. This book provides a historical analysis of these dynamics, while paying attention to the political, ideological, social, and economic climate in Aintab—a crucially important town and district of the time. The book investigates local and regional dynamics, with a particular emphasis on the disintegration of social relations and the breakdown of social fabric in the city of Aintab, to contextualize the developments that led to the persecution, forced deportation, and mass murder of Armenians, and the dispossession of their property. As Hilmar Kaiser and Uğur Ümit Üngör successfully did in the case of Diyarbekir, I pay particular attention to the local dynamics of genocide—its political, social, and economic legacies, and the roles of local actors and civilian and military authorities—but this book distinguishes itself from those scholars' works by combining Armenian and Turkish documentation as well as employing unmined

Armenian and Turkish sources.[16] Doing so enables me to demonstrate the complex picture of not only the relations between central and local actors but also each group's internal relations. The book thus brings together analysis at the macro level (contextualizing the genocide in a global and national context), the meso level (revealing and discussing the activities of the various "middlemen" of violence—notables, mid-ranking officers, and tribal leaders), and finally the micro level (dissecting how the process unfolded in the various regional microcosms)—an approach that has been missing in the literature. The book also provides new insights on the causes and origins of genocidal policies and their impact in the making and remaking of provincial elites and, by extension, of the modern Turkish Republic.

Thus, the scope of the book is not limited to the sale and liquidation of Armenian properties; it treats confiscation as an all-encompassing displacement process whose political and social underpinnings and historical context must be considered in tandem. At the core of the book is a series of studies of the nationalization of state practices at the local level: the expropriation and liquidation of properties and businesses of Armenians; their forced mass deportations; and extermination. The book focuses on the origins and implementation of these practices in the city of Aintab.

As Jan T. Gross eloquently remarks, the participation of local populations is "a necessary condition to ensure the effectiveness of genocidal policies."[17] The CUP relied to a considerable extent on the cooperation of the local administrations and elites, political institutions, and ordinary citizens in Aintab. With this cooperation in mind, certain questions arise. How were the CUP and their local collaborators able to mobilize society? How did Armenian properties change hands? How did the distribution of properties establish an important degree of local complicity? Collaboration as well as tensions between central and local authorities in the course of the violent appropriation of large amounts of property, with or without the permission of the central and local authorities, are also examined.

If genocide, as a practice that includes murder and plunder, is orchestrated by a central authority but implemented at the local level, what is the relationship between local and central authorities? How can we explain the support of Muslim elites in encouraging and implementing the genocidal policies of the central authority—in the case of the Armenian genocide, the CUP? Did the CUP distribute Armenian property to Aintab gentry and its inhabitants in exchange for their support? If so, which institutions were involved? What kinds of laws, rules, and regulations did state authorities enact for the confiscation of Armenian property? These will be the guiding questions in this book.[18] They cut across a number of research areas in Ottoman and Middle Eastern history, some of which have been more thoroughly explored than others. A careful examination and analysis of these issues can tell us more about the implementation of the Armenian genocide and the significance of Armenian property in the context of the entire process of destruction.

The concept of local or provincial elites is central to my understanding of the elite-making process. The term "provincial elites"[19] is generally associated with *ayan,* notables who held a dominant place in the Ottoman provinces beginning in the late seventeenth century.[20] Political, social, and economic power was the defining feature of these provincial elites. Predominantly Muslim, not only did they include members of the military, the learned institutions (institutions dedicated to education), religious personnel, administrative staff, and artisans, but they also occasionally consisted of dervish sheikhs, women, and even non-Muslims.[21] As Antonis Anastasopoulos explains, they could "facilitate the implementation of government policies and guarantee relative order in the provinces"; in turn, "state acknowledgement or government appointment enhanced" these local notables' prestige and authority.[22] More modest families consisted of local notables with some political power. These ayan had "more in common with contemporary patriciates in Europe than the military magnates of the Ottoman realm."[23]

The participation of the local populace in robbing their Armenian neighbors is seen as the product of an increasing radicalization and loss of restraint resulting from the breakdown of social ties along ethnic, religious, and economic lines. I seek to scrutinize both the role of the local population as witnesses to the Armenian genocide and also the impact of the radical Turkish economic exploitation of the Armenians, which led to bitter social conflicts over scarce resources, contributing to this development in the case of Aintab. While official CUP policy intended for all Armenian property to be confiscated for the benefit of the Turkish administration, material rewards clearly acted as an incentive for collaboration at the regional level. Administrators recognized this motive and tolerated or encouraged it as they saw fit, often taking their own cut. Consequently, the Armenian genocide was much more complicated than the outcome of a simple top-down decision-making process in which the CUP leadership assigned, enforced, and oversaw exterminationist policies while local Muslims acted as passive, indifferent bystanders.

This book holds not only that the relationship between the central power and regional and local authorities was one-directional and hierarchical, but also that regional offices and the central authority mutually influenced each other. Jongerden and Verheij's poly-centricity and poly-activity theory, in *Social Relations in Ottoman Diyarbekir, 1870–1915*, is useful in understanding and explaining the dialectic, dynamic, and complicated structure of the relationship between the center and periphery.[24] With "poly-centricity," the authors refer to a "shift of attention from the so-called center to the so-called periphery," and with "poly-activity," "a move from an exclusive focus on the acts and deeds of the elite alone, to one that includes also those of multiple subaltern categories."[25] In a similar fashion, local actors in Aintab were not simply engaged in implementing orders or opposing them; these actors functioned as a structural element that was present throughout the process. Thus, beyond serving as intermediaries between the outside authority and the locals or patrons of the local populace, these local actors were an authority in their own right.

Following this conceptual framework, it can be claimed that as much as the Armenian genocide was a top-down process, it was equally led from the bottom up via a multitude of multifaceted relations between the central power and local authorities. Beyond any doubt, genocide and plunder were centrally planned, yet I argue that mass participation arose primarily from local incentives and motives. At the same time, one would not expect these motives to be unanimous or lacking nuance and change. They were both economic and social. On the economic side, the prospect of loot, for example, incentivized local collaborators to support massacres and deportations. Realizing the potential, the CUP leadership deliberately instrumentalized the promise of spoil and plunder to cajole public participation. The central government was well aware of the fact that provincial notables, local landowners and bigwigs, officials, and a range of other people with vested interests tried to take possession of Armenian wealth. These actors found themselves in a fortuitous position. Not only did their actions fulfill the ideological requirements of the regime, but these actions also brought material gain in the form of expropriated and pillaged Armenian properties. These factors in combination served to catalyze further the persecution of Armenians. Thus, a "reward mechanism" was created by which the CUP could draw political and social support for decisions to deport and massacre Armenians.[26] The profiteers justified their confiscation and seizure of Armenian wealth not as robbery or plunder but as fair reward for their participation in the elimination of "harmful and traitorous elements."[27] Beyond base greed, the fervor with which they executed the genocide on the local level must be understood in part as a result of the rationalization that they were acting in the service of the Ottoman state.

On the social side, it is important to consider the role of stolen and confiscated Armenian assets in the integration and consolidation of the process of "Turkification" or a Muslim-controlled *Milli İktisat* (National Economy).[28] The main purpose of "Turkification" was the dispossession of countless thousands of Armenians and their systematic removal from virtually every sector of the economy by transferring Armenian movable and immovable properties and businesses to "Turkish" hands.[29]

To date the literature has largely ignored the participation of many "ordinary" Muslims from manifold classes in the massacres of Armenians. Motivated in large part by material profit, the actions of these actors reflected the prevailing attitude of Turkish-Muslims, that of indifference and dispassion. One of the main tasks of my study is to explicate the economic and social atmosphere in Aintab, which allowed the local administrators, members of the Aintab gentry, and ordinary Muslims (Aintab's inhabitants) to radicalize their views and policies against the Armenians and to disclose how this atmosphere expedited the deportation. By focusing on Aintab, I hope to shed light on the origins of the property and wealth of Muslim elites, as well as the means by which properties of massacred and deported Armenians changed hands.

Aintab was a frontier city that lay at the crossroads of various states, cultures, and civilizations; and control of the city over its history changed hands among Muslims, Byzantines, and numerous crusading armies including the Mamluks and the Turcomans. The city, situated on a high and fertile plan to the east of the Taurus Mountains, has long served as a border between the Byzantine Empire and Arab Syria, beginning as early as the seventh century, and was incorporated in 1516 into Ottoman lands following Selim I's Syria campaign.[30] Armenians were some of the first residents of Aintab, having settled there in the sixteenth century. As we will see, at the turn of the nineteenth century, as the living conditions of Armenians improved considerably, the Muslims of Aintab developed a growing resentment toward their affluent Armenian neighbors, resulting in part from the Muslims' demoted status within the community. The Armenians experienced various positive social, political, sociocultural, and economic transformations in the second half of the nineteenth century. They undertook key intermediary roles in relation to the outside world mostly as a result of their language skills and their religious confraternity with the European powers. However, neither the Ottoman state nor the Muslim community welcomed these transformations, which led to an aggravation of ethnic divisions and brewing of local animosities. These underlying sentiments created a tense atmosphere, foreshadowing the storm to come in 1895. Yet this storm would pale in comparison to the events that would begin in 1915.

Agitation from the Armenian community for political reform and autonomy, boiling since the 1870s, was further intensified by large-scale massacres that occurred across the empire in 1894–1897 and in Cilicia in 1909; additionally, the more seemingly benign expressions of oppression and discrimination faced by Armenians, which had increased throughout the second half of the nineteenth century, also contributed to growing discontent.[31] Though they had already suffered grave injustices, the previous misfortunes of the Ottoman Armenians paled in comparison to the genocide of 1915–1916. As Bloxham notes, the massacres of the 1890s and genocide of 1915 differ in significant ways—notably in their motivations as well as in participation by centralized versus localized actors—but share a common time frame at the twilight of the Ottoman Empire.[32] Finally, the massacres of 1894–1897 themselves charted the course of what was to come, conditioning the mentality of both perpetrators and victims.

This study discloses the differences and discrepancies between the assumed impact of Young Turk policies on the Armenian-populated areas and the actual dynamics of the implementation of mass murder, genocide, and spoliation in these areas. Aside from the grave consequences, this analysis shows how Muslim elites and Aintab's inhabitants in the community at large benefited from the implementation of genocidal policies and what I call "the economy of plunder." There was, in other words, an explicit desire at the local level for the depredation of assets and property of the Armenian community, rather than solely the generally assumed ideological pressure emanating from the political center. My localized focus tackles the chronological complexities of the genocide, especially with respect to possible antecedents in the late nineteenth century and postgenocidal developments during the Turkish War of Independence (*İstiklâl Harbi*) of 1919–1922 and the early years of the Republic in the 1930s.

Accompanying the massacres, the confiscation and plunder process of Aintab Armenians' properties can be divided into three periods. In the first period—World War I—both the CUP itself as well as Muslim elites and ordinary Muslims pillaged Armenian wealth. In terms of the CUP policy regarding the removal of Armenians from the economy, a clear legal framework was required.[33] These laws and statutes came to be known as the *Emval-i Metruke Kanunları* (Abandoned Properties Laws).

In the second period—post–World War I (1918–1921), after the Ottoman defeat—the process of restitution commenced in the city but was later discontinued. In the Sykes-Picot Agreement, concluded secretly on 19 May 1916, France and Britain carved the Arab territories of the former Ottoman Empire into spheres of influence. Under Sykes-Picot, the Syrian coast and modern-day Lebanon was annexed by France and Britain took direct control of central and southern Mesopotamian territories. Based on this agreement and the seventh article of the Mudros Armistice from 30 October 1918, British forces occupied Aintab in December 1918. The primary and most urgent tasks of the British occupation forces were to facilitate the return of the Armenians to their homes, to restore their properties and assets, and to find and deliver Armenian women and children who had been held in Muslim households to their families or relatives. Armenian survivors started to return to their hometowns in December 1918, most immediately concerned with discerning how their movable and immovable properties would be returned to them. This issue of restitution of properties was of pressing importance for the Ottoman government; related orders were sent to localities, and necessary legal regulations were issued.

However, the British decided to cede the city to the French by signing the Syrian Agreement with the French government on 15 September 1919. According to this agreement, the French forces would replace the British in October 1919, a situation that disrupted the restoration process. Local authorities became reluctant to return the Armenian properties to the survivors, even if ordered to do so by the Ministry of Interior. Though houses were occasionally returned to their rightful owners, in most cases local authorities refused to evict the present occupants. Additionally, the rise of the Kemalist nationalist movement in the city in 1919–1920 put a halt to the restitution process.

In the face of French occupation, local nationalist-Kemalist forces instigated armed struggles against the French. Throughout the Turkish-French war in Aintab, which started on 1 April 1920 and ended with the Kemalist defeat and the city's surrender to the French military forces on 9 February 1921, the Armenians of Aintab allied with the French. Yet, despite their victory, the French ultimately decided to retreat from the city in February 1921, leaving it on 20 October 1921 to the Kemalist forces in accordance with the Treaty of Ankara.

In the third period (post-1921), with the total departure of the Armenians from Aintab, the confiscation and plunder process was completed. With new administrative and legal regulations implemented under the domestic laws following the Lausanne Treaty in 1924, and with other bilateral agreements signed between France and Turkey in 1926 and 1932 invalidating the return of properties, all movable and immovable assets of the Armenians who were forced to move to Aleppo and Beirut were appropriated. Armenian properties were mainly sold by auction to Aintab's local elites who participated in the Turkish-French war and who supported the national forces financially and logistically. These auctions were organized by the *Defterdarlık* (Internal Revenue Office) of the city and the local administration's initiative. This book provides a concise history of these three periods.

Abandoned Armenian Property

Much of the literature on the destruction of the Ottoman Armenians tells the story of a state captured by a radical party that enforced genocidal measures throughout the land.[34] Scholarship about genocidal activity at the local level, however—what social scientists would call "the periphery"—is still in its infancy.[35]

Despite the paramount importance of the property issue in the execution of the Armenian genocide and its aftermath, few studies to date have addressed the issue. Lut'fik Kuyumdjian's research, published from 1927 through 1933 in the General Almanac of *So'wrp P'rgich Hiwantano'c* (The Holy Savior Hospital of Istanbul),[36] is one of the earliest attempts to contemplate the significance of the subject of abandoned properties, discussing the laws and regulations promulgated during the Republican period. Haygazn Ghazarian studied the confiscation of Armenian properties by establishing an empirical foundation mostly derived from the eastern provinces of the Ottoman Empire.[37]

The first comprehensive study to scrutinize Ottoman and Turkish laws and regulations in relation to Armenian abandoned properties was undertaken by Levon Vartan.[38] In his pioneering work, Vartan examined the enforcement of legal instruments with respect to the abandoned properties of Ottoman Armenians. From another perspective, Kevork K. Baghdjian designated the confiscation of Armenian properties as a decisive process that was constitutive of what in due course followed it: the perpetration of the genocide in 1915.[39]

Dickran Kouymjian introduced an early categorization of expropriated properties, including gold, bank assets, insurance policies, immovable wealth, and inventories.[40] Kaiser's studies on the dispossession of Armenians have contrasted "the promises of the legal veneer and the actual events" that transpired on the ground.[41] He argued that no Ottoman law existed to keep the confiscation process within legal boundaries, nor did the Young Turk regime seem to have any interest whatsoever in safeguarding Ottoman Armenians' property.[42]

A more precise analysis by Taner Akçam indicated an overview of the demographics of the new owners of confiscated assets. Relying solely on Ottoman documents, he identified six types of recipients of the Armenian properties: Muslim immigrants, the Muslim bourgeoisie, the Ottoman army, the operational costs of conducting the Armenian deportation itself, the state's own infrastructure, and militia organizations.[43]

Bedross Der Matossian's work provides another perspective. He argued that "whereas the CUP confiscated Armenian property, the subsequent Kemalist movement gladly accepted the crime as *fait accompli* and could move towards appropriation" without obstacles; "this distinction between confiscation and appropriation is a matter of active versus passive expropriation."[44] Der Matossian discussed the fate of "Armenian capital" as an important component of the annihilation process of the Ottoman Armenians, approaching the confiscation of "Armenian capital" as a process thinly veiled under the guise of legality. Furthermore, he put forth questions to invite further research on the possible connections between this capital and the material foundations of the later Republican era.[45]

In *A Perfect Injustice: Genocide and Theft of Armenian Wealth*, Hrayr Karagueuzian and Yair Auron aimed to fill yet another hole in the existing literature, an academic void resultant from a lack of sufficient documentation of how and why the Young Turk government forcibly annexed Armenian life insurance policies. Their book provides an interesting but fragmented discussion that ultimately fails to expound on how the Armenian properties were transferred at the local level.[46]

Sait Çetinoğlu placed the expropriation of Armenians during the 1915 genocide in a much wider historical context and discussed the fate of Armenian properties through a linear historical understanding. He argued that the period of 1895–1955 (including the Hamidian massacres of 1895, the Adana massacres of 1909, the genocide of 1915, and the pogroms of 6–7 September 1955) brought the complete elimination of the economic life of the Armenians.[47] Nevzat Onaran's voluminous studies on the confiscation of Armenian and Greek properties offered a narrative account of the dispossession of these two Ottoman Christian groups and examined the entire body of legislation that had been passed by the Ottoman and Republican states.[48]

Claiming to be the first comprehensive study devoted to the mass sequestration of Armenian property during the genocide, Üngör and Mehmet Polatel's work detailed the emergence of Turkish economic nationalism and creation of a Turkish bourgeoisie,[49] offered insight into the economic results of the genocidal process, and described how the plunder was organized on the ground.[50] This important study relies on two interconnected concepts that played a pivotal role in the nationalization of Turkish economy: confiscation and colonization. By "confiscation," the authors mean "the involvement of an extensive bureaucratic apparatus that perpetuated a legal façade during the dispossession of Armenians." As for the concept of colonization, the authors refer to the redistribution of Armenian property to Muslims "as a form of internal colonization."[51] Additionally, the authors explored the interrelated nature of property confiscation carried in cooperation with the local elites within two provinces of the Empire, Adana and Diyarbekir.[52]

Anahid Astoian analyzed the factual history of Armenian expropriation throughout the Ottoman Empire in 1914–1923 based on archival documents as well as Armenian, Turkish, and other sources.[53] Oya Gözel Durmaz's dissertation constituted an exception within the existing literature regarding this topic. Her study distinctively illustrated how the Abandoned Properties Laws were implemented for Kayseri Armenians, while also bringing to light the active role of the local elites in the confiscation process of 1915–1918.[54] In her recent study, on the other hand, Ellinor Morack delved into how abandoned property and the discourses and practices surrounding its distribution were used for the creation of a Turkish bourgeoisie and the foundation and internal legitimization of a Turkish nation-state during the early Republican period.[55]

In *The Spirit of the Laws*, Taner Akçam and I directly focused on the legal framework of the abandoned properties and, in particular, provided information on the Lausanne and post-Lausanne periods.[56] We also examined the confiscation of Armenian properties during the genocide and subsequent attempts to retain seized Armenian wealth. Through close analysis of laws and treaties, we revealed that decrees issued during the genocide constituted central pillars of the Turkish system of property rights, retaining their legal validity; although Turkey has consented through international agreements to return Armenian properties, it has continued to refuse to do so. The book demonstrated that genocides did not depend on the abolition of the legal system and elimination of rights; on the contrary, the perpetrators of genocide manipulated the legal system to facilitate their plans. While a few studies touch upon this issue, they do not primarily address the topic.[57]

These noteworthy studies share one major drawback: insufficient use of primary and secondary Armenian materials. The scholarship on the Armenian genocide in general and economics of genocide in particular lacks focus on the local or micro level and the Ottoman periphery, in part as a result of the absence of Armenian sources. This book includes the confiscation, liquidation, and plunder process as an integral element of the entire destruction system within a particular region, using Armenian and Turkish as well as Western sources to analyze and document with specificity the liquidation of Armenian movable and immovable properties. The book demonstrates how the Abandoned Properties and Liquidation Commissions carried out Abandoned Properties Laws and performed transactions on the wealth of deported Armenians, including the newly unearthed report and records of the Aintab Liquidation Commission that clearly reveal how "the economy of plunder" created intersecting political or ideological and material interests among the local collaborators.

While there are a number of existing books regarding the history of Aintab Armenians, almost none contains studies on property issues or describes in rich detail the social, economic, and political lives of the various ethnic-religious groups living in the area, as well as the relations among them.[58] My work fills this gap by dealing closely with the problems specific to the origins of property and wealth of the Aintab gentry.

The objectives outlined here can hardly be met given the present state of research. There is no lack of regional histories of the persecution of Armenians under the CUP regime, but the economic expropriation of the Armenians and economic "Turkification" for the most part appear only marginally. Most local and regional studies limit themselves to a summary overview; though they contain useful strands of information, they cannot stand in for a comprehensive investigation. Even today, little is known about the destruction of Armenian economic and material power in centers of Armenian life in the Ottoman Empire. I see this book as both a foundation for such work at a regional level and also a stimulus for further comparative research.

The core of this study focuses on the 1915–1916 period, with chapters detailing the late nineteenth century through 1914, as well as a legal and an economic overview of 1920–1923 and the early Republican years. Chapter 1 explores the massacres of 1895 in Aintab, examining why and how the anti-Armenian violence took place and how two communities—Armenian and Muslim—that lived in relative harmony until the last quarter of the nineteenth century began to clash with each other on ethnic grounds. The chapter aims to investigate the process through which ties between the two ethno-religious communities turned hostile—how and why this atmosphere was transformed into a series of violent and panic-stricken events. The principal question I raise here is how a region that had not experienced any significant level of sustained, systemic, or intercommunity violence until the turn of the nineteenth century became a region synonymous with ethnic conflict.[59] Most prominently, my attention is focused on how the events revolving around the Aintab Armenian massacres unfolded. The Hamidian massacres clearly demonstrated that when specific circumstances would present themselves in the coming years, the relations between these two ethno-religious communities could rapidly gain a violent character.

The southeastern Ottoman provinces of Greater Cilicia were—much like the rest of the Empire—composed of manifold ethnic groups, as was the case for the Aintab district within the Aleppo province. Christians and Muslims seemed to live together harmoniously but both knew that the latter had the upper hand in an imperial-monarchical structure. Yet, beginning in the second half of the nineteenth century, the Armenians of Aintab went through various social, political, sociocultural, and economic changes. These changes became evident in several areas: economy, trade, education, and religious institutions. Advancement of the Aintab Armenian population in all these areas altered the imperial hierarchical context. I analyze how this multifaceted change culminated in the disintegration of social relations and violence.

In Chapter 2, I first examine how the tense relations between the two communities further went amiss with July 1908's restitution of the 1876 *Kânûn-ı Esâsî* (the first Ottoman Constitution) by a new generation of leaders, the CUP. With a bloodless revolution, empire-wide elections, and the reintroduction of the Parliament in 1908, "the Ottoman Empire had, it seemed, transformed itself into a liberal, constitutional monarchy."[60] Subsequently, I explain how the news of the April 1909 Adana massacres was received in Aintab. This chapter also explores the nature of the relationship between Armenians and Muslims before World War I to understand whether the ideal of *Ittihad-ı Anasır*, an Ottomanist unity (Ottomanism), actually existed following the restoration of the constitution. Additionally, I address the impact of the Young Turk Revolution on the Armenians of Aintab, the sociopolitical structure of ethnic groups, the sociopolitical power dynamics between them, the political attitudes of both the government and the ethnic groups toward each other, and Muslim and Armenian perceptions of the constitutional era.[61] I elucidate why a powerful escalation of ethnic tensions as a result of ethnic politics appearing in the first year of the constitutional period erupted in a counterrevolution and why an incident similar to the Adana massacres of 1909 did *not* occur in Aintab, as well as identifying and analyzing the factors and processes that led to restraint.

Since Aintab Armenians were no longer as defenseless and unorganized as they had been in November 1895, they were not subjected to the killing and looting that erupted in Adana. Relatively speaking, there was a period of peaceful though tenuous coexistence in Aintab. Because of its fragility, Armenians had fortified themselves in the Armenian neighborhoods and protected these neighborhoods against any mob attack.

My findings demonstrate that the attitudes of Muslim inhabitants and administrators, as well as the firm stance of local CUP rulers, prevented the possibility of a new upheaval.

"Union and progress" and "liberty, justice, and brotherhood" were the mantras of the Young Turk revolution. These major pillars of the revolution were emphasized in many postcards and placards thanks to the birth of a lively press within the empire. However, as Mustafa Aksakal remarks, the years that followed the revolution were also marked by "deep crises of internal violence, including the massacre of 20,000 Armenians in the Adana region in 1909, wars in North Africa and the Balkans in 1911–13, and continued financial insecurity."[62] Lastly, in the context of the Balkan Wars, the CUP attained absolute power politically and administratively in 1913 and controlled the state apparatus over the course of the war years. I end up by tracing the policies of the Young Turks that plunged them into the war and genocidal acts.

Chapter 3 describes and attempts to explain the mass violence that was inflicted upon the Ottoman Armenians in the Aintab district during World War I. The chapter explores the persecution of Armenians and how that process evolved into genocide. The chapter analyzes the extant political and social context, which radicalized the views of local authorities, provincial elites, and ordinary Muslims regarding Armenians and paved the way for the deportations. I assess how the behavior of local elites affected the genocidal process and how they interpreted, organized, and intensified the destruction of Armenians. The decision-making processes and policies of the Ottoman central government and its regional as well as local representatives against Armenians will also be discussed.

Additionally, it is important to investigate the path taken from the decision to deport to actual massacre. Deportation and extermination are not the same, though a number of similar historical situations have demonstrated that one can easily lead to the other under ripe conditions. Hardly planned from the outset, genocidal spasms and their related events were fostered by certain situational dynamics.[63] One thing gave rise to another as actors calculated their next steps in response to previous actions and decisions that had been unplanned. The momentum of events frequently led participants to find themselves in situations they had not envisioned. Thus, genocidal motives did not prefigure any actual genocidal design, intent, or target.[64] No genocide is an "*a priori* given." Further, human agency in genocidal processes "depends on forces that often go beyond any sense of rational action."[65] Hence, genocides are not inevitable events; to the contrary, as Yektan Türkyılmaz stresses, a genocidal process has its own specific spatial, temporal, and political dynamics, as well as potential discontinuities. It is precisely these local situational and structural dynamics and contexts that can both explain and give rise to genocides. The orders and policies of the center constitute only one side of the story of the deportation process in Aintab; equally important is the implementation of these orders and policies.

Therefore, as Üngör and Kaiser have, independently, suggested in the case of Diyarbekir, it is essential to explore how local elites established, preserved, and broadened their control over Aintab. To reveal the dynamics that shaped the annihilation, I illustrate the local power structures, focusing on the deeds of Ali Cenani,[66] a CUP parliamentary deputy from Aintab, and Ahmed Faik (Erner),[67] the *mutasarrıf* (district governor) of Aintab. Through this approach, I hope to capture the complexity of processes governing mass violence.

Chapter 4 has two sections. The first fundamentally examines the Abandoned Properties Laws. In doing so, I also document the expropriation process of Armenian properties that changed hands under the veneer of legality. Properties belonging to Ottoman Armenians were seized through various laws, decrees, and other legal regulations passed by the CUP government and later the cadres of the Republican regime. Both governments concocted ways of making this illegal process look legitimate under the veil of the law. Central to this process were the economic outcomes of violence committed against Armenians. Principally, what "economic violence" refers to here is the appropriation of movable and immovable properties and assets left behind by the deported Armenians. The process was abetted by the legal system, through which an entire community was reduced to the status of nonexistence. A similar process took place in the Third Reich and various European countries invaded by Hitler's army (the *Wehrmacht*). All the appropriated wealth and proceeds from the Jews were transferred to the treasury of Nazi Germany through the appropriation of law and the extension of legal boundaries. As a result, Germany was able to finance its war. These resources were distributed among central and local actors that supported the regime as well as various social classes that belonged to the Aryan race.[68]

By the same token, after the CUP issued the decision for deportations, Ottoman Armenian citizens were prohibited from selling, renting, or transferring their properties. Thus, the state systematically managed to confiscate these assets, and highly detailed laws were prepared regarding how these properties would be appropriated. This whole process was put into action by commissions established by the CUP government. These commissions were called Abandoned Properties Commissions and Abandoned Properties Liquidation Commissions. Through the laws and regulations issued during the period of the CUP government, an intricately detailed action plan was presented regarding what was to be done with the properties left by the Armenians, but no legal arrangements were introduced regarding the values of these properties that were supposed to be returned.

The second section details how these regulations were executed specifically with the Armenians of Aintab in mind, concentrating on the appropriation of Armenian abandoned properties. I investigate what happened to these properties primarily by using Armenian sources and other archival materials. This chapter presents a unique report of the Aintab Liquidation Commission—previously undiscovered—that documents the liquidation process on the ground. It is the first of its kind in demonstrating how numerous government officials and other individuals from different classes (particularly Aintab Muslim elites)—including property assessors, auction houses, trustees, estate agents, notaries, and transport companies—were employed to manage the administration and sale of Armenian assets through the Abandoned Properties Laws.

Additionally, I review a number of documents from the Ottoman archives that show that laws and decrees passed in the period of 1915–1918 constituted the basic components of the extermination process. Hence, these laws and decrees could be regarded as the most important legal documents of the Republican era. Furthermore, I extensively use coded telegrams sent by the Ministry of Interior, particularly telegrams dispatched to Aleppo regarding abandoned properties, as Aintab was located in the province of Aleppo.[69] The relationships between the CUP, local merchants, and local officials who participated in the despoliation and distribution process of properties are illustrated.

Chapter 5, also consisting of two sections, focuses on the period between 1918 and 1920. One section discusses the legislation that came into effect regarding Armenian survivors who returned and demanded the restoration of their assets following the end of the war, after the Ottoman Empire signed the Mudros Armistice on 30 October 1918. The second section specifically explores the return of Aintab Armenians and reveals the process for the restitution of their properties. In this period between 1918 and 1920, the most complicated topic was the restitution of abandoned properties to the survivors, as their properties had already been liquidated.

After Kemalist forces came into power in Aintab in December 1921, the dispossession of Armenians who were forced to migrate to Syria and Lebanon en masse between 1921 and 1922 continued. In Chapter 6, my main focus is to elucidate how Aintab Armenians' properties and assets were used after their absolute departure. Having flourished between 1915 and 1918, the city's newly emerging wealthy Turkish-Muslim class consolidated its economic status by seizing these properties, with the complete departure of the Armenians in 1921–1922. This chapter provides a unique systematic analysis that demonstrates how properties were used for various purposes by the central government, local municipality, and Aintab Muslim elites, and how they were sold at auction and distributed in accordance with the orders of Mustafa Kemal himself, founding father of modern Turkey.

Additionally, I discuss how Armenian properties were expropriated through a series of domestic laws, rules, and regulations, and a complex legislative framework prior to the promulgation of the Lausanne Treaty on 6 August 1924 and mutual agreements signed between France and Turkey in 1926 and 1932. In order to come to an agreement with Turkey, France rescinded its claims for some combination of the return of or compensation for the properties of Armenians who had acquired Syrian or Lebanese citizenship, leaving Armenians isolated on the international stage.

The practice of selling Armenian assets, including shops, estates, and houses in different neighborhoods, at auction to Muslims at very low prices continued through the 1930s and 1940s. The Muslims who acquired these immovable properties became rich, creating the base of what would become the urban bourgeoisie of Aintab in the 1960s and 1970s. Today, the majority of these Muslims still retain these assets at their disposal.

The Sources Problem

The existing research on violence in the Ottoman Empire suffers from an important methodological problem: the lack of sources from ethnic groups subjected to violence. Some works reconstruct the history of violence solely through the prism of the Ottoman archives, while others rely only on European sources; both are deficient in terms of Armenian sources. Using sources from as many of the parties involved as possible provides us with a better understanding of the factors that led to the eruption of violence in the region and its culmination in the massacres.[70]

It is evident that there are neither sufficient studies that draw upon Armenian, Ottoman-Turkish, French, British, and Turkish archival sources nor ample research within the literature focusing on one particular province or district. The scope of books on the history of Aintab is rather narrow, relying entirely on a nationalist narrative grounded in the sources of the proponents of this nationalist narrative. The main problem is the absence of a comparative analysis of existing archival documents. Within this context, it is easy to understand the difficulty in conducting studies on the seizure and plunder of Armenian wealth at the local level.

To compensate for the gaps in the literature, this book is based principally on archival documents and primary and secondary sources in Armenian, Ottoman-Turkish, English, French, and modern Turkish languages. These include correspondence and reports of state authorities, periodicals, local newspapers, and personal documents such as letters, memoirs, personal papers, and oral testimonies, scattered in archives in

Armenia, Turkey, Lebanon, France, England, and the United States. This study also uses a wealth of untapped local archival sources in Gaziantep, including the private archive of Mahmut Oğuz Göğüş. However, Armenian materials are most central to the work.

Many of these documents, introduced to scholarly discussions for the first time, allow for an in-depth examination of the period spanning the 1890s all the way up to the 1940s. They provide for an integrated historical narrative that takes into consideration the rapid changes seen in institutions such as the military, political elite, and local community, as experienced by the inhabitants of Aintab in the first quarter of the twentieth century. Accounts of the perpetrators (local elites) and of the victims are integrated with accounts from third parties to reveal in full the plunder and murder of the Armenians of Aintab.

One caveat must be given: the *Emval-i Metruke Tasfiye Komisyonu Defterleri* (The Principal Record Book and Record Book of Current Accounts from the records of the Liquidation Commissions), as well as the archives of *Tapu ve Kadastro* (Land Registry and Cadaster), are inaccessible in Turkey. Two circulars of the General Directorate of Land Registry and Cadaster were issued in 1983 and 2000, stipulating that deported Armenians and their heirs were prohibited from accessing any information regarding the fate of their properties or disclosing the identities of those who acquired the properties. Since the Turkish state itself utilized and benefited from Armenian properties, dissemination of information and of documents concerning this issue has been regarded as a threat to the national security of Turkey. The Turkish National Security Council found the transfer of land records covering the 1915 period from the Land Registry Archives to the Prime Ministry Archives against the interests of the state and prohibited researchers from accessing these records starting in 2006.[71]

Without access to these books and records, the liquidation of the abandoned properties cannot be fully understood. Only the documents in the Land Registry and Cadaster Archives, the record books of the abandoned properties, and records of the Liquidation Commissions can provide detailed accounts of the distribution of confiscated houses, workshops, and movable properties, as well as auctions of property in Aintab. Nevertheless, the documentation of the liquidation of Sarkis

Yacoubian's properties detailed in Chapter 4 is an attempt to overcome this problem and unveil records that belonged to the Aintab Liquidation Commission.

As Lemkin points out, genocide is a process not only of destruction but also of construction. By the time genocide perpetrators are destroying one group, they are also constructing another group or identity. Expropriation is one of the most indispensable and effective mechanisms for perpetrators to realize the process of destruction and construction. Therefore, the entire process of expropriation can be construed as both an ideological principle and economic motivation. These two aspects cannot be separated from each other. The ideological principle was hugely supported and complemented by economic motivation and material stakes. In some instances, ideology played a more significant role than economic motivation, and in other instances economic interests came into prominence vis-à-vis ideology. These two parameters, as important aspects of the political economy of the Armenian genocide, were implemented and constituted dynamic and effective mechanisms in the confiscation, plunder, and seizure of Armenian material wealth.

The CUP deported the Armenians for various reasons, and while deporting them promised that the government would look after their properties and give them their equivalent values in the new places where they would be resettled. All the promulgated laws and regulations repeated that the Armenians were the true owners of their properties and that the state undertook their administration only in the name of the owners. However, the entire legal system was based on deception and a fiction of caring for Armenian wealth and assets. In reality, these laws and regulations were used to eliminate both the material and physical existence of the Armenians in Anatolia. The same practice continued in the Republican era. The Armenians' right to the properties they left behind was repeated in the international treaties signed during this period. Turkey promised to give back properties to owners who as of 6 August 1924 were at their properties. Afterward, Turkey's borders were fortified, and not even one Armenian was able to enter the country.

The Armenians not allowed back were declared to be *fugitive* and *missing,* and the process of confiscation of their properties continued. Furthermore, as all this occurred in the Ottoman and Republican periods, it was not and could not be said that the Armenians had no rights to their properties. Legislation held that the Armenians possessed rights to their properties—if properties could not be returned, their equivalent values were supposed to be paid—but that same legislation was used simultaneously to prevent restitution. The goal was to completely remove the Armenian presence in Anatolia. What was occurring was a legal operation of theft. The use of the legal system was both an attempt to deny and legitimate the Armenian genocide under the cover of legality. The law was used to provide a legitimation of what was an act of power and destruction.

As in most of Asia Minor, the physical removal of Armenians to the Syrian deserts proved decisive in separating them from their property, because it was clear they were not meant to return. The confiscation and sequestration of Armenian properties were not just politically complex but also involved an economic process. The expropriation of Armenian wealth in the Ottoman Empire clearly evinces how an essentially ideological process came to incorporate highly diverse motivations and interests, especially material ones. These then contributed to a progressive and deepening radicalization of the whole process.

·1·

The 1895 Massacres in Aintab

The bulk of existing studies view the outbreak of mass violence in the Ottoman Empire as a by-product of the imperial collapse and subsequent invasion by Western powers that took place in the aftermath of World War I. Yet this process can be traced back to the period of the *Tanzimat* (Edict of Gülhane of 1839) and *Islahat* (Ottoman Reform Edict of 1856) reforms of the nineteenth century. The aim of the reforms was to eliminate the imperial hierarchy that institutionalized discrimination between Muslim and non-Muslim (Christian and Jewish) communities, laying the groundwork for the equal citizenship law that would come into force following the promulgation of the Ottoman Constitution of 1876.[1] The reforms were fiercely contested by the Muslim community, which perceived them as a direct threat to their social and economic status.[2] Central actors in this response were factions of ayans (local Muslim dignitaries wielding administrative authority), tribal leaders, and landowners on one side and Christian nationalists on the other. Muslim clergy as well as local elites, especially in eastern Anatolia and Cilicia, were also influential in this process.

In eastern Anatolia, outside the major towns, "central government control was mostly nominal. The countryside was dominated by shifting groups of local notables, insurgents, semi-nomadic Kurdish and Turkmen tribes."[3] Reactions were particularly fierce in borderland and religiously mixed areas such as Kosovo, Trans-Jordan, Albania, and the Kurdish tribal zones. Such reactions served to stall reforms in these borderlands, where the Tanzimat and the Islahat were effectively dead on arrival. Yet, disenchantment with these reforms was not only a matter of bigotry. The nineteenth century was, for the Empire, a period of immense territorial loss and painful separatist movements. The Ottoman government, engrossed in European politics with the 1856 Treaty of Paris and seeking to preserve its integrity, attempted to gauge the shifting tides of international political balances yet suffered a vast loss of power. This era also saw the emergence of Greek independence; French control of Tunisia; British control of Egypt and Cyprus; and the Empire's loss of Bessarabia, Serbia, Abaza, and Mingrelia. The shrinking of territory persisted, with Crete in 1908, Libya and Tripoli in 1912, and Macedonia and Albania in 1913.

These developments had a profound effect on Ottoman society. Military defeat produced successive waves of migration and resettlement. The mass exodus of Muslim refugees fleeing the Crimean War (and intensified by the 1877–1878 Russo-Turkish War), the Russian annexation of Kars, Ardahan, and Batumi, and the nascent Balkan nations (born of the 1878 Treaty of San Stefano) exacerbated grievances against the Armenians and other Christian populations, as these refugees had suffered greatly at the hands of Christian regimes. The European powers, however, quickly grew wary of the treaty, which emboldened Russia in the Balkans and eastern Anatolia. Hence, the treaty was allowed to collapse shortly after its signing, and the European powers convened in Berlin in 1878 to produce a new agreement that would be more advantageous for the Ottomans. Macedonia and eastern Thrace reverted to Ottoman control, the nascent Bulgaria was reduced in size, and the Ottomans retained control of the Dardanelles and the Bosporus Straits, with an understanding of their unimpeded control of maritime trade.[4]

Nonetheless, the new agreement failed to dispel anxieties within the Ottoman administration, especially regarding the status of the Armenian communities. The treaty included reforms but contained no provisions on foreign enforcement mechanisms, and Ottoman authorities feared Article 61 (explained in the following pages) could be used as grounds for Armenian secession.[5] The distrust the Ottomans felt for the Christian citizens of the Empire prior to the Berlin treaty deepened into a conviction that the non-Muslims sought to collude with foreign adversaries in order to bring about the state's downfall. The Great Powers, with an eye on Russia, further stoked Ottoman paranoia of a subversive Christian movement, leading to the Ottoman Empire further imperiling the Christian groups for whom the Europeans had previously shown concern.[6]

Making matters worse for the Armenians, the Ottoman state encouraged displaced Muslim citizens to settle in Armenian-populated regions, heightening security concerns for Armenian communities.[7] This combination of defeat, out-migration, and belated efforts toward institutional modernization via reforms exposed and exacerbated the religious polarization occurring in the Ottoman Empire. Such feelings were intensified by the rapid social and economic changes that were taking place within the state and society. The nineteenth century was a period of steady demographic decline and diminishing social mobility for the Muslim population. In many areas, commerce, agriculture, and industry passed into the hands of an emerging Christian elite that benefited from foreign power intervention, the Empire's gradual entrance into European economies, and a newfound sense of collective ethnic identity among the Ottoman Christians.

Ethno-religious disputes coalesced in this context. For the Armenians and other Ottoman Christians, these developments elevated their grievances, without the implementation of reforms; for the Ottoman statesmen, they led to a growing suspicion of the Ottoman Christians because of their sudden international prominence. The Ottoman Christian question thus emerged as the amalgamation of issues of territory, agriculture, demographics, and an incipient collective consciousness. The unrest caused by the Tanzimat reforms, military defeats, and weakening of the government's control over more distant reaches of the Empire compelled a stronger state response during the reign of Abdülhamid II. In such a heightened political atmosphere, ethno-religious relations deteriorated in the decades preceding the massacres of the 1890s.

The breakdown in Muslim-Christian relations was not limited to Anatolia; intercommunal violence broke out in numerous provinces. In 1860, intercommunal tension between the Maronite and the Druze communities of Mount Lebanon resulted in violence and massacres.

Such incidents were no less conspicuous in the Balkans, including the April 1876 uprising in Bulgaria and the Cretan revolts of 1866–1869 and 1894. In 1894–1897, the predominantly Kurdish and Armenian eastern provinces of the Ottoman Empire witnessed the massacre of the Armenian population. In 1909, shortly after the Constitutional Revolution of 1908, the Armenian population of Adana endured pogroms and massacres. In 1912–1913, the Balkan Wars resulted in a diminution of the Muslim population caused not only by forced migration, starvation, and disease but also by mass killings committed by Bulgaria, Greece, and Serbia. With the commencement of the Armenian genocide in 1915, the ruling CUP took a drastic step toward one of its long-standing goals—the Turkification of Anatolia. This series of state-initiated persecutions and intercommunal violence continued throughout the post-Ottoman Middle East, with ruthless policies carried out by newly established nation-states.

The overall Ottoman state decline, changes in landownership laws benefiting Christians (specifically, the Land Code of 1858, which transformed use rights on land into exclusionary land rights),[8] the increase of a sense of "relative deprivation" among Muslims,[9] *muhajir*-immigration, the "second Ottoman invasion of Kurdistan" throughout the 1830s and 1840s (which constituted a state attack on the effectively sovereign Kurdish regions in eastern Anatolia),[10] "modernizing" policies that disaffected Muslims, along with the legacies of the Treaty of Berlin in 1878 and the Treaty of Paris in 1856, all contributed to a sense that external powers were working clandestinely with Christian minorities. It was the totality of these grievances that made possible the coming massacres in Aintab.

The eastern provinces of the Ottoman Empire became the primary site of a series of massacres of Armenians between 1894 and 1897. These killings centered initially in the urban centers of the six *vilayets* (provinces) of Sivas, Erzurum, Ma'muretü'l-aziz, Diyarbekir, Bitlis, and Van—where the great majority of Ottoman Armenians lived—but spread after November 1895 not only to rural districts but to western and southern

Anatolia. Violence claimed the lives of hundreds of thousands under the last significant sultan, Abdülhamid II. Tens of thousands converted to Islam to escape death, and tens of thousands fled to the Russian Empire. Thousands of Armenian women and girls were abducted and forced into marriage to Muslim men. Systematic and repeated violence was coupled with the plunder of residences and businesses, ruining countless families.[11]

The opening act took place in the Sasun district of Bitlis vilayet in summer 1894, when Muslims killed Armenians after the latter mounted armed resistance to administrative encroachments, unfair taxation, and the depredations of the local Kurdish *aghas* (chieftains, reportedly backed by Turkish regulars).[12] The second stage, in which events discussed later play a part, erupted in Istanbul and then Trabzon in September and October 1895. The outbreak of violence motivated British and Russian diplomatic pressure to improve political and social conditions for the Christian populations inhabiting the Empire's eastern provinces. The Sultan's October 17, 1895, promulgation of reforms consequent to that pressure seems to have only encouraged the violence. As Selim Deringil notes, the massacres "spread like shockwaves" after the announcement of the Sultan's concessions.[13] Muslim resentment provided the hostile political atmosphere prerequisite to anti-Armenian disturbances. Though several important studies of the eastern vilayets have appeared recently, there has been little research into the unfolding of violent events in the region of Cilicia (southern Anatolia), though these took place in provinces and districts such as Adana, Osmaniye, Düzce, Kilis, Zeitun, and Aintab.[14]

Surrounded by hills and valleys, Aintab is situated on the boundaries of Cilicia and Syria near both the Mediterranean Sea and the Gulf of Alexandretta. Toward the south lies Düz Tepe, Mardin Tepe, and Kurban Baba. Aintab's layout at the time of these events consisted of the citadel in the north, the downtown, and the ethnic quarters (Figure 1.1). Aintab rose from a valley to three hills called Hayik, Kayacık, and Kurd Tepe, with the Armenians living chiefly on Hayik (though some lived on Kayacık as well).

FIGURE 1.1 Aintab in the early twentieth century. Courtesy of the Mihran Minassian Collection.

A populous and prosperous Armenian community lived in Aintab and its surroundings. Records indicate that there was not a significant Armenian community in Aintab until the onset of the fifteenth century, when Armenians immigrated and settled in the city from various parts of Greater Armenia, Anatolia, and Persia. The size of the Armenian population in Aintab began to increase beginning in the sixteenth century.[15] For example, according to some sources, there were 236 Armenians living in Aintab in 1536.[16] Of the city's twenty-nine neighborhoods in the sixteenth century, only one was Armenian.[17] In this period, the prevailing spoken language was Turkish, though the Turkish population of the city used Armenian words and expressions in their daily lives. Armenians also spoke Turkish, and the Arabic language was used occasionally.[18]

Aintab was fairly developed in trade and artisanship in the sixteenth century and became a center of commerce, as various trade roads passed through the city. This enrichment in economic life contributed to the growth of the city's population. Aintab was within the boundaries of Aleppo, which was one of the greatest provinces of the Ottoman

Empire, after Istanbul and Cairo. This connection with Aleppo played a pivotal role in the commercial and cultural life of Aintab.[19] The Egyptian invasion of Aintab by Ibrahim Pasha, son of Mehmet Ali (the *khedive* [governor] of Egypt), took place in 1830–1839. During Ibrahim Pasha's short-lived rule, the Armenian population of Aintab prospered materially.[20] In 1839, Ibrahim Pasha defeated the Ottoman army of Hafız Pasha, but the city came under Ottoman rule again in 1840.[21] After the Ottoman Empire seized Aintab, the greatest threat at hand was attacks from Arabic and Kurdish tribes, who harassed the Armenians and Turcoman tribes.[22] These attacks became increasingly violent in the seventeenth and eighteenth centuries.[23] In 1870–1871, the general structure of Aintab was as follows:

> Aintab was the biggest district of the Aleppo Province. There were thirty-six mosques, fifty-seven prayer rooms, twenty-one Muslim seminaries, four dervish lodges, thirty-six schools, five churches, thirteen baths, 1,938 shops, four covered bazaars, ten *khans* [large commercial buildings], thirty-six coffee shops, nine pubs, fifty paint shops, three soap shops . . . thirty-seven bakeries, two police stations and one hospital.[24]

According to estimates by Turkish historians Solmaz and Yetkin, in 1832, the population in Aintab and its surrounding villages was 15,000,[25] consisting of approximately 12,000 Muslims and 3,000 Christians, mostly Armenian. While the Armenian population increased significantly starting from the second half of the nineteenth century, Muslim Turks maintained the majority status they had occupied since the eleventh century. Turkish sources show that the Muslim-Turkish population continued to surpass that of Armenian Christians both in the nineteenth century and at the beginning of the twentieth century.[26] An important hub inside Aleppo, Aintab was home to 10,802 Muslims, 4,933 Christians, and 274 Jews in 1868.[27] By 1883 that population had doubled to 31,486, two-thirds of whom were Muslims and one-third Armenians.[28] According to the city's 1895 Yearbook, the total population of Aintab had more than doubled to 84,135, of whom 15,390 were Armenians.[29]

As a trade center and gateway to Syria and Palestine, Aintab attracted Armenian entrepreneurs who took a great deal of initiative in commerce. By the turn of the nineteenth century, Armenians had become economically more powerful than Muslims. Armenians owned caravansaries, covered bazaars, and other businesses.[30] For example, the Kürkçü Hanı, an inn, was owned by the Kurkchuians, one of the most prosperous families in Aintab.[31] These lodgings and bazaars enabled Armenians to become even more active in economic life.

Among Aintab's Muslim and Armenian communities, no specific ethnic or religious conflicts existed. Having always been close to Turkish culture and having even adapted their language to the Turkish language, Armenians also embraced many aspects of Turkish culture, such as music, dance, dress, and customs. In order to settle their legal problems, which also included intracommunal issues, Armenians often appealed to Şer-i mahkeme (the ecclesiastical court), the civic authority of the Muslim community. Armenians could serve as witnesses in lawsuits of Muslims, they could represent Muslim plaintiffs, and they could even challenge Muslim testimony.[32] Armenians faced no challenges at the ecclesiastical court in claiming their rights regarding issues of credits and debits, commercial transactions, and properties such as shops, vineyards, and gardens.[33]

Status Change

In an attempt to explain potential causes for the outbreak of communal violence, describing status changes between the two societies is of great value. Residential organization in seventeenth-century Aintab was not predicated on socioeconomic segregation, and most neighborhoods retained their mixed demography until the nineteenth century.[34] By that time, however, "the overall distribution of wealth in Aintab's residential topography and the ethnic composition of the wealthy had changed significantly."[35] Beginning in the second half of the nineteenth century, the Empire's Armenians underwent accelerated economic, educational, cultural, religious, and political change. Especially evident in economic life, the changes were likewise apparent outside the Armenian community.

First, economic power gradually shifted to the Armenians. Ali Nadir Ünler (1895–1986), a local notable who played an important role in Aintab's official historiography, emphasizes that the Aintab Armenians were considerably ahead of the Turkish-Muslim community in terms of economic and commercial activities. The vast majority of artisanal businesses were in Armenian hands: soapmaking, jewelry making, copper working, tailoring, shoemaking, construction, blacksmithing, weaving, saddlemaking and more.[36] Ünler describes how they protected their craftsmanship jealously and refused to train Turks. Besides most fields of artisanship, Armenians controlled nearly all of Aintab's trade, domestic and foreign. Most doctors, dentists, pharmacists, and lawyers were Armenian.[37] Muslims, on the other hand, tended to earn less money as grocers, butchers, and the like.[38]

Second, education factored into Armenian status change. Two institutions founded by American missionaries in 1876, the American Central Turkey College and the Girls' Seminary, enrolled primarily Armenian students. At the onset of the twentieth century, there were twenty Armenian schools: eleven "national schools," eight Evangelical schools, and one Catholic school.

Prominent Armenian schools were the Cilicia Tchemaran (College), founded in 1912;[39] the Vartanian and Atenagan Schools for boys, founded in 1882 and in 1885, respectively;[40] and the Hayganushian School for girls, founded in 1878.[41] By contrast, Aintab's Muslim-Turkish community remained loyal to the traditional education model and continued to attend madrasahs (Muslim theological schools).

Armenian schools helped to strengthen a national identity while encouraging cultural modernization. In Aintab, Armenians' educational and cultural programs led some speak of Aintab as "the Athens of Cilicia and Anatolia."[42] Thus advantaged, Armenians gained new positions. A considerable number of members of the Ottoman lower court (court of first instance), as well as both the administrative and town councils were Armenians;[43] two of the four members of the Ticaret Odası (Chamber of Commerce) were Armenians, and Armenians occupied posts in the

Ziraat Bankası (Agricultural Bank) and the Tarım Kurulu (Agricultural Assembly).[44]

Third, some Armenians now could entertain thoughts of conversion from Apostolic Orthodoxy to other forms of Christianity. There were seven Armenian churches in Aintab by the early twentieth century: an Apostolic church,[45] three Evangelical churches, an Anglican church, and a Catholic church and Franciscan monastery.[46]

The history of an organized church community in Aintab dates to the seventeenth century, when the old church was built at the time of Michael I, Catholicos of Cilicia (1738–1758). The Armenian Church of Aintab underwent repairs on three occasions, with the major repairs made in 1807. When a fourth repair was necessary in 1873, the great plan of a new church was submitted. The Armenian people themselves worked diligently to construct the church. They began to build in 1873 but were interrupted during the years 1875–1877 because of an epidemic and the outbreak of the Turkish-Russian War.[47] Eventually, Surp Asdvadzadzin (Saint Mary's Church) took its final form and shape in 1893.[48]

There were three Armenian Protestant churches in Aintab: the Kayacık Church, built in 1848; the Hayik Church, in 1865; and the Alay Beyi Church, in 1880. The first Protestant church of Aintab Armenians was formed by the efforts of American missionaries such as Dr. Azariah Smith and Van Lennep in 1848.[49] Each of the Armenian Protestant churches in the city had primary or elementary schools for both the boys and girls of their congregations. At the Kayacık Church, there was also a middle school funded by the Kurkchuian family called the Kurkchuian Varjaran.[50] The middle school associated with the Hayik Church was built by a wealthy member, Adour Agha Niziblian. Niziblian also donated a large building known as the Niziblian Tankaran, to be used for youth activities, public cultural gatherings, and lectures.[51] In addition, the Seminary School for Girls was also founded in Aintab. Benjamin Schneider began to teach a group of girls in his home in 1852, which was to become the forerunner of the Kız Koleji (Seminary for Girls),[52] which was introduced in 1860. The school was originally housed in a group of buildings near the Kayacık Church. Owing to a significant rise in the Protestant community in Aintab, the third Protestant church was founded in 1880. Yet this church was not as successful as the first two churches.[53]

The Armenian Catholic Church was built in 1862. Armenian Catholics in Aintab constituted a small minority. While they taught Armenian in their schools, the sermons were preached in Turkish. According to Sarafian, this was because Aintab Armenians, as a result of Turkish persecution, had abandoned the Armenian language as of the eighteenth century.[54]

Improvements in welfare made Aintab Armenians more politically aware, and Armenians throughout the Empire gained increased self-consciousness and a collective assertiveness. Foreign Christian missionary activities played a key role in this process.

Activities of American Missionaries

American missionary efforts gained momentum in 1848 when the first Protestant church was established in Aintab. Its missionary activities were successful, generating a number of converts equal to that in the entire remainder of the Empire.[55] The advance of Protestantism in the 1870s and 1880s became associated with Aintab's reputation as a center of Armenian prosperity. To understand the success of Protestantism among Armenians in an Ottoman periphery, one needs to bear in mind the context of economic, societal, and political transformations. Thanks to the city's proximity to Aleppo, Aintab Armenian businessmen might connect to a broader world system. The Armenian middle class of Aintab flourished, which seemed to some Turks to threaten the traditional *millet* (confessional community) system that had long regulated the lives of non-Muslims within the Empire.[56] In this context, Protestantism, which seemed to reflect American values, offered relative autonomy from traditional forms of oppression and presented a more flexible religious and legal structure—features that in turn promised social mobility.

Nor were Protestant missionary activities limited to the confessional sphere. Most important, two institutions established by missionaries focused on modernization: Central Turkey College (established in 1876) and Azariah Smith Hospital, founded in 1878 under the college's medical department.[57] The latter, notably, enjoyed the financial support of a number of wealthy Muslim families.[58] Its chief was American missionary Dr. Fred Shepard (1855–1915). The college was established by Rev. Dr. Tilman C. Trowbridge (1831–1888), who became its first president, with the collaboration of Professor Alexan Bezjian (1856–1913).[59] While the official language of instruction was Turkish, the study of English, Armenian, and Arabic was mandatory. The college contributed to Armenian intellectual development, ethnic self-awareness, and social advancement.[60] Its high level of Anglo-Saxon education enabled sharp growth in the political and national consciousness of Armenians.[61]

In the eyes of many Muslims, unfortunately, the college was an infamous place where Armenians honed their national objectives. The Ottoman government considered American colleges in Merzifon and Aintab "harmful" threats, labeling them "subversive places, striving to train young Armenian students to instigate disorder."[62] According to government officials, most of the professors took part in "incidents" as activists of Armenian political organizations.[63]

Perceived Muslim Inferiority and Envy

In Muslim eyes, a number of significant factors underlay the superior position of Armenians by the late nineteenth century. Endless unsuccessful war spelled conscription for young Muslim men, many fated never to return. Most of those who did return were either sick or disabled. Muslim peasants not drafted (like their Armenian counterparts) bore the cost in heavy taxes. Wealthier Armenians could buy exemption by paying the *bedelat-ı askeriye,* an exemption tax, and thus continue their economic activities.[64] Such factors permitted some affluent Armenians to take over businesses and land that previously belonging to Muslims.

Although the Armenian population in the villages near Aintab was small, much of the land there belonged to Armenians who lived in the city. At the beginning of the twentieth century, more than half of the commercial, industrial, and agricultural wealth of the Aintab district was owned by Armenians, who constituted less than a quarter of the population.[65] To be sure, Muslim imaginations exaggerated this wealth. *Terekeler* (probate inventories) and inheritance documents prove that Armenians became only *comparatively* rich. Property holdings of wealthy Armenians from 1830 to 1908 are reflected in the following:

> Forty-eight out of 576 law estates in this period [1830–1908] belonged to Armenians. In 1840–1849 jewelry dealer Agob, the son of Sarı Kirkor . . . was the richest person out of eighty-four people. . . . In 1850–1874 twenty-two out of 277 law estates belonged to Armenians. Among the richest people, Kirkor Karabet, the son of Karamenek, was in third place with his vast amount of land and Okancian, the son of Keşişoğlu, was in fifth place. In 1880–1890 seventeen out of 180 law estates belonged to Armenians. Amongst them, Artin Agha from Nizip was the wealthiest person. Most of his wealth was composed of vineyards near Aintab and pistachio lands in the vicinity of Nizip. . . . Especially in the aftermath of the Second Constitutional Period, Armenians increasingly flourished by means of commercial relations, which they established with Europeans, and immense amount of land that they acquired in war times.[66]

It is possible to see concrete manifestations of the relative prosperity of the Armenian community in comparison to the underdevelopment of its Muslim counterpart by looking at the structure of neighborhoods where the two communities widely exhibited their living practices. The missionaries observed that the orderliness, splendor, cleanliness, richness, and architectural magnificence of houses in Aintab's Armenian quarters were much more sophisticated than those in Muslim neighborhoods. This striking visual difference contributed to the crystallization of economic fault lines. The missionaries noticed this difference, stating that "we are much impressed by what we see here, both as regards the conflict between civilization and barbarism."[67]

Skewed socioeconomic, political, and cultural developments, and the failure of the Muslim community to keep pace, generated a sense of disadvantage. This feeling diluted earlier feelings of "harmonious coexistence" between the two groups. Enlightened nineteenth-century reform programs also upset many Muslims, for instance because of their rhetoric of religious equality.[68] Envy and resentment opened the door to a hate-mongering atmosphere. Toward the end of the nineteenth century, this open enmity found expression in many of the Ottoman newspapers:

> They [the Turks] are ordered to die on Crete, they have been slaughtered on Samos, massacred in Rumelia, cut into pieces in Yemen, mowed down in Hawran, and strangled in Basra. But it's not the Greeks, the Bulgars, the Vlachs, the Jews, the Arabs or the Armenians . . . who are sent there, is it? Let them sit in their houses, in their homelands, in their tents! Let them put all their energies into their work and grow rich! Let them marry and multiply! It wouldn't be right to upset them, to trouble their lofty souls, to tire their delicate bodies. If it were otherwise, how could we have warmed them to the idea of Ottomanism? We had to please them so that they would beg and plead to remain Ottomans.[69]

Economic, social, and political asymmetries upset earlier balances, enabling opportunistic actors to foster a social climate in which violence seemed to be justified, as would become evident in 1894–1897. The momentum of this violence first became evident in 1895 and resurfaced again in 1909, but it was not fully put into action for various reasons. Finally, in 1915, it erupted. As Mark Levene persuasively demonstrates, "while the form of killing remained remarkably constant" in these three violent moments, the framework and particular circumstances rooted in different historical trajectories in which these massacres came into existence "markedly changed."[70]

The "Armenian Question" as an International Issue

The Hamidian massacres were a turning point from the nineteenth-century history of the "Armenian question" of the Ottoman Empire. Therefore, it will be useful to clarify a few points about that "question" as an *international* issue before discussing how the 1895 massacres unfolded. The great European powers were becoming an increasingly determining factor in the Ottoman Empire. The Treaty of Berlin of 1878 marked a crucial shift after Turkish defeat by Russia (itself cheated of the benefits by other European powers). Article 61 of the treaty stipulated that "the Sublime Porte agrees to implement, without further delay, the improvements and reforms . . . in those provinces inhabited by Armenians, and to assure their security against the Circassians and Kurds. It will regularly keep the powers who oversee the implementation informed of the measures taken."[71] The European powers thus extracted from Abdülhamid II a promise to carry out the necessary reforms in the eastern provinces. Instead, fears for the Empire's demise moved him to evade these commitments. Even the opposition forces within the ranks of the Young Turks perceived these reforms as foreign intervention in the Empire's internal affairs, encroachment on the sovereignty of the state, and a genuine menace to the territorial integrity of the Empire.

Until the Sasun massacres of 1894, the Great Powers (at this time, Britain, France, and Russia) did little besides sending various proposals and notes to the Sublime Porte. In Asia Minor, these interventions produced the reverse effect of causing Abdülhamid II to intensify his policies of centralization and repression.[72] In Sasun, Armenian peasants had been mobilized by members of the Hunchakian Revolutionary Party (founded in Geneva in 1887) to resist exploitation, unfair taxes, and predations by local Kurdish aghas (chieftains, reportedly backed by Turkish regulars).[73] Fearful in particular of interference by Britain and Russia, the sultan ordered an "immediate and brutal response"[74] during which, according to European reports, up to twenty thousand Armenian villagers were killed and numerous villages burned in 1894.[75]

After the Sasun massacres and violence elsewhere in eastern and southeastern Anatolia, the oppression of Armenians and other Christians by the Ottoman authorities elicited serious responses from European governments. Through their embassies in Istanbul, the latter pushed reforms on the Empire calculated to improve the conditions of Christian populations in rural areas.[76] Finally, the Great Powers, led by Great Britain and Russia, sent an ultimatum on 11 May 1895. While Abdülhamid II was severely offended by this move, he dragged his feet for months before issuing an official response. Finally, on 17 October 1895, after much haggling, the Porte informed the Great Powers that it had accepted the proposed reforms, after which the reform program was published in the Istanbul press.[77] Yielding, Abdülhamid II sent instructions to the provinces, stating that the reforms were to be carried out, all court cases were to be handled by impartial judges, and discrimination based on race and religion was to be prohibited.[78] Most local governors did not welcome the sultan's orders. In reality, going through the motions served primarily to appease the European states,[79] and indeed the orders themselves became the triggers to anti-Armenian violence.[80]

The Hamidian massacres of 1894–1897 started in Sasun but spread widely through eastern Anatolia and Cilicia, from Bitlis, Muş, and Diyarbekir to Sivas, Trabzon, Samsun, and Erzurum; and then continuing to Merzifon, Tarsus, Zeitun, Marash, Adana, Urfa, Birecik, and Aintab.[81] Massacres and pillaging were organized with the large-scale participation of local elites as well as the Turkish and Kurdish Muslim populations. Ordinary members of the dominant community enjoyed the "permission" of governors, subprefects, the police, and the gendarmerie.[82] Material gain and personal grievances seem to have underlain ordinary people's assaults on neighbors, employers, employees, customers, and even friends. It is also true that many Muslims outside the state hierarchy thought they were acting in the interests of the state and with the support of the sultan.[83] As Donald Bloxham notes, the sultan could not very well oppose actions that had "emerged in large part from the general policies he had sponsored"; his entire program was predicated on not alienating the provincial Muslim population.[84] The course of the massacres in Aintab supports this general observation.

Alarm

In order to understand events in Aintab, one needs to consider certain revolutionary political organizations. Among these, the Hunchakians occupied a significant place in the political awakening of Armenians. The Aintab branch of the Hunchakian Revolutionary Party was established at the Central Turkey College in 1890.[85] Nationalistically inclined

Armenian youth tended to be directly involved in or at least sympathetic to the Hunchakians.[86] The movement maintained a presence in Aleppo, Marash, Kesap, Kilis, Talas, and Urfa.[87] Aintab was especially closely linked to events in the town of Zeitun, some ninety miles away. In fact, to understand Aintab's political climate on the eve of the massacres, one would do well to keep Zeitun in the picture.

Zeitun witnessed early and strong Armenian resistance against the oppressive policies of the government in 1895. Already aware of the ongoing empire-wide massacres in the nearby regions, Zeitun Armenians prepared themselves for armed resistance under the leadership of the Hunchakian Party on 24 October 1895. Like Sasun, the traditionally rough mountain town of Zeitun offered all the advantages for armed resistance. A force of 1,500–6,000 men, armed with guns and rifles, fought against the state.[88] Ottoman forces, despite their overwhelming advantages in numbers (20,000 troops) and technology, were repeatedly defeated. In this area, "something resembling a civil war between Armenians and Muslims raged for months before being brought to an end through mediation by the Great Powers."[89] Thanks to the European diplomatic intervention, Zeitun Armenians ended the resistance in early February 1896. As a result, Hunchakians activists were allowed to go into exile, the tax burden on Armenians was mitigated, and a Christian subgovernor was appointed.[90] According to the report of the British Consulate on January 1896, "at least 5,000 [Ottoman soldiers] have been killed though common report swells the number to 10,000."[91] The British Consulate estimated that fatalities among Armenians numbered approximately 6,000.[92]

Soghomon Bastadjian, a leading figure in the Aintab branch of Hunchackian Revolutionary Party, was of the opinion that Armenian rebellion in Zeitun was a heroic struggle of self-defense and self-preservation.[93] In this manner, the Zeitun rebellion was treated as a collective and national movement. It was a victory won against the Ottoman administration, and it made a considerable mark upon the European powers.

At the beginning of summer 1895, one of the prominent figures of the Hunchakian movement, Aghasi (Garabed Tour-Sarkissian) arrived in Aintab to plan a resistance in Zeitun,[94] strengthen links to the central organization, and arrange financial support.[95] Local supporters formed an administrative board in Aintab including prominent figures such as Armenag Nigoghos Nazaretian, Hırand Sulahian, Berc Mumdjian, and Soghomon Bastadjian.[96]

According to British consular reports, Aghasi and other revolutionaries stirred "younger Armenians" in Aintab to actions likely to provoke Turkish "retaliation."[97] However, the reports offered no concrete evidence, and missionaries in the city suggested quite the contrary: the Christian population had behaved with the "greatest forbearance" in the face of the "grossest and most wanton insult, abuse and violence."[98]

Despite the fear caused by the 1894 Sasun massacres, along with news of similar atrocities in Harput, Sivas, and other towns, schools and shops remained open in Aintab—although many Armenians locked themselves in their houses.[99] Abdülhamid's May 1895 reformist promises reassured Aintab's Armenians, who gathered to celebrate at Surp Asvadzadzin Church in September.[100] Aintab native Sarkis Balabanian, then a schoolboy, later recalled:

> That day was different from any other day. The streets and squares of Aintab took on a festive air. The expression of satisfaction on Armenians' faces was extraordinary. . . . At school, our teacher was talking about the benefits and freedoms brought to us by European states' reformist program.[101]

These celebrations disturbed the Muslim population. Great power interference undermined whatever feelings of trust remained between Muslims and Christians. Then on October 9 local authorities received an order from the Sublime Porte to "arrest the Protestant Pastor and a College professor who were guilty of sedition and the organization of [revolutionary] societies."[102] Troops repeatedly passed through the town, "followed by crowds of Muslim women weeping and cursing the infidels."[103] Over the following days fear gripped the Christians, who locked themselves in their homes. "Thousands were without food," reported a missionary, though the more fortunate cared for them. "Over 1000 men" fled for shelter to "mosques, khans, and powerful Muslim houses," where they lived as virtual prisoners.[104]

The missionaries still believed that Aintab might avoid the violent fate of neighboring Armenian communities. Deeming circumstances here different, the missionary doctor Rev. Americus Fuller wrote that "the leading Muslims . . . [were] intelligent and able men and have shown themselves to a degree tolerant of and even friendly to Christians." Moreover, "the Governor of Aleppo . . . seemed disposed beyond most Turkish officials to respect the rights of Christians," and the town had a relatively large contingent of foreigners "sure to be witnesses of any violence" against them. Furthermore, according to Fuller, the missionary hospital and college had generated "good will" among "all classes," and the town's Christians had "given very little countenance to the [Armenian] ultra-revolutionists."[105]

Reassuring hopes notwithstanding, threats against the Christians were repeatedly heard during the weeks before the massacres. Orders to confiscate arms from the locals reached the governor of Aleppo,[106] but the local government focused only on disarming the Christians. Concurrently, Muslims armed themselves to confront any Armenian "rising."[107] British consul Barnham later learned that "a number of persons from Constantinople dressed as dervishes" had arrived in Aintab shortly before the massacre and "were received with extraordinary honor" by the authorities, who spent hours meeting with them.[108] An American missionary reported that a *firman* (edict) ordering a massacre arrived a few days before the outbreak of violence, along with "a wink from Constantinople."[109]

İhsan Bey, *kaimakam* (local prefect) of Aintab at the time, repeatedly warned the central government that inevitable violence would break out between the two communities. Upon receiving the news on 12 November that the *redif* (military reserve) battalion[110] stationed in the district would be dispatched to Zeitun in order to suppress the Armenian resistance, he informed the government that such military action would present an extremely significant threat to the safety of Aintab.[111] Despite his protest, stationing of the military troops to Zeitun continued until 14 November.[112]

On Friday, 15 November 1895, Ali Bey, son of the notable Rasim Pasha, secretly organized a meeting with the softas (madrasah students) and other provincial elites to organize massacres.[113] The brothers Nuri and

Süleyman Bakkalzâde planned the raids according to instructions from the central government.[114] The doors of Armenian homes in the Muslim quarter were marked.[115] As such preparations continued, large crowds of villagers poured into town.[116] When there was no news regarding the ongoing stationing of the redif battalion in Aintab, İhsan Bey wrote to Istanbul on the morning of November 16 that an uproar was imminent and unless the government interfered, he would be forced to resign.[117] Yet the redif battalion in Aintab had already departed for Zeitun. Finally, on the evening of November 15, the mufti (religious official of the state) and qadi (a Muslim judge) issued a fatwa stating that "the lives and property of Christians were lawful prey for Muslims."[118]

The Massacres

A mob of Turks and Kurds began the slaughter the next morning, continuing bloodshed until the evening of November 19.[119] The events began in the Arasa marketplace, where Armenian shops and businesses were located.[120] The mob butchered shopkeepers and pillaged stores, killing all Armenians in sight.[121] Attackers used stones, clubs, and axes.[122] When an Armenian blacksmith was caught by the mob, one of his neighbors pleaded with him to convert "so we can save you."[123] The blacksmith refused and was killed. In the nearby Kalealtı district, five Armenian smiths were murdered with cries of "peace be upon the Prophet," and their bodies were carried away and thrown into ditches. In the same neighborhood, fifty to sixty Armenian-owned jewelry stalls were robbed.[124] Hoping to find hidden gold and silver, the looters dug up the floors.

The violence then spread to the Armenian residential neighborhoods that were least defensible. Dr. Shepard, the missionary in charge of the hospital, heard the "terrible [cries] of Kurdish and Turkish women cheering on their men" and saw "a crowd of Kurds armed with guns, axes, clubs, and butcher-knives . . . swarming out of their quarter . . . to attack their Armenian neighbors."[125] Fuller also remarked on "the loud shrill '*zullghat*' [wedding ululation]" of the Turkish women crowded on their roofs and cheering on their men.[126]

Approximately eight hundred people surrounded the Debbağhane neighborhood, armed with axes and pistols. In four hours, they burnt and destroyed this quarter and massacred Armenians.[127] The twin brothers of the Duzdjian family were butchered in their own home. Peasants from the Keçe Inn area slaughtered the shoemaker brothers Sarkis and Abraham Apoian. In Rahen Street, Krikor Kabakdjian's house was pillaged and then burned down. Chests, cases of wares, and everything else were plundered from the homes of brothers Melkon, Khacher, and Harutyun Kabakdjian.[128] Some parts of the Alaybeyi neighborhood were set on fire.

The mob's next stop was the grand and spacious house of the Babigian family, another distinguished Armenian family of Aintab. Crying out, "Wood does not make a tong; an infidel does not make a pasha,"[129] they first looted the Babigians' house and then burned it to the ground. Across from the Babigians' house, the Kadehdjians barely managed to escape from their own burning house, only to find the arsonists waiting outside with clubs in their hands.[130]

A Franciscan monk who witnessed the massacres told the investigating British consul that "butchers and tanners . . . armed with clubs and cleavers" were prominent among the killers.[131] They screamed "*Allahu Akbar*" ("God is great") as they broke down doors "with pickaxes and crowbars or scaled the walls with ladders" and then slaughtered Armenians. "Then when midday came they knelt down and said their prayers and then jumped up and resumed the dreadful work. Wherever they were unable to break down the doors, they torched the houses with petroleum."[132] The fact that petroleum was scarce at the time suggests that it had been purchased in Aleppo and sent to Aintab in advance of the massacre. In some areas, the uproar went on until midnight. Then, the crowd settled down, and the initial panic subsided. Armenian watchmen guarded the gates of the Armenian quarters all night.

On November 17, a group of people from the Kozanlı neighborhood reached the Sarı Mahsere gate; there, they attacked houses lining both sides of the street.[133] Horrified young girls and boys were chased through the streets, screaming. To establish peace and order, İhsan Bey requested at least one battalion be sent to Aintab on the same day.[134] This request again went unheeded, for the incidents in Zeitun prevented the government from supplying military support to the district.[135] Shepard and Fuller witnessed Armenians being assaulted as their homes were plundered; people—particularly Armenian women—defending their homes from the rooftops with "stones and firearms,"[136] to the horrid shouts of the Kurdish women, the screams of the "wounded and dying [and] the hoarse cries of the men."[137] At times, as in the case of two large Armenian compounds, the mob was fended off; in other cases, where Armenian houses were adjacent to Muslim homes, the mob broke through the doors and began massacring and plundering.[138]

On November 18, the same mob resumed the atrocities, on this occasion singling out the house of Haroutioun Agha Nazaretian, who had inherited the building of the former Iranian Consulate in Aintab from his father, Kara Nazar (Figure 1.2). This act of despoliation went on until late that evening. With its large and spacious courtyard, garden, and guest facilities, the two-story house was scoured. Fortunately, the mob did not burn it down. To protect their houses and neighborhoods, Armenians had built *tebirges* (strong gates) as a precaution. During the massacres, the tebirges of the Armenians' quarters were not breached, principally because the mob preferred the shops and warehouses of the market.[139] These gates spelled the difference between life and death for many.[140] At noon the attacks on private homes promptly ceased; however, the looting of the market went on into the night.[141] A large convoy of Turkish and Kurdish villagers "with bundles . . . on their backs, and some with donkey loads and camel loads, showed too plainly that the looted area must have been considerable."[142] As they walked, the villagers chanted limericks like, "Queen of England, the owner of Armenians, come quick, save the infidels."[143] Muslim women swarmed around the now-homeless Armenians, mocking their destitution.

On the 19th, the government finally issued an order instructing the fourth and fifth military commands to put an end to the disturbances in Aintab at once.[144] Then, the killings and looting abated.[145] Nevertheless, on 24 November, a Turkish mob accompanied by mostly Kurdish peasants from surrounding villages invaded Haroutioun Agha Nazaretian's house again from the garden gate facing the Çınarlı mosque to scour it for the last valuables.

FIGURE 1.2 Nazaretian family, 1880s. Standing on the left is Nigoghos Agha; seated left to right are Nazaretian Nazar Agha (Kara Nazar), Garabed Agha, and mother Zmrout Khatun; and standing on the right is Haroutioun Agha. Courtesy of the Mihran Minassian Collection.

In the course of three days, all houses in the Alaybeyi, Debbağhane, Sıçancı, Paşa Street, Akyol, Kalealtı, and İbn-i Eyüp quarters and the Arasa marketplace were robbed; except for covered bazaars in Gemlikli and some inns, all shops and businesses owned by Armenians were pillaged. The churches and school buildings were filled with cold, hungry women and children: "The husbands and fathers [were] in prison or dead: . . . Houses [were] not only sacked, but even doors and sash windows [were] carried away: . . . Except for the few wealthy ones, and the few who [had] assured salaries . . . all [were] plunged into destitution."[146]

Perpetrators, Rescuers, Victims

Often those best situated to reduce the violence were themselves complicit. Numerous members of the local elites and minor officials played an active role in the pogroms. Fuller commented that the local government was "wholly in sympathy with the rioters and . . . that it [had] incited and directed nearly all the disturbances."[147] The principal organizers were Ali Bey, Bakkalzâde Nuri, and the Süleyman brothers. Additionally, Cenanizâde Ali Bey, a prominent wealthy citizen, seized goods and property from the looted Armenian houses. Veli Agha, a local official and lieutenant in the Ottoman Army, also benefited.[148] The bigoted yet influential member of Aintab's *ulema* (religious scholar), Bülbülzâde Abdullah, supported the massacres. Another prominent local who took part was Dayızâde (Dai) Ahmed Agha,[149] notably in the pillaging of the Nazaretian house.[150]

Some soldiers sent by the government "to maintain order" also took part in the pillage, and, in Shepard's words, the majority made "not the slightest attempt to prevent the attack, or to scatter the mob."[151] Neither the government nor the notables attempted during "the whole of that terrible Saturday [16 November]"[152] to stop the killing and looting, other than hurrying "a large force of soldiers out for the defense of the foreign residents [missionaries]."[153]

Taşçızâde Abdullah Effendi, Tuzcuzâde Hafız Ahmet Effendi, Ahmet Muhtar Bey, Kethüdazâde Hüseyin Cemil Bey, Bulaşıkzâde mufti Hacı Arif Effendi, Mahmut Çitçi, Cenanizâde Rıza Bey, Nizipli Hacı Mehmet Effendi, Battal Beyzâde Tahir Bey, Daizâde Hasan Sadık Bey, and Mennazâde Mustafa Bey were other Muslim notables who had actively participated in the massacres.[154] They incited the Turkish and Kurdish rabble (also including Arabs from adjacent villages) with provocative speeches and declarations, providing them with instruments to enact violence. Additionally, contacts in the underworld were called upon to amass and guide this mob.

However, not all Muslims of Aintab participated in the pogroms. Some "behaved with great humanity" to protect "nearly 2,000" Armenians.[155] The sheikh of the dervish lodge welcomed many Armenians into his lodge.[156] On the afternoon of 16 November, a number of Ottoman soldiers came and transported those remaining in Armenian neighborhoods to the compound of the sheikh of Tekke.[157] Another such individual was Mazlum Effendi, a lawyer who had Armenian clients, lived close to the heavily Armenian Kozanlı market, and harbored Armenian neighbors during the pogrom.[158] For this, some Muslims later called him "Gavur [Infidel] Mazlum."[159] Another Muslim who resisted the persecutions was Ubeydullah Effendi, an educated, religious, and successful lawyer, antagonistic to Abdülhamid's regime.[160] Ali Bey, the Muslim *mukhtar* (headman) in charge of the Armenian quarter, persuaded the mob to stay away.[161]

A shop owner, Hagop Acoian, was saved by his friend and business partner, a Muslim named Ahmed, who warned him the day before the massacres began: "Partnership is off, stay at home tomorrow, don't come to the shop!"[162] Thanks to Ahmed's advice, Acoian did not go to the store the next day and thus survived. During the raids, two Armenian workers appeared in front of their shop. Ahmed hid them inside and went out, locking the doors and calling out to the howling Muslim crowd approaching his shop, "That infidel Aco sold and left this place a long time ago, this shop is mine now."[163] A few Muslim elites, such as Iztırapzâde Şefik Bey, Iztırapzâde Celal Kadri Bey, Patpatzâde Nuri Bey, and Patpatzâde Bahtiyar Bey, also sought to protect their Armenian neighbors.[164]

In another instance, as the mob approached the majestic Niziblian home, a rugged-looking Muslim prevented its looting by addressing them furiously: "You merciless people, what kind of Muslims are you, how are you going to stone this house? Isn't the owner . . . a charitable person? He gave you free wheat when the famine hit us, how quickly you forget, you treacherous sons of traitors."[165] Future research may uncover other examples, but surely numerous courageous acts of protection went unrecorded.

Armenian Resistance

The Armenians of Aintab were not all passive victims of this persecution. Those who were able to, resisted the Muslim mob's assaults, particularly in the Armenian quarters. For instance, Kevork Tanelian, from one of the well-known Armenian families, killed one of the mob's leaders with his rifle. The terrified crowd fled, carrying the body away. As they were leaving, one shouted to warn the others: "Hey, do not come in, it is raining fire here."[166]

Another crowd from the Tepebaşı quarter attempted to attack the Armenian neighborhood, whereupon the Armenians called for help. Thirty-six Armenian fighters had already gathered in the two-story house of the Sulahian family to guard the tebirges. Upon hearing this call for help, Hırand and his brother Yenovk Sulahian quickly gathered more men with them and positioned themselves in houses near the tebirge, shooting warning shots in order to disperse the Muslim bands.

In another instance, a diverse crowd of Turkish and Kurdish villagers and "roughs to the number of fifteen hundred or so" made a rush for the Christian quarter of Haik.[167] That quarter had a strong tebirge, and thirty to forty Christians were gathered upon "the housetops, commanding the approach to this gate, armed with stones and two or three guns; and with the advantage afforded by their position on the flat roofs they held the mob at bay for three-fourths of an hour, and finally drove them off."[168] In the Haik quarter, the Armenians were prepared and were able to "beat off their assailants."[169] Yet the mob returned, and through the fortified, chained tebirges, they attempted to gain access to Mahsereci Street. A group of Muslims managed to break into one or two houses.[170] Meanwhile, Kevork Tanelian aimed his Martini rifle on the mob from the upper window of the neighboring Topchuians' house. An individual from the mob was hit by Kevork's bullets. Thereupon, the panic-stricken people began to run in all directions. Springing from the barricades they had built earlier, a few young Armenians closed the tebirge on their street. To prevent the Muslim group from reentering, they quickly erected a wall behind the wooden gate.

With the exception of tebirges, Armenian neighborhoods were practically defenseless. In many places, responding to the armed mob, the Armenians tried to defend themselves by opening fire on groups passing by Armenian houses. In response, the attackers dispersed.

Attempts on the Missionary Institutions

The mob also attempted to attack missionary institutions. However, government troops effectively protected both the missionary schools and the hospital, as Ottoman authorities both in Aintab and in Istanbul made painstaking efforts to protect the lives and properties of American missionaries.[171] The Ottoman archives are replete with telegraphs in regard to that matter.[172] In fact, Alexander W. Terrell, the US minister in Istanbul, expressed his high appreciation of the soldiers of the Ottoman Imperial Army stationed in Aintab, as well as the Beridjik (Birecik) contingent, for protecting Americans on 16 November.[173] In contrast, Terrell did not express any concern for the Armenians.

On 17 November, a group of Kurds and villagers brushed past a cordon of soldiers around Central Turkey College.[174] Crying out "*Allahu Akbar*" with flags in their hands, thousands of people marched with the apparent purpose of setting the college ablaze.[175] The army commander positioned the soldiers around the college and gave orders to repel the mob. Ignoring the guns aimed at them, the mob continued to draw near the college, when suddenly the soldiers opened fire, injuring some among the crowd. As a result, panic ensued, and a stampede broke out, causing people to be trampled while trying desperately to save themselves.[176]

Another attack was made upon the hospital gate.[177] At that time, Dr. Shepard was in the hospital. When he opened the gate to confront and reason with the mob, he found his closest neighbor, "a burly Turk, Hadji Hussein Agha, standing in the hospital gate holding the mob at bay, and protesting that no one should enter."[178] Mehmed Agha of Haik Baba Street was also active in saving the lives of Americans at the college and the hospital during the mob attack on 17 November. In his telegram to Tevfik Pasha, Terrell acknowledged his gratitude to Hadji Hussein Agha and Mehmed Agha, stating that "the noble conduct of such men in time of popular frenzy distinguished them as heroes in the cause of humanity and entitled them to the gratitude of the human race."[179] Later, some two hundred soldiers filed into the street below, forcing back the crowd.[180]

Aftermath

The period including the massacres of November 1895 was remembered as "Balta Senesi" (the Year of the Ax) and "Talan Senesi" (the Year of Spoliation): most victims were felled by knives, axes, and bayonets—though firearms were also used; numerous Armenian houses, shops, and businesses were looted.[181] The exact number of victims remains unknown. According to various records, the approximate number of Armenians killed in Aintab from 16 November to 19 November is between 300 and 400.[182] Official Ottoman sources (not realistically) report approximately sixty Muslims and 110 Christians dead.[183] The estimated number of plundered shops and stalls ranges from 900 to 1,500, that of pillaged houses from 500 to 600.[184] In addition, "Christian graveyards were desecrated, the bones carried off and scattered. Christian-owned orchards were destroyed."[185]

After the killings, a "peaceful atmosphere" was reestablished. In each Armenian neighborhood, a garrison of thirty soldiers was deployed. Yet these continued to rob and tyrannize the Armenians.[186] In June 1896 an effort by Lutfi Pasha, the newly appointed major general of reserve battalions in Aleppo, to arrest the plunderers and restore Christian property came to naught after Muslim demonstrators forced him to release all prisoners.[187] Some of the outraged looters burned stolen property in the street rather than return it.[188]

For weeks, even months, the Armenians feared leaving their homes. Many took refuge in Surp Asvadzadzin Church. In January 1896, the British consul reported that some 750 Armenians still sheltered there, while all Armenian shops remained closed.[189] On 5 and 6 January 1896, soldiers in the redif battalion were assigned to protect the Armenian quarters. Commanding these soldiers, Lieutenant Hacı Hilmi gently tried to convince the Armenians that they could go on with their lives as before, open their shops, and continue their business.[190] While the Armenians found a degree of comfort in Hacı Hilmi's attitude, they did not dare to return to their normal routines.[191]

Five priests in charge of the church tried to calm the people's fears, though they also were horrified by the massacres. Protestant churches were filled with homeless and destitute Armenians. After things settled down, families who survived the massacres continued to stay in Atenagan School's large courtyard and its adjacent rooms.[192] In total, there were four thousand Armenians "dependent on charity for daily bread."[193]

After the massacres, leading Armenians were arrested: "sixty four of [Aintab's] most influential and wealthy Christians" remained in jail as of early March,[194] some there and others sent to Aleppo.[195] Among the prisoners were Artin and Garabed Nazaretian; Kevork Leylekian; Kevork and Movses Shamian; Agop, Babik, and Movses Babigian; Artin Boshgezenian; Avedis Hasırdjian; Kirkor Kabakian; Agop Araklian; Anton Gaberlian; and Garabed Barsamian. Of these, two prominent Armenians—Artin Agha Nazaretian and Kevork Leylekian—stood out. Coming from affluent families whose houses had been severely attacked during the massacres, they sent a letter to the sultan, begging to be pardoned.[196] Thereupon, Aleppo governor Raif Pasha sent a follow-up telegram to Sadaret detailing the alleged offenses committed by Nazaretian and Leylekian: "Nazaretian got involved in a murderous incident during the events in Aintab, and that Leylekian attempted to murder a man but only injured him. They were put on trial and condemned alongside their wives."[197]

A few weeks later, thirty-two more were arrested, including Rev. Hovannes Krikorian, an Armenian Protestant pastor.[198] The number imprisoned continued to increase, and Aintab's jails were soon "crammed with Armenians."[199] The arrested were charged with conspiring with coethnics in Zeitun. British consul Barnham suggested that the continued arrest of wealthy Armenians was largely designed to facilitate their expropriation.[200] Another possible motivation was to pressure them to convert. Aintab's "leading Muslim notables," including the new kaimakam, repeatedly warned that there was now "no hope of [the Armenians] living in security unless they . . . [became] Muslims."[201]

By appealing to the Ottoman Ministry of Foreign Affairs, the British Embassy was able to obtain the release of the Aintab Armenians.[202] In April 1896, twenty-seven Armenians were released from the jails in Aleppo and Aintab after the sultan amnestied Armenians connected with the armed resistance in Zeitun.[203] Eventually, the remaining Armenian jailees of Aleppo were released with bail or under amnesty.[204]

No Muslims were punished in the wake of the massacres, and the authorities "systematically" portrayed Christians as "the aggressors,"[205] a perspective occasionally represented in Turkish historiography even today.[206]

According to current consensus, the massacres of 1894–1897 were ordered and arranged by the central government, with the active participation of *Hamidiye* cavalry regiments—quasi-irregular units founded in the early 1890s under Abdülhamid II and overwhelmingly composed of Kurdish tribes—often aided by the gendarmerie and regular army.[207] Both Richard Hovannisian and Ronald G. Suny write that the massacres were intended to put the Armenians "in their place" for engaging outside interests.[208] Norman Naimark observed that Abdülhamid II aimed to reinvigorate his domination by dehumanizing the Armenian minority,[209] weakening it economically and socially, and sending a message to both the Ottoman populace at large and the outside world that he would not tolerate any further interference with the integrity, or in the domestic affairs, of the Empire.[210] Selim Deringil contends that "Abdülhamid intended to cow, decimate, and humble the Armenians, but not to destroy them."[211] It has also been argued that Abdülhamid II's approach was to execute policies of reform and persecution simultaneously: after the reform program that he declared under British pressure,[212] he encouraged massacres in the provinces of Eastern Anatolia and Cilicia.[213]

However, some recent studies have urged greater caution regarding the role of the sultan and the government. Although the timing of the Armenian massacres overlapped and intensified throughout the Empire shortly after the declaration of the October 1895 reform plan, and although the fact that each massacre had a beginning and an end point implies the existence of a central scheme, the overall picture was more nuanced. Certain studies contend that there is no proof of the direct involvement of the sultan. According to Jelle Verheij, the development of events suggests an impression that "the situation veered out of control and that the Sultan could not even decide how to act, far less direct events."[214] As sole ruler of the Empire, Abdülhamid II sought to preserve social tranquility as order took priority over any other matter for him and he knew that violence, once unleashed, was very difficult to control.[215] Donald Bloxham argues that the extent of Abdülhamid's direct complicity "in the full spectrum of the massacres is, [however], unclear"[216]—this is not to absolve the sultan, since he bore "the primary responsibility of inculcating the atmosphere of anti-Christian chauvinism in which the massacres took place."[217] Moreover, recent studies have suggested that the roles of the Hamidian troops and local governors deserve to be reevaluated.[218] Verheij, for instance, asserts that the involvement of Hamidian regiments in the massacres in Diyarbekir province is uncertain.[219] In Mardin, a Hamidian regiment of the Arabic Tay tribe was reportedly involved in restoring order,[220] and Hamidian regiments protected Armenian towns and villages in certain places.[221] The attitude of local officials varied from place to place: in some provinces governors actively attempted to prevent killings.[222]

In other words, a complex web of relationships preconditioned and constrained the massacres: common perpetrators internalized their criminal roles as religious and patriotic duty when the sultan and his government signaled their tacit or explicit consent. In the particular case of Aintab, it would be hardly accurate to suggest that the 1895 massacres were directly ordered by the central government or the sultan. However, it is possible to claim that they were carried out to a certain extent with "permission" from the center. As the representative of the central government in Aintab, İhsan Bey's appeals to the center for securing public order and safety in the district were fruitless, as suppression of the Armenian resistance in Zeitun was the government's priority. Therefore, the center condoned the Armenian slaughters in Aintab for three days, without taking any security measures.

Consequently, the 1895 Aintab massacres manifested a climate of enmity enabling direct violence against a minority. The precondition of the massacres was mobilization of the grievances of lower-class Turks, Kurds, and Arabs by political leaders and organizations, including local notables, provincial elites, and the Muslim clergy. These groups stoked the majority's deep sense of collective frustration and the identification of Armenians as the fundamental cause of the difficulty of the Muslims' lives, as well as their society's social, political, and economic backwardness.

As a result, each channel and physical space signifying the superiority of Armenian community over Muslims eventually became an object of this extreme violence. The perpetrators' focus of rage was initially economically valuable assets, such as shops and businesses in the market area, and the Armenian quarters. Violence was later directed at houses, churches, school buildings, and cemeteries. Exposing these spatial planes to violence or turning them into objects of physical violence was a manifestation of feelings of economic envy and resentment in the eyes of Muslims.[223] The Armenians were painted and seen as traitors dissatisfied with their already superior position and eager to overturn the status quo ordained by Islam.

The most important elements in the massacres in Aintab were the roles of elites and the voluntary popular participation. Many ordinary Muslims were so eager that they attacked even when the local government or the sultan himself sought to restrain them. The year 1895, often seen "as a bloody apogee of the Sultan's power, appears here much more like the collapse of his system." As Verheij cogently observed, Abdulhamid "appears to have been caught between his own inclination to 'teach the Armenians a lesson' and the multiple forms of other opposition (from the Powers, of the Muslim citizens) that were unleashed."[224] But the case of Aintab shows that once people at the street level perceived the implicit consent of their immediate superiors (or authorities higher still), they took matters into their own hands.

·2·

Ethnic Politics after the Young Turk Revolution

After Abdülhamid II's abolishment of the Kânûn-ı Esâsî and Meclis-i Mebusan (Ottoman Chamber of Deputies) in 1878, a group of reform-oriented political activists called Jön Türkler (Young Turks) led a network of exiles and reformers, establishing the CUP in 1889. During the summer of 1908, the CUP convinced the commanders of the Ottoman army in Macedonia to revolt against the sultan. They threatened to march to Istanbul unless the group's demands were met. As a result, the sultan announced the restoration of the constitution and established a parliamentary government, which was led by members of the CUP. More important, civil and religious liberties were guaranteed to all citizens again on 24 July 1908.[1] Thus, the Young Turk Revolution of 1908 revitalized the Ottoman reform ideal of equality among its citizens before law and provided for empire-wide elections. Having reinstated the constitution by military action, the CUP presented itself as the savior of all Ottomans. The revolution also created a liberal political atmosphere, which enabled a number of different political parties and social organizations to come into existence.

Toward the end of July, a telegram was dispatched to Aintab's post office from the CUP headquarters, stating that citizens of Aintab were subject to the Ottoman constitution and that the Empire would protect their freedoms.[2] After the Hamidian pogroms, Aintab Armenians welcomed the news of revolution with enthusiasm. The CUP's Aintab branch was officially formed after news of the coup in the capital reached the district.

The Aintab CUP Branch and Dashnaksutiun

After the Young Turk Revolution of 23 July 1908, new political currents and empire-wide political changes resonated strongly in Aintab, and the heroes who carried out the revolution—particularly Resneli Ahmed Niyazi and Enver Bey—were met with a massive outpouring of support.[3] A general feeling of contentment abounded.[4] Lieutenant Yahya Bey of the military reserve battalion stationed in Aintab began organizing meetings to establish the local CUP branch. At least eighteen representatives of the Muslim elites of the city took part in the branch's foundation and formation.[5] Although the lieutenant had founded the organization, he believed that it would be more appropriate to have a civilian leader. Therefore, Ali Cenani Bey, parliamentary deputy for Aintab, was elected president. Taşçızâde Abdullah Efendi was the vice president.[6] Two other founding members, Rüştü Attaroğlu and Mahmut Çitçi, served on its administrative board.[7] Bulaşıkzâde mufti Hacı Arif Effendi was the general secretary.[8]

Prominent members of Aintab's Armenian community also actively participated in the foundation of the CUP branch, including Zenop Bezjian, one of the directors and professors of Central Turkey College, as well as Hırand Sulahian and Hovsep Kendirjian.[9] In fact, Sulahian later became a deputy, winning one of the CUP seats.[10] Additionally, several officials became members.

Immediately the new branch began to operate vigorously in Aintab, organizing various conferences, and as part of its activities, founding branches of the nationalist organizations Türk Yurdu (Turkish Homeland) and Türk Gücü (Turkish Power).[11] By taking up the cause of the CUP and Turkish ethnic nationalism, the dominant notable families of Aintab secured their control over the local party organization, parliamentary representation for the district of Aintab and Aleppo province, and a seat on the CUP's central committee.

On the other hand, to strengthen the revolution, the CUP had worked jointly with fellow clandestine organizations of various ethnic stripes, in particular the Armenian Revolutionary Federation (ARF; hereafter Dashnaksutiun), founded in Tbilisi in 1890.[12] The Aintab branch of Dashnaksutiun was established as an underground movement in 1895, following the Hamidian massacres. These events greatly impacted the Hunchakians, causing fractures in the organization and allowing the empowerment of the revolutionist Dashnaksutiun movement.[13] One important element that increased the support for Dashnaksutiun was the fact that this organization did not oppose the church and opened its doors to everyone. Lead by Hagop Bekarian, it was founded by Nerses Bagdoian, Nerses Poladian, Nerses Mahdesian-Hagopian, Harutyun Der Bogossian, and Hagop Muradian—all from the Central Turkey College—as well as tradesmen Kevork Sivajian, Nazaret Yemenidjian, and Kirkor Poladian.[14] Their main goal was to organize the Armenian youth and train them in self-defense. With the declaration of the second constitutional period, Dashnaksutiun officially proclaimed itself as a political party and continued to grow in strength until 1915.[15] It also had ardent members in various schools, including the College, Atenagan, and Cilicia Tchemaran.[16]

In the Aftermath of the Revolution

At the time of the revolution, the population of Aintab was around 90,000.[17] Armenians constituted a minority, with a population of 18,963. The Armenian community consisted of 4,584 Armenian Protestants and 477 Catholics, with the remainder being Orthodox, belonging to the Surp Asvadzadzin Church. The Muslim population numbered 69,920.[18]

The revolution seemed to resolve tensions between the two communities in the aftermath of the Hamidian massacres. As Nerses (Mahdesian) Hagopian observed:

> Everywhere, national songs-anthems were sung freely and bravely. Avenues and streets were too narrow for the political heroes leading the parades. Mosques, churches, schools and

> other closed buildings were opened. Greeted by a great shower of applause and cheering, Muslim and Christian orators were giving their speeches and expressing themselves freely. The elderly were embracing and kissing each other, shouting "Brotherhood" with a great enthusiasm. The motto of the day was "Liberty," "Justice," "Equality," and "Fraternity." Niyazi's and Enver's names were echoing in the songs; these two names were in everyone's mouth—even the puppies. Political leaders of Unionists, Dashnaks and Hunchakians were having a good day. They were close friends now. They were inseparable. Things went back to normal. Everything was "new"; they were supposed to be new.[19]

Religious functionaries from mosques and churches walked arm in arm and forgave each other for the "unwanted" losses of the past.[20] Political campaigns of Muslim notables and sheikhs, who had mistreated the Armenians before, were condemned.[21] A political campaign was initiated to enlist all as members of the CUP, a call answered by Armenians, Turks, and Kurds who swore on the Koran to protect the constitution with their lives. Although a telegram sent by the Dashnaksutiun center in Istanbul warned Aintab Armenians that they were prohibited from becoming a member of any organization, Dashnaks did not hesitate to join forces with the Unionists (members of the ruling CUP) and cooperated with them for the protection of the constitutional regime. Shortly after the revolution, Khatchig Bonapartian, a Dashnaksutiun representative, visited Aintab and gave speeches on "how to protect the constitution in cooperation with the CUP," addressing thousands of Muslims and Armenians. Cheers of "Long live the CUP!" and "Long live Dashnaksutiun!" echoed through the halls.[22]

In general, Armenians benefited from the constitution more than any other ethnic group.[23] Newspapers in the Armenian language were published freely on all subjects, including articles on national, local, scientific, and historical topics. Prior forms of censorship ceased, and Armenian history and literature came into prominence. Poetry, odes, and dramas on the national past of Armenians were published and performed. Above all, critiques of the regime and its officials became possible. The revolution also brought about a different attitude toward the Armenians, putting them on equal ground with Muslims. Marksmanship, hunting, and bearing arms were now allowed. The directive of *Seyahat Tezkeresi* (safe conduct), which had prohibited Armenians from traveling within the Empire and going to Istanbul, was repealed, and Armenians regained the right to travel freely. Unjust and biased judicial decisions were reviewed. The CUP initiated attempts to return plundered Armenian lands and other properties. When phrases like "pis gavur" (dirty infidel) were no longer used, everyday life was eased for Armenians.[24]

This atmosphere allowed Armenian political organizations to become more active. In fact, Dashnaksutiun became the most active Armenian party. In the summer of 1908, a major conference was organized, which concluded with the following points:

1. Dashnaksutiun will be kept secret, and discipline will be a priority.
2. In order to help people and to accommodate books and publications, a secret place for a library will be arranged, and these books and publications will be placed in the garden building in the courtyard of Surp Asvadzadzin.
3. Two people will be assigned to establish communication with the government/administration officials, Unionist administrators/directors, and foreigners. These two individuals will be Tatul Kupelian and another clerk.
4. In order to preserve the constitution, it is decided to collaborate with Unionists.
5. In order to consolidate the Dashnaksutiun, it is decided that new comrades will be recruited.
6. We will arm ourselves and design a new plan for self-defense.[25]

To enlighten the public on political and economic issues, Dashnaksutiun also built the first auditorium, Azgayin Lesaran (National Auditorium), and initiated a series of public lectures. However, the euphoria of the revolution did not reflect the actual attitudes of the different ethnic groups. In reality, a great change had taken place in the power dynamics, and the euphoria soon faded, bringing real problems to the surface. Different fragments of the Turkish and Kurdish population, especially the extremely religious and conservative elements, gradually realized that the constitution favored Armenians greatly.

The constitution gave Armenians greater political power at the expense of those who previously held considerable cultural and political capital. For example, a career in military, civil service, or politics was no longer off limits for Armenians. Already jealous of the Armenian minority's economic success, this change was difficult for many Muslims to accept.[26] For Armenians to gain equality on every level further aggravated these feelings of anger and resentment, which hardened ethnoeconomic identities and resulted in antagonism between the Muslim majority and the Armenian minority. Cemil Alevli, a prominent local literati, offers an example of this resentment from his memoir: "Ignorant peasants borrowed money from rich Armenians with very high interests" in order to marry their sons and daughters, and "Armenian moneylenders usually used tricky methods to collect their money."[27] Thus, landed properties of Muslims who failed to pay their debts on time were appropriated by Armenians. Moreover, Armenians were even described as "bloodsuckers" and "traitors" who benefited from the wealth Aintab provided.[28]

Previously ossified ethnic and economic affiliations and the ensuing enmity were amplified further during the Ottoman Empire's political and economic decline. The dominant group thought that they were being deprived of their ruling nation status and felt degraded.[29] Subsequently, opposition emerged from among the local Muslim population. Many of the strongly religious citizens had been antagonized by the CUP's slogans of "equality" and "fraternity" and feared that their superior social and economic status was at risk. Even as the Aintab Armenians tried to enjoy this new liberty, memories of massacres from Abdülhamid II's reign led them to arm themselves in preparation for what might come.[30]

The first cracks in this new union surfaced in September 1908, when Necmeddin Bey, kaimakam of Aintab, was beaten and expelled.[31] This incident calls for careful examination because it reflects the impact of the revolution on different ethnic groups. Additionally, it offers some useful clues regarding how the CUP as a political organization and its policies were received on a local scale.

Power Structure of the CUP and the Beating of Necmeddin Bey

After the revolution, the CUP initially failed to establish the required local governmental control mechanisms. In Feroz Ahmad's words, the state seemed to cease to function with the sudden declaration of the constitution.[32] Within the state, no one realized which powers they held and to what extent they could use their power.[33] An order stating that local representatives were not to interfere with the local government's conduct was sent to various provinces.[34] However, noticing the authority gap, some groups exploited this confusion to establish their own law and order. In rural areas, locals confronted officials, with the intention of settling the score.[35] Rural functionaries of the CUP also began to dismiss the unwanted governors and officials, sometimes by resorting to violence.[36]

For example, some state officials in Izmir were arrested and sent to Thessaloniki; in Edirne, military pashas and civil officials were sentenced to execution; in Bursa and Diyarbekir, after raids, governors' offices were handed lists of undesired officials to be dismissed; in Manisa, Isparta, Antalya, Izmit, and Rize, governors were forced to leave their offices as a result of telegrams sent by citizen proponents of the reforms; in Kayseri, as the people were raiding the government building, the governor died of a heart attack; in Zara, officials were banished; in Trabzon, district governors and officials were forced to flee, leaving no clear authority; and finally in Aintab, kaimakam Necmeddin Bey[37] was overthrown by force, beaten brutally, and subjected to insults.[38]

As a civil servant, Necmeddin Bey's general attitude toward his duty was to maintain all control in his own hands and avoid any interference. Unable to embrace the values of the new constitution, he openly rejected Constitutionalists who stood against his authority.[39] As a response, local members of the CUP gathered approximately one hundred people to march to the district governor's office in Sera[40] in September 1908.[41] As a witness to this incident, Şakir Sabri Yener,[42] recalled, lawyer Ali Rıza Bey (a local CUP member)[43] and Mennanzâde Mustafa Bey (another local CUP member and well-known elite) were the organizers of this protest.[44] Roughly fifteen of the demonstrators went upstairs and dragged

Necmeddin Bey out to the street.[45] He was beaten, insulted, taken barefoot to the barn of the Emirali Inn, and imprisoned there. A merciful citizen, gatekeeper Ali Effendi, saved Necmeddin Bey from being lynched and helped him escape to Aleppo.[46] Fueled by this victory, certain local notables from the CUP demanded a guarantee from the government that no other officials like Necmeddin would be sent to Aintab again.

However, the mayhem continued in the city. In a ciphered telegram dated 31 October 1908, Aleppo governor Reşid Bey informed the Ministry of Interior that a telegraph written by Dikran Cemil had been sent to them via the Aleppo Telegraph Office. In his telegram, Dikran Cemil wrote that Aintab Armenians were living in horror and terror. However, Reşid reported that "this statement is baseless. I have investigated the situation with the Aintab kaimakam and have been told that this information is inaccurate." Thereupon, the Ministry of Interior asked the Aleppo governor, "Why is this feeling of horror and terror diffused in Aintab? What is the reason behind creating this fear even if there is no such a thing? What kind of precaution has been taken by the Aintab kaimakam so as to avert such alleged horror and terror which Armenians were allegedly in?" and ordered Reşid Bey to inform the ministry about this matter.[47]

In November 1908, three CUP officials from Istanbul arrived in Aintab to investigate the beating of Necmeddin Bey. As a result, Ali Rıza Bey, a Muslim barber, Mennanzâde Mustafa Bey, painter Jirgi Barsumian, and tax collector Robert Tashdjian were arrested.[48] To maintain peace and order in the district, Aleppo governor Reşid Bey asked the Ministry of Interior to send the arrestees to Aleppo for trial, to which the ministry agreed.[49] Reşid Bey's persistence in having the prisoners tried in Aleppo was the result of their close ties with Armenians, of which he had been informed by the Aintab kaimakam. Thereupon, Reşid Bey shared this information with the ministry and reiterated his suggestion through a telegram sent on 21 February 1909.[50]

Upon receiving this news, local Dashnaksutiun administrators immediately visited the local CUP functionaries, ostensibly to discuss the situation of the two Armenian prisoners. Yet the investigating CUP officials were intent on punishing these five men. After holding several meetings among themselves, the Dashnaks decided to draw up three petitions and to collect signatures for the two Armenians' release. However, most Muslims were unwilling to sign the petitions.[51] The new spirit of brotherhood invoked by the constitution was falling apart. In the end, after remaining in prison for ten days, the prisoners were released and taken to Aintab.[52] Following this incident, political institutions and organizations in the city were divided into "Constitutionalists" and "opponents of the Constitution."

Nonetheless, Necmeddin Bey continued to serve as district governor in various districts.[53] Aintab Armenians encountered him once again in 1915, as most of them were deported to the Syrian town of Salamiyya, where he was the district governor. Ironically, he saved a number of Aintab Armenian families by recruiting them in various construction works.[54] Here, a conscientious, conservative, and pro-Hamidian Ottoman bureaucrat disobeyed the orders of the central government and used his power to save Armenians. In other words, during mass murders, one could argue that there is not always a direct connection between personal ideologies and individual actions of a person. On the other hand, it should also be noted that Necmeddin Bey was ultimately a government official with various duties. By saving those Armenians, he was also taking advantage of their labor, as he selected Armenians with certain skills to settle in Salamiyya.

Furthermore, of note here is that the CUP government—which overturned the Hamidian regime, revived the constitution, and reestablished the Parliament—chose to protect Necmeddin, an opponent of both Constitutionalists and Unionists. Most probably, one of the reasons for this was the reflex to preserve the state's authority and dignity. Even though he belonged to the bureaucratic cadres of the autocratic former regime, any insult or assault on his person was taken as an attack on the state itself, for Necmeddin Bey was a representative of the government, regardless of his political views. This fact elucidates that the CUP did not wish to reveal any authority gap, aiming to maintain law and order at all costs.

Another reason for this tolerance toward him was the CUP's lack of mass support and control on the local level. Historian Ali Birinci, known for his work on this period, stresses that crowded demonstrations that were held immediately after the declaration of the constitution—like the ones staged in Aintab—prevented people from realizing the true weakness of the CUP.[55] In fact at the time, the number of members registered to the CUP was considerably low.[56] Furthermore, the CUP had only limited information on its local representatives and members. As it assigned officials from party headquarters to investigate the Necmeddin Bey incident, the CUP unsuccessfully attempted to form a local organizational structure that submitted absolutely to its central authority through a strict hierarchy.[57] Lacking its own local bureaucratic and administrative cadres, the CUP was forced to form working relationships with leaders of the autocratic regime at the beginning of the constitutional period. Indeed, after the revival of the constitution and before the centrally planned purge in the summer of 1909, there were still bureaucrats throughout many provinces and towns of Anatolia who remained loyal to Abdülhamid II's regime.[58]

In this sense, one could say that the CUP government remained a *supervising* government until the military coup d'état, known as Bâb-ı Âli Baskını, on 23 January 1913 and the assassination of Mahmud Şevket Pasha on 11 July 1913.[59] After these two incidents, however, the CUP attained absolute power politically and administratively and was adamant about not sharing it with anyone else. In other words, the takeover of the Sublime Porte in January 1913, under the leadership of Enver Bey, brought to power a new government and marked the beginning of increased one-party rule under the CUP.[60]

The Adana Massacres and Self-Defense Preparations

Although the atmosphere calmed down relatively following the beating of Necmeddin Bey, the initial excitement over the 1908 revolution faded, leaving behind a climate of sociopolitical tension. This tension first manifested itself at the Central Turkey College in February 1909. A disagreement between the Armenian students and the college administration on the limits of the newfound "liberty" arose. The college instructors described this condition as a "delirium of liberty."[61] The students felt free to disobey the college's rules, while the faculty insisted that true liberty lies in faithfulness and obedience to the constitution and the authority of the college. The leading students of the unrest were Dashnaksutiun members. The situation quickly escalated when students insisted they had the fundamental right to bear arms. A critical moment came after the college administration rejected the students' seemingly moderate demand to recognize Vartanants Day,[62] a commemoration of the Battle of Avararyr, as a school holiday.[63] On 18 February, a large group of Armenian students gathered in front of the college to commemorate Vartanants Day. Student Sarkis Demirdjian addressed the group:

> Friends, liberty was declared in the Ottoman Empire. The inconsiderate faculty administration ignored our demand. We must commemorate our greatest national and religious holiday. And we will do so in spite of them. . . . Today, we are not going to school. We are going to the church to take part in the ceremony.[64]

Out of 200 students, 170 did not attend classes that day.[65] A more serious incident occurred when an expelled student entered a classroom with a revolver, threatening Professor Zenop Bezjian and demanding to be readmitted. To establish order and peace at the college, the local government was asked to provide an armed force.[66] Ultimately, suspecting secret propaganda of Armenian revolutionary organizations, the administration decided to close the college in early March 1909. Upon completing a detailed two-week investigation that concluded with the dismissal of seventy students believed to be Dashnaksutiun sympathizers, Central Turkey College reopened its doors.[67]

Shortly afterward, the Adana massacres, the second series of large-scale massacres of Armenians, broke out on 14–17 April and 25–27 April 1909, claiming more than twenty thousand Armenian lives.[68] Several factors hastened the arrival of conflict, including Muslim sentiments toward the elevated status of Christians, resentment created by increasing economic inequality, and demographic changes brought by both natural and man-made disasters. Cilicia would eventually become a melting pot of various ethnicities—Christians escaping the massacres of the 1890s, Caucasian *muhajirs,* Muslim economic migrants, Kurds,

Turcomans, and Circassians—all of whom (except for the Christians) had participated in the violent assaults on Armenians. The environment of rivalry resulting from the emerging national and ethnic groups and budding Armenian political freedoms gave rise to wild notions and rumors about the aspirations of Armenians in Cilicia. The constitutionally granted right for Armenians to bear arms and Armenian leaders' advocacy to exercise this right further inflamed the tensions.[69] This led to accusations being lobbed at both Muslims and Armenians of a collective arms race, which the Armenians admittedly had deemed imperative, given the increasing number of Armenian murders in the community.[70] Bedross Der Matossian, a renowned historian of the period, views the Adana massacres as part of the revolutionary process that resulted from "the erosion of social and political stability in the [Cilicia] region, the creation of weak public-sphere institutions, and the intensification of the existing economic anxieties, all of which led to the enactment of violence against the vulnerable Armenian population of Adana."[71]

At the same time, these slaughters coincided with the counterrevolution staged by supporters of Abdülhamid II. As the most powerful political force after the revolution, the CUP faced two types of opposition: the followers of Prince Sabahattin, united in the Ahrar Fırkası (Liberal Party); and conservative religious circles, namely, the lower ulema and sheikhs of the *tarikats* (religious sects). These religious circles were mostly represented by Nakhsbandi Sheikh Dervish Vahdeti and his Ittihad-i Muhammedi (Society of Muhammad), its extensions within the army, and the newspaper *Volkan*.[72] The counterrevolution of 31 March 1909 (13 April 1909 in the Gregorian calendar) was not "a spontaneous outburst by dissatisfied elements" in Istanbul; rather, "it was organized by oppositional elements and reactionary forces mainly represented by conservative religious circles."[73] On the next day, false rumors of an Armenian insurrection—fueled by the instigation of Muslim clergy, articles published in the newspaper *İtidal* (Moderation, an organ of the Young Turks), and the schemes of local notables, the gendarmerie, and high-ranking officials, including Governor Cevat Bey—drove waves of clashes, massacres, and looting in Adana.[74]

Aintab experienced its share of these developments. A dozen professors, teachers, and other respectable figures from Aintab's Protestant community participated in the annual meeting of the Evangelical Union held in Adana on 11 April.[75] On 14 April 1909, the news that they were burned alive in a Protestant church in Osmaniye reached Aintab.[76] This contagion of violence, presaged by fearful rumors, spread swiftly across the breadth of the Empire.[77] Dr. Shepard wanted to leave for Hassan Beyli to help the poor, but he was convinced that Aintab was in such a critical state that a massacre might occur at any moment.[78] Nerses Hagopian, a Dashnak leader, relays one provincial notable's view on the Adana massacres: "You Armenians, you covered a long distance in modernism. We weren't able to follow your lead; we weren't able to rise up to your level. . . . So we need to slaughter you every twenty to thirty years, to make you run with our pace!"[79]

Confronted with this mindset, the Armenian community in Aintab decided to form a resistance force following the Adana massacres, and prominent members of Dashnaksutiun gathered under the leadership of Hagopian.[80] Dashnaksutiun made every effort to work with CUP functionaries to prevent an unfortunate incident. Meanwhile, the organization used its power and resources to supply weapons, create funds, and send its members to Aleppo, Alexandria, and Beirut to organize further support.[81] However, these visits did not prove as beneficial as hoped.

On the other hand, the ideal positions for self-defense were identified from the residential areas on the west side of the city. If an attack were to be launched against Armenians, the Kozanlı and Akyol police stations and military guard posts in the surrounding areas would be invaded first. Therefore, the Armenian section of the district was divided into different zones, and at each post a band of warriors stood guard day and night. Weapons were distributed to children, who were encouraged to maintain vigilance.[82]

In the political sphere, it was clear that ARF's relations with the CUP would never be the same after the massacres. Fundamentally, ARF's commitment to the constitutional process and a possible alliance between the two parties were undermined.[83] A significant representative of the local Dashnaksutiun organization, Hovhannes Araradian, remarked:

> In those days, when Armenian and Muslim preachers gave their speeches in Çıkrıkçı Mosque's courtyard, an Armenian orator

> was speaking with a bouquet of flowers in his hands. He told his audience: "The Empire's unique population came together for the Constitutional Monarchy, like the flowers in this bouquet. Unless this bouquet of different flowers is held by capable and reliable hands, it will be watered by blood." And the Ottoman's constitutional regime was watered with Armenian blood in Adana on 31 March 1909. Turks who took a vow of "brotherhood" with Armenians were the ones who shed their blood. [84]

Soon, Armenians received news that Muslim notables were meeting with various groups and discussing preparations for massacres, but, according to rumors within the Muslim community, there were individuals who opposed massacring Armenians. Since Armenians were no longer as defenseless and unorganized as they had been in November 1895, Muslims believed that "the time for such cheap plundering, looting and easy slaughtering had now passed."[85] Thus, Aintab stayed relatively calm, and a period of peaceful coexistence—though fragile—prevailed in the district.[86]

In the meantime, a coup attempt launched on 13 April 1909 to topple the CUP government, during which the military called for a return to Islamic law, was suppressed on 24 April by Hareket Ordusu (the Action Army) from Macedonia, under the command of Mahmud Şevket Pasha.[87] This attempted coup incited the massacres that would erupt in Adana, rapidly spreading to the rest of Cilicia and concluding on 27 April with sporadic bursts of violence the following month. Local police and military forces, in an ominous and troubling manner for the Armenians, actively partook in the killings.[88]

The Case of the Severed Head

On 3 May 1909, an event that came to be known in Aintab as *Kesik Baş Vakası* (the case of the severed head) took place.[89] Given the historical context and rising tensions between Muslims and Armenians, it is necessary to give attention to this incident. A basket containing a severed head was thrown into the lot adjacent to an Armenian Protestant church, leaving the impression that an Armenian had murdered a Muslim.

A Muslim woman discovered the severed head and ran wailing to the Muslim neighborhood to break the news.[90] She screamed, "Infidels killed this Muslim, cut his head off and threw it to the garden."[91] Upon hearing the news, Muslims were filled with anger toward local Armenians and were intent upon taking revenge. Massacres similar to those that took place in Adana seemed imminent. In response, Armenians closed their shops and withdrew to their houses. All young Armenian men took their positions and waited.[92] To uncover the truth and calm the agitated Muslims, kaimakam Ali Kemal Bey and Ahmed Agha, a local notable, worked tirelessly.[93] In addition, certain Muslim citizens, local administrators, and local CUP rulers contributed to these efforts.[94]

Meanwhile, an old Muslim woman approached the kaimakam's office, asking to view the severed head. Upon examining the head closely, it was discovered that one of the teeth in the dead man's mouth was missing. The woman right away recalled that her son had had a tooth removed the previous week and got up from her seat, claiming, "This is my son!"[95] The old woman blamed her son-in-law, who was also her son's business associate. The police chief and other policemen arrested him, as it was evident from bloodstains that the severed head had come from his house.[96]

The perpetrator of the Kesik Baş case was tried in Aleppo, with the attendance of a number of Armenians and Muslims. Ahmed Agha made significant efforts to have the guilty man hanged in Aintab, and Ali Kemal Bey used all his power to maintain the peace.[97] The murderer was executed publicly at Arasa Market Square (Figure 2.1).[98] Later, Ali Kemal Bey was rewarded with a letter of appreciation from Aleppo Province for preventing a potential disturbance.[99] After the execution, relations between the two groups evolved into a "relative state of normality." Yet this "normality" no longer had a solid foundation and was vulnerable to break at any moment.

The presence of local CUP authorities in Aintab in 1909 was intended to prevent similar massacres. Specifically, the authorities tried to preclude anti-CUP softas, as well as Turkish, Kurdish, and Arab tribes in and around Aintab, from provoking Muslim citizens.[100] Thanks to the

FIGURE 2.1 Execution of the culprit of the *Kesik Baş* (severed head) incident in May 1909. Reproduced from *Badmo'wt'iwn Ah'nt'abi Hah'o'c*, vol. I, 980.

efforts of pro-CUP district governor Ali Kemal Bey and Ahmed Agha, one of the influential Aintab CUP club members, as well as some men of religion, sheikhs, and other local administrators, no massacres took place in the district.[101] In fact, Ali Kemal Bey was rewarded by the CUP government for his efforts. More important, organized defense mechanisms of Aintab Armenians were the main deterrent for local Muslims.

The Adana pogroms and the massacre attempts in Aintab are significant indicators of the interaction between the central government and local actors. Armenians gained an important lesson from the 1895 slaughters, preparing themselves for other potential atrocities, developing various self-defense mechanisms, and arming themselves. Despite the CUP's and Dashnaksutiun's joint efforts in 1909, a lack of trust between them was reflected by Aintab Armenians, who maintained their vigilance until 1915. Meanwhile, rather than seeking to repair this distrust, the CUP's actions in Aintab further aggravated the situation. The determination of the Armenian political leaders at the time was that their community should be prepared in some measure to defend themselves in case of future attempts at massacre.

Overall, the six years following the declaration of the constitution was a constructive period of economic, cultural, and educational improvement for Aintab, especially for Armenians. Nevertheless, Armenians came to know the unpredictability of violence and the unreliability of Ottoman justice, bearing in mind their still-recent experiences of mass killing in 1894–1897 and the Adana massacres in 1909. As Ronald G. Suny asserts, young political activists "moved between optimism that they would be able to protect their vulnerable compatriots and pessimism about their ability to organize and mobilize them." The emotional world of Aintab Armenians was "colored by vulnerability, uncertainty, and mistrust tinged with condescension" directed at the Muslim community.[102] As demonstrated by incidents in the Central Turkey College, Adana massacres, and the severed head case, the relations between Armenian and Muslim communities undulated, filled with ethno-political tensions until the mobilization of 1914.

The second constitutional period was replete with political failures for the CUP, especially in the international arena. At the very beginning of the July 1908 revolution, Austria-Hungarian officially annexed Bosnia-Herzegovina. Following the annexation, Bulgaria declared outright independence, and the Cretan deputies proclaimed unilateral union with Greece by taking advantage of domestic turmoil in the CUP government. The counterrevolution started by followers of Abdülhamid II culminated in his dethronement. Subsequently, the CUP cracked down on the political opposition, imposing martial law to curtail fundamental liberties. Strikes were banned for all public services, labor unions were dissolved, political demonstrations were forbidden, and the Press Law was enacted to restrict freedom of the press.[103] The Turkification process was codified and expanded in 1910 and 1911, including the settlement of foreign Turkic and Muslim groups around transportation hubs and cultural and linguistic prohibitions for Albanians and Arabs, increasing their marginalization within the Empire.

At the same time, the CUP had to turn its attention to revolts led by the Druses south of Damascus, as well as uprisings in Albania and Yemen.[104] In the immediate aftermath of the Tripolitania (Italo-Turkish) War, which saw Italian victory, the Balkan Wars of 1912–1913 broke out. Greece allied with Bulgaria, Serbia, and Montenegro in the Balkan League against the Ottoman Empire. They wrested Macedonia from the Empire, though then proceeding to fight among themselves over how to divide the territorial spoils of war. The total and permanent loss of the Balkan Peninsula in 1913 and the secession of the Muslim province of Albania "accelerated the transition from a general Muslim consciousness in the CUP to a specifically Turkish one."[105]

During this period, economic boycotts developed out of the CUP's political response to these defeats. Having begun to protest the annexation of Bosnia-Herzegovina, the boycotts had as their main target European companies and business enterprises of Ottoman Christian subjects.[106] In fact, by 1910–1911, the systematic boycott movement was initiated to target the shops owned by Christian Ottomans (particularly Greeks) and Jewish Ottomans as well. A coordinated campaign of atrocity propaganda, intended to heighten the stigmatization and consequent dehumanization of Ottoman Christians, was implemented following the routing experienced by the Ottomans in the Balkans.[107]

Sensationalized stories of Muslims being abused and violated at the hands of Christians were spread, stoking enmity against the Muslims' fellow countrymen and setting the stage for the violence to come.[108] According to this atrocity-propaganda discourse, non-Muslims were "sucking blood of Muslims." As Yusuf Doğan Çetinkaya quotes, for instance, in public lectures on hygiene delivered in the province of Aydın, medical students Behçet Salih, Mahmed Halit, and Mustafa Muzaffer depicted the Christians as vipers:

> We are brokenhearted at finding you Muslims are still asleep. The Christians, profiting from our ignorance, have now for ages been taking our place and taking away our rights. These vipers whom we were nourishing have been sucking out all the lifeblood of the nation. They are the parasitical worms into out flesh whom we must destroy and do away with. It is time we freed

> ourselves from these individuals, by all means lawful and unlawful.[109]

All manner of actions—public meetings, demonstrations, boycotts, picketing, destruction of property, pogroms—were used to foment hatred against non-Muslims. The effort extended across all societal lines, with elites and workers, artisans and officers all contributing to the "othering" of Christians, a crucial step in preparing the public for collective violence.[110] The 1912–1913 Balkan Wars, which chipped away at the Empire's remaining European territory and resulted in a loss of its most fecund farmland, marked the end of any possibility of political compromise within the CUP. In addition, as displaced Muslim refugees from the Balkans sought shelter in Anatolia, great pressure was exerted on the minorities who had resided there for centuries, further polarizing social relations. Yet perhaps the most significant impact was psychological. For the first time in Ottoman history, the dominant Turkish Muslim majority experienced the fear of annihilation.

The loss of most of the territory of Macedonia at the end of the Balkan Wars was a source of acute national humiliation. At this juncture, for the CUP, the only remaining option was to establish a cult of ethnic nationalism and Islam in the rechristened Turkish homeland, Anatolia. Mehmed Emin, a leading nationalist and CUP intellectual, assured his readers that the Turkish nation would not succumb. In his poem "Young Turk," published in *Turkish Homeland,* he wrote: "The Turkish state will not die. No, I am a noble Turk. I descend from a lineage the blood of which makes the essence of history. I know how to die as well as how to kill. I lower any hand that threatens the Turks, even if that enemy hand would be mine."[111] The trauma of defeat and the exacerbated fear of the erasure of the Turkish state and nation demanded a national revival. "The Bulgarians—the milkmen—the Serbians—the swineherds—even the Greek—the tavern keepers" defeated the Ottomans, "who had been their masters for 500 years."[112] The Balkan nations, Armenians, and other Christians were portrayed as being goaded by the West to seek (illegitimate) privileges at the Turks' expense.

With the conclusion of the Balkan Wars, the issue of reform still unresolved for the eastern provinces, and the failure of collaboration between Armenian political organizations and the CUP government,

Armenians again turned for assistance to Russia, which viewed the circumstances as ideal to further entrench itself in areas of withering Ottoman influence. Mirroring the process that the Russians had pursued in 1878 with the Armenians, and with support from the Armenian Catholicos, a reform scheme arose in the midst of waning Ottoman strength and the Empire's acceptance of its diminishing territory.[113] The reform package, as enacted in February 1914, mandated the establishment of two zones, comprising the six Armenian provinces and the Black Sea province of Trabzon, which would be governed by impartial inspectors general (Westenenk from the Netherlands and Hoff from Norway) endorsed by the central Ottoman authorities.[114] In the eyes of the CUP triumvirate (Enver-Talat-Cemal), the reform agreement was viewed as a violation of national sovereignty, national security, and national honour. In the words of Zaven Der Yeghiayan, then Armenian Patriarch of Istanbul, "the Ittihadist government had not forgiven the Armenians for having asked for European controls. . . . Because of this, the Ittihadists were filled with vengefulness toward the Armenians, perceiving them as an element that was inviting foreign interference and letting itself become the tool of foreign states."[115] This imposed reform agreement reinforced Turkish resentment toward non-Muslims.

On the eve of World War I, this mindset of the CUP leaders—fostering and legitimizing radical ideas in the Empire—paralleled the rise to power of Enver, and with him a radical militant segment within the Young Turks, including those who would become two major perpetrators of 1915, Dr. Nazım and Dr. Bahaeddin Şakir. This reform plan fueled radical voices in the CUP, evident in Talat's reprimand of the Armenians at the onset of the deportations the following year. The plan, moreover, signaled the injection of fury into discourse for decades to come.[116] While the CUP started the revolution to restore the Ottoman constitution and Parliament, the euphoria was short-lived. Both domestic political developments and international geopolitics contributed to the failure of the *Ittihad-ı Anasır* (Ottoman unity), and the experience of total war sealed the Empire's fate. The 1915 Armenian genocide marks the end of Ottomanism. It dispenses whatever hope there was remaining for the making of a multicultural, multireligious, and multiethnic modern polity based on relations of mutual obligations between the sultan and his subjects.[117]

·3·

Wartime Deportation and Destruction of the Aintab Armenians

The CUP leadership became hostile to the Great Powers following the empire's failures in foreign policy and defeats in the front in 1908, 1911, and 1912–1913. Nonetheless, the Unionists were keen to search for protectors among these countries.[1] First, Cavid Bey, the minister of Finance, communicated with the British Foreign Office. His request in 1913, however, was rejected by Sir Edward Grey. Then the Unionists sought partnership with Austria-Hungary in February 1914, with Russia in May of the same year, and finally with France in July. The only power to return the Ottoman's call was Germany, in August.[2] Meanwhile, the Great Powers were in conflict themselves. Archduke Franz Ferdinand's assassination in 1914 was the final stroke that brought them to war.

On 24 July 1914, the Ottoman General Staff issued a draft. Four days later, when Austria-Hungary declared war on Serbia, the Ottoman minister of war, Enver Pasha, made a proposal to Ambassador Wangenheim for a defensive alliance, which came to fruition on 2 August, a day after Germany declared war on Russia. A general mobilization was issued by the CUP government a day later.[3] On 6 August, Austria-Hungary joined the Turco-German alliance, finalizing the Central Powers bloc. Russia, France, and Britain, on the other hand, took sides under the Entente Powers. Over the next four years, the Ottoman Empire enlisted approximately three million men from all across the empire. Roughly "a quarter of them died in combat and of disease, half a million deserted, and some 250,000 were captured and taken prisoner."[4]

News of the mobilization was disseminated by the state, being called out by town criers and printed in newspapers. Local officials hung posters on any available wall—in municipal buildings, mosques, coffeehouses, schools—as well as distributing them to village headmen.[5] Accordingly, on 3 August 1914, the news spread about the declaration of general mobilization throughout Aintab. The town criers announced the decision with joy, and the town square filled with people. Everyone was excited; flags with a crescent and star were hung in front of all shops and on minarets.[6] An eyewitness described the scene: "Chants of 'Allah-u Akbar!' echoed from minaret to minaret. The town criers were running around shouting, 'Compatriots, long live Turks; let's march against the enemy.'"[7]

Heading the procession led by soldiers and officials, mullahs were murmuring verses from the Koran, and dervishes from *tekkes* (convents) were praying with a religious zeal. Disciples of dervishes were carrying *Sancak-ı Şerif* (the banner of the Prophet).[8] The people were promising that they would destroy the "infidels" without fear and mightily take Sancak-ı Şerif to the highest level.[9] Armenian religious leaders and notables also joined the celebrations. At the same time, the ARF, at a party congress in Erzurum, were conducting back-channel negotiations with CUP representatives. Hoping to capitalize on the ARF's sizable base of Russian-Armenians, the CUP presented a plan wherein the Dashnaksutiun's Transcaucasia organization would be used to facilitate an Ottoman attack behind Russian lines. The ARF swiftly refused to participate in such a scheme, upon which the CUP withdrew any pretense of alliance with the Armenians.[10] Thus, on 6 September 1914, Minister of Interior Talat Pasha ordered provincial authorities to "follow and monitor the behaviour and movements of people there from among the leaders of the Armenian political party and committee leaders who do not refrain from the dissemination of sedition and abominable deeds against Ottomanism and who for a long time have pursued political aspirations."[11]

Allied with Germany, the Ottoman Empire entered the war in October 1914. Until late October, "the Ottoman political leadership had maintained an armed neutrality, hoping that Germany would win the war before it became necessary" to enter the fray. As Eric J. Zürcher observes, after the German defeat on the Marne in mid-September, it was evident that "the war on the western front would not be won quickly, and German pressure on the Ottomans to join the war effort increased."[12] By late October, the CUP leaders in Istanbul agreed to send an Ottoman naval squadron to attack Russian Black Sea naval bases. A month after the naval attack that culminated in "the Russian declaration of war (followed by those of France, Britain, Serbia and Montenegro), the Ottoman sultan proclaimed a Jihad" on 14 November 1914 to mobilize the support of its Muslim subjects in a time of war.[13] This declaration provided Turkish-Muslims with a particular sense of "holy war" that had to be waged against both local Ottoman Christians and the occupying forces of France, Britain, Russia, and Italy. The introduction of this ideology reframed the political struggle as a millenarian one with no room for compromise or moderation, facilitating the extremes of violence perpetrated against the Christian populations.

The Ottoman government launched two military campaigns, both focusing on regions with Muslim inhabitants and hoping to draw on their support. December 1914 marks the first campaign orchestrated by Enver Pasha, which took place across the Russian border and extended into the Caucasus, where the Ottoman military pushed to regain the three provinces it lost in 1878, as well as the oil-rich Baku. A year later, in January 1915, the campaign for Sinai and the Suez Canal was launched, this time run by Cemal Pasha, minister of the Navy, governor of Syria, and commander of the Fourth Army.[14]

On the supposed basis of the principle of equality for all Ottoman subjects, the CUP government adopted conscription for all citizens.[15] Delivered in the May 1914 Mükellefiyet-i Askeriye Kanun-ı Muvakkatı (Law of Military Obligation), all male Ottoman citizens between the ages of twenty and forty-five, regardless of ethnicity or religion, were required to perform military service.[16] Everyone was expected to fight wholeheartedly for and provide financial support to the Empire. In each household, articles that would be of use for military personnel were claimed.[17] Those who most bore the brunt of this financial support were non-Muslim merchants. Available goods in these merchants' hands were subjected to a process of *müsadere* (seizure). In Aintab, mainly Armenians were left to shoulder the entire burden.

Besides the palpable political and social fear and anxiety, the mobilization yielded a destabilizing effect on Aintab's economy. As the production mechanisms of the time relied overwhelmingly on manual labor, this large-scale conscription of the male populace essentially halted the region's commerce. Without their able-bodied men to provide, many families fell into destitution. However, there was a sense of unity among the citizens of Aintab. For instance, in mid-November 1914, a group of sheikhs, imams (Muslim religious leaders), mullahs, priests, rabbis, civil servants, aghas, teachers, and intellectuals distributed bags of bread and ground wheat to thousands of soldiers while seeing them off from Aintab's Akçakoyunlu train station.[18] But this atmosphere was to be short-lived, suffering a complete breakdown following the Sarıkamış disaster.

The Ottoman army attempted to regain Kars, formerly an Ottoman province, under the leadership of Enver Pasha in late December 1914. The campaign had catastrophic results for the army, where thousands of soldiers froze to death in the frigid mountains of Sarıkamış, Kars.[19] The Third Army, entering with 90,000 troops, ultimately retreated with its numbers reduced to 12,000; of those who perished, the majority did not die in combat but succumbed to the elements.[20] At the same time, smaller campaigns with irregular forces led by Enver's brother-in-law Cevdet and Enver's uncle General Halil (Kut) Pasha in northern Persia harassed and attacked Armenian and Syriac villages but again failed in their military objectives. Believing that their calamitous failure was a result of "treacherous Armenian elements," the CUP leadership embarked upon an extensive purge, focusing on the provinces of Erzurum, Bitlis, and Van.[21] In a decree on 26 December 1914, Talat called for "the dismissal of all Armenian police officers, police chiefs, and government employees, and the deportation of anyone who opposes these measures."[22] This represented a new level of state distrust of the Armenians.

Another setback was experienced in Egypt, when Cemal Pasha's Fourth Army was decisively defeated by the British in February 1915 in what became known as the First Canal Expedition. Following its defeat on the Caucasus front and amid swirling rumors of Armenians voluntarily surrendering to the enemy and divulging Ottoman military plans, the army's suspicion of non-Muslim soldiers boiled over. On 25 February 1915, the army's high command stripped these troops of their uniforms and weapons before removing the soldiers from combat duty and reassigning them to labor battalions.[23] The twin recent failures of the Entente's unsuccessful attempt to force the Dardanelles and the crushing blow received at Sarıkamış catalyzed a shift in the mentality of the Ottomans, who now viewed themselves as besieged on all sides.

In the meantime, in February 1915, the Catholicos of Cilicia Sahag II Khabaian (1849–1939), accompanied by Fahri Pasha, second in command in the Fourth Army, paid an unexpected visit to Aintab.[24] In his visit, the Catholicos advised the Armenians to properly obey the government's orders and urged them to lend their assistance to the government. Fahri Pasha stressed that Armenians needed to consider what was beneficial for the empire and to collaborate in order to crush the Ottomans' enemies. This visit and Fahri Pasha's message reassured Armenians to some extent and assuaged their fears.[25] However, in March 1915, news from Zeitun and Marash alarmed Aintab Armenians again, causing them to doubt the promises of Sahag II and Fahri Pasha.[26]

Furthermore, the local Young Turks launched a campaign against French and British organizations and then conducted an anti-Armenian boycott and propaganda tour through the villages.[27] In fact, since 1913 an economic boycott against Greek products and producers was in place. This Muslim boycott came as a result of the Balkan Wars and was orchestrated by the CUP.[28] The 1914 ethnic cleansing that the Ottoman government carried out, particularly targeting the Greeks in Thrace and the Aegean littoral, was "initially attempted through a severe economic boycott and by other intimidating measures."[29] The Greek presence in Thrace and the Aegean coast was seen as a threat. The CUP had a plan to exchange non-Muslim populations with their Muslim counterparts, for the Muslims were considered a more loyal group. Both socially and politically, the environment was set to justify actions by the Muslim population and commands by the members of the nationalist movement, with both groups exultant to prioritize Muslim gains over the welfare of non-Muslims. A xenophobic milieu was created that would eventually culminate into genocidal policies.[30] Also instrumental in the Greek expulsions were CUP efforts to form a Turkish-Muslim middle class, while eroding the foundations of the Christian community.

Not only Greeks but also Armenians suffered from the boycott movement between 1913 and 1914. Local nationalist cadres and notables who actively participated in the boycott movement against Greeks took advantage of this political climate and targeted Armenians as well. The local CUP leaders encouraged a general boycott of Armenian businesses; more specifically, they encouraged peasants from surrounding villages to default on their debts to Armenians and refuse to cultivate their lands. Peasants were told that soon there would be not one Armenian left in Aintab. Similar sermons were given at the district's mosques.[31] These developments were harbingers of the coming genocide.

Aintab as Outlier

The demography of Aintab at the onset of World War I remains crucial context for the deportation process. Various Armenian, French, and British sources estimate the Armenian population of Aintab in 1914 as somewhere between 32,000 and 37,000.[32] According to Turkish sources, the total number of Armenians was between 20,000 and 30,000.[33] The deportation of Aintab's Armenians began in August 1915,[34] late compared with the deportations in most eastern regions. The first such deportations, from the Cilician towns of Dörtyol and Zeitun, commenced in mid-February 1915.[35] These deportations were an informal, small-scale response to local events. Dörtyol, because of its location on the shores of the Mediterranean Sea, was vulnerable to Entente military landings, and Armenians there were not trusted.[36] Using the pretext that Armenians were in collaboration with foreign submarines, Cemal Pasha ordered an operation against the Armenians of Dörtyol, leading to the arrest of 1,600 men.[37] After this operation, fighting broke out with Armenian draft dodgers from Zeitun who had taken refuge in the mountains.[38] As these clashes continued, in a coded telegram dated 26 February 1915, Cemal Pasha made a proposal to the interior minister to deport Armenian families from these two locations.[39] In his response, dated 2 March, the minister ordered the Armenians to be "sent to the locations that had been set for this purpose," adding, "It is necessary not only to let develop conditions that might lead to revolution or revolt, but also to act forcefully and speedily in areas where Armenian operations and activities increase, and to extinguish every incident, with effective and definitive methods, together with the local causes that have caused the incident."[40]

The first formal decision for deportation was issued on 8 April 1915, following an exchange of coded telegrams between Enver, Talat, and Cemal.[41] Essentially, it was Cemal Pasha himself who ordered deportation for Zeitun and who dictated to Talat the relevant instructions. Stating in his telegram dated 8 April to the interior minister that the rebels in Zeitun were "harb-i şedid ile kahr [violently suppressed]" and were now "kuzu gibi [like sheep]," Cemal Pasha ordered the deportation of certain families to Konya.[42] In order to resolve the Zeitun issue once and for all, he requested that more than one-third of Zeitun Armenians be sent to Konya and settled in its Muslim-dominated neighborhoods.[43]

In a telegram sent to Enver, Cemal had declared that "the transfer of those whose residence in Zeitun and Marash is deemed to be harmful [to Konya], is absolutely necessary," because "otherwise the enemy's landing" would "make it necessary to station many troops in this area."[44] Zeitun's deportations began with the departure of thirty-five Armenian notables and their families.[45]

The moves were not aimed at extermination; they were strategically motivated and resulted from political anxieties.[46] The transition from strategic to genocidal deportations occurred during the Van uprising on 19 April 1915. Having failed in his military campaign in Iranian Azerbaijan, Governor Cevdet Bey entered Van with his henchmen and installed his reign of terror in the city in late March. First, his demand for drafting four thousand Armenian males came to naught. Then, Cevdet ordered the assassination of ARF leader Ishkhan and Van Deputy Vramian on 16 and 17 April, respectively. On the following day, news of the massacres executed in the surrounding regions reached Van. At the same time, Cevdet Bey ordered the Armenians of Van to surrender their weapons to the authorities. Surrounded by Turkish forces, Armenians responded to his call by instigating an uprising on 19 April.[47]

Because of Armenian resistance in Van and the fear of enemy landing in Gallipoli, the final destination of deportations was changed from Konya to quasi-desert areas of Syria on 24 April 1915.[48] Because "a collective presence" in a place like Konya, where the Armenians of Zeitun and Marash had been exiled, "would after a while lead to a coordination of activities with local Armenians," orders were issued "not to send other Armenians to that area [Konya] in addition to those sent up now." Instead, "those, whose expulsion from places like İskenderun, Dörtyol, Adana, Hacin, Zeitun, or Sis [was] deemed necessary" were to be sent to the southeast of Aleppo, as well as Deir ez-Zor and Urfa.[49] On the same day, house raids and arrests of leading Armenians began in Istanbul and then spread to other provinces. Including many Hunchakian and Dashnaksutiun members—as well as cultural, intellectual, educational, and church leaders—these arrestees were sent to central Anatolia, where the majority of them were killed.[50]

In early May, deportation in the region of Cilicia gained momentum. In fact, on 9 May, orders were sent for the deportation of all Armenians from Zeitun, as well as Furnuz (north of Zeitun), Kaban, and Alabahçe.[51] Meanwhile, Armenian resistance in Van followed by the arrival of the Russian army on 19 May led to the widening of the deportation's scope.[52] Once Van had been controlled by the Russian forces, "the distinction between 'innocent' and 'guilty' Armenians was rendered meaningless, both ideologically and practically in CUP eyes."[53] For the CUP, the Van uprising was the realization of "a prophecy of Armenian treachery."[54] As Türkyılmaz argues, Van was "the site in the Ottoman Empire where the genocidal intent of the Young Turk government first materialized."[55] In the same vein, Bloxham hints at the Van episode contributing to the "exacerbation of existing CUP policy and the unleashing of its most extreme tendencies."[56] In this regard, "Van is precisely illustrative of a process of cumulative radicalization towards a policy of genocide," as well as the extension of the scope of the deportations.[57]

Indeed, in May 1915, the Ottoman government embarked on a deportation policy that would evolve into an empire-wide program, ultimately targeting the Empire's entire Ottoman Armenian population. On 23 May 1915, new regions were added to the deportation list.

According to the list of instructions received by Cemal Pasha, the Armenian population was to be removed from:

> (1) The provinces of Erzurum, Van, and Bitlis, (2) Besides the provinces of Adana, Mersin, Kozan, and Cebel-i Bereket, the population of the cities of Adana, Sis, and Mersin. (3) The provincial district of Marash, besides the population of the city of Marash. (4) The town and villages inside the counties of İskenderun, Bilan, Cisr-i Şuğur, and Antalya, besides the central county of the Aleppo province.[58]

That same day, Talat Pasha "urged the Fourth Army Command to court-martial any Muslim who collaborated with Christians."[59] The large-scale deportations of 24 April 1915 and 23 May 1915 "signified an intensification of the anti-Armenian measures, escalating in the summer of 1915 into genocidal destruction."[60] On 24 May, under Russian leadership, the Entente (Britain, France, and Russia) issued a declaration "promising to hold Ottoman leaders and officials accountable for atrocities against Christians."[61] Nevertheless, the atrocities intensified still further on the very next day. On 26 May, Talat Pasha requested permission from the grand vizier to promulgate a temporary deportation law.[62] This was the "official legal cover for the deportation of Armenians to the Syrian desert."[63] The execution of the deportation program rested with the Ministry of Interior and especially with the ministry's İskan-ı Aşair ve Muhacirin Müdüriyeti (Directorate for the Settlement of Tribes and Immigrants; hereafter IAMM).

On 21 June, the CUP government issued new orders to deport "all Armenians, without exception" from Trabzon, Diyarbekir, Canik, Sivas and Ma'muretü'l-aziz.[64] Aintab, however, had not yet become an "area of displacement."[65] In fact, in a coded telegram sent by Talat to Cemal regarding the deportations, its Armenians were not mentioned among those to be expelled from Aleppo province.[66] On 20 July, Talat Pasha asked all governors and district governors to prepare maps and statistical tables of the ethnic composition of all villages and neighborhoods.[67]

Only at the end of July 1915 was Aintab included in the planned deportation scheme.

Provocateurs and Protectors

In late March 1915, Aleppo's provincial governor Celal Bey reported to Cemal Pasha that some Armenians living in Aintab's Muslim quarters were discreetly moving their belongings to the Armenian quarters. The news was creating great concern among the Muslim population, who feared that the Armenians were preparing to revolt. Cemal Pasha informed the Ministry of Interior, which in response ordered Aleppo province to make the following announcement in Aintab on 29 March: "No Armenian shall be allowed change of place [*tebdil-i mekan*]; those who have done so shall return to their prior neighborhood." But it added the reassuring promise that "the properties, lives, and honour of the population loyal to the Government shall be protected against any attacks, and the slightest assault by the Muslim population against any Armenian, even if they were revolutionaries or rioters, shall be subject to immediate disciplinary action."[68] As it turned out, Aintab's Armenians eventually *were* deported—but only in August 1915, after much of the rest of Eastern Anatolia had already been "cleansed." Why were Aintab's Armenians spared for so long?

Aram Andonian, an Armenian journalist and intellectual who survived arrest and deportation in late April 1915 and found refuge in Aleppo, had immediately begun collecting information on the government's annihilation campaign and would continue to do so throughout the war. His files contain material on Aintab that provide an invaluable source for the dynamics driving the fate of Aintab's Armenians.[69] Andonian learned that as early as March 1915 the leaders of Aintab's CUP branch—led by Ali Cenani, the district's parliamentary deputy; Fadıl Bey, the former district governor of Kilis; and Hacı Mustafa Bey, a prominent Kilis notable—began taking advantage of the incidents in Zeitun and Marash to depict Aintab's own Armenians as a harmful element. The CUP leaders repeatedly appealed to Istanbul, hoping to obtain a deportation order for the Armenians of Aintab and Kilis.[70] The appeal was thwarted, however, by Mehmed Şükrü Bey, Aintab's district governor, and Hilmi Bey, Aintab military commander, even though both men—as Armenian survivors noted—were themselves Unionists. The military commander simply informed the central government that there was no valid reason for deportation. Other Armenians in the district, Kirkor Bogharian and Sebuh Aguni, confirm Andonian's picture of Mehmed Şükrü Bey's and Hilmi Bey's opposition to deportation.[71]

Not daunted by this official opposition, the three Aintabi notables, with the assistance of their Marash counterparts, then organized provocations.[72] They also sent telegrams to the central government claiming that Aintab Armenians had attacked mosques with weapons, killed Muslims, raped Muslim women, burned down Muslim houses, and plundered their properties.[73] Hilmi Bey responded by personally requesting Cemal Pasha to punish the notables as provocateurs. Although his opponents countered by branding Hilmi as an Armenian sympathizer, Celal Bey added his support for the commander by reporting that this situation was causing great panic among Aintab Armenians.[74] His investigations revealed an Armenian community that feared general massacre (*umumi kıtal*).[75]

In light of these charges and countercharges, Cemal Pasha dispatched Fahri Pasha to Aintab on 8 April 1915 to investigate in person.[76] Police searches of the Armenian neighborhoods failed to provide any confirmation of the accusations of deputy Ali Cenani and his cronies.[77] In fact, the American consul of Aleppo, Jesse B. Jackson, noted that Fahri Pasha announced to Aintab's leading Muslims, in the presence of Christians, "If any Muslim frightened Christians [Armenians] or in any way treated them unkindly, he would himself hang him even if the offender were his own brother."[78] He himself behaved toward Christian leaders in Aintab in a very friendly manner. However, according to the German consul at Aleppo, Walter Rössler, the Christians were deceived by Fahri, to whom he attributed "the harshest and most merciless implementation of the deportation."[79]

In fact, after Fahri Pasha left Aintab, the situation worsened. Following the Van uprising, Ali Bey, a ranking member of Teşkilat-ı Mahsusa (the Special Organization, hereafter SO) and bandit leader, was summoned by Ali Cenani and in late April arrived in Aintab. The SO emerged primarily out of the experience of the CUP in the Tripolitanian and Balkan wars. An early unconventional warfare organization, the SO officially existed from 13 November 1913 to 30 October 1918. Its operations included "the recruitment, training, and supervision of armed groups tasked with conducting asymmetric warfare to weaken enemy morale and fighting strength."[80] Units of this organization were involved in executing the deportations, boycotts, and massacres directed at Armenians and other Ottoman Christians during World War I.[81] Ali Bey, a fierce member of the SO, came to Aintab along with a squadron of bandits, mostly consisting of Kurds and Arabs from villages surrounding Aintab, who began organized pillaging and the first murders outside the city.[82] Then, on 30 April 1915, the first raids *inside* the city took place.[83] To obtain the weapons and "harmful" writings, alleged to be hidden in Aintab, the houses of prominent Armenians, including Dashnaksutiun and Hunchakian members, were raided. Nothing incriminating was found.[84] Nevertheless, many Armenians were arrested. Another wave of house searches was conducted on 1 May, and ten men were arrested and brought before the military court in Aleppo.[85] In addition, thirty leading political figures from the Armenian community were sent to Aleppo for interrogation. Following the questioning, eighteen were returned to Aintab.[86] Again, no incriminating evidence was found, and all were set free. On 12 May, house raids and individual arrests of intellectuals peaked with the collective arrests of 200 people,[87] but the provincial governor, Celal Bey, helped release most of those apprehended.[88] Some detainees were freed on the same day and others a few days later.

Watching Their Future

Meanwhile, Aintab's Armenians became witnesses to the deportations of those from less fortunate regions. As house raids and police searches in Aintab continued, on 3 May they saw the first convoy, comprising three hundred women and children from Zeitun, pass through their city.[89] The deportees had suffered greatly on their way. Some were injured, their wounds infected and their clothes in tatters.[90] Miss Frearson, an American missionary worker, noted that Aintab's Armenians could form a relief committee for the deportees. John Merrill from the Central Turkey College and Dr. Hamilton and the nurses from the American Hospital also exerted strenuous efforts to aid the deportees, many of whom—children included—were suffering from serious knife wounds.[91] More deportees followed. In fact, the US consul of Aleppo, Jesse B. Jackson, observed:

> From Zeitun, 350 families, or about 2,000 persons, have been sent to Marash and from there to Aintab, and are expected to arrive in Aleppo about May 1915, to be sent to Meskené, while about 250 or more families are expected to follow before 20 May to report to the Governor of Aleppo.[92]

Indeed, throughout June and July 1915, convoys from Zeitun, Marash, Elbistan, Gürün, Sivas, and Furnuz continued to fill the streets of Aintab, on their way south toward Syria.[93] All of them were in a similar destitute condition, having suffered continual attacks on their persons and property along the way.[94] All deportees were kept in the Kavaklık neighborhood, fifteen minutes from the city center, near a spring where they had to pay gendarmes a quarter of *mecidiye* (five kurush or piasters—the smallest denomination of Turkish currency; one piaster equals fifteen pfennigs) per glass of water.[95] Aintab's Armenians bribed the gendarmes and tried to supply the deportees with food and water themselves. Yet while the Armenians in Aintab bore witness to these horrors, they did not consider the possibility that they could face a similar fate.[96] Vahe N. Gulesserian, who was there, described this state of mind with this striking passage:

> In spite of everything that was happening around us and in spite of all the facts standing right in front of our eyes, the number of those who buried their head in the sand like an ostrich was not small. These people convinced themselves that they were happy, and they tried to deceive themselves into believing that a similar deportation was not possible for Aintab and that nothing bad would happen to them.[97]

Previously, Armenians had relied upon the honesty and kindness of Celal Bey, Mehmed Şükrü Bey, and Hilmi Bey as a shield against deportation.[98] The period of wishful thinking ended when Cemal Bey, general secretary of Aleppo's CUP branch, arrived in late June, accompanied by a few propagandists.[99] The mission of this Unionist cadre was to convince Aintab's notables to repeat their entreaties to Istanbul to issue a deportation order. Cemal Bey succeeded in pressuring the local CUP and other Muslim leaders to send new slander letters to the capital. On 21 June 1915, Rössler reported that Governor Celal Bey was to be removed from his post because of his refusal to deport Armenians.[100] And, indeed, on 30 June, in a reshuffling of provincial governorships, Bekir Sami Bey was given the Aleppo seat, while Celal Bey was moved to Konya.[101] On 5 July, Celal left Aleppo. Aram Andonian mourned, noting in his Aintab file: "Aintab Turks collaborating with Unionists in Aleppo [have] succeeded in removing the honest, charitable, and reasonable governor of Aleppo from his post."[102]

Still, as late as 17 July, Aintab's own district governor, Mehmet Şükrü Bey, was able to inform the Ministry of Interior that no Armenian had been deported (*harice çıkarılmadı*) from Aintab.[103] Dissatisfied with that state of affairs, Talat replaced Mehmed Şükrü with Ahmed Faik on 26 July 1915.[104] Around the same time, Hilmi Bey, Aintab's military commander, also resigned.[105] On 29 July, the local CUP at last received a "positive" reply to its entreaties from the central government, and Aintab was added to the deportation list.[106] By the time Ahmed Faik Bey reached Aintab on 26 August, the deportation had already begun.

Once they received the news from Istanbul, local Young Turks called an emergency meeting and prepared the list of Armenians to be deported.[107] On 31 July, in his report to Imperial Chancellor Bethmann Hollweg, Consul Rössler stated that deportation would be "particularly unjustified and especially hard from the town of Aintab, in which a large percentage of educated and relatively wealthy families live because urban dwellers are even less used to the hardships of the road than people living in the country."[108] Additionally, he underlined that Aintab was situated neither in a war zone nor along the military road. Subsequently, he notified his superiors that the order to deport Armenians from Aintab and Kilis "had just been issued."[109]

The American representative passed the news "along to his ambassador a few days later, adding that the order also applied to Antakya, Alexandretta, and Kesab."[110] Meanwhile, in the village of Beşgöz, between Aintab and Kilis, the people of the village were discussing the looming onset of the deportation in Aintab the next day. "After a while, a well-dressed gentleman, by his appearance a Circassian, wearing partly civilian and partly officer's clothing, joined the people and inquired from" which part of the town people would leave, which road they would take, what kind of people it would be and what one could possibly pilfer from these people.[111] "When one of those present asked him if he was a civilian or a member of the military," he grinned slyly and questioned rhetorically, "Is there a more opportune moment to be a soldier than the present one?"[112] At the same time, on 29 July, all the prominent members of the Armenian community gathered in CUP Armenian Deputy Hırand Sulahian's house to discuss the deportation decision.[113] In this meeting, Dashnaksutiun was represented by Armenag Maksudian, Toros Merjenian, and Arshag Kalusdian; Dikran Sebouh Tchakmakdjian represented Huncakian.[114] Kevork Barsumian, a Dashnaksutiun supporter, took notes of this meeting:

> Our suggestion was that we should defy the order and take up arms; but unfortunately our call was not heeded and in the end we were forced to remain silent. . . . Towards the end, Avedis Kalemkerian[115] said that weapons must be taken out of their hidden places and people must get ready to resist. The attendees of the meeting put pressure on him and he had to succumb to their decision.[116]

On 30 July, fifty Armenian families were ordered to leave Aintab within the next twenty-four hours.[117] Their deportation began on 1 August 1915.[118] The persistent efforts of some of Aintab's most prominent citizens to get the central government to expel the district's Armenians seem to have enjoyed locally a considerable level of social support. Yet for some time these demands encountered resistance from several powerful civil and military figures. The result was that Aintab's Armenians were deported later than most of their eastern neighbors.

Deportation of Orthodox Armenians

At first, only Orthodox Armenians were deported. On 1 August, the fifty families (approximately 400 Armenians)[119] departed with a few light belongings, locking their doors and leaving behind nearly all their assets.[120] The first convoy was not given time to gather all their valuables. According to instructions, each family was expected immediately to pack a few of their belongings. They would be allowed to take food, bedding, jars, clothes, and blankets.[121] The testimony of Yervant Derentz, a survivor from Aintab, vividly recollects this very first day of deportation: "Children, elders, were all on the road. Our neighbors, the Turks, were singing from their homes, we could hear them: *İt yola bindi . . . İt yola bindi . . . İt yola bindi* [The dog is on its way . . . the dog is on its way . . . the dog is on its way]."[122]

Even then, comforting rumors softened the blow: that this exile was only for three or four months; that the deportees would be sent to places like Aleppo, Damascus, Hama, and Homs, where life could continue; that no one would be managing the convoys; and that only individuals suspected of subversive political activities would be deported.[123] The first convoy, consisting primarily of notable and affluent families, such as the Jebejians, Demirdjians, Pirenians, Kabakians, Kurkchuians, and Leylekians,[124] along with members of the deportation relief committee, left for Aleppo, after which the convoy continued on to Hama.[125] Walking in a line, these deportees proceeded to Akçakoyunlu with their carts, hired camels, and other draught animals. Akçakoyunlu was a transition camp for many deportees. According to the directions of IAMM, they were initially to be transferred to Aleppo and then dispersed to various districts and towns of Syria. At Akçakoyunlu station, they were housed in tents under close surveillance, only nine hours from the desert area to which they would be sent (Figure 3.1).[126]

As this convoy was making its way from the western side of Aintab, bands—comprising four hundred men and led by Ali Bey, Yasin Bey, and Hacı Fazlızâde Nuri Bey—set off from the east side, intending to assault them in the nearby Sazgın village, where deportees would spend the night.[127] İsmail Bey, nephew of Hacı Fazlızâde Nuri, helped his uncle as chief of the bands; Hacı Hamza Bey, mukhtar of Sazgın village, was the

FIGURE 3.1 Armenian deportees from Aintab in Relief Committee tents around Akçakoyunlu railroad station, camping and waiting for the train to be dispatched to Aleppo. Library of Congress Prints and Photographs Division, Washington, DC, LC-DIG-ggbain-50064.

chief of other bands.[128] Fortunately, these bands departed later than the first convoy and missed most deportees. However, they were able to catch Nazareth Manushagian, a member of the municipal council who fell behind the convoy, whom they murdered.[129]

Two days after the first convoy left Aintab, another wave of house raids took place. On the grounds that Armenians had connections with people outside the Empire's borders, many houses and shops were turned upside down; consequently, seven people were arrested and sent to prisons in Birecik and Aleppo.[130] It is interesting to note that the small Greek population of Aintab was not subjected to the same treatment. According to a secret message sent by the district governor of Aintab to his Rumkale counterpart on 5 August, the Greek subjects were to be treated in a friendly manner, and unless a special order was issued, they were to be exempted from deportation.[131]

On 7 August, the second convoy of fifty Armenian families was deported.[132] On the same day, bands—this time formed by peasants from the villages of Tılbaşar, Mezra, Kinisli, Kantara, Ekiz Kapı, Bahne Hameyli, and Sazgın—carried out attacks on deportees. The bandits were led by Emin Effendi, the manager of Agricultural Bank and an important figure in Aintab's "good society." Indeed, he was a member of Aintab's "Deportation Committee (*Sevkiyat Komisyonu*)."[133] The second convoy was systematically pillaged by bands less than a day's march away from the city.[134] As deportees from this second group were able to take their valuable belongings with them, the attackers (locals) looted a huge amount of money and jewelry with the consent of several government authorities. Assigned to protect the deportees, Kurd Hacı Nuri collaborated with these bands and beat Nazar Nazarian, a wealthy Armenian and permanent member of the city council, to death.[135]

Following the departure of the first and second convoys, discrimination against the remaining Armenians prevailed in the city. An Armenian jeweler disappeared, and her body was found in a well a few days later.[136] No official investigation was conducted. Two Armenians from Mush and an Armenian from Aintab were killed at the mill of deputy Ali Cenani. The politically motivated public prosecutor selected Armenians as scapegoats and found them guilty of the crime.[137] The mukhtar of Aintab's Tılfar village murdered six Armenian children by throwing them off a mountain.[138] In this time, bands formed by surrounding Kurdish villages operated on a regular basis between Aintab and Nizip, robbing and murdering all deportees who crossed their path.

Meanwhile, early on 8 August, the third convoy, composed of one hundred families from the Kayacık and Akyol neighborhoods, departed, again with carts, camels, and draft animals.[139] After spending the night at Sazgın village, they were led to Akçakoyunlu station.[140] The fourth convoy was led out from Aintab on 11 August.[141] This convoy consisted of more than one hundred families, many of them well off, from the Kayacık, İbn-i Eyüp, and Kastelbaşı neighborhoods.[142] Priest Nerses Tavukjian, Professor Armenak Chamichian, and dozens of teachers were also included in this convoy.[143] The fifth convoy set off on 13 August.[144] The convoy numbered more than 120 families (approximately 1,200 people) from Eblahan and Akyol.[145] When the fifth convoy arrived in Akçakoyunlu, Bogharian, one of the deportees in this convoy, described the scene he witnessed in his diary:

> The fourth convoy and deportees from other regions were gathered here, waiting for the train. Therefore, our convoy had to

> wait for these people to be sent away first. We stayed in tents but the heat was scorching; dust and straw were everywhere. We had food to eat but our water was limited. . . . We were waiting for the train. But the train never returned from the East with empty wagons.[146]

Around 20 August, based on a rumor that an armed hoard of Armenians was marching toward the town, some members of the Young Turk Committee in Aintab called for a massacre of the local Armenians in the city. The rumor turned out to be a hoax.[147] In response, on 23 August, the sixth convoy reached Akçakoyunlu.[148] There were around 120 Armenian families from Kayacık, the neighborhood of Surp Asvadzadzin Church, Eblahan, İbn-i Eyüp, and Kastelbaşı. Unlike other convoys, those who came from Aintab included men, women, and children over ten years old.[149] From Akçakoyunlu, the first two groups (the ones from 1 and 7 August) were sent to Damascus. The rest were held in a transit camp surrounded by barbed wire while waiting to be loaded into stock cars for transport to Aleppo. These deportees were later sent on foot to the region of Deir ez-Zor.[150] Surprisingly, in a telegram to the Ministry of Interior, Aleppo's new provincial governor, Bekir Sami Bey, claimed that deportees from Aintab, Kilis, and the province's border regions were sent only to Hama, partly by train and partly overland.[151] As of August, to prevent them from fleeing, all Armenians were prohibited from leaving Aintab unless a deportation order was issued for them.[152]

Deportation of Catholic and Protestant Armenians

On 4 August 1915, Talat Pasha ordered that Protestants and Catholics be exempted from deportations.[153] A week later, he annulled the exemption for Armenian Catholics in Adana and Aleppo provinces and ordered their deportation.[154] However, with a general and secret regulation dated 19 August, Catholics and Protestants were again exempted from deportation.[155] This regulation also stated that they would be deported if they behaved suspiciously or if they lived in areas with very high concentrations of Armenians.[156] These exemptions were invariably cases of placating Western powers. Both the initial exemption order of 4 August and this subsequent reinstatement resulted from German and Austrian pressure combined with international public opinion. Nevertheless, these groups were also deported.[157]

By 24 August, the population of Protestant Armenians in Aintab was approximately 5,100,[158] and that of Catholic Armenians around 350–370.[159] The new district governor, Ahmed Faik Bey, arrived in the city on 29 August and launched the preparations for the deportation of Catholic and Protestant Armenians as well as the remaining Orthodox. Ahmed Faik was "a harsh man who spread terror all around" and held "radical opinions towards Armenians."[160] It was during his term that the route of the deportation was changed from Aleppo–Hama–Hauran to Meskené–Deir ez-Zor.[161]

In the eyes of Talat, Aintab was still the center of activity for Armenians; he referred to it as "Little Armenia" and considered it to present a serious threat.[162] Thus, the deportation of Catholic and Protestant Armenians was also deemed necessary.[163] Only after the Orthodox Armenians had been expelled did the authorities issue the order, on 19 September, to deport the Catholics of Aintab. On the same day, another announcement was made:

> (i) No Armenians shall stay in Aintab; (ii) Among Protestants, only the notified shall leave, that is, those with a Protestant husband or an Armenian wife shall stay. Those with an Armenian husband or a Protestant wife shall leave; (iii) *Vesika* [certificate] holders who are exempt from deportation must have them approved; (iv) Those issued with a deportation order but still remaining in Aintab shall be deported; (v) The government shall only help the poor.[164]

The implicit addressee of this announcement was the Catholic Armenian community and its leader, Der Vartan Vartabed Baghchedjian. In late September 1915, Father Vartan and his community were taken to Akçakoyunlu. At the station, Father Vartan was visited by a delegation of Armenian Catholics from Aleppo. The delegation hoped to take him to Aleppo, but he refused to leave with them, saying, "I set off with my congregation and I will accompany them to death."[165] A report sent by American Consul Jackson in Aleppo to Henry Morgenthau, the American ambassador in Istanbul, on 29 September noted that "in Aintab, before the deportation, there were seventy-five Catholic families; after the deportation there were none! Twenty of them were [now] located in Aleppo; fifty-five in Bab. The situation of Catholic Armenians in Aleppo was fair, whereas in Bab, it was miserable."[166] Eventually, all Catholic Aintab Armenians, including Father Vartan, were sent to Deir ez-Zor.

As Kévorkian notes, by late September, three-quarters of the Armenian population had been deported.[167] After the official announcement of Protestants' exemption from deportation, the majority of the Protestant community carried on with their normal lives.[168] They even held a thanksgiving service, at which a Protestant Armenian leader stated:

> Now that we are permitted to stay in our city we must be very careful to give no occasion of complaint to the Government. If they ask for our sons as soldiers, we must give them up without murmuring; if for money, or goods, or clothing for the soldiers, let us give as if we appreciated the privilege of staying in our homes. Let us show them that we are loyal to the country. Let no one take into his home a child or anyone else who has been told to go, whether they be of those passing through the city as refugees or from among our own friends and relatives in the town. Let us show to the Government that we will do all that is asked of us.[169]

However, in early October, Ahmed Faik and his allies then organized raids on Protestant houses and made numerous arrests.[170] The process they had been witnessing eventually eroded the Armenian Protestants' belief that they would be spared the deportation suffered by the Orthodox and the Catholics. But there were no measures the Armenians could take against it. Around mid-October, Ahmed Faik mobilized the remaining Armenian men between the ages of sixteen and twenty and assigned them to a labor battalion that was put to work on the Bagdadbahn (Baghdad railway) construction site in Rajo.[171] He had eight Ar-

FIGURE 3.2 Ali Cenani Bey, CUP deputy of Aintab, orchestrator of the deportation and genocide in the city. Courtesy of the Mihran Minassian Collection.

menian young men executed in the town square on the grounds that they were involved in "perfidious activities" against the government.[172] It became apparent that Ahmed Faik Bey enjoyed a remarkable degree of freedom of action for executing central government orders. In fact, he was so adamant about the removal of all Armenians from Aintab that he did not hesitate to confront the local elites who protected certain Armenians for their own benefit. For example, on 19 October, he discovered that, acting purely out of selfish and material intentions, Ali Cenani Bey (Figure 3.2) was hiding Bedros Ashjian[173] and Sarkis Krajian,[174] two prominent and well-off Protestant Armenians, at his farm and therefore reported Ali Cenani to Ismail Canbolat Bey, the director of general security in Istanbul.[175] This case also reflects that slight conflicts between Ottoman officials and the local elites could arise.

On 20 November, Protestant pastors were arrested, and house raids increased.[176] All the coffeehouses and other places where people congregated were shuttered, and a curfew was imposed.[177] Circumstances deteriorated further when Colonel Galib Bey, commander of a military reserve battalion from Urfa, arrived in Aintab on 30 November.[178] After meeting with Ahmed Faik Bey, he gathered Armenians around the Armenian cemetery, where they were detained.[179] Central Turkey College was emptied on 2 December.[180] Positioning armed troops and cannons to elevated vantages around the city, he ordered his soldiers to decimate the Armenian neighborhoods that were still inhabited.[181] Galib Bey held certain Armenians responsible for the resistance to deportation in Urfa in October, and he aimed to use that as a pretext to deport Aintab's Protestant Armenians. However, Draft Office President (Askerlik Şubesi Reisi) Yusuf Effendi, military commander Osman Bey, and Mayor Sheikh Mustafa Effendi objected to Galib Bey's plan.[182]

Despite this disagreement, on 15 December the officers registered the names of Armenian Protestants who would be deported.[183] On 19 December, the first convoy was sent, again via Akçakoyunlu, to Deir ez-Zor.[184] The first was followed by the second, third, and fourth convoys, until 23 December.[185] By now Aintab's Protestants had ample time to learn what deportation to Deir ez-Zor meant and did not hesitate to use every means (such as bribery, personal contacts, and social capital) to ensure that they would be deported via the Homs–Hama–Damascus route instead.[186] It was to no avail. On 24 December, it was announced that deportations would be suspended until January 1, 1916, thanks to Christmas.[187] They recommenced on 4 January when the fifth convoy was sent away.[188] Of 600 Protestant families in Aintab, 200 were deported,[189] the majority of whom were annihilated in Deir ez-Zor.[190] In total, by January 1916, the number of Aintab Armenians who had been exiled exceeded twenty thousand.[191]

At the same time, Armenians from Sivas and Harput remained in Aintab, waiting to be deported. On 11 January, Governor-General of Aleppo Mustafa Abdülhalik Bey sent a ciphered telegram to district governor Ahmed Faik Bey, demanding information about the process of destroying these Armenians.[192] The telegram instructed: "Do not give them any opportunity of settling there, and by the methods you are acquainted with, which have already been communicated to you, do what is necessary and report the result."[193] On 18 January, the district governor informed the governor-general that there were approximately five hundred people from these provinces in the vicinity of Rumkale, which was under the district governor's jurisdiction.[194] The subprefect of Rumkale reported that "most of them were women and children, and that, in accordance with the methods with which the Turkish officials were acquainted, communicated to them earlier, these women and children have been sent under Kurdish watch with the understanding that they are never to return."[195] However, the number of people subjected to massacre was in fact much higher than the number Ahmed Faik Bey provided.[196]

By February 1916, deportation of Armenians from Aintab—especially Protestants—was still underway. On 7 February, in his ciphered telegram, Ali Suad Bey, the district governor of Deir ez-Zor, informed the Ministry of Interior that 2,500 Armenians from Aintab and Izmit had arrived in Deir ez-Zor.[197] The following day, he relayed that 1,440 Armenians from Aintab, Tekfurdağı, Karahisar, and Akşehir had arrived.[198] Concurrently, Jackson reported that "the last three hundred to four hundred Armenian families in Aintab were given a clear choice between conversion and deportation."[199] On 26 February, Aintab's district governor ordered the registration for deportation of fifty more families, who then departed two days later.[200] On 29 February, twenty-five more households were deported. On 3 March, a population census was taken, after which it was announced that the Armenian population was still too high, and thus more Armenians would be deported.[201] On 16 March, two more families were deported. Appointed to the post of director-general of police in Istanbul, Ahmed Faik Bey left Aintab on 23 March 1916. Talat promoted him because of his "success" in deporting Aintab Armenians.[202]

Exempted Groups

The authorities decided to exempt three categories of Aintab Armenians from deportation in order to provide public services and meet the army's needs.[203] The first, comprising 370 people, was made up of craftsmen employed in a factory that produced clothing, shoes, and ironware for the army. The second consisted of sixty-five to seventy pharmacists,[204] dentists, jewelers, goldsmiths, tinsmiths, kettle-makers, veterinarians, tailors, masons, painters, saddlers, and bakers, accompanied by their families. As the local Muslim population lacked these skills, these artisans were considered valuable assets.[205]

In the third category were the families of soldiers, officers, and medical officers who had been drafted into the Ottoman Army.[206] The number of families falling under this category was somewhere between thirty and thirty-five.[207] Avedis Jebejian (1876–1952), one of those military physicians, kept a diary regarding his experiences within the army. After serving in Gallipoli, he was sent to eastern Anatolia to continue his service. His family was first deported to Aleppo and then returned to Aintab, as Jebejian was serving as a medical doctor for the Ottoman Army (Figure 3.3). In his diary, he also described the destitute conditions of evacuated Armenian houses in the eastern vilayets.[208]

Although the Ministry of Interior sent telegrams to provinces and provincial districts regarding the deportation-exempt status of family members of ranked Armenian soldiers who officially served in the army, in reality, these exemptions were not put into practice. Families of Armenian soldiers—some ranked as high as captain—who served in the Ottoman Army on various fronts were also deported. One such example is Captain Movses Babikian, a native of Aintab, who was on duty in Gallipoli as the operator of the 44th Mobile Hospital of the 24th Division. His whole family was deported to Deir ez-Zor.[209] Another example is Captain Hagop Effendi, son of Ohan, who commanded the 63rd Regiment of the 2nd Company of the Kastamonu Gendarmerie Regiment. His aunt and sisters were expelled to Hama.[210]

From the large Armenian population in Aintab, only around two thousand Armenians were allowed to remain.[211] Among them, thirty families converted to Islam and thereby managed to stay.[212] Nevertheless, those Armenian converts were regarded with suspicion as late as 1918.[213]

Demographic Restructuring of Aintab

Muslim *muhacirs* (immigrants) and *mültecis* (refugees) displaced by the war were settled in Aintab following the deportation of Armenians.[214] Talat Pasha himself stated that Aintab was a settlement zone.[215] In his

FIGURE 3.3 The Jebejian family, Aintab. Standing from left: Roza, Krikor, Avedis, Negib, Salihe; sitting on the left: Hovhannes and Azniv (children of Krikor), Sultan (the wife of Krikor), Mennoush Hanum, and Hovhannes Agha Jebejian. Courtesy of the Mihran Minassian Collection.

various cipher telegrams, he instructed that in case of overcrowding, Muslim immigrants from Bitlis en route to Diyarbekir would be relocated to Urfa, Aintab, and Marash, where they would be supported with supplies obtained from the abandoned properties.[216] From 31 March to 12 April 1916, approximately six hundred Turkish and Kurdish immigrants from the province of Diyarbekir were sent to Aintab.[217] On 4 May, the IAMM informed the provincial districts of Urfa, Marash, and Aintab regarding the allocation of financial support to Muslim immigrants and the resettlement of Kurdish refugees.[218] The resettlement of Muslim immigrants and refugees in Aintab was accelerated in June and July 1916.

On 4 June, Tahsin Bey, governor-general of Diyarbekir, sent a cipher telegram to the Ministry of Interior, reporting that sixty-two Muslim and eleven Kurdish refugees had been relocated to Aintab.[219] On 7 July, the governor-general of Aleppo informed Talat Pasha that 113 Circassian refugees were living in thirty-six houses in Aintab left behind by the deported Armenians.[220] On 24 July, thirty-five people sent from Diyarbekir to Urfa were resettled in Aintab.[221] Chechen refugees were also settled in the vacated houses of Aintab Armenians.

This resettlement process continued until July 1917. Immigrants from Hoy, a town located to the northwest of Urmiyya with a majority Azeri and Kurdish population, were settled in Aintab because the topography of the region resembled that with which they were already familiar, thus facilitating their resettlement.[222] It was initially planned that the immigrants in question would be settled in Urfa, but since immigrants from Erzurum and Bitlis had already been settled there, Aintab was chosen instead. This constant relocation of Turkish, Kurdish, Chechen, and Circassian immigrants and refugees in the city demonstrates that Aintab was regarded as a settlement area within the framework of the CUP's population policy, highlighting the creation of an ethnically homogenous Anatolia.[223]

Main Perpetrators

It is important to underscore that the deportations organized in Aintab were supervised by a Deportation Committee, presided over by the district governor Ahmed Faik Bey. In the Deportation Committee, every branch of respectable Aintab society was represented: the district's parliamentary deputy and his brother; the head of the provincial cabinet and a local prefect; the president of the municipality; financial officers of the municipality, including the head of its treasury, two officials in the tax department, and two secretaries; a census officer; and two judges, a magistrate, and the first secretary of the court. Law enforcement was also prominent, including two gendarmerie commanders, a sergeant in the gendarmerie, two police lieutenants, and a prison warden. The military was there, including a regimental commander, a member of the general staff, a regimental secretary, and the commander of a *chete* squadron of four hundred, along with several religious leaders—a former mufti, two imams, two ulema, two sheikhs, and the secretary of a religious charity. And a physician, a lawyer, the director of an orphanage and the director of the agricultural bank—and local leaders of the CUP—were also on the committee's rolls.[224] The list points to the breadth of social support that underpinned the regime's genocidal policies in Aintab. Perhaps more important, men such as these legitimized the process of genocide. Not one of these local worthies did anything to protest the deportations, hide the vulnerable, or stop the convoys. Many of them benefited enormously from the deportations and expropriations.

The Armenians of Cilicia, in general, and Aintab in particular, were deported to three places. The first group was sent to the Deir ez-Zor region in the Syrian desert, where very few survived. The second group was sent to the region of Hama, Homs, and Salamiyya, located in the central part of the Syrian desert. Except for very young and old deportees, the majority there survived thanks to local Arabs. The third group was sent to the region of Jebel Druz and the desert areas of Jordan, where most survived.[225] The exact number of deportees, the total death toll, and the number of survivors for Aintab are not known. It is estimated, however, that the number of Armenians deported from Aintab by the end of the war was approximately 32,000, with 20,000 perishing as a result of genocide and 12,000 surviving (approximately 4,000 Armenians were exempted from deportation).[226] Survivors were most numerous among those deported via the Homs–Hama–Damascus route.[227] A great number of Aintab Armenians, mostly Orthodox, were deported to Salamiyya, a district of Syria province in the southeast of Hama, where—thanks to the efforts of district governor Necmeddin Bey—a large number were able to survive.[228]

The testimony of Sarkis Patanian, a survivor from Aintab, reflects the terrible fate of Armenians who were deported to Deir ez-Zor. According to his account, thousands of Aintab Armenians perished as a result of attacks by bandits, gendarmes, and military soldiers, as well as disease, famine, and exposure.[229] There was no food and no drinking water. The deportees cooked dogs, cats, and other animals for subsistence.[230] Ottoman military officers let loose groups of wild Chechen and Circassian tribesmen, who robbed the deportees, kidnapping and raping the girls.[231] After they had disposed of the majority of the deportees with similar atrocities, they compelled the remaining group to march on. By the shores of Habur, Chechens filled the boats with "teen-age boys and in midstream they intentionally tipped the boat, to see their agonizing death by drowning."[232] In the summer of 1916, convoys with Aintab Armenians were brought to camp on the banks of Habur River, near Shedadieh.[233] There, a band of Circassians on horseback surrounded the convoys, attacking the deportees with axes, machetes, and bayonets.[234]

It is clear that the deportation depended on close coordination and collaboration between central authorities and various Aintab actors. In fact, administrative, political, local, and civilian agents proved far more efficient than the central authority. In this regard, Aintab is a microcosm of the CUP's genocidal policies as they unfolded throughout the country. Without enormous efforts put forth by these locals on the periphery, it would have been impossible for the CUP at the center to carry out the expulsion and ultimate dispossession of almost the entire Armenian population of Aintab. The prospect of personal enrichment served effectively to implicate and integrate local collaborators in the national process of displacement and destruction—and perhaps also to inoculate them against moral misgivings.

As Üngör and Kaiser have indicated in the case of Diyarbekir, an analysis of how local elites established, maintained, and expanded their hold over Aintab is indispensable for comprehending the shape the massacres and depredation took. During his term in Aintab, Ahmed Faik Bey cooperated with local notables and their allies in the extermination of the Armenians, along with Ali Cenani. Thus, his newly won allies were able to shape the execution of government orders. Despite occasional disagreements, they served as an interface between central authorities and local elites. Extensive reports submitted to the Ministry of Interior by Ahmed Faik and other high-ranking officials provide a sound basis for a detailed account of the forced removal and destruction of Aintab Armenians.

Central CUP members intervened when they sensed opposition to or a lack of enthusiasm for the party's agenda among local officials. Thus, in the case of Aintab, Ahmed Faik's appointment as district governor was a step to ensure the execution of the central authority's directives or their party factions' goals. The activities of two CUP extremists, Ali Cenani and Ahmed Faik, point to a strategy by which this faction tried to radicalize the deportation scheme and thereby increase Armenian fatalities. These two perpetrators did not need encouragement, but less compliant men were threatened and dismissed. Talat did not stop the activities of this radical faction, which could apparently operate without much interference from the government's executive branch.

The implementation of the genocide and the significance of the confiscation of Armenian wealth are two inextricably linked processes in the context of Aintab. Expropriation and plunder of movable and immovable properties were essential to the process of destroying Armenians. For parts of the local population in Aintab, the acquisition of Armenian property was a strong incentive to participate in the anti-Armenian measures.

·4·

Confiscation and Plunder under the Abandoned Properties Laws

In the aftermath of the Aintab War (Antep Harbi), there was this town crier, walking around town and inviting those who had participated in the war to come to Tuz Hanı (the Salt Caravansary). Many locals of Aintab, including Ali Beşe (a prominent member of the Aintab's gentry and a leading figure of the Aintab CUP club), headed over. A guy told them to queue up in twos, as they would let people in two at a time. It was Ali Beşe's turn. He went in, and saw some keys placed on a rug. "Each person takes two," commanded the guy in charge. There were also these medallions lying on the rug. Ali Beşe took a quick glance and said, "So, that's what we saved Aintab for? For two keys and a piece of tin? Thanks." And he left. Who would have guessed that those two keys belonged to the Armenians? They were keys to two Armenian houses.[1]

What would happen to the properties Armenians left behind, and how would they be managed? Beginning in May 1915, a series of laws, decrees, and regulations that were known as the Abandoned Properties Laws was introduced to address these questions, with the intention that the state should assume control of these properties and liquidate them based on certain self-serving priorities.[2] As we will see, not a single legal arrangement was enacted to ensure that values equivalent to the seized properties would be provided to Armenians at their deportation destinations. In the case of Aintab, the Aleppo Abandoned Properties Commission managed the confiscation and liquidation of properties; more specifically, the Aintab Liquidation Commission, founded in late September 1915, oversaw this process. Each decision made in Aleppo and each coded telegram sent by the CUP government to Aleppo regarding the Armenian properties was binding for Aintab Armenians. Records of the Abandoned Properties and Liquidation Commissions, including any archival materials on the original records of both the Aleppo Abandoned Properties Commission and the Aintab Liquidation Commission, are contained in the Ottoman archives but are inaccessible. Therefore, it is nearly impossible to paint a complete picture of how the legislation of abandoned properties was implemented in Aintab.

However, certain documents from the relatives of survivors may help to demonstrate how movable and immovable properties were liquidated and auctioned by the Aintab Liquidation Commission.

The Abandoned Properties Laws

The first law, known as *Tehcir Kanunu* (deportation law), was introduced on 27 May 1915.[3] This law gave army commanders the authority to take preventative measures against any sort of opposition, armed aggression, and resistance to government orders in wartime. Although the confiscation of Armenian goods had begun much earlier, the first decrees on the systematic expropriation were issued on 17 and 23 May. The first decree was limited to those who left the country, military deserters, and their families. According to this decree, properties of those Armenians were to be confiscated on behalf of the Treasury.[4] The second decree was far more significant. The Ministry of Interior wrote to the command of the Fourth Army, noting that "Armenians being transported can take with them all their movable properties and goods. Detailed instructions concerning immovable properties are ready for notification."[5]

On 30 May, the IAMM sent a regulation, organized in fifteen articles, to the relevant provinces.[6] It provided the basic principles in accordance with which all deportations and resettlements would be conducted and began with the listing of the reasons for the Armenian deportations.

The most important provision concerning Armenian properties was the principle that their equivalent value would be provided. According to this decree, properties and land are going to be distributed to the Armenians in their newly resettled areas in proportion to their previous financial and economic situations. The state is going to construct houses for the needy, distribute seeds to farmers, and distribute tools and equipment to those with professions who need them. The things and goods that remain in the places they left or their equivalent values would be given to them in the same form.[7] Two procedures would be applied to goods left behind. First, "immigrants and tribes" would be settled in the vacated Armenian villages; once the value of the land and property was determined, it would be distributed to the new settlers. In cities and towns, "immovable property belonging to people who [were] being transported . . . after its type, value, and quantity [were] determined" would also be distributed to the settlers. Second, properties which produce income such as olive, mulberry, grape, and orange orchards, and stores, factories, inns, and warehouses, which remain outside of the scope of the work that new settlers know and do through being sold in public auction or being rented, their total equivalent value "*will be placed temporarily in accounts of* [local treasury directorates] *in the names of their owners so that it be given to the latter* [italics added]."[8]

In order to implement these procedures, three-person commissions were to be formed with a chairperson and one member each from the Ministry of Interior and the Ministry of Finance. These commissions, to be sent from central locations to various regions for their work, would have the authority, if necessary, to establish subcommissions or appoint officials. In regions where there were no commissions, the work would be conducted directly under the highest local administrative authority (for example, the governor or provincial district governor).[9]

The general principles mentioned here informed the fifteen-article regulation of 31 May 1915, but this new set of instructions essentially concerned the steps to be taken during the deportations and how the Armenians would be resettled. It repeated the principle that "land [would be given] in a sufficient quantity to each family being deported, taking into consideration its previous economic situation and present needs."[10] In addition, this regulation discussed topics such as the characteristics of the new settlement areas, the requirement that they be twenty-five kilometers from railway lines, how the Armenians would be registered in the population ledgers, and the prohibition of travel. The regulation stated that Immigration Commissions (Göçmen Komisyonları) would be formed to arrange all settlement matters. There was no mention of what would happen to the properties that were left behind.

The Regulation of 10 June 1915

The ordinance of 10 June 1915, in thirty-four articles, put forth in a detailed manner how the property and goods the Armenians left behind would be impounded by the state.[11] Article 1 announced that "committees formed in a special manner" would be created for the administration of the immovable properties of the Armenians. The most important of these committees were the Abandoned Properties Commissions. The commissions were each to be composed of three people—a specially appointed chairperson, an administrator, and a treasury official—and would work directly with the Ministry of Interior. Their first task was to affix their seals to goods and buildings belonging to those being deported and place them under the protection of a Heyet (Special Committee) found suitable by the commission. After the kind, quantity, and estimated value of the goods being taken under protection were registered in a detailed fashion together with their owners' names, the goods were transferred to places like churches, schools, or inns suitable for use as storehouses. Record books indicating their places of safekeeping were to be prepared.

After this procedure, animals and items that might spoil among the movable goods at hand were to be sold at public auction by a committee created by the commission, and their equivalent value was to be surrendered to the accounts of the local treasury directorate in the name of their owner when this could be ascertained; if the owner could not be ascertained, the value would be tendered in the name of the village or town where the goods were found. The type, quantity, value, original location, purchaser, and sales price of the goods being sold were to be registered in detail in special record books. Articles 10 and 22 are the most important articles contained in this regulation. Article 10 prohibited the Armenian owners from conducting any transactions concerning the properties, even if a power of attorney existed.

In Articles 6 and 22, the principle that the equivalent values of the properties left behind by Armenians would be given to them in the places where they were sent was repeated. Article 22, after stating that the revenues obtained from Armenian properties sold in public auctions or leased were to be deposited in "the accounts of the local treasury directorate in the names of their owners in trust," added, "they are going to be given to the owners according to an announcement which is going to be made later."[12] However, this giving "to the owners" procedure never took place, for it was understood that the Armenians would never return to reclaim their properties.

The issues of the Armenians' settlement and the presentation of the value of their properties or their revenues ceased to be topics of laws and decrees and would never again be addressed.

Toward Appropriation

The most important steps toward the appropriation of Armenian cultural and economic wealth were the eleven-article temporary law of 26 September and the twenty-five-article regulation of 8 November 1915 on how the aforementioned law would be implemented.[13] Many matters were covered in detail in the law and regulation. The law stipulated the creation of two types of commissions with different tasks: the Heyetler (Special Committees) and Emval-i Metruke Komisyonları (Liquidation Commissions).[14] Additionally, the law regulated the manner in which these bodies were to be formed and the conditions of work, including wages. The distribution of positions and powers among these bodies and various ministries and departments of the state were specified. Rules to be followed during the process of liquidating properties, the different ledgers to be kept, how the ledgers were to be kept, and examples of relevant ledgers were also set out.

This characteristic of the law and regulation is the most significant indication of the desire not to return to the Armenians their properties or the equivalent values. According to the law's first article, Liquidation

Commissions were to prepare separate reports for each person regarding the properties, receivable accounts, and debts "abandoned by actual and juridical persons who are being transported to other places."[15] The liquidation would be conducted by courts on the basis of these reports.

The second article explained at which institutions the properties would be registered. In order to be liquidated, places like income-producing houses, inns, and stores, as well as revenue-producing properties of pious foundations, would be registered in the name of the Evkaf Nezareti (Ministry of Pious Foundations), while the remaining properties would be registered in the name of the Ministry of Finance. After properties were liquidated—when the procedures concerning debts and receivable accounts were concluded—whatever remained was to be returned to the original owners. Another issue included in this article is that if lying, fraud, and collusion occurred in property transfers transacted more than fifteen days prior to deportation, the transfers would be annulled.

The other articles of the temporary law discussed the stages of the liquidation procedure and the details of how it would be conducted. The law stated that the commissions would carry out procedures such as the collection of the receivable accounts or the payment of the debts of each person. After all transactions were completed, properties that were not subjects of lawsuits would be sold by auction, and the gains produced would be placed in the accounts of the local treasury directorate in the names of their true owners. Detailed record books would be kept for all these procedures. Of note, the fifth article of the law stated that the courts' "verdicts were not protestable, refundable, contestable, or appealable."[16] In other words, the decision of a court on the credits and debits of accounts was final. The purpose of the article becomes clear when considering that no deported Armenian could be present at any of these courts.

Following the temporary law of 26 September, the regulation of 8 November 1915 was introduced. It regulated in a detailed fashion the protection of the movable and immovable properties of deported Armenians, the creation of new committees for liquidation issues, and the working principles of the commissions. The two-part regulation of twenty-five articles moreover included explanatory information on what had to be included in the record books to be kept during the liquidation process and how these record books were to be used. The regulation stated that two bodies would be created, one a committee and the other a commission, and defined their tasks and powers in detail.

The first three articles concerned these bodies and their duties. In every district where real estate belonging to people being deported was found the day after this regulation was officially announced, a committee was to be established with one official each, chosen by the highest-ranking civil service official from the Tax, Register of Deeds, and Civil Registry Offices; and, if it existed locally, the Pious Foundations Office (Vakıflar Dairesi). The committee would be chaired by the highest-ranking finance official of that locality.

This committee first would prepare a record book regarding all sales transactions conducted either in a period of fifteen days prior to the date of transport of the abovementioned individuals or after the communication of the order for transportation by extracting from the minutes books in the Title Deed Registry (Tapu Sicili Kayıtları) within three days. This book would be given to the Liquidation Commission. Article 13 regulated the work of this commission on these transactions. The commission would apply to the courts for the cancellation of sales transactions indicated as fraudulent in tables that would be prepared. Moreover, in accordance with the second article of the regulation, the commission would prepare two copies of a record book concerning the various types of real estate—including those of foundations—belonging to deportees, by means of a comparison of tax and title deed registry documents. After determining the location, street, and document number of each immovable property, this information, along with the total number of properties and their total value, was to be registered in record books in the names of the properties' owners.

One copy of the record books to be prepared would be given to administrative councils for study and a second to title deed registry directorates in order to be available for consultation by interested parties. The third article stipulated that the administrative councils, after conducting investigations, would ascertain the value of each approved immovable property according to its cadastral records and tax valuations. The councils would prepare two reports on this matter and send one copy each to the Ministry of Pious Foundations and the Ministry of Finance, as well as informing the Liquidation Commissions.

The majority of the remaining articles of the regulation concern the establishment, duty, and authority of the Liquidation Commissions. These commissions were to be composed of a chairperson appointed by the Ministry of Interior, with the Ministry of Justice and Ministry of Finance appointing one person each. For the people being transported, the commissions would maintain watch over their money, abandoned movable properties, the sum of money on deposit, receivables, and restitution; oversee collection and if necessary the initiation of lawsuits; conduct the sale through auction of abandoned goods when there was no opposition; and make any necessary decisions concerning payments, as well as other matters within their purview. All documents and transactions regulated and conducted by commissions[17] established through the regulation of 10 June 1915 prior to these new rules coming into effect on 8 November 1915 would be transferred to the Liquidation Commissions.[18]

After their organizational and logistical deficiencies were corrected and they began to work effectively, these commissions would accept petitions from those making claims about loans, debts, and abandoned properties. Those who claimed to have money owed to them by deportees were obliged to add to their petitions receipts and other documents they possessed (certified copies were accepted in cases where the originals were inaccessible) and proof of power of attorney if the application was made by proxy. The court would evaluate applications of people with a document demonstrating that they followed all the proper procedures concerning their claimed debts.

While such protocols were in place, they were in many ways moot, as both Muslim inhabitants and the commissions themselves openly disregarded them. Armenian survivor Ephraim Jernazian, who served as a chief government interpreter for a Liquidation Commission in Urfa, provided unique insights into the workings of a Liquidation Commission. Specifically, he was tasked with the disposition of Armenian properties. In November 1915, the commission announced to the Muslim inhabitants that any who had debts to collect from Armenians should present their petitions. He noted:

> More than two thousand bills were presented, most of them false. It did not matter because to this day, not one cent has been

> paid, neither to legitimate nor illegitimate claims. . . . The commission began its work of disposition by breaking into Armenian stores one by one and selling their contents at auction. The chairman of the commission, Nabi Bey, took me with him so that I could keep a record of the merchandise sold. With us were two policemen and an auctioneer. The ritual was the same at each store. First they examined the door seal, then broke it. Next they forced the door open and then put up the merchandise for auction. Neither the sellers nor the buyers knew the actual value of the goods. As a result, items would sell for many times their worth, or conversely, many times less than they were worth. In the evening, Nabi Bey took the account records home with him. At night he juggled the accounts, pocketing a share of the proceeds. The following day, when I saw the recorded entries in the office files, the figures were in his handwriting—not my originals—and the amounts altered. Actually, we found relatively little in these stores because the local government officials would enter these buildings at night through a hole made in the roof or a wall, and they would steal a large share of the goods.[19]

The tasks of the commissions included confiscation of the money and goods taken under guard by the government from the people being deported, along with the rest of their belongings. In addition, the commissions would ask banks, other institutions, and individuals for the accounts of money and properties left by people being deported. All those being asked were required to immediately provide the accounts and, if necessary, documents, receipts, and letters to substantiate them. In this way, the government also was able to seize the belongings Armenians had left to others. The Liquidation Commissions would later sell these belongings by public auction.

According to the regulation, all goods, pictures, and holy books in churches would be registered in record books and preserved. Later they would be sent to the location where the people of the relevant village or quarter settled. The right of use of any type of building or object connected to education, like schools or monasteries, that were left from the Armenians would be given to the Ministry of Education. The other significant articles of the regulation were that on the demand of the chairperson of the commission, the government would send police officers and gendarmes for the accomplishment of the tasks of the commission. The work of the commission would be conducted under the supervision of the government. And the members of the commission would be held financially responsible for damages caused by any negligence, laxity, or delay shown in their duties. The regulation noted that of the two different record books to be kept by the commission, one would be the principal book and the other the accounts book.

The first book, specified as the Principal Record Book of the Abandoned Properties Liquidation Commissions, treated the classification of abandoned properties, expenses, and revenues separately from their sale in fourteen distinct sections. There was a detailed section at the end of the regulation called the Principal Record Book Sample, which gave examples of the forms of these books to illustrate how and where to document information. The second book was called the Record Book of Current Accounts of Abandoned Properties. Detailed information on its recording and use were given. Each page of the book was to be divided into four tables.

After the neighborhood or county of the person being transported together with her or his name and the number of the dossier kept by the commission were noted, the record book could be used. The regulation gave an explanation of the tables in a detailed manner. After the publication of the regulation, Liquidation Commissions were to be established in various sites across Anatolia, and the regions for which they would be responsible would be specified.[20]

Some changes were made to the temporary law and the regulation. For example, on 5 October 1916, this amendment was added: "This much that in the places where the aforementioned people being transported to other places are settled, to the degree that it can assure their subsistence with overnight stays and dwellings, assistance may be given by providing real estate, land transferred to the Treasury, and habitation and land at no charge from the land of the Treasury."[21] The second important change took place on 5 October 1916, and all transactions of the Abandoned Properties Liquidation Commissions commencing from this date became connected with the Ministry of Finance.[22]

Enlargement of Confiscation

Nothing existed in the laws or regulations regarding how equivalent values of the Armenians' properties were to be paid beyond the repetition of the general principle of the 30 May 1915 regulation and the 10 June 1915 ordinance. In the second article of the temporary law of 27 May 1915, the principle was merely reintroduced that "after liquidation the remaining quantity would be given to their owners" of the revenue and value of the properties.[23] In addition, Article 17 of the decree says only that "the value of properties the owners of which are not known . . . [would be sent] later by the government to the neighborhood in which the people of the aforementioned village or neighborhood would be settled."[24] Two points are extremely important about this law and regulation, which do not include even a single regulatory provision concerning how Armenians would be compensated for the equivalent value of their properties, instead focusing on how and which of their properties would be confiscated, as well as how their debts would be paid.

First, the extent of the properties and wealth that were to be confiscated was widened, in three ways: (1) It was announced that any type of transaction conducted up to fifteen days prior to the Armenians' deportation pertaining to their goods and wealth could be annulled. (2) If any type of sequestration decision had been previously taken by courts concerning the properties of Armenians, it would be annulled and the properties would pass to the state. (3) If there was money owed to Armenians by others, it was decided that the state would collect this debt directly. In this way, the law blocked the possibility for the Armenians to collect what was owed them through other channels.

Second point, it was announced that the debts owed by Armenians to local and foreign people and organizations would be paid. In this way, any possible intervention of foreign powers, especially Germany, would be prevented. Moreover, and perhaps most important, the legal paths for the Armenians to act against these official decisions were completely blocked.

Worth noting is that long before the publication of the 26 September law and the 8 November decree, confiscations were already being conducted. A telegraph from 11 July 1915 sent to Trabzon is illustrative. It asked that all receipts concerning the debts owed to Armenians be collected and recorded. Moreover, it informed the Trabzon governor that permission was not given for the transfer of Armenian properties to others or their sale to foreigners.[25] On 10 August 1915, the IAMM announced that a regulation was about to be issued concerning how the Armenians' debts and money owed to them would be settled and that these should be recorded in special record books.[26]

On 11 August 1915, the same office stated that it had been ascertained that the properties of the Armenians were being sold to foreigners in particular at below market prices. The IAMM asked that all these sales be annulled and that the foreigners opportunistically canvassing the provinces immediately be removed.[27] In a telegraph sent on 28 August 1915 to nearly all provinces, including Aleppo, the office asked that within three days a list of the buildings and lands belonging to Armenians in the pertinent provinces that had been sold to foreigners as early as eight days before the deportations began or during the deportations and transferred to others be prepared and sent to the central government.[28]

In summary, through the laws and regulations issued during the period of the CUP government, a very detailed action plan was presented for what should be done with the properties left by the Armenians, but no legal arrangements were made for returning the value of these properties to the deportees. In the eyes of the Unionists, from the moment Armenian citizens were deported, they ceased to exist.

Abandoned Properties in Aintab

To provide a clearer picture of the situation in Aintab, I briefly analyze the socioeconomic conditions of the city, with a particular focus on the role of Armenians in the economy on the eve of war. Prior to World War I, Armenians were dominant in profitable economic sectors such as textiles, agricultural goods, tobacco, and cotton. They were also prominent in almost all artisanal fields—photography, ironworking, copper working, silver plating, jewelry making, tailoring, shoemaking, painting, multicolored weaving, dyeing, bakery, and bread making.[29] Armenians held the majority of places in professions that required a high level of education and brought the highest level of income, such as doctors, pharmacists, lawyers, and dentists. Sectors like banking and brokering, too, were generally in the hands of Armenians. For example, the type and number of businesses owned and operated by 684 Aintab Armenian families in 1914 were as follows:

Founder or smelter 22
Goldsmith or silversmith 50
Coppersmith or brazier 50
Blacksmith 25
Gunsmith 25
Cutler 30
Farrier (horseshoe maker) 33
Shoemaker 40
Tailor 25
Stonecutter or mason 300
Baker 50
Wheat miller 4
Saddler 30[30]

Economic wealth began to change hands following the Armenians' deportation. This wealth was liquidated by the commissions and was used for various purposes. With the redistribution of Armenian properties, a new, wealthy Turkish-Muslim elite class emerged in Aintab after 1915. It is possible to divide the emergence of this new class into two periods. The first period took place between 1915 and 1918, when Aintab's new elite bourgeoisie was born. The second period was from 1921 to 1922, when this new class's social status was consolidated through the liquidation of Armenians' wealth and property.

Fire Sales and Profiteering in Aintab

The first deportees who left Aintab were promised that this was a temporary arrangement and that they would return to their homes in a few months.[31] According to some survivor accounts, Armenians were told that they could leave everything, lock their doors, and either hold on to their keys or leave them with a neighbor or the mukhtar.[32] They were also assured that the government would carefully seal their properties and protect them.[33] However, those who received their deportation notice started to put their belongings up for sale at fire sale rates.[34] Many Armenian families sought to rent or buy draft animals to be able to endure the long and hard road that lay ahead. Those who bore the heaviest brunt were well-off Armenian families from middle or higher classes, particularly Armenian merchants and tradesmen. After the deportation decision became definitive, they wanted to convert as many of their assets as possible to currency; thus, they put everything they owned on the market. Some trusted their Muslim neighbors with their valuables and other properties, hoping that they would eventually be able to reclaim them upon their return. Harutyun Nazarian, a survivor, explains the fate of his father's property after receiving the deportation news:

> My father had pistachio groves and 100 beehives. He was doing this business in partnership with a mukhtar from a nearby village. The morning he received the news about our deportation, my father's [business] partner came to our house and told him that my father should entrust all the belongings in his house. He would store these somewhere with the intention of returning them when we got back. . . . In fact, he knew what was going to happen to us but he was not able to express this frankly.[35]

For Muslims, this was "a lifetime opportunity to seize the spoils."[36] Kayacık and the other Armenian neighborhoods surrounding it were transformed into a huge open bazaar in early August 1915.[37] Hundreds of thousands of gold coins were sold for a fraction of their worth.[38] Everything movable was displayed in the streets, and "Muslims began to purchase these items for as cheap as dirt."[39] Massive amounts of bedding, furniture, and utensils were piled up in the Armenian quarter and sold at auction, seldom bringing more than one-fifth of their value and often far less than that. Buyers determined the prices. On the one hand, there were those who offered, "If you don't want to leave these behind, here is the price"; on the other hand, there were those who tried to deceive Armenians, saying, "Let's put this stuff in my storeroom, it is yours when you return; do not sell them in the auction."[40] In his report sent to Henry

Morgenthau on 19 August 1915, Aleppo Consul J.B. Jackson describes the extent of this profiteering:

> The Armenian community of Aintab [was] the wealthiest of the kind in this part of the Empire, offering a splendid opportunity for pillage. Their household belongings were left behind to be taken by the first plunderer to arrive. Most of the merchants of the city being Armenians, their stocks likewise [disappeared]. It [was] a gigantic plundering scheme as well as a final blow to extinguishing the race.[41]

The Ottoman government was aware of the fact that people were buying the abandoned properties at extremely low prices and then selling them at higher rates. Considering this chaotic situation against the state's own interests, it attempted to manage the process more systematically so that the state could reap the greatest profits. Furthermore, disorderly plunder would not promote the development of Muslim businesses but rather serve to enrich some at the expense of others.

Therefore, the CUP government warned various provinces and districts, including Aintab, over such abuses and ordered the prevention of illegal exploitation.[42] All transactions conducted at extremely low rates, auctions for depreciating goods, protection of goods on behalf of their owners, and procedures such as conveyance and sequestration of real estate were prohibited.[43] In fact, the street crier went from door to door accompanied by two policemen to guarantee people that "anyone who sells or buys anything, if caught, will be sent to the court-martial and the goods will be confiscated." In doing so, the government intended to acquire "for itself all the remaining property of the Armenians."[44] Despite these measures, fire sales carried on for months, and movable assets could be sold for 20 percent of their real value.[45] This process of profiteering was one of the reasons for Armenian destitution and starvation.

Landed Properties of Aintab Armenians

There were 6,000 residential homes and 7,000 parcels of land that belonged to Aintab Armenians.[46] It is possible to divide seized landed properties into four categories: (1) major immovable properties of the wealthy families,[47] (2) middle or second-class immovable assets,[48] (3) public properties, and (4) national properties or properties owned by religious institutions.

Families in the first category had numerous properties in and outside of Aintab, including villages, farms, pistachio groves, fruit orchards, fields, vineyards, inns, coffeehouses, houses, shops, and watermills. In the second category, people owned relatively smaller properties: all but hotels included in the first category. In the third category, there were 700 Armenian families. Of these, 100 did not own a house; they had landlords or lived with other people. The remaining 600 families resided in their own houses. Among them, there were also low-income families who possessed two to five orchards. The properties within the fourth category belonged to Surp Asvadzadzin and other churches. These included buildings surrounding these churches, twenty-five shops, two mills owned by Armenian Catholics and Protestants, the library that bore the name of Niziblian, a coffeehouse, the Millet Inn building (as well as several other inns); and the buildings of the Vartanian, Atenagan (along with six shops inside), Nersesian, Haygazian, Hayganushian (seminary), and Cilicia Tchemaran schools.[49]

It is possible to expand the list of estates mentioned. Together with houses and uncultivated lands that belonged to Surp Asvadzadzin in various towns and villages such as Cibin, Ehnesh, Orul and Nizip—as well as small churches and land owned by Sis Catholicate throughout these areas—a clear picture of the confiscated Armenian estates comes into view.[50] All these estates were at the disposal of the CUP government under the Abandoned Properties Laws.

The Requisitioning Commissions

Additional mechanisms were utilized to confiscate Armenian wealth. During World War I, the CUP government introduced the law of *Tekalif-i Harbiye* (requisitioning and special war taxes) in August 1914 to meet military necessities, a law that was binding for all Ottoman citizens. To implement these taxes, Tekalif-i Harbiye Komisyonu (Requisitioning Commissions) were founded in various provinces, headed by two CUP members who were also local Muslim notables.[51] The officials specifically targeted non-Muslims, while Aintab's Muslim notables were left largely untouched. Under the pretext of military necessity, the commission seized without compensation all merchandise, livestock, and household items. They regularly deprived families of their much-needed winter supplies. At the same time, Armenian artisans were obliged to work for free and produce needed equipment for the army.[52]

A telegram sent from the Treasury to the Ministry of Interior on 20 March 1916 demonstrates how the government and army used Armenian assets in the Aintab branch of the Ottoman Bank through the Aintab Requisitioning Commission. The commission confiscated commercial goods belonging to deported Armenians from the bank, promising to return these assets after the war. However, it estimated their values at half of their market prices, obscuring what the bank owed to the real owners.[53] For example, in late July 1916, the Aintab Requisitioning Commission confiscated *alajas*[54] (ginghams) deposited by Armenian deportees at the Ottoman Bank and valued them at twenty-eight piasters, when in fact their real market value was fifty-five piasters.[55] Ultimately, the alajas in question were treated as abandoned property and allocated to the military.[56] In this fashion, commercial goods were sold below their market value without the consent of their owners, who received no compensation.

The Active Participation of Local Elites in Plunder

Motivated by the promise of acquiring movable and immovable Armenian properties, local elites meticulously carried out orders sent by the Unionists from the central government. To ensure the "success" of Armenian destruction, an executive committee was established with the encouragement of the district governor Ahmed Faik and Ali Cenani. Its members included local notables, local CUP members, and civil and military officers. These members were the son of Debbağ Kimiazâde; local merchant and well-known provincial elite Kadir, the son of prominent local notable and large landowner Nuri Bey; the son-in-law of Seyyafzâde; prison warden Zeki, the son of gendarmerie commander Hacı

Halil; Seyyafzâde Abdo Effendi; Nafi and Asaf, sons of Seyyafzâde Abdo Effendi; Hacı Halil Ağazâde Ahmed Ağa; Hacı Halil Ağazâde Zeki Bey; Taşçızâde Abdullah; Mennanzâde Mustafa; Bulaşıkzâde Arif Effendi; and ulema Bülbül Hoca.[57] The committee selected four representatives and sent them to Deir ez-Zor to see the actual living conditions of Aintab Armenians firsthand and ensure that the circumstances rendered it impossible for them to return to Aintab. Having done so, they could seize Armenian properties without reserve. These four representatives were the son of Debbağ Kimiazâde; Kadir, the son of Nuri Bey; the son-in-law of Seyyafzâde; and Zeki, the son of Hacı Halil.[58] After confirming the dire situation of Aintab Armenians in Deir ez-Zor, committee members freely participated in auctions organized by the Liquidation Commissions. As they were close with Tevfik Bey, the president of Aintab Liquidation Commission, they were able to purchase valuable Armenian items at very low prices.[59]

The very existence of this committee demonstrates that deportation, expropriation, and extermination constituted a party policy and that a dual-track mechanism was in place. Alongside the government's official channels, another special network dealt with the process of confiscation and seizure through the CUP. In other words, local actors close to the CUP club in Aintab were active agents of the process. Government officials could receive orders and implement them, but it was these local agents who personally went to Deir ez-Zor, illustrating the degree of their involvement. They were well placed to reap the benefits of the situation. They had already obtained a prominent role in the local organization and execution of the government's campaign against Armenians. These urban notables also possessed crucial knowledge about Armenian businessmen, their wealth, Armenian-owned real estate, and Armenians' other properties and economic activities. Thus, the Muslim elite had a decisive advantage over government officials. The notables could quickly identify desirable properties and take action to obtain them. Moreover, with the notables' influence over the local administration, necessary official paperwork was an easily surmountable obstacle.

Ali Cenani, one of those notables, conceded the fact that most of the well-off Armenians left their money and valuable items with the Ottoman Bank right before their deportation.[60] He claimed that district governor Mehmed Şükrü Bey issued an order "warning the Armenians and helped them to deposit their goods and belongings" in the charge of the Ottoman Bank. For that purpose, "he rented Nazarian Han and deposited all the [A]rmenian goods therein."[61] Later on, the Ministry of Interior, after having corresponded with the bank, gave an order that a commission should be formed with the right to sell these goods.

The Ottoman Bank's employees also tried to persuade Armenians to entrust their valuables to the bank, assuring them that after the sale, the money would be sent to the actual owners. However, when Aintab Armenians who were to be deported sent letters to the Ottoman Bank asking for their money, the bank did not heed these requests.[62] Leon Rahern, the manager of the bank's Aintab branch, played a significant role in the confiscation of Armenian properties. He attended meetings organized by Muslim notables and encouraged them to expropriate Armenian properties by deception.[63] Initiated and organized by Aintab CUP branch members—such as Seyyafzâde Abdo Effendi and his sons, Nafi and Asaf; Hacı Halil Ağazâde Ahmed Ağa; Hacı Halil Ağazâde Zeki Bey; Taşçızâde Abdullah; Mennanzâde Mustafa; Bulaşıkzâde Arif Effendi; Ali Cenani; and Ahmed Faik—these meetings were attended by provincial elites such as Hacı Fazılzâde Hacı Mehmed, Battal Hocazâde Halil Effendi, Müftüzâde Abdo Effendi, Fazlı Ağazâde Nuri Bey, Rıza Cenani Bey, Emin Beyzâde Sadık Bey, Battal Beyzâde İsmail Bey, Kethüdazâde Abdülrahman Effendi, Kepkepzâde Abdülrezzak Effendi, Kafadarzâde Hasan Effendi, and Obarizâde Fadıl.[64] Others included pro-CUP civil and military officers such as police captain Körükçü Hafızzâde Mustafa, police officer Hacı Sabitzâde Ahmed Effendi, gendarme sergeants Musluzâde Mehmed and Çubukçu Ali, ulema Kurd Muhammed, ulema Talibzâde Arif Effendi, ulema Bülbül Hoca, Head of Treasury Besim Bey, and Judge Bilal Hilmi.[65]

Furthermore, Rahern encouraged Armenians to deposit their money, gold, jewelry, notes, personal assets, and bills of exchange in the bank before deportation. While some Armenian tradesmen considered the Ottoman Bank a safe place to store their wealth, once the deportations had commenced, Rahern founded a company along with certain Muslim elites and put the bills and commercial documents Armenians had entrusted to the bank up for sale. These assets were then purchased for 40–50 percent of their real value by Rahern or on behalf of his company.[66] He was also present (along with M. Tahir and his Armenian secretary) at the sales of gold and other valuables deposited by Armenians to the Ottoman Bank through auctions organized by the Aintab Liquidation Commission.[67]

Ahmed Faik Bey, too, exploited the situation, purchasing for only a nominal amount of money handmade embroidered silk clothing Armenians had entrusted to the Ottoman Bank before their deportation. Later, these articles were sent to Enver, Cemal, and Talat pashas, misrepresented as a gift of "the handmade work of Muslim women."[68] Besim Bey, another local leader and provincial treasurer in Aintab, participated in the massacres and the looting during the deportations, and he later stole gold from Armenians during the genocide. While attempting to escape British custody, he was apprehended in Pozantı (a town in the Adana Province) with this gold on 23 January 1919. The gold was confiscated by the French Extraordinary Commissariat under the orders of British general MacAndrews.[69] On 1 May 1920, the Ottoman government petitioned the French Extraordinary Commissariat to no avail for the return of Besim Bey's gold.[70] The same Besim Bey would also play a significant role in the "National Liberation War" against French forces in Aintab in 1920–1921.

The Aintab Liquidation Commission

Prior to deportation, Armenians were required to submit a petition to register their movable and immovable properties. An instruction was in effect stating that these petitions had to be delivered to the Aintab Liquidation Commission within a day of receiving notice for deportation.[71] Accordingly in early December 1915, Armenians (mostly Protestants) who were in preparation to leave Aintab submitted their petitions to have their houses registered by the Liquidation Commission.[72] At the same time, the commission had already begun sales of Armenian movable goods and assets by auction. For instance, on 23 January 1916, houses of bakers, jewelers, shop owners, edge tool makers, and other artisans were registered by the Liquidation Commission so that the owners could be deported to Diyarbekir, Urfa, Sivas, and Adıyaman.[73] On 6 March, the Liquidation Commission started to sell the goods and other objects preserved in the Surp Asvadzadzin Church by auction.[74]

On 23 May, Ahmed Faik Bey informed the Ministry of Interior that estates and goods of "those who were relocated were sold and there was more to be sold."[75] The Aintab Liquidation Commission also confiscated fifty to sixty trunks of books, taken from the Catholic church.[76] They were considered abandoned property and handed over to the *Mahalli Maarif İdaresi* (local administrative branch of the Education Ministry).[77] On 18 June, the Ministry of Interior asked to be informed regarding how many Armenians were deported, the value and quantity of the deported Armenians' properties, and how these properties were utilized.[78]

Confiscation and Liquidation under the Citizenship Law of 1869

The CUP government used the fifth and sixth articles of the Law on Ottoman Citizenship of 1869 to confiscate and liquidate the property of Armenians who, though having obtained foreign citizenship, were formerly citizens of the Ottoman Empire. These articles regulated the principles of becoming citizens of other countries. According to Article 5, an Ottoman citizen could become a citizen of another country only if permitted to do so by the Ottoman government. Without the required permission, the new citizenship would not be recognized. The person in question would still be considered an Ottoman citizen and would be treated as such. According to Article 6, the Ottoman citizenship of a person who became a citizen of another country without government permission could be revoked *if the state wished to do so,* and such person would be inadmissible to the Ottoman Empire.[79]

The citizenship law of 1869 was generally used by the Ottoman government as a convenient means to not recognize the foreign citizenship of Ottoman subjects. In fact, the dual citizenship of Armenians who had become American citizens had constituted a problem between the Ottoman Empire and the United States since the second half of the nineteenth century. Armenians who had become American citizens would return to the Empire and demand their rights as American citizens be recognized. According to American law, the United States was obligated to address problems of its naturalized citizens in their country of origin. Nonetheless, the Ottoman state refused to recognize the American citizenship of these people, since that process happened without its permission under the citizenship law of 1869; thus, they continued to be regarded as Ottoman citizens. This created serious legal and diplomatic problems between the state parties.[80] By classifying such persons as Ottoman citizens, the Ottoman state created a legal framework for subjecting them to the Abandoned Properties Laws. These cases clearly indicate that the CUP government took advantage of the fifth and sixth articles of the citizenship law of 1869 to liquidate the property of Armenians who were formerly citizens of the Ottoman Empire but had acquired American citizenship.

Many Aintab Armenians had already left the Empire long before the deportations began. Some went to the United States, returning to the Empire as American citizens. Some of these returns coincided with the Armenian deportations in 1915. In this period, the American citizenship of returning Armenians was not recognized. According to the Law on Ottoman Citizenship of 1869, these individuals were to be treated as Ottoman citizens, and their movable and immovable properties were to be subjected to the liquidation laws.

One such person was Garuj Karamanougian, one of the richest Armenians in Aintab. He had immigrated to the United States and earned his citizenship prior to the deportations. He was the representative of a New York company that exported handkerchiefs to Turkey. Despite his American citizenship, the Liquidation Commission in 1916 confiscated his property of US$70,000 in value, the sum of which was then deposited in the Aintab branch of the Ottoman Bank. Subsequently, Karamanougian appealed to the American Consul in Istanbul. Ambassador Morgenthau contacted Talat Pasha, asking him to restore Karamanougian's property, upon which Talat Pasha sent a cipher telegram to Aleppo Province on 16 March 1916, ordering an investigation of this issue.[81]

Mustafa Abdülhalik Bey, the governor-general of Aleppo, stated in his response that Karamanougian was still an Ottoman national. According to his telegram, upon hearing the deportation order, Karamanougian had deposited his assets under the name of his son, who was in the United States. Moreover, Abdülhalik Bey claimed that Karamanougian's US citizenship was not valid.[82] Thus, he reported that "Karamanougian and his sons were regarded as Ottoman nationals, and their abandoned properties were confiscated per relevant articles of the Liquidation Law."[83] Abdülhalik Bey further emphasized that if Karamanougian sought to claim ownership of his property, he should apply to the Aintab Liquidation Commission with proper documentation.[84] For the same reason, the assets of Movses Karamanougian from the same family were also liquidated. However, the pressure exerted on the Ministry of Interior by the American Consulate of Istanbul eventually succeeded, and the liquidation procedure on Karamanougian's assets was stopped.[85]

Brothers Movses and Nerses Demirdjian faced a similar situation. Residing in New York, the Demirdjians had acquired American citizenship but still owned real estate in Aintab. They were partners at the Walter and Wood Company, which had machinery in Aintab.

Additionally, they had commercial commodities, which were produced by Belfast Lunien Cooperation in New York and exported to Aintab. The Aintab Liquidation Commission expropriated all of their assets in May 1916. American Consul of Aleppo Jackson protested the commission's decision and reported it to Morgenthau.[86] Thereupon, Morgenthau asked the Ministry of Foreign Affairs to cancel this transaction.[87] As a result of two investigations conducted in Aintab on 15 August and 14 November 1916, the Ministry of Interior was informed that no official record existed that proved that the Demirdjian brothers were US nationals.[88] It was also noted that although they were not subjected to the general deportations, the Liquidation Commission appropriated their goods and estates because they had abandoned their place of residence.[89]

However, the American Embassy insisted that the Demirdjian brothers were US nationals. Therefore, on 19 December 1916, the Directorate of Nationality in the Ministry of Foreign Affairs (*Hariciye Nezâreti Tabiiyet Müdüriyeti*) requested that the Embassy should prove when and where the Demirdjian brothers had obtained their US citizenship.[90] Finally, on 29 January and 6 March 1917, the Directorate of Nationality confirmed that Movses and Nerses Demirdjian were still Ottoman nationals.[91]

Distribution of Armenian Properties

Military and governmental needs. Generally, most Armenian properties were used for the necessities of the army and government. For this purpose, by 12 August 1915, a central government order was sent to various provinces and districts stating that Armenian properties could be transferred to the military if needed.[92] Therefore, a list of properties allocated to the military had to be prepared and sent to the Ministry of Interior.[93] The abandoned stock in the stores would be appropriated by the authorities in accordance with the needs of the military. On 22 August, Surp Asvadzadzin Church was sealed, after which all movable items in it were sold at auction (Figure 4.1).[94] Shortly afterward, it was turned into a military station by government order.[95]

During the deportations, all of the non-Muslim schools were seized by the government, except those belonging to the American Board.[96] The Ottoman Army also appropriated the buildings of Vartanian and Barsumian Schools.[97] On 19 February 1916, Cilicia Tchemeran was transformed into a military hospital.[98] In 1916, when the war was at its most violent, Armenian neighborhoods were completely evacuated and ceded to the army.[99] Some of those houses were rented out for a pittance, the rent of which was collected by the government.[100] Among the numerous wealthy and prosperous Armenians who lived in Kayacık were Nazaretian, Ashjian, Uzun Toros, Garuj Effendi Karamanougian, Hovhannes Jebejian, Barsumian, Harutyun Nazarian, Garabed Agha and his son Artin, Postal Rupen, Bezjian Hagop, the well-known Bezjian family, the Kurkchuian family, Hovhannes Levonian Effendi, T. Levon's father, the Bozyakhalians (their house was very spacious and large), the Hadidians, and the Kalfaians; Ottoman soldiers were settled in their houses. The Aintab Liquidation Commission later sold these houses to pro-CUP local elites and notables of Aintab by auction in early 1916.[101]

Needs of refugees and immigrants. Armenian properties were utilized for the purposes of facilitating the settlement of Muslim refugees and immigrants in Aintab. By late September 1915, Muslim refugees were being settled in Armenian houses.[102] On 25 October, a letter was sent to the liquidation commissions stating that immigrants who had been sent

FIGURE 4.1 Interior of Surp Asvadzadzin (Saint Mary), the Armenian Apostolic Church. Courtesy of the Near East Relief Collection, Houghton Library, Harvard University.

to resettlement areas should be placed in vacated homes and all their needs should be addressed.[103] They also acquired shops and businesses "abandoned" by Armenians.[104] In fact, on 2 November, the Ministry of Interior ordered the distribution of Armenians' shops and paraphernalia to the refugees.[105] In addition, in his cipher telegram of 26 February 1916, Talat Pasha instructed the IAMM that in case of overcrowding, the Muslims en route to Diyarbekir would be rerouted to Urfa, Aintab, and Marash, and they should be supported with supplies from the abandoned properties.[106] In some instances, there were attempts to sell Armenian vineyards, gardens, mulberry groves, and so on to Aintab locals, but the Ministry of Interior ordered the cessation of such attempts, stating that the estates in question must be used for the immigrants.[107]

Yervant Kuchukian, a survivor, describes how an Armenian house was given to the refugees settled in Aintab: "After the Daghlians were exiled, another tenant came. He came in with a goat and directly tied it to the room with red marble floors. . . . One thing I remember was that the new tenant was a Turkish family."[108]

The Fate of Three Families' Properties

Having demonstrated the various mechanisms of the process of confiscation, next I will examine how Armenian properties were plundered and liquidated by focusing on the personal histories of three Aintab Armenian families, the Yacoubians, Danielians, and Nazaretians, which shed light on how thousands of Armenian families lost their wealth. On the one hand, the wealth of the Danielian and Nazaretian families is reviewed on the basis of their title deeds.[109] These two families present only two examples of numerous Aintab Armenians who lived abroad and still held their deeds. On the other hand, two documents provided by Sarkis Yacoubian's family offer a previously undiscovered aspect of the liquidation process in Aintab.[110]

Yacoubian's lists are of great significance, as they hint at what information on liquidated Armenian movable and immovable properties the Ottoman archives might conceal. Nevertheless, part of the correspondence of the IAMM may be overlooked amid the documents scattered among the Republican Archives of the Prime Ministry (BCA) and Archive of the General Directorate of Land and Settlement (TİGMA). Among these records, some documents are directly relevant to the duties and functions of the Liquidation Commissions. These documents clearly demonstrate how movable and immovable properties of the resident Armenians of Balyan, Muradiye, and Beylan (all within Aleppo province) had been registered by early January 1916 for liquidation.[111] Information pertaining to the quantity and value (in piasters, an Ottoman subunit of currency) of "abandoned" properties registered under the name of deported Armenians from the aforementioned places can be found in these documents. This information is drawn from the assessments of official state authorities of the Liquidation Commissions.[112] The availability of these documents also suggests the existence of identical lists issued to the district of Aintab.

Yacoubians. The first Yacoubian document includes a list of the family's properties registered by the Ottoman Bank in order to be submitted to the Aintab Liquidation Commission immediately following the family's deportation. The second document consists of another list, which indicates the commission's auction results along with detailed information on buyers and prices of these assets. Thus, this record is an original document of the official transaction, revealing, for the first time, the processes of liquidation and auction executed by the Aintab Liquidation Commission.

The properties listed in the Yacoubian documents were registered at the Ottoman Bank on behalf of Sarkis Yacoubian and his family on 19 October 1915. The bank surrendered these properties to the Aintab Liquidation Commission on 13 May 1916. Soon after, on 1 June, the commission auctioned these properties. The list dated 13 May includes the number and type of the movable goods and items as well as real estate, whereas the list dated 1 June offers the details of who purchased these assets and at what price. As can be seen in Table 4.1, most of the Yacoubians' possessions consisted of household goods, and most of the buyers were members of Aintab's CUP (including provincial elites) and civil and military officers (local state officials).

Among the household items, the majority came from the kitchen, bathroom, and salon. From the kitchen, pots, soup bowls, plates, sets of cutlery, and a yogurt container were sold. From the bathroom, multiple basins, a laundry boiler, and a bath vessel were sold. Ahmed Agha in particular took advantage, purchasing more items than any other buyer. A total of seven rugs were sold, with one fetching 1,405 piasters from Demir Muhsin.

Beyond the household goods, a number of valuable items were included for sale. There were a few pieces of silver, but most were of gold: four gold bracelets, one gold watchband, ten gold rings, and two gold earrings. Additionally, a handful of other assorted items were listed, such as one steelyard, one child's pillow, and five trade notebooks (see Table 4.2).

Many of the landed properties lost had been in the Yacoubian family for roughly five to ten years (see Table 4.3). Nartuhi bin Kolancı Yacoub and Yacoub's son Agopcan had title deeds for houses from 1903, and Yacoubian Agopcan Agha had one from 1905. Sarkis Yacoubian, Nurcan Gazarian, and Agopcan Yacoubian's daughter Elisa signed quittances in 1911. More recently, Dikran Yacoubian signed a quittance in 1914, and Agopcan Yacoubian's daughter Elisa signed another in 1915. The oldest of the lot was the deed for a shop in the name of Yakup's son Agopcan from 1893.

Table 4.1 Liquidated Movable Goods and Assets Owned by Yacoubians

Item	Number	Price (piasters)	Buyer
Pot	2	62	Tevfik Effendi
Bath basin	1	91	Pekmezci Muhsin
Fez	2	30	Gendarmerie Ali
Bath basin	1	57	Pekmezci Muhsin
Hayler-style set of soup bowls	1	23	Ahmed Agha
Copper basin	1	161	Ahmed Agha
[Text illegible]	1	51	Demir Muhsin
Bath vessel	1	25	Hasan Hüseyin
Laundry boiler	1	130	Ahmed Agha
Meşruba [Translation unknown]	1	51	Hüseyin Bağdadi
Pot	1	18	*Dellal* [Crier] Yakup
Vessel	4	35	Ahmed Agha
Plate	4	46	Ahmed Agha
Plate	10	115	Ahmed Agha
Yogurt container	1	25	Yakup
Narghile head	4	431	Ahmed Agha
Basin	1	60	Pekmezci Muhsin
Fez	1	36	Dellal Mustafa
Small pot and vessel	2	20	Yakup
Basin	1	25	Ahmed Agha
Plate	3	17	Hacı Halil Effendi
Rose basin	1	7	Pekmezci Muhsin
Coffee mill	1	41	Habib Effendi
Candelabra	1	26	Oturakçı Osman
Water vessel	2	41	Musa Effendi
Fez	1	20	Yakup
Fez	1	50	Hacı Halil Effendi
Yellow tray	1	132	Mennanzâde Mustafa Effendi
Yellow tin spirit lamp	1	20	Habib Effendi
Set of forks and spoons	32	62	Hacı Kadirlikli
Red barbecue grill	1	210	Hüseyin Bağdadi
Fusty red barbecue grill	1	65	Demir Muhsin
Rug	2	1,405	Demir Muhsin

Item	Number	Price (piasters)	Buyer
Rug	1	400	Mennanzâde Mustafa Effendi
Rug	1	380	İbrahim Veysi
Rug	1	900	Mennanzâde Mustafa Effendi
Fusty piece of rug	1	15	Acem Said
Fusty piece of rug	1	27	Kurd Muhsin
Light rug	1	91	Halilzâde Ahmed

Total: 6,860 piasters

Table 4.2 Liquidated Valuable Items and Additional Liquidated Assets Owned by Yacoubians

Valuable items[a]	Number	Quantity (grams)	Price (piasters)
Gold bracelet	4	15	950
Golden watchband	1	10	400
Silver watch	1	1	[not given]
Golden rings	10	8	400
Nuhas watchband	1	1	10
Golden earring	2	5	100
Silver small vessel, hookah tube, golden earring	14	60	50

Additional movable assets[b]
1 bundle of clothing and clothes for Madam
2 skins
1 steelyard
6 mattresses
8 quilts
1 child's pillow
5 trade notebooks

381.20	21 *batman* 800 *dirham*, kernel of seed (17 kilograms)[c]	Oturakçı Osman
5,225	200 *kıyye*[d] alajas	Tekalif-i Harbiye
[Requisitioning levy]		

Total: 10,974.20 piasters

[a] These items were found in a tin and submitted to the Aintab Abandoned Property Liquidation Commission as they were on 30 April 1332 (13 May 1916).

[b] These assets/items were submitted to the Aintab Abandoned Property Liquidation Commission as they were on 19 May 1332 (1 June 1916).

[c] *Batman* and *dirham* are Ottoman units of measurement. One batman equals 7.7 kilograms; one dirham equals 3.2 grams.

[d] *Kıyye* is an Ottoman unit of measurement; one kıyye equals 1.3 kilograms.

Table 4.3 Yacoubians' Liquidated Land and Estates

1	Title deed, numbered 215, dated 27 February 1327 (11 March 1912) in the name of Sarkis Yacoubian and his partners
2	Title deed, numbered 832, dated December 1319 (1903), a house, Nartuhi bin Kolancı Yacoub
3	Title deed, numbered 867, dated December 1319 (1903), a house, Yacoub's son Agopcan
4	Title deed, numbered 92, dated May 1321 (1905), a house, Yacoubian Agopcan Agha
5	Title deed, numbered 121, dated October 1326 (1910), a house, Abraham's daughter Vartuhi and his partners
6	A quittance signed by Nubrin Gazarian, dated 21 July 1910
7	A quittance signed by Agopcan's daughter Elisa Gazarian, dated 11 February 1910 and 12 February 1910
8	A quittance signed by Agopcan Yacoubian's daughter Elise, dated 17 December 1915 and 31 August 1915[a]
9	A quittance signed by Dikran Yacoubian, dated 21 May 1914
10	A quittance signed by Sarkis Yacoubian, dated 11 May 1911
11	A quittance signed by Nurcan Gazarian, dated 21 July 1911 and 21 July 1910[b]
12	A quittance signed by Agopcan Yacoubian's daughter Elisa, dated 14 October 1911
13	A quittance signed by Babak Sarkis, dated 25 June 1899
14	A quittance signed by Kirkor and Rupen Ubuian, dated 13 June 1905
15	Certificate of receipt signed by Kazakçı Melkon and Toros, dated 23 April 1895
16	One title deed for a shop in the name of Yakup's son Agopcan, numbered 868, dated December 1893.

[a] The original document included two dates in that order.
[b] The original document included two dates in that order.

Upon close examination, the list of buyers includes various familiar names from Aram Andonian's perpetrator list (see appendix). For example, although his participation in the auction was prohibited, Tevfik Effendi, chairman of the Aintab Liquidation Commission, was one of the buyers. Among the other buyers were Dayızâde Ahmed Hurşid Bey, Hacı Halil Effendi, Mennanzâde Mustafa (president of the CUP club at the time), and Halilzâde Ahmed, all permanent members of the Aintab's CUP branch who played active roles in deportations.

Besides these figures, additional buyers of the Yacoubian properties can be found in the perpetrator list provided by Aram Andonian. Additionally, 200 *kıyye* of alajas were sold by the military authorities under the guise of special war taxes at a price far below normal market value on 31 October 1916.

These documents methodically demonstrate that local actors assumed direct roles in the deportation and annihilation of Armenians. They were motivated by material gain from liquidated Armenian properties and benefited from a legalized regime of plunder. The Yacoubian documents indicate how meticulously organized the looting was and offer a glimpse of the similar documents locked in the Ottoman archives.

Danielians. The example of the Danielians is similar to many Aintab Armenians from the diaspora living in Europe and the United States who still hold their title deeds. Esther Danielian- Barsumian was born on 3 March 1876 in Aintab. She was the daughter of Artin Danielian and married Jirgi Barsumian on 4 January 1900. Her properties were liquidated during the deportation. The following immovable properties belonged to Esther Danielian-Barsumian, according to the deeds in the hands of her true heirs:

1. A pistachio and mulberry orchard located at İbrahimli near Battal Höyük within the city limits of Aintab. This orchard contains 600 pistachio and 200 mulberry trees. This property is bounded on the north by the property of Kazkanju Nerses, on the east by the property of Anzerli Ohannes, and on the south by the property of Leylekian.
2. A pistachio and mulberry orchard located at Battal Höyük within the city limits of Aintab. This orchard contains 400 pistachio and 150 mulberry trees. To the north of this property is the property of Kazanju Nerses, to the west is the property of Leylekian, to the south the property of Kazanju Krikor, and to the east, the property of Anzerli Ohannes.
3. A two-story residence made of stone construction, containing sixteen rooms, located in Haig *Mahallesi* (neighborhood), Aintab. In the same yard surrounding this house is another two-story store building used exclusively for storing pistachio nuts, raisins, and other provisions. To the north of this property is Eshek Oğlu's property, to the east is the residence of Karamanougian and Topjian, to the south is the property of Tutunjian Krikor, and to the west is the property of Terzibashian.

4. A pistachio orchard located in the Beylik section about one and one-half miles from Aintab. This orchard contains about 1,000 pistachio trees.
5. A vineyard located in the Beylik section in Aintab. This vineyard contains seven thousand grape vines. This Beylik section is used exclusively by the Aintab people as summer homes, and for that reason the property is very valuable. The only neighbor mentioned in the deed is Hovhannes Levonian.
6. A vineyard located at Gujeh and Jeideh Kariye sections in Aintab. This vineyard contains 3,200 vines. The neighbors are not mentioned in the deed.
7. The stock of goods in her father Artin Danelian's store, consisting of imported silk, woolen goods, cotton goods, linen, velvet, and so on.
8. Six complete sets of bedroom furnishings, consisting of twenty-eight woolen beds, twelve Turkish carpets, six kilim (rugs), and miscellaneous bedroom articles.
9. One complete set of guesthouse furniture, including silk draperies, six Persian rugs, antique gold vases, and antique furniture.
10. One complete set of dining room and kitchen furniture, including copperware, utensils of copper, silverware, and china.

Nazaretians. However, there were certain exceptions to the Abandoned Properties Laws. For example, Nazar Agha Nazaretian, also known as Kara Nazar, was a well-off jeweler, dealer in antique coins, and merchant. He built a magnificent home for his family in Aintab's Kayacık neighborhood. He founded a *masmahane* (soap factory) and an inn, today known as Kara Nazar's Inn (Figure 4.2).[113] A successful businessman and a leading member of the community, Nazar Agha was appointed *Başşehbender* (chief consul) of Persia in Aintab by the shah and was later appointed as the American vice consul.

Upon Nazar Agha's death, his youngest son, Garabed Effendi, became the consul of Persia. Garabed Nazaretian and his family were exempted from deportation because of his position as the consul of Persia, and they settled in Aleppo in 1915. Following his death in May 1916, the Aintab Liquidation Commission inquired to the Ministry of Interior regarding

FIGURE 4.2 Kara Nazar's Inn, which was converted into a hotel called Çınar Oteli. Courtesy of Gaziantep Kent Arşivi, Gaziantep Photograph and Postcard Collection.

the procedure for Garabed's property, though the commission had already registered his majestic house.[114] The Ministry of Interior responded on 17 May and stated that the deceased Iranian citizen Garabed Nazaretian's property should not be liquidated under any circumstances.[115] Nevertheless, following the Armenians' total departure from Aintab after the Franco-Turkish War of 1920–1921, Aintab's local administrative authorities decided to sell his house.[116]

As can be seen from the Yacoubian case, numerous government officials and other individuals—including property assessors, auction houses, trustees, estate agents, and notaries—were employed to manage the administration and sale of Armenians assets through the Abandoned Properties Laws.[117] At the direct level of implementation, the prospect of looting motivated the local collaborators from different classes in Aintab. In most areas, the CUP relied to a considerable extent on the cooperation of the local administration, institutions, and state officials, as well as provincial elites and ordinary citizens. The deportation and genocide of Aintab Armenians were not implemented by a rabble brought in from the countryside to carry out an act recognized as too despicable for respectable people, nor performed by Aintab's more ordinary have-nots, but rather were brought about by the district's Muslim notables, landowners, dignitaries, and the city's elites. They prospered through the acquisition of Armenian property and wealth, elevating them into an even *more* privileged position. This process of redistributing Armenian properties illustrates the close relationship between CUP officials and local Muslim elites.

·5·

The Flawed Restitution Process for Armenians

With the disastrous conclusion of the war drawing inescapably nigh, on 8 October 1918 the CUP government resigned and fled. The rest of the party, meeting at its final congress, dissolved on 4 November.[1] The first new cabinet was established by Ahmet İzzet Pasha on 11 October 1918, and a series of eleven governments held office in the period leading to 4 November 1922.[2] Among the first actions of these governments were the initiation of legal proceedings against members of the CUP and the granting of permission for surviving Armenians to return.[3] The return of the Armenians also raised new issues such as the delivery of Armenian women and children to the Armenian community and restitution of the abandoned properties. In the first part of this chapter, I examine the legal and administrative regulations concerning the return of the Armenians after World War I and the restitution of their properties and estates. In the second part, I focus on the implementation of the return process of Aintab Armenians and the restitution of properties upon their return.

First Returnees and Restitution Attempts

The first permissions for the return of deportees, though limited in scope, were granted by the CUP regime at the start of 1918. On 21 October 1918, the order giving permission for deported Armenians and Greeks to return was sent to all relevant provinces.[4] On 23 October, it was requested that the necessary steps be taken to enable Armenians and Greeks to return to their homes safely.[5] Later, this request was elevated to a strictly defined set of orders regarding the return process. These orders stipulated permission for Armenians and Greeks to travel without travel documents; the assignment of special trains for them; provision for their needs, including food, drink, and travel expenses; and their secure arrival to their destinations.[6] The key moment occurred on 4 November 1918, when the temporary law of 27 May 1915, known as the deportation law, was found unconstitutional and was rescinded.[7]

It is very difficult to estimate how many Armenians were able to return to their homes after 1918. According to figures reported on 20 November 1918, 7,163 Armenians returned (of a total 10,601 returnees).[8] On 21 December, it was announced that 2,552 Muslims, along with 19,695 Greeks and 23,420 Armenians, returned. The minister of interior, who had made the announcement in the Parliament, stated that these people had been resettled.[9] In a report prepared in March 1919 by the Ottoman Ministry of Interior after complaints by the occupying forces that insufficient aid was provided to returning refugees, the number of those returning was given as 232,679.[10] The report did not state how many of these were Armenians and how many were Greeks. According to news that appeared in Ottoman newspapers on 12 March 1919, 118,352 Greeks and 101,747 Armenians returned and were resettled.[11] In a 17 June 1919 report given to the British High Commissioner in Istanbul, Prime Minister of the Istanbul government Damat Ferit Pasha cited a figure of 276,015 returning Armenians and Greeks.[12] On 3 February 1920, newspapers quoted the figure of 335,883 "Armenians and Greeks who by means of the government were able to return to their homelands since the armistice."[13] The biggest question concerning the repatriates was how their movable and immovable property should be returned to them. The restitution of the Armenian properties was a pressing issue for the Ottoman government, and related orders were sent to the localities.

According to some studies in line with the official historiography, the government went to great lengths and great expenditures to ensure the safety of Armenians during their return and resettlement.[14] This historiography asserts that "abandoned properties of the returnees were mostly restituted or compensated by the Ottoman government."[15] The returnees had to be relocated as quickly as possible upon their arrival to their hometowns. For instance, on 28 October 1918, following the return of the Armenians, the Ministry of Interior sent a telegram to the province of Diyarbekir ordering the vacating of abandoned properties and the prevention of the destruction of these properties.[16] However, enforcement of this dictate was not easy under the existing circumstances. In some districts, the properties abandoned by Armenians and Greeks had already been destroyed; therefore, the Ministry of Interior issued a further warning to the provinces and districts to prevent the continuation of such events. In addition, the community properties of the deported Armenians—such as schools, churches, chapels, and other similar institutions, which had been occupied during the war—had to be vacated.[17]

Following problems surrounding the restitution of abandoned properties, a detailed circular was prepared on 18 December 1918 and sent to various provinces. The circular asked for the return of the confiscated properties of the Armenians and the most rapid vacating of their homes by officials, police, and other individuals who might be living in them.[18] The Armenians' houses and lands were to be surrendered to the former owners. Immigrants and refugees living there had to vacate these houses and lands; if this was impossible, several such families would be given shelter together in appropriate houses, and those remaining homeless would be settled in immigrant villages.[19]

It was important for the Ottoman government not to cause suffering to the Muslim immigrants while restituting the abandoned properties. In order to prevent Muslim immigrants from "being left homeless until they could find a permanent residence, two or three Greek and Armenian families could be temporarily placed together."[20] In a communication dated 22 December 1918, the Ministry of Interior declared that a law was quickly being prepared that would provide for the "complete and whole return" to the owners of "properties and claims" that had been subject to liquidation in accordance with the temporary law of 22 September 1916.[21] As a result of a delay to this proposed law, the government attempted to solve questions pertaining to the return of goods and properties, as well as settlement, primarily through telegrams sent from Istanbul.[22] Attempts to solve these issues through instructions from the capital continued throughout 1919. Additionally, it was instructed that "movable properties, which had been entrusted to the Liquidation Commissions, were to be redeemed and restituted to their original owners."[23]

Restitution of the abandoned properties was executed "in accordance with the registry books" that had been kept during the deportation and "included proceedings and existing status of the mentioned properties."[24] The IAMM—as the institution in charge of restitution, settlement, and housing of Armenians[25]—sent instructions to the local authorities setting an example for the registration process, according to which,

> the watches and the jewelry shall be registered by defining their types and values under the names of their owners, if they are known; otherwise they shall be registered under the name of the place where they are found and shall be put in a separate case in the bank, by being registered in the presence of a special committee.[26]

In addition to registration of the abandoned properties, the government employed officials for their protection.[27] In towns where Armenians returned, "officials from the local departments of the IAMM and Ministry of Finance were charged with restitution of the left properties."[28] As Adem Günaydın notes, these officials would distribute "the properties to their former owners with regard to the registry books and would note down the restitution proceedings into the same books in detail."[29] Officials who purposefully failed to fulfill their duties would be severely punished, as their disregard "would cause damage to the treasury and peoples of the Empire."[30]

The military occupation of Cilicia at the end of 1918 was executed by three battalions of the Armenian Legion, a special corps in the French Army of the Levant known as Légion d'Orient. As Vahé Tachjian indicates, some ten thousand Armenian survivors of the genocide were repatriated speedily from the Arab provinces of the dismantled Ottoman Empire to Cilicia.[31] Armenian properties appropriated during the war and genocide by the CUP were being restituted by the French administration to their owners in Cilicia. In fact, from April to June 1919, Colonel Brémond issued three decrees that "formed the legal base of the restitution to the Armenians of all confiscated movable and immovable properties."[32] Under a legal decree published on 3 April 1919, sales of immovable Armenian properties carried out by Agricultural Bank were declared null and void.[33] Additionally, sales of movable properties and goods conducted by the CUP were also rescinded.

In accordance with the regulations mentioned above, Armenian survivors who managed to return to their hometowns were restituted in different forms. For instance, all the properties and arable lands seized in the Osmaniye, Cebel-i Bereket, and Dörtyol districts were restituted to their original owners on 10 and 12 April 1919 as a result of the efforts of Colonel Brémond, the military governor who was appointed on 19 December 1918 to the Cilicia region, following the French occupation.[34] In this restoration process, Hüsnü Bey, the district governor of Cebel-i Bereket, cooperated with Colonel Brémond as chief administrator of Cilicia. In addition, a list providing information about the number, type, and extant owners of the restituted properties was prepared.[35] Another restitution process was implemented in the province of Kayseri in November 1918,[36] where sixty-nine houses were evacuated for the returnees on 7 November; by 23 November, the number of vacated houses in Kayseri and its districts reached 136.[37]

In cases in which "movable properties like currency, jewelry, household goods, implements of husbandry, gains from the sale of the abandoned properties, etc." were being saved in the "revenue authorities or in the banks, and registered definitively, they were restituted at once."[38] For instance, a package including gold and Ottoman piasters that had been left by Vagarshak Saatchian at the Erzurum branch of the Ottoman Bank during the deportation was handed over to him by the Istanbul Liquidation Commission on 10 July 1919.[39] In another instance, valuable items owned by Boghos Djigherjian, who was deported from Erzurum in 1915, were given back to him by the Istanbul Liquidation Commission on 27 April 1920.[40] Upon arrival of the returnees, "the movable properties saved by the Commission for the Administration of Abandoned Properties were delivered."[41] Indeed, "those that had been saved in the banks were also demanded by the authorities to be distributed to their Armenian owners."[42] Together with the movable properties, the real estate of the Armenians—including houses, religious and educational institutions, shops, factories, hotels, and so on—were "immediately restituted if they were empty or evacuated" if occupied.[43] In the event that abandoned properties "which had been sold to the local individuals were demanded [back] by their original owners[,] instead of the cash gained from their sale, if possible, the government repurchased these properties" so as to properly return them.[44] One of the means of restitution in the event of seizure and stealing was opening inquiries for the people who were responsible in active seizures and plundering. For instance, on 29 April 1920, a lawsuit was filed against Ahmed Agha, a mukhtar of the Taş neighborhood in Bitlis who embezzled an abandoned property during the genocide.[45] Similarly, on 26 April 1921, Osman Effendi, former head of the finance office in the Harran district, and his assistant Reşid were put on trial on the charge that they had embezzled abandoned property.[46] Another means of restoring abandoned properties was to create special commissions, which aimed to reconcile the current and the original owners of a property and to help them reach a mutual settlement among themselves. These commissions included salaried clerks, officials, and leading figures from the Greek and Armenian communities.[47]

Another important issue of the return process pertained to the restitution of properties of deceased deportees. When the families of deportees tried to claim their inheritance, they encountered "a procedural problem regarding the death certificates." According to Article 31 of the Law of Civil Registry, inheritance procedures would be initiated upon the submission of death certificates, which were to be obtained from "the quarters or villages in which the deceased [used] to reside." However, as Oya G. Durmaz states, many returnees could not obtain such an official paper in cases where their *muris* (legator) had died in the deportation process. To resolve the problem, the Ministry of Interior issued the following instruction:

> The death certificates which were prepared by *heyet-i ihtiyariyye* [the commission of elders], who had also been generally deported along with these deportees, would be accepted, and the

procedures would be implemented upon the submission of these death certificates.[48]

Despite the instructions from the Ottoman government for the restitution of Armenian properties, numerous problems arose regarding the transferred and liquidated properties. Many complaints were made about the restitution of movable goods, many of which had changed hands or had been utilized in government offices. In some places, these goods were not returned to their real owners but instead remained in government offices. Thus, the Ministry of Interior again requested the restitution of these goods, and in cases in which the owners had not yet returned, the goods were to be held in custody until their return.[49]

One partial reason for the failure to restitute many properties was the chronic inability of the central Ottoman government to control the events and processes in the provinces. Local authorities in the provinces were unwilling to take any action toward facilitating Armenian restitution and resettlement. Their resistance to obeying the directive could be seen in the correspondence between the Ottoman administration and its Armenian citizens.[50] The Armenian Patriarchate and the British High Commissariat in Istanbul found the attempts of the government to restitute the movable and immovable properties of deported Armenians insufficient. The Patriarchate repeatedly protested the failure to have their properties returned, while the British High Commissariat continued to pressure the government.[51]

Annulment of CUP Liquidation Laws

The long-anticipated regulation concerning the return of abandoned properties was finally issued on 12 January 1920. It contained thirty-three articles and delimited in a detailed fashion how Armenian properties were to be returned. Its thirtieth article revoked the temporary law of 26 September 1915 and the regulation of 8 November 1915.[52] The most important point of the regulation was that immovable properties impounded by the state and registered in the names of the treasuries of the Ministry of Finance and Ministry of Pious Foundations were to be immediately returned to their original owners. If the owners were not alive, then the properties—regardless of whether they were registered in the names of the aforementioned ministries—would be immediately surrendered to the rightful heirs and registered in their names. If no heir was found, the properties would remain in the hands of the state. Furthermore, if the original owners of the properties did not accept the monetary value of the sales conducted by the Ministry of Finance and Ministry of Pious Foundations, then the owners could have their properties returned.[53]

Revenues gained by the state from confiscated properties were to be given to the original owners after the deduction of taxes or any other item specified by the law. The government would also pay compensation for any damage to the properties. The regulation stipulated that the money amassed by the Liquidation Commissions would be repaid with interest. If the original owner of the property did not accept the rental agreements made by the treasuries of the Ministry of Finance and Ministry of Pious Foundations with Muslim and refugee tenants, it was decreed that within a period of ten days after the original owner applied to the government, the renters were to be expelled and the property returned to the owner.[54] With this regulation, all practices of the CUP period concerning Armenian properties were revoked, and the process of returning of usurped Armenian properties, which had already started, became official.

The Return of Armenian Survivors to Aintab

British occupation (December 1918 to October 1919). Established by Ahmet İzzet Pasha on 11 October 1918, the Ottoman Empire's new cabinet signed the Armistice of Mudros on 30 October. In the seventh article of the armistice document, the Entente Powers reserved the right to occupy any Ottoman lands in cases where the security of their armies was threatened. For that reason, British forces occupied Kilis and Aintab.[55] To better understand the British invasion of Aintab, district governor Celal Bey's coded telegram to the Ministry of Interior on 28 December is crucial. In his telegram, Celal Bey reported that Aintab Armenians in

Aleppo appealed to the British commander for their safety, as they feared Muslim attacks upon their return to Aintab.[56] Armenians informed the British commander that unless British forces occupied Aintab, the Armenians would not return. Heeding this request, the British commander sent cavalry units stationed in Kilis to Aintab.

Even though Celal Bey had informed Major Mills, the liaison officer and commander appointed by Sir Mark Sykes (a military commander), that public order was assured in the city and that there was no reason for the involvement of British soldiers—which would have been against the terms of the armistice—the general told him that British soldiers would not interfere in any matters and that their sole intention was to ensure public order in cooperation with the local government.[57] On 18 December 1918, the British entered Aintab on the grounds that they needed to procure food for the cavalry's horses and to ensure the security of their units in Aleppo.[58] Central Turkey College was used as headquarters for the British troops.[59] On the next day, Sir Mark Sykes visited the Protestant chapel, the main Orthodox church, and the Vartanian and Atenagan School buildings, along with Professor Lutfi Hodja Levonian.[60] On the way, they noticed half-ruined buildings festooned with graffiti—for example, "We have desecrated this Protestant Chapel and turned it into a wasteland, we turned this Catholic Church into a stable and we turned that Armenian Church into a barrack and a wasteland."[61] Sykes reported this situation to General Clayton, stating that "Turks systematically demolished empty Armenian houses."[62] On 25 December, regiments of the Indian Cavalry entered Aintab.[63] They encamped in the vicinity of the college. Afterward, Antep Kalesi (Aintab Fortress) and the Belediye Hanı (the Municipality Inn) were occupied by the British forces.[64]

The British occupation enraged the Muslim community, who claimed that not a single event endangering the safety of returnees had occurred in Aintab and that therefore the occupation was illegal. However, the well-organized British troops quelled this dissent. Aside from restoring peace, Sir Mark Sykes dealt with four main issues: (1) the collection of documents regarding deportations and the disarmament of Muslims in Aintab and its surroundings; (2) the arrest of the ex-CUP members who took part in the deportation and plunder; (3) the return of the Armenians; and (4) the restitution of seized Armenian goods, commodities, and properties.[65]

Collection of documents regarding deportations and disarmament of Muslims. As soon as the British arrived in Aintab, they demanded all documents concerning the deportations of Armenians.[66] In February 1919, a British officer visited Celal Bey to "ask him to turn over all the telegrams and letters exchanged between the *vilayet* [province] and the Imperial Ministry on the one hand and the *mutesarifat* [district governorship] on the other in the period running from 1330 [1914] to 1334 [1918]."[67] Confronted with Mayor Sheikh Mustafa Effendi's refusal to comply, the British had the building surrounded and seized the relevant documents. According to official Turkish historiography, the British troops in Aintab sent those records to Egypt.[68] This procedure was implemented after the dispatch of "a circular telegram from the head of the telegraph office in Diyarbekir instructing the agencies under his jurisdiction to destroy the originals of obsolete documents."[69]

The British occupation forces seized control of all official correspondences in January 1919. Major Mills confiscated the records at the governorate, raided the post office, and appointed Haykazun Levonian as censor.[70] In late January 1919, Turks from Adana, İçel, Marash, Aintab, İskenderun, Beylan, Rithanin, and Antakya who resided in Istanbul decided to form a committee in order to provide support for resistance organizations composed of former CUP members in their hometowns.[71] As a result of the British and French invasions, they felt that such a committee was urgent and necessary. The aim of this committee would be to make every effort in order to claim before the public their absolute right to retain these towns and their surroundings. Delegates to these districts were sent from Istanbul, but the committee thought it first advisable to prepare public opinion in these towns and their surroundings and to undertake the necessary measures for opening new branches. Therefore, Aintab, as well as Marash and Urfa, became a center of petty conspiracy organized by local former CUP members and received support from this committee. Attempting to prevent this organization from gaining public support and consequently arming itself in Aintab, Major Mills ordered the disarmament of the Muslim population in late February 1919.[72]

General MacAndrew, commander of the British occupation forces, announced that the notables of Aintab would be held responsible for even the slightest disturbance and took extraordinary measures against the conspiratorial activities of former CUP members in the city.[73] MacAndrew was also convinced that newspapers published in Aintab had collaborated with such conspiracies.[74] At Central Turkey College, he summoned prominent local figures—including Daizâde Ahmed Hurşid Effendi,[75] Doctor Hamid Bey, reputable young literati, Muslim judges, accountants, and the mayor of Aintab—to convey that threats to public order in and outside of the city should not be tolerated.[76] Following a British decision, Celal Bey ordered the newspaper *Antep Haberleri* (Aintab News), published by Hüseyin Cemil Bey and Ali Kemal Göğüş (two former members of Aintab's CUP club), to be shut down in February 1919 for spreading anti-British sentiments. Hüseyin Cemil Bey, son of Kethüdazâde İbrahim Effendi of the Muslim gentry and graduate of Central Turkey College, published this newspaper with his friends in protest of the British arrival to Aintab, the predicament of the country, and the excesses of Armenians. The mottos of the newspapers were "Aintab is Turkish and will remain Turkish," and "Aintab is the fortress of Turkishness."[77]

Arrest of former CUP members. In early 1919, prominent figures from Aintab's branch of the CUP, men who had been active in the deportation and dispossession of Armenians and knew that they would be targets of the occupiers' justice—Taşçızâde Abdullah, Mennanzâde Mustafa Effendi, Kethüdazâde Hüseyin Cemil Bey, Kurd Hacı Osman Agha, and Mamat Ağazâde Ali Effendi, and Hafız Şahin Effendi, who was still a parliamentary deputy—met together. Their objective was to build a resistance front against the occupiers and to provoke the Muslims to continue the struggle. For that purpose, they founded Müdafaa-i Hukuk Cemiyeti (Society for the Defense of Rights) as a resistance front to foment discontent within the Muslim populace.[78] But they failed. British troops were able to keep the lid on the situation, while their commander, Major Mills, worked on disarming the Muslim population, salvaging whatever documents could be found pertaining to the exile and expropriation of Aintab's Armenians, and bringing to justice those former CUP members who had participated in those activities. In late January 1919 Mills started arresting the masterminds of the Armenian deportation:[79] Besim Bey, an accountant; Hakkı Bey, clerk of *awqaf;* Eyüp Sabri Bey, title deed officer and influential CUP member; Mennanzâde Mustafa Effendi; Kurd Hacı Halil Bey; *Kasap* (Butcher) İncozâde; Taşçızâde Abdullah Effendi; and Hüseyin Cemil Bey were summoned to the Central Turkey College, where they were taken into custody by orders of General MacAndrew and Major Mills, with the cooperation of Celal Kadri Bey.[80] They were charged with "vandalizing Armenian houses while they were sent away, committing murder and prospering on Armenian wealth."[81] Major Mills openly explained to Eyüp Sabri Bey the reasons for his arrest:

> You were present here during the deportation of Armenians and you sent them away. The lives and goods of those helpless people were under attack on the roads. You caused all of this and you are still involved in certain activities that would violate order and peace in this place. That is why you are a villain. You will be kept far away until a peace treaty is signed.[82]

Eyüp Sabri Bey, a founding member of the local CUP and onetime official at the land registry office (and thus a key figure in the redistribution of Armenian lands, for which he was also summoned by Mills to Central Turkey College) expressed his disgust that the British occupiers had met with absolutely no resistance, not "even the smallest attempt" from any side. Taking a dim view of the "remarkable tranquility" of his Aintab countrymen, which only increased the hopes and ambitions of the British, he charged municipal functionaries with supplying the occupiers' every need, even producing propaganda on their behalf, paid for off the books (without entry into the municipality's budget). All this, he said, was done with the permission and direction of district governor Celal Kadri Bey, whom Eyüp Sabri damned as "a collaborationist."[83] It is worth remarking that Celal Kadri was, like Eyüp Sabri himself, one of the founders of the Aintab CUP.

Ultimately, General MacAndrews transferred these arrestees to Aleppo for their trial on 23 January 1919. *Teminat*, a local Aintab newspaper, printed in its 22 and 25 January 1919 issues that the accountant of Aintab, officers of the Land Registry and Pious Foundations offices, as well as two leading figures from among the local notables were surrendered to the commander of British occupation forces by the district governor, Celal Bey. These people were subsequently sent to Aleppo to be investigated regarding their roles in the deportation of Armenians from Aintab.[84] Later, Dişikırıkzâde Halil Agha, Sedat Bey,[85] Patpatzâde Nuri Bey, Abdülvehhab Bey, Celil Bey, Sabri Bey, Hadji Mehmet Agha, Hadji Süleyman Effendi, Sergeant Yusuf, and Hüseyin Bey[86]—all active members of the dismantled local CUP club—were also sent to Aleppo.[87] On 2 March 1919, they were exiled to Egypt.[88] In the meantime, British forces continued to search for Ali Cenani Bey, another perpetrator and a former deputy from Aintab. At the time, he was one of the most influential figures of the Kemalist movement in Aintab and had formed a secret militia corps after the armistice.[89] Ali Cenani was later exiled to Malta in 1919 along with other leading CUP members.

Return of Aintab Armenians. After disarming the Muslim population and arresting individuals responsible for deportations and looting, the most urgent task for British occupation forces was to facilitate the return to their homes of those Aintab Armenians who had managed to survive the genocide, to restore their properties and assets, and to find the women and children who were now dispersed among Muslim households and return them to their families. With military control of Aleppo in the hands of British forces under General Edmund Allenby, the Allied commander-in-chief, this matter had been specifically mentioned in a twelve-article instruction given by Allenby to the Ottoman Sixth Army Command. In fact, Article 6 stipulated that Allenby reserved "the right to send Armenian refugees home and that their houses, lands, and other possessions should be immediately restored to them."[90]

Yet the precarious political-military situation in the Anatolian hinterland and the scarcity of sufficient transportation were two major hurdles for immediate repatriation. Significantly, by its Circular No. 69-9 of 18 December 1918, the Ottoman government agreed to "defray the repatriation expenses but subsequently failed to fulfill its obligation."[91] As Vahram L. Shemmassian emphasizes, in early January 1919 the Ottoman government "issued a decree of repatriation" amounting to "a permission to the Armenians to return to their homes," but as reported by the special correspondent of the London *Times,*

> many of them find their property occupied. Before and even for some time after the armistice, a Commission was appointed by the [Ottoman] Ministry of the Interior providing for the settlement of Mohamedans [Muslims] from Thrace and Macedonia on the land of the expatriated Armenians. These Moslem emigrants will presumably be evicted, but the authority of the Central Government is a dead letter in the provinces. The local officials are obstructive, and the process will not be easy until we have troops on the spot. Some time must pass before there is any security for Armenians in the outlying districts.[92]

Sir Mark Sykes had the same viewpoint as he stressed the urgency of repatriation: "Indications show that unless steps are taken by the Entente to supervise repatriation, Turks will grow more obstructive, as they know that while Armenians remain exiled, birth rate is diminished and death rate has increased."[93] He accordingly offered a plan "to organize, cover and protect the repatriation of deported Armenians."[94] Notwithstanding these difficulties, some Armenians, beginning with those in Kilis, did venture to return to Cilicia as early as 1918.[95] In January 1919, other convoys of Armenians—from Dörtyol, Mersin, and Tarsus; Alexandretta, Kırık Han, Hacin, and Toprakkale—followed the Kilis refugees and began the return to Cilicia-Adana in trains. This tremendous effort was organized in Aleppo by the Armenian National Union (hereafter ANU), a group that formed in Egypt in early 1917, and promoted by the Allies, brought together an array of Armenian parties and organizations.[96] A cipher telegram of 6 January 1919, sent by the Interior Ministry to the Ottoman Ministry of War, requested the transfer of two thousand liras from the *seferberlik tahsisatı* (mobilization allowance) to the district of Aintab, to reimburse it for the return expenses of those surviving families.[97]

So far, repatriation had been confined to the core areas of Cilicia. Beginning in February, it was extended to Aintab, Marash, and Urfa, in an area now called the Eastern Territories. According to statistics produced jointly by the Ecumenical and Armenian Patriarchates early in 1919, only 430 Armenians had by this point managed to return to Aintab.[98] On 12 May of that year, the director of the Central Service of Armenian Repatriation issued an order respecting the disposition of the

FIGURE 5.1 Armenian orphans under the protection of British forces in Aintab. Courtesy of the Near East Relief Collection, Houghton Library, Harvard University.

Marash and Aintab refugees.[99] By the end of the month, 4,221 Aintab Armenians had returned.[100] By 20 July 1919, the number on record had risen to 5,607.[101]

The exact number of Aintab Armenians who came back to their homeland, however, is unknown. Armenian and Turkish sources give contradictory figures. Turkish sources put approximately 18,000 Muslims and 37,000 Armenians in Aintab in 1918–1919 and estimate the number of Armenians who returned with the support of the British at around 25,000 (Figure 5.1).[102] Based on Armenian sources, 18,000 Armenian survivors managed to return to Aintab by the end of year.[103] Of these 18,000 returnees, 1,500 Armenians from Sivas, Gürün, and Kayseri, as well as 600–700 Armenian orphans from various places, returned to Aintab.[104] These estimations became very important for the ANU Committee of Aintab in 1920, as it used the numbers to calculate the distribution of food rations as equitably and economically as possible.[105]

Individual property restitution. After restoring peace and resolving provision issues, the British forces began to adopt measures to improve Aintab's economy and thus return the community to a state of self-sufficiency. Throughout this short period, the financial situation of

FIGURE 5.2 Ransacked and plundered houses in the Armenian quarter of Aintab. Courtesy of Gaziantep Kent Arşivi, Gaziantep Photograph and Postcard Collection.

Aintab's population, particularly that of the Armenians, improved. Major Mills negotiated with certain leading notables of the city and subsequently summoned Celal Bey to order the return of confiscated immovable properties to Armenians.[106] Following this order, the process of returning properties began, facilitated by the British military forces.[107] The surviving Armenians also filed petitions about properties that had been entrusted to the Aintab Liquidation Commission or that were taken hostage or sold to others.[108] Following the assessment of each petition, the Ottoman government would conduct a proper return if deemed necessary. In some cases, it was impossible to return immovable properties, as special teams deployed in Aintab by the CUP government had systematically looted and then destroyed 2,400 abandoned Armenians houses during the genocide (Figure 5.2).[109] Therefore, the owner was paid compensation instead.[110] In Aintab, the local government would inform central authorities by sending a wire that the property in question was impossible to repair, and hence it would be more reasonable to pay compensation.[111]

However, many properties were returned to their rightful owners. A list of movable and immovable Armenian properties sold by the Aintab

Liquidation Commission was prepared; as a result, fifty appropriated houses, still intact, were returned to their actual owners.[112] Similarly, seized villages were also given back to their owners.[113] Turkish and Kurdish peasants, who had been benefiting from the Armenian vineyards and crops, relinquished them to their rightful owners. For example, a number of Armenian landlords—such as Hovhannes Beredjiklian, Manug Matossian Agha, and Yusuf Babigian—were able to repossess their pistachio orchards, after which they harvested their crops to be transported to Aintab.[114]

Community property restitution. Armenians also had to restore their damaged churches and schools. According to a missionary report dated November 22, 1919:

> The present condition of the church [Surp Asvadzadzin] was in strange contrast from that in which it was at the time of the meetings in the spring of 1914. Efforts had been made to destroy the church. The galleries had been removed; the iron braces had been taken away, the woodwork torn out and the building left as a refuse dump, into which was thrown every description of filth and abomination. It had been somewhat . . . cleared out, and somewhat repaired and stood as an emblem of the desolate community. The three large evangelical churches in Aintab have been so desecrated that they are now worshipping in one church as one congregation.[115]

Karnig Panian, who came to Aintab from the Antoura Orphanage along with other Armenian orphans after the armistice, recalled that the Armenian neighborhoods of the city were eerily empty. Now and then, "we saw someone exiting a home. We also saw a few people repairing homes that had recently been damaged."[116]

On 19 January 1919, the repair of Surp Asvadzadzin Church and the second Protestant church was completed.[117] The Barsumian and Nersesian Schools were reopened, and Adour Agha's house was used as a school for boys. The houses of the Kurkchuian family and Nigoghos Agha were turned into seminaries, and Hayganushian College resumed instruction. In April 1919, the Atenagan School for boys was reopened with 1,300 students under the direction of Professor Krikor Sarafian.[118] The process of restitution of movable goods—such as rugs, oil lamps, and other goods confiscated from Armenian churches, monasteries, and schools, which were then auctioned by the Liquidation Commission—was initiated on 15 May 1919.[119] On 13 July, the Ministry of Interior ordered that each item of immovable property that once belonged to the Armenians and to their churches was to be returned to its original owner.[120] In late July 1919, the British demanded the stones of the Aintab Protestant church, which had been sold to local Muslims by the Aintab Liquidation Commission during the deportation. These stones were later used for the restoration of this church.[121] Having been occupied by the Ottoman military during the deportations, the Catholic church was also returned to the Armenians. On 21 December, the Aintab district governorship requested financial aid from the central government to repair the damage done to the church.[122]

The example of Pascal Mumdji's petition offers insight into the restitution process in Aintab. An Armenian from Aintab, Mumdji held British citizenship and resided in Aleppo. He filed a complaint regarding his immovable properties in Aintab directly to the British authorities on 16 April 1920. According to his statutory declaration, when the war broke out, the Ottoman government authorities confiscated his house located in Kurbu-Kayacık (an Armenian neighborhood). Before he inherited it from his deceased father, John Mumdji, the house had served as a consular residence for almost two decades.[123] In his petition, Pascal Mumdji claimed that government authorities had completely ravaged and destroyed his large house. His two water mills were left in ruins: his pistachio, walnut, olive, fig, and poplar orchards and vineyards were pillaged: and his horses and large wheat stocks were expropriated. The estimated value of these assets was 37,500 sterlings of gold.[124] In addition, the entire revenues of his properties had been confiscated. He also held the government responsible for the death of his wife, Emilie. According to his claim, on 17 December 1915, his wife was alone at home when a group of Ottoman soldiers entered and beat her to death.[125] It is not clear whether Mumdji was compensated for his losses.

From British to French Occupation in Aintab

By July 1919, the attitude of British military authorities toward Ottoman Muslims had evolved from hostility to open friendship, a change that seems to have been reciprocated. The shift came at the expense of justice for Armenians, as arrests of perpetrators slowed, along with efforts toward restoring Armenian property.[126] *Chagadamard* (Struggle), an Armenian daily published in Istanbul, reported that the Armenian populations in Aintab and Kilis were in a desperate situation. Letters of complaint from Armenians addressed to local authorities were left unanswered.[127] Conversely, the Muslim residents of Aintab, particularly local elites, were rather content with the British occupation. Turks were redistributing arms in Aintab and Kilis, and armed bands were created throughout the territory to resist the occupation.[128] British military forces no longer searched Muslim houses, instead mostly focusing on Armenian homes, and "if anyone was caught with a gun, they would be sentenced to prison."[129] Around the same time, a new nationalist resistance movement under the leadership of Mustafa Kemal began to emerge in various cities of Anatolia, gathering all opposition forces to unite against the foreign occupation. Mustafa Kemal organized a conference in Sivas on 4 September 1919, which resulted in the formation of Anadolu ve Rumeli Müdafaai Hukuk Cemiyeti (Society for the Defense of the Rights of Anatolia and Thrace). Afterward, various defense fronts, resistance organizations, and irregular forces, known as *Kuvayı Milliye* (national forces), emerged in Anatolia and Thrace. Although the British were aware of this movement in Aintab, they chose to overlook it.[130]

The British were in fact preparing to leave Aintab. This considerable attitude adjustment reflected larger developments in the imperial policy of the British Empire. In order to acquire oil resources in Mosul, Britain now reversed the Sykes-Picot Agreement and ceded Marash, Urfa, and Aintab to France by signing the Syrian Agreement with the French government on 15 September 1919.[131] Desiring to depart Aintab without leaving behind problems with the Muslim people, the British became more lenient. For instance, Major Mills's first action after the Syrian accord was to end the censorship of Mustafa Kemal's telegrams and letters.[132] The cipher telegram sent by Sabri Bey, the deputy to the district governor of Aintab, to the Ministry of Interior on 11 October 1919 revealed that according to the agreement reached by the British and the French, Britain would withdraw from Syria and Aintab by the end of the month.[133] Syria would remain under French occupation.[134]

In fact, the final British brigade did not leave Aintab until 19 November. Significantly, before they left, they returned to the Muslims the weapons that had been confiscated.[135] By October 29, 1919, two companies of French mounted infantries and a battalion of volunteers from the Armenian Legion—a special corps, formerly a Légion d'Orient (Eastern Legion), in the French Army of the Levant—had arrived, welcomed by Armenians in the city.[136] Sabri Bey officially protested the French occupation on 1 November.[137] On 4 November, Aintab was officially handed over to French troops.[138] The fate of the Armenians now lay in French hands, beginning a period that all inhabitants experienced as uncertain and insecure.[139]

The reoccupation of the Cilicia region by French forces had indeed caused deep resentment among the Muslim inhabitants.[140] Muslim residents, especially local elites, were extremely distraught over the presence of Armenian soldiers within the French forces, as well as the large number of Armenian returnees. Muslims expressed their overreaction to the occupation and support of the Armenians with the following menacing words: "İngiliz ve Fransız babalı deyyuslar, başınızdan onca şey geçti, hala akıllanmadınız [You, panders who are sons of the British and French. While you had passed through all these things, you haven't still become wiser]."[141]

The possibility that seized Armenian properties might be more systematically and thoroughly restored to their owners and that local notables involved in the genocide might be brought to trial without delay led many frightened Muslim notables and inhabitants to support the nationalist movement, which they had been reluctant to do until the arrival of French and Armenian soldiers.[142] Historian Sabahattin Selek describes the situation:

> With the Armenian properties they bought for a song, nouveau riche had emerged; the fortunes of the already established rich

> had become even larger. When the Great War ended with the defeat of the Ottoman Empire, the Turkish people from eastern and southern eastern regions, which had been densely populated by Armenians, were faced with a terrifying threat. The common people were afraid of what Armenians would do in revenge, whereas local notables were not only concerned for their lives but also for their fortunes.[143]

Therefore, in the eyes of Aintab's Muslim population, the real force behind the French occupation was the Armenians, which they saw as evident from the French determination to expedite the restitution process.[144]

Realizing that they would soon lose their fortunes, these elites agreed upon armed resistance with the foundation of Antep Heyet-i Merkeziye (Aintab Central Committee) on 23 November 1919 and, more important, decided to provide economic and logistical support to Kemalist forces.[145] The president of the committee was Hocazâde Ferit Bey, and most of its members were local notables, civil and military bureaucratic elites who were former members of Aintab's CUP club.[146] These elites began working closely with the underground CUP movement, which was in partial cooperation with the Kemalist movement. Additionally, local elites and civil and military bureaucrats, who had been arrested and sent to Egypt during the British occupation, either were released or escaped from prison during the French siege. Most of these arrestees returned to Aintab and joined the national forces.[147]

The French military occupation proved utterly ineffective. Although some reinforcements were sent, the High Command was unable and, it would appear, unwilling to undertake adequate offensive measures against the resurgence of Turkish nationalists. As a result of local Kemalist resistance, the French army was forced to retreat from Marash in early February and from Urfa in April 1920. After withdrawal from Marash and Urfa, the French occupation forces started disarming the Armenian volunteers in keeping with a new partial appeasement policy, which would lead to the eventual rapprochement with national forces.

The entire process of restoring Armenian properties was a casualty (perhaps a preordained one) of what we can call "the Turkish-French war in Aintab," which started on 1 April 1920 and ended with the city's surrender to French military forces on 9 February 1921.[148] According to mutual agreement, set down in the Ankara Treaty between Turkey's Grand National Assembly and the French government, signed on 20 October 1921, all activities on Turkish-French fronts ceased, and the French withdrawal from Aintab was sped up. For the sake of ensuring a long-term French presence in Syria and Lebanon to counterbalance British gains in the Levant, Cilicia was left to the Kemalists. In the end, the French failed, not only to protect the Armenians, but also to allow them the means of protecting themselves.[149] Henri Franklin-Bouillon, former president of the French Senate's Foreign Relations Committee and a former minister of propaganda in the war cabinet, who negotiated and signed the Ankara Agreement for France, stressed:

> In Cilicia, France was expending five million francs a year and had buried some 5,000 of its sons. . . . France had incurred these losses in defense of the Armenians. . . . France could make such sacrifices no longer and that there was no need, in view of these facts, to defend the decision to arrange a peace with the government of the Grand National Assembly of Turkey.[150]

Even under the best of circumstances, restitution in Aintab would have been a political hornet's nest. The return of Aintab's Armenians led to conflicts between the "new" arrivals and the Muslim immigrants and refugees, also relatively new, who had been settled in their houses, as well as those local officials and prominent Turks to whom Armenian houses had been rented, given, or in some cases, sold by the government. Thus "return" for some necessarily meant "eviction" for others. The issue was made worse by the fact that many of the houses' current occupants had no place to go.

Given the immense difficulties involved in recovering the documents that would have established rightful ownership, British military authorities had often had no choice but to rely on the claims of the conflicting parties themselves. Initially, at any rate, it was the Armenians who were given the benefit of the doubt. Thus if an Armenian pointed to one of the "Turkish" houses, declaring "this house used to belong to me, Turks took it away by force," then the Turk would be immediately forced out and the house would be given to the Armenian.[151]

In the case of Aintab, however, it was the attitude of the local Muslim authorities that was key. These men were reluctant to restore properties to the returnees even after the new Ministry of Interior ordered the restoration. Thus while occasionally houses were given back when demanded by their original owners, in most cases local authorities simply refused to evict the current occupants, so that returning Armenians were made to suffer considerably as a result.[152] Furthermore, the Ottoman authorities were returning the Armenian houses only to those whose names were written in the title deeds. Thus, if the father of a family died during the deportation, it was impossible for the other members of that family to take back their properties. According to the report, the Ottoman authorities were completely aware that most of the Armenian families lost their male head of household. Therefore, this policy was simply a pretext for the government to not return the Armenian properties to their owners.[153]

On 15 February 1919, the Ministry of Interior informed various provinces that "a new law was being prepared for the restitution of the abandoned properties, compensation for losses, and other related subjects. In order to prevent any further problems, provinces were warned not to give permission for the sale or pledging of the abandoned properties, since such transfers among individuals could interfere with the restitution process."[154] However, there was a certain ambiguity as to which authority was actually in control. The legislative regulations of the Istanbul government were not fully accepted, and local actors and officials, who were reluctant to restore the Armenian properties despite the Ministry of Interior's orders, acted as sole authority.[155] In some cases, instead of following the relevant legal regulations, local authorities and citizens applied individually to the Ministry of Interior regarding their problems. This unstable environment and the lack of regulatory enforcement disrupted the restitution process.[156]

The growing insecurity within Aintab itself was another factor that hindered restitution. The city's initial "tranquility," of which the CUP stalwart Eyüp Sabri Bey had once complained, evaporated as the return of increasing numbers of Armenians allowed local CUP networks to exploit the anxiety and anger of the townsfolk at the loss (real or prospective) of their homes and to raise a hue and cry. This environment, and the uncertainties of the British and especially the French occupations, turned the restitution process toxic, despite the orders of the new government in Istanbul. Aintab's townspeople responded by forming national defense organizations within the city. Violence broke out when such national forces attacked returning Armenians, and the homes of non-Muslims more generally again became targets for pillaging brigands.[157] From late 1918 through 1921, as nationalist forces, led by the Antep Cemiyet-i İslamiye (Aintab Society for Islam) and Antep Heyet-i Temsiliye (Aintab Committee of Representation), fought the French, and Armenians sided with the latter, Aintab became a theater of war. In Armenian historiography, the war is referred to as "the struggle for the existence of Armenians" or "the self-defense war of Armenians." Turkish historiography codifies it as the "Aintab War" or the "Aintab Resistance and Defense." In it we can see the emergence of two diametrically opposing historiographies—alike, ironically, in their nationalist point of view.

In totality, this restitution process directly affected the national resistance movement in Aintab, so much so that the famous battle of Aintab against the French—which resulted in the gifting of the honorific prefix *Gazi* (veteran), rechristening the city as Gaziantep on 8 February 1921—seems to have been as much the organized struggle of a group of genocide profiteers seeking to hold onto their loot as it was a fight against an occupying force. This resistance methodologically sought to make it impossible for the Armenian repatriates to remain in their native towns, terrorizing them in hopes of causing them to flee. In short, not only did the local notables, landowners, industrialists, and civil and military bureaucratic elites lead the resistance movement, but they also financed it in order to cleanse Aintab of Armenians.[158]

·6·

The End of the Armenian Community in Aintab

Seeing the handwriting on the wall, Armenians had begun gradually leaving Aintab, beginning in March 1921, ceding their properties (or prospective properties) to so-called French protection, and settling in Aleppo and Beirut, both now French mandates.[1] On 4 November 1921, the French officially declared their evacuation of Aintab complete, creating a great panic among those Armenians who still remained and who now saw themselves delivered into the hands of Kemalist forces—which would bring about their final destruction.[2] In early December, eight thousand Armenians had managed to quit Aintab by their own means—even though French authorities had prohibited migration and declined to issue passports (albeit *temporarily*) that would have allowed these Armenians to go to Syria and Lebanon.[3] On 1 January 1922, France forbade Armenians to enter Syria, over which they now held a League of Nations mandate.[4] In a letter full of pain to Arshak Chobanian, in Paris at the time, the deputy of the Armenian Catholicate, Father Nerses Tavukjian, revealed the Armenians' sense of abandonment, especially by the French, who had betrayed their promises to protect their lives and property. But Tavukjian's bitter reproaches were also aimed at the Armenians, including himself, for their naivete in believing the promises of French civil and military authorities, when in fact, he said, "the French sacrificed Armenians to the enemy [the Kemalists]."[5]

In November 1922, the Kemalist government declared that the goods of any Armenian who failed to return to Turkey within three months would be seized. Meanwhile, the government announced that it would not recognize the validity of passports that had been issued earlier by the French authorities to the Armenians for the purposes of crossing over to Syria.[6] Rather, all Armenians of Anatolian descent were to be counted as Ottoman citizens. Apparently, by not voiding Armenians' Turkish citizenship, the new Republic could more easily confiscate their properties. The Armenians did not take the bait. When, under the terms of the Ankara agreement, Cilicia was returned to Turkish rule, and the final French contingents left on 4 January 1922, the Armenians left the region too.[7] They settled mainly in Syria and Lebanon. A year later, on 4 January 1923, the Armenian population of Aintab numbered eighty persons.[8]

During these turbulent years, some Armenians *had* been able to sell their properties—however rare these people may have been.[9] Although the sales had been made under compulsion, and for prices considerably lower than the properties' real value, the fact that they had been technically "purchased" gave a color of legality to their new Turkish owners. As for the properties that had been (briefly) restored to the Armenians, which they now had to leave behind: these were henceforth listed under the rubric of "abandoned properties" according to the Abandoned Properties Laws. As such, they were now at the disposal of the government and local administrations.[10]

In this chapter, I discuss how the properties of Aintab Armenians who were forced to migrate to Syria and Lebanon were expropriated by the Ankara government through a series of domestic laws, rules, and regulations, as well as a complex legislative framework. I also elucidate in what ways Armenian properties were used after the Armenians' total departure from Aintab and demonstrate how the city's newly emerged wealthy Turkish-Muslim class (or local elites) consolidated its economic status by seizing those properties. Finally, I conclude by examining the Lausanne Treaty and mutual agreements signed between France and

Turkey, which hindered property claims of Aintab Armenians at the level of international law.

The Grand National Assembly on Abandoned Properties

With the departure of the Armenians along with the French forces from Aintab in December 1921 and January 1922, the Kemalist government in Ankara reintroduced the Abandoned Properties Laws with certain amendments. Thus, the second phase of confiscating Armenian properties in Aintab began. This phase was completed with the enforcement of the CUP's liquidation laws of 1915 again on 15 April 1923.

The 20 April 1922 Abandoned Properties Law. The 20 April 1922 law was the first abandoned properties law to be issued by the Grand National Assembly.[11] Although it is known as an abandoned properties law, it should not be confused with the 26 September 1915 Liquidation Law. The 20 April 1922 law addresses the abandoned properties of people who fled and went missing after 1919. According to its fifth article, the law covered "the movable and immovable property and the agricultural products of people about whom it was determined legally that they were in difficult circumstances due to war or political reasons and fled to other places or were lost."[12] The law said that movable goods abandoned and left by owners who fled or went missing would be sold at auction according to procedures set by the government, while immovable properties and agricultural products would again be administered by the government. After subtracting expenses, their revenues, rent, and other incomes would be placed in treasury accounts in escrow. If any of the property owners returned, the immovable properties belonging to them as well as the sums of money placed in trust in treasury accounts would be returned to them.

According to the third article of the law, those who seized abandoned, ownerless properties and agricultural products would be required to surrender these things to the government within one week after the law was issued. Legal procedures would be initiated against those who did not comply. With the fourth article, those who reported secretly held abandoned properties would be given one-tenth of the value of these properties as a reward. Another important regulation stipulated that the transactions would be accepted and considered valid if the property owner gave power of attorney. As can be understood from these articles, the 20 April 1922 law—stating that properties would be returned to their owners—did not contradict the 12 January 1920 regulation issued under Sultan Vahdettin. In this sense, this law can be seen as an adaptation of the earlier regulation to new conditions.

The regulations of November to December 1922. The Council of Ministers on 29 October and 14 December 1922 gave permission to non-Muslims, in particular to Greeks, to freely leave the country. Two separate regulations were issued concerning the management of the properties that these people would leave behind. First, a regulation issued on 12 November 1922, together with the 29 October regulation, made "the decision that harm is not seen in the transmission of immovable properties to others and the transfer and sale of movable properties [by those given permission to leave the country]."[13] That is, these people could transfer or sell their properties as they wished. However, the practice of free transfer and sale was temporarily halted on 14 December 1922, the same day that all non-Muslims were freely allowed to leave the country.[14]

This sudden change in the regulations is grounded in logic. Turkey, having won the war against Greece, considered demanding "significant money as war reparations and compensation for destruction and repair from Greece."[15] However, it was also known that "due to Greece's known financial circumstances," it would not be able to provide "the assurance of a full cash indemnity."[16] Therefore, it was planned to seize these properties left behind by Greeks as the equivalent of this indemnity. If this were to be realized, it was expected that two purposes would be simultaneously served: "In this way, the collection of reparations will be facilitated, and the financial connection of Greeks to Anatolia will be found to be cut off."[17] This proposal, originally put forth by the chief of the general staff, was later placed on the agenda of the cabinet by the president of the Council of Ministers. In taking such a decision, it was desired that "it be ordered that the wealth and real estate belonging to Greek nationals, and to emigrating *Rums* [Ottoman Greeks] and Armenians quickly be determined by local governments."[18]

The 14 September 1922 "abrogation of property regulation." The Grand National Assembly began to amalgamate procedures connected to abandoned properties created in the period of the Armenian genocide and those created in the period of 1919–1922 starting on 14 September 1922. On that date, the 12 January 1920 regulation, which I refer to as the Vahdettin Regulation, was annulled by way of an extremely short one-sentence decree: "The regulation dated 16 Rebiülahir 1338 and 8 Kânunısani 1336 [both dates translate to 8 January 1920] on the properties subject to liquidation of people transported to other places is abrogated."[19] Through this decree, which in practice came to be called the "abrogation of property regulation," the 26 September 1915 law and the 8 November 1915 regulation again came into use, and the Republic began the legal process of reconstructing the CUP's genocide policies. As circumstances had changed in the seven years since the initial promulgation of these laws, certain alterations were deemed necessary. The first change was made on 31 October 1922 with the alteration and deletion of articles from the 8 November 1915 regulation.[20]

These changes concerned the composition of the Liquidation Commissions. The commissions, henceforth under the chairmanship of a local treasury official appointed by the highest-ranking civil servant of the region, would consist of one person each from the administrative and municipal councils, and if it existed locally, the chamber of commerce.[21] The new regulation added a fourth article to the 8 November 1915 rules. According to this new article, the movable and immovable properties of people who traveled to foreign or occupied lands *in any manner whatsoever* either before or after World War I and still had not returned would be administered by the government until the return of these people.[22] In addition to this change, the scope of application of the 1915 law was broadened to include the property of those who left the country in a new wave of migration after 1918, and a new law in place of the 26 September 1915 one was issued on 15 April 1923.

Return to the CUP Genocide Laws

Parliamentary discussions of the abrogation of the 12 January 1920 regulation make clear the reasons for the return to the CUP's genocide laws. After the war had been won, it was likely that the abandoned properties issue would appear on the agenda of the forthcoming peace negotiations with the Allied Powers, and Turkey could be asked to return the properties to their owners. Yet, Turkey could not tolerate the existence of Armenians inside the country, let alone the return of their confiscated properties, as the state considered the abandoned properties an important source of revenue. However, there was an obligation to relinquish these properties to their owners according to the Vahdettin Regulation, which was still valid. Consequently, it was necessary to abrogate this regulation prior to the commencement of the Lausanne negotiations.

Since the parliamentary discussions on this subject were secret, Minister of Finance Fehmi Bey explained the reasoning to deputies in a direct manner. While the regulation remained in force, the return of all goods and properties that had passed into Muslim hands to their original owners would be unavoidable. The Western states would employ pressure on this topic at the approaching Lausanne Peace Conference. In the words of the minister, "I think that if the minorities while this topic is being discussed say we do not want anything else if you carry out once again the provisions which you accepted on this issue and up until today implemented, we will have no answer to give in response."[23] The most thought-provoking point of the minister was that "the Treasury [will be] obliged to pay the cost of the entire financial and moral responsibility." He said that "the implementation of this regulation is one-tenth of the existing provisions of the law," meaning that 90 percent of goods and properties still had not been returned. "However," he continued, "while this regulation exists as law, naturally it should be implemented, [and] they [foreign powers] will pressure us to carry out its provisions. For this reason, the abrogation of the regulation is necessary as soon as possible."[24]

The discussions of the parliamentarians revealed why it was necessary to eliminate this law and, if not, what would await Turkey. Hakkı Sami Bey, the deputy from Sinop, said, "When we were forming the

Assembly here . . . we were unable to find . . . time to deal with such regulations."[25] Trabzon deputy Hasan Bey said, "Peace is near. It is necessary before the problems of peace begin to clear away such things. . . . It is necessary to make this regulation decompose from its roots."[26] The words of these two deputies reflected the collective sentiments expressed by other deputies.

Return to the CUP Mentality

The 26 September 1915 law and 8 November 1915 regulation were reenacted together with the 14 September 1922 abrogation of property regulation. As mentioned earlier, some changes were necessary to adapt to new conditions. These changes, which were delayed for many reasons, first were made through the 15 April 1923 Liquidation Law.[27] This law, with nine articles in all, took as its basis the 26 September 1915 law in modified form. Its seventh article annulled the 20 April 1922 Abandoned Properties Law. Articles 2, 4, 7, and 8 of the 26 September 1915 law were revised, while the ninth article was removed completely, and a new article added.

The sixth article is perhaps the most significant addition, as it broadened the scope of the law, including in it those who fled or disappeared after 1919. Henceforth, the 26 September 1915 law and the altered form of the 15 April 1923 law would be applied together "to movable and immovable properties, debts and assets abandoned by those disappearing in any way whatsoever, or leaving a place, or fleeing to foreign and occupied lands, or Istanbul or connected places."[28] With this change, people covered by the law in the first and sixth articles were defined as those who were "*fugitives, lost,* or *fled* to other places" (italics added). This definition, primarily referring to Armenians, would form the basis of all civil lawsuits in the Republican era.

The first article of the 15 April 1923 law is no more than the second article of the 26 September 1915 law with some revisions, a point of extraordinary importance. The 1923 law annulled the provision existing in the 1915 law, which would return to the original owners the money remaining after the liquidation of their properties. The 1923 law presumed that people who had fled or disappeared would not return. In its stead, according to the kind of movable and immovable properties, records would be made in the Ministry of Foundations or Ministry of Finance, and "the sum that will remain after liquidation from the values at which the properties would be appraised [would be registered as] revenue in trust *in the name of* the aforementioned owners" (italics added). In any lawsuits that might arise concerning the properties, the Treasury would be the defendant.[29]

The critical point is that in official texts after this date concerning abandoned properties, the identifications "13 Eylül 1331 [26 September 1915] and 15 Nisan 1339 [15 April 1923]" would be used together. Consolidation with the CUP regime was complete. The natural conclusion to this amendment process was the issuance of a regulation concerning the application of this law. This was the regulation of 29 April 1923, number 2455, and it took the place of the 8 November 1915 regulation.[30] The 1923 regulation was nearly identical to the 1915 regulation, also consisting of twenty-five articles. The first article extended the scope of the law to entail "people being transported or who in any manner whatsoever by going from the place at which they are located to another place disappear, or are leaving a place."[31] The distinction between *heyet* (committee) and *komisyon* (commission) was maintained, and the duties of both were separately detailed. According to the regulation, in every county in which the aforementioned people were to be found, the day after this regulation was officially communicated, a committee would be formed by that locality's highest ranking civil servant under the chairmanship of that locality's highest ranking treasury official, with one member each from the tax, title deed registry, and population registry administrations; the local police; and, if it existed locally, the foundations administration. The first five articles described in detail what work the committees were to do.

The second part of the regulation, concerning the commissions to be formed and their duties, again modified the 8 November regulation. The activities of the commissions in essence remained the same. The power to seize all money, goods, and other properties of departing people was given. The commissions would complete all transactions concerning the assets and liabilities of these people. The provision existing in the

8 November 1915 regulation stating that "the values of properties the owners of which are not known are going to be registered in the name of the village or neighborhood in which the articles are located and later will be sent by the government to the place where the people of the aforementioned village or neighborhood were settled"[32] was changed, as it was now moot. Under the new arrangement, the prices of these properties would be registered as revenue in accounts of the local treasury directorate.

In brief, throughout the Republican era, abandoned property transactions were carried out according to the 15 and 29 April 1339 (1923) law and regulation. Once more, the dominant logic of the CUP era was maintained. Only the provision that the sum remaining after the liquidation of properties would be returned to the original owners was eliminated. Henceforth, it was considered that those people who fled and disappeared would not return. The state issued a detailed list of properties belonging to disappeared people, which were documented in record books. After the necessary transactions concerning the elimination of debts and assets were concluded, they were registered in the treasuries of the Ministries of Finance and Foundations. Similar to other immovable properties belonging to the Ministries of Finance and Foundations, these would be managed by means of administrative councils.

Total Confiscation of Aintab Armenians' Properties

Here I attempt to present how and which individuals and institutions acquired Armenian properties and wealth; as the archives of the Land Registry and Cadaster in Turkey are closed, a full study of these properties is not presently possible.[33] First, an overall list of abandoned Armenian properties prepared by Priest Karekin Bogharian immediately prior to his departure in December 1922 is reviewed. Second, individual cases of Armenian property seizures from various sources are analyzed under five headings. Finally, Çukurbostan, a former Armenian neighborhood in Gaziantep, is examined as a case study to demonstrate how abandoned properties were used.

Bogharian's list of Armenian properties. As a distinguished man of religion and one of the last persons to leave Gaziantep, Priest Karekin Bogharian compiled a comprehensive list of properties owned by the Armenian community just before his departure in December 1922 (Table 6.1). Included in this list of fifty-two articles, he recorded the names, locations, owners, types, and values (in Ottoman gold) of these properties, most of which were landed estates that had been liquidated by the Treasury after April 1923.[34] Some of them were used by Gaziantep Belediyesi (Gaziantep Municipality) for local administrative needs, while others were sold through auctions organized by Gaziantep Defterdarlığı (Gaziantep Internal Revenue Office) in the early 1930s. The majority of buyers were the city's local notables, most of whom had participated in the Turkish-French war. The remaining properties were also distributed among refugees and immigrants.

The Gaziantep Municipality purchased a significant array of properties. This lot included a number of schools, such as Hayganushian, Saint Mariam (Lusovarichian), and Vartanian. The municipality also acquired properties including a graveyard, churches and their associated buildings, and a store in Eblahan bazaar. Other schools went to private individuals (Cilicia College, Atenagan School) and unknown buyers (Ahmed-Vahanian, National Haygazian, Armenian school in Ibn-i Kör, Hripsimyan) or were demolished (Sahakian). Private individuals claimed a number of businesses, including stores in Çukur-Balıklı bazaar: three stores in the jewelry bazaar in Kalaaltı; and a hotel, coffeehouse, and stores in Akyol. Two former homes—Kavukdjian's house in Akyol and Lusia Andiliani's House in Kayacık—are now coffeehouses.

Armenian Property Seizures

Distribution to the needy, refugees, and immigrants. From 1922 to 1928, some of the houses that belonged to Armenians were used for charitable purposes, distributed at no charge by the state and the Aintab municipal authority to Muslim families who had lost their own dwellings during the Turkish-French war.[35] According to a local, these impoverished Muslim

Table 6.1 Karekin Bogharian's List of Armenian Properties, 1922

Number	Property	Value[a]	Present-day owner
1–8	Old church, new church, house of the arch-priest, cottage of the priests, house of the people who assist priests, kindergarten, classrooms at the school, Hayganushian School, fourteen shops, and a mill that belonged to the church	1,000	Gaziantep Municipality
9	House of Sarkis Karamanoukian	1,000	Gaziantep Municipality
10	A store in Eblahan bazaar	100	Gaziantep Municipality
11	Sahakian school in Akyol	800	Demolished
12	Sarkis Kavukdjian's house in Akyol	200	Coffee shop
13	Land and houses in Akyol	2,600	Private individuals
14	Ahmed-Vahanian School in Kurbu Munya	300	Unknown
15	Saint Mariam School (Lusovarichian) in Kurbu Kozanlı	300	Gaziantep Municipality
16, 17	National graveyard and *sumaklık* (type of land) in Kurbu Kozanlı	40,000	Gaziantep Municipality
18	National Nersesian School in Çukurbostan	16,000	Former Gaziantep Court House
19	Houses and mill in Çukurbostan	8,000	Private individuals
20	Stores in Çukur-Balıklı bazaar	2,500	Private individuals
21	Lusia Andiliani's house in Kayacık	300	Coffee shop
22	National Haygazian School in Kurbu Zincirli	3,000	Unknown
23	Hagop Istanbulian's house in Kurbu Zincirli	500	Unknown
24	Haygazian's flower house, bakery, and two stores in Ehl-i Cefa	1,500	Private individuals
25	Millet Inn in Ibn-i Şeker	30,000	Mustafa Geylani
26, 27	Millet coffee house and three stores in Ibn-i Şeker	800	Private individuals
28	Three stores in jewelry bazaar in Kalaaltı	200	Private individuals
29	Armenian school in Ibn-i Kör	200	Unknown
30, 31	Hotel, coffeehouse, and stores in Akyol	12,000	Private individuals
32, 33	Eight stores, one bakery, and one house in Kozanlı	5,000	Private individuals
34	Uzun Kız's (Long Girl) house in Ibn-i Eyüp	100	Private individuals
35, 36	Hripsimyan school and stores in Ibn-i Eyüp	2,500	Unknown
37	Vartanian School and its houses in the Haig Zımyan	10,000	Gaziantep Municipality

Number	Property	Value[a]	Present-day owner
38, 39	Cilicia College, its buildings, and land in Akyol	12,000	Private individuals
40	Yacoubian's house in Kayacık	300	Private individuals
41	Lusia Khanum's house in Kayacık	1,000	Unknown
42	Bilemdjian's house and their stores in Kozanlı	250	Private individuals
43	S.G. Nazarian's paint house in Kurbu Kozanlı	1,000	Kimya family
44	Koca Kevorkian's store in Haig Baba	50	Dai family
45	Der Nerses and H. Hamalian's garden in Akyol	500	Private individuals
46, 47	Hamamlı land and gardens in Akyol	2,800	Gaziantep Municipality
48, 49	Atenagan School and stores in Haig Zımyan	9,800	Turgut Gündoğdu
50	Deghirmendjian's house in Haig Zımyan	200	Private individuals
51	Land with 10,000 acres in Akyol	500	Private individuals
52	Young Men's Christian Association (YMCA) house and stores in Karagöz	3,000	Unknown

Total: 269,500[b]

Source: Kevork A. Sarafian (ed.), *Badmo'wt'iwn Ah'nt'abi Hah'o'c* [History of the Aintab Armenians], vol. I (Los Angeles: Union of the Armenians of Aintab, 1953), 442.

[a] Value given in Ottoman gold; unit of currency unknown.
[b] While the sum of the property values does not equal 269,500, these numbers are taken directly from a document originally written in Armenian.

families were given small or neglected Armenian houses.[36] This was the fate, in 1922, of the house owned by the father of Harutyun Nazarian, who was forced to leave Aintab and settle in Aleppo along with the rest of his family when he was fifteen. In a memoir, Nazarian recalled the event:

> Before we left the house, a state official accompanied by two women came into our yard early in the morning. Then the official said, "as you are leaving Aintab and the houses of these two women were demolished due to the battle and bombardments, and in addition to that, since the state and local government have authorized you to leave Aintab, your house along with other empty houses will be occupied by others." He also asked these two women how many rooms there were in their wrecked houses. In this manner, our house was registered into the list of other occupied houses.[37]

Several years after the war, abandoned houses and estates of the Armenians were still being used to settle immigrants and *muhajirs* (refugees). A telegram of 17 August 1924 sent by the Ministry of Population Exchange, Development, and Settlement (Mübâdele, İmar ve İskân Vekâleti İskân Şubesi) to Gaziantep Province reported that there had been 19,500 Armenians in the province, whose houses and estates, following their departure, could accommodate a large number of muhajirs, and directed that these muhajir families be settled on these properties according to their needs.[38]

As late as 1928 the distribution of immovable properties of the Armenians to Muslim immigrants who had been settled in Gaziantep was still going on. For example, on 3 November 1925, the Ministry of Interior approved an application submitted by Hasan Effendi, an immigrant from Kars, to settle in Gaziantep.[39] On 7 November, the provincial government was instructed to provide housing for Hasan Effendi and his family from abandoned properties.[40] When an immigrant from the Adilcevaz district in Bitlis province applied to the "Administration for the Settlement of the Gaziantep Province" for relocation to the city, his request was referred to the Ministry of Interior.[41] In the ministry's 5 March 1927 response to the Gaziantep administration, it was stated that the settlement of Abdullah, son of Haji Reşid in Gaziantep, posed no problem, and that a house from the remaining "abandoned Armenian properties" of the Aintab Armenians be given to him, so that he and his family could live comfortably.[42] In another telegram sent to the Gaziantep Governorship by the Ministry of Interior on 23 November 1925, it was stated that twenty-six households of refugees from Mersin were to be settled in Gaziantep.[43] Yet the Gaziantep Governorship replied that no housing or estates remained in the city in which to settle more refugees.[44] Furthermore, on 31 December, it was underlined that even the existing refugees could not be settled properly.[45]

However, Tables 6.2 and 6.3, which include information on the numbers and types of abandoned properties—and the recipients thereof—demonstrate that the distribution process was ongoing in Gaziantep and two of its districts, Kilis and Nizip, on 11 November 1926.[46]

The most properties in Gaziantep (135) went to exchanged people, and the fewest (19) to eastern refugees. In Kilis, the most properties (76) were

Table 6.2 Distribution of Abandoned Properties in Gaziantep Province, 1926

	Gaziantep	Kilis	Nizip
Mübâdil (exchanged people)	135	17	26
Gayr-ı mübâdil (nonexchanged people)	39	76	—
Syrian refugees	65	19	10
Eastern refugees	19	—	—
House	143	86	38
Shop	15	—	—
Land (acreage)[a]	5,868	2,218	620
Vineyard (acreage)	2,171	51,100	—
Küruh[b]	—	—	—
Orchard (acreage)	104	—	79
Garden (acreage)	6,186	—	—
Fig and pistachio groves (acreage)	464	—	6,238
Olive trees	49,393	9,028	21 *kıta*[c]

Source: BCA / TİGMA 272.00.00.12.55.136.13, 11 November 1926.

[a] Acreage refers to a land measure of about 920 square meters.
[b] *Küruh* is a unit of measurement.
[c] *Kıta* is a unit of measurement.

Table 6.3 Allocation of Abandoned Properties in Gaziantep Province, 1926

	Gaziantep	Nizip	Behisni
Shop	—	—	3
House	15	15	16
Land	—	—	48
Vineyard house	—	—	116
Vineyard	—	117 plots	119
Estate (acreage)	2,738	4,283	9,474
Pistachio trees	—	144 plots	277
Orchard	—	2 plots	3 acres
Olive groves (*kıta*)	—	119	—
Garden (acreage)	—	—	24
Mill	—	—	4

Source: BCA / TİGMA 272.00.00.12.55.136.13, 11 November 1926.

distributed to nonexchanged people and the fewest (17) to exchanged people (Table 6.2). In Nizip, on a lesser scale, properties were distributed to only nonexchanged people (26) and Syrian refugees (10). In terms of land acreage, Gaziantep allocated 5,868 acres, Kilis 2,218, and Nizip only 620. However, when it comes to fig and pistachio grove acreage, Nizip allocated 6,238 acres to Gaziantep's 464 (no fig or pistachio groves were allocated in Kilis).

Within the province, Behisni allocated 9,474 estate acres, Nizip 4,283, and Gaziantep only 2,738 (Table 6.3). Beyond houses (15), allocation was not recorded for any other property types in Gaziantep. Similarly, Nizip allocated 15 houses, and Behisni allocated 16. Nizip and Behisni again had similar numbers of vineyard plots that were allocated, 117 and 119, respectively. However, Behisni had significantly more pistachio tree plots (277) than Nizip (144).

On 25 December 1927, the Statistical Description Unit of the General Directorate of the Interior Ministry sent a telegram to Gaziantep Province asking for the exact numbers of nonexchanged, immigrant, fire victim, and other such families in the city, for the ministry intended to distribute more abandoned properties to these groups.[47] In its response, Gaziantep Province informed the Ministry of Interior that 2,445 nonexchanged persons, immigrants, and fire victims were settled in 529 houses.[48] However, in some cases, this distribution process was abused. For instance, two abandoned houses were distributed to *Vilayet Muhasebecisi* (bookkeeper of Gaziantep Province) by Vilâyet İskân Komisyonu (Province Settlement Commission) in January 1925.[49] Upon hearing this, the Ministry of Interior warned Gaziantep Province that abandoned properties were to be used for the settlement of refugees. As a result, said houses were evacuated in May 1925.[50] Ultimately, a law enacted on 12 March 1928 enabled current occupiers to register their abandoned Armenian properties at the Deed Office.[51] Thereafter, the new settlers became the official owners of these properties.

Illegal seizures after the Aintab War. In the immediate aftermath of the Turkish-French war, large Armenian houses were looted by prominent and affluent local elites without any legal repercussions.[52] According to local sources, Ali Api obtained Garuc Karamanougian's mansion in 1924; after changing hands a few times, the building was bought and restored by Hasan Süzer, a businessman from Aintab, in 1985 and donated to the Ministry of Culture and Tourism on the condition that it would serve as Hasan Süzer Etnografya Müzesi (Hasan Süzer Ethnography Museum).[53] Ahmed Hurşid Bey and Mustafa Kayaalp, both members of Aintab Central Committee and financiers of national forces, seized Armenian estates (Ahmed Hurşid Bey claimed Pirenian's large house in 1922 and later paid a symbolic price for it at an auction);[54] and Nuri Patpatzâde usurped the houses of Hagop Bezjian and Harutyun Aghian in 1923.[55]

It is possible that in an effort to embezzle the spoils, the state organized symbolic auctions through the Gaziantep Municipality and Gaziantep Internal Revenue Office to complete official sale transactions. These so-called transactions were even announced in *Gaziantep Gazetesi* (Gaziantep Newspaper) in 1930–1935, the notices of which detailed the quantity, date, time, approximate location, type, value in liras, and—most important—previous owners.[56] However, information on the buyers was not provided. To illustrate, a parcel of land owned by Hanna Kurkchuian, valued at 250 liras, was auctioned for thirty liras in 1934; a parcel of land owned by Avedis Nacarian, valued at sixty liras, was sold for ten liras in the same year;[57] Zenop Bezjian's shop, valued at 216 liras, was auctioned for 150 liras in 1935; and around the same time, Abraham Babikian's vineyard was sold for fifteen liras, far below its actual value.[58]

Auctions for local elites. The houses, fields, lands, vineyards, orchards, and estates, along with other properties that Armenians left behind, were sold for very low prices by auctions organized by the Gaziantep Municipality in the 1920s. Many prominent families enlarged their fortunes by purchasing these assets. Furthermore, certain local notables collaborated to decrease the price of the abandoned properties by manipulating these auctions and bought these properties for a pittance.[59] Some of these individuals were Abdullah Göğüş, Daizâde Mahmut, Kepkepzâde Mustafa and Abdullah, Mayor Lütfü Effendi, Attarzâde Abdullah, Bakkalzâde Ali, Körükçüzâde Mustafa, Helvacızâde Ali and Abdürrezzak, Hanefizâde Ahmet, Müftüzâde Süleyman, Hocazâde Mustafa, Mahmut Atay, Ali Cenani, and İncozâde Hüseyin. They lived in the houses of well-known Armenian families such as the Nazaretians, Demirdjians, Leylekians, Krajians, Ashchians, Kurkchuians, Matossians,

FIGURE 6.1 A former employee of the Nazaretian family, Daizâde Mahmut, known as the first Muslim industrialist of Gaziantep. Courtesy of Gaziantep Kent Arşivi, Gaziantep Photograph and Postcard Collection.

Bezjians, Hadidians, Jebejians, Bulbulians, Nacarians, Barsumians, Karamanougians, and Bireciklians.[60]

Among these individual buyers, Daizâde Mahmut is of particular interest (Figure 6.1). As a member of a leading wealthy Aintab family, he served as the chairman of *Gaziantep Ticaret Odası* (Gaziantep Chamber of Commerce) from 1921 to 1924.[61] In 1923, he purchased Garabed Nazaretian's house, which was put up for sale by the Gaziantep Municipality. The deceased Garabed Nazaretian's daughters, who held Iranian citizenship, objected to this sale through the Iranian Embassy. Thereupon, the embassy sent an oral notice to the Istanbul Office of the Foreign Affairs Commissariat of the Turkish Grand National Assembly on 5 February 1923. The embassy requested a halt of the sale of the property of the deceased Garabed's daughters. The sale procedure, the Iranian Embassy added, was illegal, and the property in question had to be returned to its real owners. This oral notice was later presented to the ministry of Foreign Affairs, but to no avail.[62] Despite this protest, the sale transaction was realized.

A former employee of the Nazaretian family, Daizâde Mahmut became an affluent merchant and used this house as a mansion until it was donated to the military to be used as a gendarmerie station in 1965.[63] After the departure of military forces in 1967, the Daizâde family sold the house to its current owner, Abdülkadir Kimiazâde (today known as Kimya), a wholesaler and real estate agent. The building was used as a residential house, warehouse, and drying room until the 1980s. The Kimya family rented the house in the 1990s, when it was in a state of dilapidation. Until its restoration in the mid-2000s, it was used as a dormitory. Today, with its eight owners from the Kimya family, it serves as Papirüs Kafe (Papyrus Café).[64] Both the Daizâde and Kimiazâde families actively supported and participated in the deportations in return for Armenian properties.[65] Additionally, Daizâde Mahmud bought Nazaretian's other estates in Aintab. For example, the Kara Nazar Inn, later called Büyük Pasaj (Grand Bazaar), was transferred to the Gaziantep Internal Revenue Office as a national estate and sold to Mahmut Dai. A few years later, his son İhsan Dai purchased Sarkis Krajian's house at an auction in 1934.[66]

A house belonging to Dr. Avedis Jebejian was acquired by the Konukoğlu family, the most well-off industrialist family of Gaziantep. In 2011, this family donated the house to the Gaziantep Metropolitan Municipality. In 2013, the municipality opened it to the public as Gaziantep Atatürk Anı Müzesi (Atatürk Memorial Museum of Gaziantep; Figure 6.2).[67]

One of the Nazaretian houses was used as the building for Konukoğlu Vakfı (Konukoğlu Foundation) in 1989. Currently, one of the houses belonging to Hagop Aslanian's family is being used as a boutique hotel, the Anatolian Houses Boutique Hotel.[68]

FIGURE 6.2 Gaziantep Atatürk Anı Müzesi, former house of Dr. Avedis Jebejian. Courtesy of Gaziantep Kent Arşivi, Gaziantep Photograph and Postcard Collection.

The Ankara government further encouraged sales of large Armenian commercial estates. One of those estates was the Millet Inn, which was built in 1869 by the Armenian Apostolic Church and later sold by the Treasury to third parties after the last Armenians had departed.[69] In a book sponsored and published by the Gaziantep Valiliği (Gaziantep Governorship) in 2005, titled *Gaziantep Kültür Envanteri* (Gaziantep Cultural Inventory), the Millet Inn was designated a "Turkish cultural asset."[70] Since 2000, both the inn and the stores within it have been owned by a single individual.[71] The inn known as Kürkçü Hanı (Kurkchuian Inn), founded by Hanna Kurkchuian in 1890, was sold to Mustafa Humanızlı, a local entrepreneur, by the Treasury in the early 1950s.[72] Similar in status to the Millet Inn, Kurkchuian Inn is yet another Armenian building that would acquire the honor of being named a "Turkish cultural asset."[73] It has also been under personal ownership and used as a warehouse and storehouse since 2000.

Mustafa Kemal's rewards for war contributions. Through the personal directives of Mustafa Kemal in 1924–1925, Armenian land assets were sometimes also bestowed on individuals as rewards for noteworthy accomplishments during the national struggle.[74] These consisted of the Aintab Central Committee *Semt Komutanları* (district commandants) who took part in the 1920–1921 war and local notables who financially or logistically contributed to the war.[75] Such individuals included Hüseyin Effendi İncozâde, Mahmud Effendi, Kabakzâde Şakir Effendi, Attarzâde Abdullah Effendi, Kepkepzâde Abdullah Effendi, Ağazâde Hüseyin Effendi, Hacızâde Hacı Şerif, and Mütevellizâde Ramazan Effendi.[76] A good majority of the immovable Armenian properties ended up in the hands of these men, as well as in the hands of the local gentry and other veterans of the 1920–1921 war. These men had bought the abandoned properties through the Milli Emlak (National Estate) and the Defterdarlık (Internal Revenue Office), which had put them up for sale for very convenient prices. Local notables colluded to hold down the price and obtain the properties at cut-rate prices.

For example, one such beneficiary was Türkmenzâde Ahmet Effendi, a parliamentary deputy of Aleppo who hailed from a family of Antioch notables and had resided in Gaziantep ever since the Middle East's national boundaries, redrawn after the war, had left Aleppo outside the new Turkish nation-state. It was Mustafa Kemal himself who gave instructions, on 14 December 1924, that Türkmenzâde Ahmet Effendi, whose previous house in Antioch, worth thirty thousand liras, had been confiscated by the French, was to be awarded a great parcel of garden and courtyards from abandoned-turned-national assets of equal value, because of his outstanding services during the national struggle.[77] The order was approved by the decree of the Ministerial Cabinet and implemented on 23 December 1924.[78] Similar to Türkmenzâde Ahmet Effendi, Mehmet Ali Effendi, a lieutenant from Aleppo, was settled in Gaziantep to repay him for his services,[79] and his housing was provided from abandoned properties.[80]

It is important to note that certain individuals, especially those who had participated in the Turkish-French war and were the commanders on a variety of fronts (such as the Suburcu and Çınarlı neighborhoods), were appointed, after the foundation of the Turkish Republic, to vital positions in the official agencies of the state. In the meantime, certain district commanders were also elected as deputies to the Turkish Grand National Assembly.[81] In general, thanks to Armenian wealth, this group

FIGURE 6.3 Funeral of İncozâde Hüseyin, a local elite and district commander actively involved in deportation and spoliation. Courtesy of Gaziantep Kent Arşivi, Gaziantep Photograph and Postcard Collection.

formed Aintab's new wealthy bourgeoisie class and consolidated their status further during the Republican period. One such individual was İncozâde Hüseyin, who actively participated in the war as a district commander (Figure 6.3). As the Armenians left Aintab, he purchased Movses Jamgochian's house at auction for a cut-rate price. Another house classified as abandoned property was rewarded to him for his various services to the nation by Mustafa Kemal. In addition, with Mustafa Kemal's support, İncozâde Hüseyin was elected to Parliament as a deputy of Gaziantep.[82]

In another example, the buildings of the Atenagan School and Surp Bedross Yegeghetsi (Second Catholic Church) were passed on to the National Estate after the Armenians had to vacate the city. Later these buildings were turned into a *Veliç İplik ve Dokuma* (thread and weaving) factory in 1933[83] and given to Cemil Alevli, a young native of Aintab, by a special order of Mustafa Kemal, as part of the effort to create a class of entrepreneurs and capitalists in the city.[84] With a Western education as his "social capital," and with Mustafa Kemal acting as his "venture capitalist," Cemil Alevli became the biggest textile supplier of Aintab in the Turkish Republic. He admitted that he had learned the textile business from Aintab's Armenians. "Since my childhood," Alevli said, "I used to watch how Armenians in my neighborhood worked on their textile looms for hours as I headed back and forth to school. I was amazed to follow how Armenian weavers created beautiful fabrics by combining various tones of red, yellow, green, blue, and white thread cones."[85]

Known as the "founding father of the textile industry" in Gaziantep, Alevli later became a member of the Republican People's Party (hereafter RPP) and served as the president of the RPP Gaziantep Bureau from 1941 to 1946. Additionally, he served as an RPP deputy in Parliament from 1946 to 1950.[86] His factory was officially named Ömer Ersoy Kültür Merkezi (Cultural Center) after its restoration in 2008.[87] Acquiring the buildings left behind by the Armenians, Ömer and the Mahmut Ersoy brothers also established a yarn factory under the name of "Yüzbaşızâdeler Mahmut and Ömer Mensucat (Textiles)" and began production in the formerly Armenian-populated Tepebaşı neighborhood in 1927.[88]

However, a rivalry emerged between those who actively took part in the war and those who left Aintab before the war only to return after the Armenians and the French had left the city.[89] Some members of Aintab's first resistance movement, Aintab Society for Islam, opposed the Aintab Central Committee's call for armed resistance as they favored a promandate position. At a meeting organized by Sheik Mustafa Effendi, the then-mayor of Aintab, Bulaşıkzâde Arif Effendi, chair of the Aintab Society for Islam who also served as the mufti of the city, took a stance against armed resistance by making the following statement: "Because Mustafa Kemal Pasha disobeyed the Caliphate's orders, he was demoted and subsequently declared a 'asi' (rebel). Islam does not condone following the lead of such a rebel."[90] Though the Central Committee's decision ultimately outweighed the propositions extended by the opposition, this duality persisted even as the Aintab War was already underway. Some members of the Aintab Society for Islam participated in the city's defense while others left town for Aleppo and other neighboring villages.

Accused of having made no contribution to the war, the latter were deemed unworthy of acquiring any Armenian wealth, and the former considered themselves *Hakiki Antepli* (natives of Antep) and felt justified in landing abandoned properties. Therefore, there was an open struggle for control of the Armenian wealth and assets. The Şıhlar Sheikhs family (today known as Ocaklar), another well-known provincial elite family whose leader was Sheikh Mustafa, were among those who led the way for the nonparticipants. On the side of the active participants were the İncozâde family and their followers. Whereas the Şıhlar neither actively participated nor financially supported the national forces, the İncozâde provided enormous logistic and financial support to local Kemalist groups and vigorously took part in the war against the French and Armenians, and the İncozâde therefore felt that Armenian properties were rightfully theirs. This division also played a decisive role in shaping Gaziantep's political life after the founding of the Republic.

During the Aintab War, the Aintab Central Committee's executive cadre was composed of 31 percent ulema, 6 percent sheikhs, and 62.5 percent notables.[91] Meanwhile, those who effectively defended the city by taking part in local national forces were workers, tradesmen, farmers, and the poor people of the city. However, the majority of Armenian wealth was acquired through various ways by Muslim elites who already owned large amounts of land (such as the Cenani, Dai, and Ocak families).[92] This situation created tension between the elites and those who actively defended the city in the Aintab War. Until the 1940s, while this elite class played an influential role in the political and economic life of the city, the lower classes were pushed aside. On the local level, the RPP consolidated the power of this section of society.

Utilization of Armenian properties as national estate. The abandoned properties were also repurposed into schools, government offices, and prisons to meet the needs of state agencies through the National Estate Administration. The house of an affluent Armenian family in the Kozanlı neighborhood was first converted to Eytam Mektebi (Orphan School) in 1922 but later became Sakarya İlk Mektebi (Sakarya Primary School) in 1924.[93] Zenop Bezjian's house was converted to Vali Konağı (Governor's Residence) in 1923; it was later used to entertain Mustafa Kemal during his visit to Gaziantep in 1933.[94] Houses of the well-known Barsumian, Karamanougian, and Jebejian families were given to the Aintab municipal authority. On 22 June 1925, the Sahakian Inn was assigned to Gaziantep İktisat Müdüriyeti (Directorate for Gaziantep Economy) to be used as an office.[95] As a result, this property was not put up for sale. Similarly, another estate deemed a nationalized asset was given to Gaziantep School on 9 August 1925. Additionally, a coffeehouse and two ruined hotel buildings were transferred to the school by decision of the Ministerial Cabinet on the same date.[96]

Abandoned properties were also used to meet needs deemed essential to the people. An enactment dated 3 November 1926 decreed that an estate that had once belonged to a local Armenian, located in the Çukurbostan neighborhood in Gaziantep, was to be allocated to the municipality, which had built a bakery for purposes of public service, for a sum to be assessed.[97] The demolished house of Hovsep Kendirdjian, another prominent Aintab Armenian, was transferred to Hilal-i Ahmer (Turkish Red Crescent).[98] The Armenian Apostolic Church (St. Mary), in a particularly repellent twist, became a prison in the Republican era, although in 1988 it was converted to a mosque, named Kurtuluş Camii (Liberation Mosque).[99]

After the Armenians' departure, Kendirli Church and its monastery were confiscated and used by the government in the early Republican period. It was first used as Öğretmen Okulu (Teachers College)[100] in 1923 before becoming the first building of the RPP's Gaziantep Office and Gaziantep Halkevi (Gaziantep People's House) in 1932.[101] According to Yervant Kuchukian, an Aintab Armenian who visited his hometown in 1951, a college that belonged to Kendirli Church had been converted into the Gaziantep Governor's Office.[102] The prayer room was used as a movie theater, and the church's cafeteria was used as a club and restaurant.[103] In the 1960s, the church was Öğretmenevi Lokali (Teacher's House Club) and its meeting hall under the Directorate of National Education, and the building later functioned as the Vocational School for Tourism and Hotel Management in the 1970s.[104] Afterward, the Gaziantep Metropolitan Municipality assumed control of the building and turned it into Kendirli Gazi Kültür Merkezi (Kendirli Veteran Cultural Center) in 2013.[105]

Many conversions occurred in 1951. One of Nazaretian's houses was converted into the Democrat Party's building (Figure 6.4).[106] Bedros Ashjian's house was transformed into a seminary.[107] A large part of a

FIGURE 6.4 The Democrat Party's building on the right in 1951, former house of the Nazaretian family of Aintab. Courtesy of Gaziantep Kent Arşivi, Gaziantep Photograph and Postcard Collection.

Protestant church was destroyed in a fire, and local government officials then used other parts of the building for offices. Zenop Bezjian's house was being used as Vali Konağı (Governor's Mansion) at this time.[108] The Vartanian School was turned into a warehouse.[109] The house once owned by the Matossian family was used as a police headquarters.[110] Today, Central Turkey College's building belongs to the Şahinbey Municipality, the American Hospital and Seminary are used by Sağlık Eğitim Vakfı (Foundation for Health Education), and the Hayganushian School is at the disposal of the National Estate.[111]

Case Study of the Çukurbostan Neighborhood

The example of Çukurbostan offers important insights into the distribution of abandoned properties by the municipality after the Armenians' departure. In 1952, the properties in Çukurbostan, a former Armenian neighborhood, were parceled out and sold as residences by the Gaziantep Municipality. In 1957, the Hükümet Konağı (Government Office) was constructed in this district.[112] In July 1963, the Gaziantep Municipality confiscated and demolished many old buildings in order to create a large square in front of the Government Office.[113]

Çukurbostan had two gates. A road was widened and renamed "Abide-i Hürriyet Caddesi" (Liberty Monument Street). Many of the properties were purchased by private individuals and remained residences, and some were demolished. Teacher Raife Özen purchased the house previously owned by Zahterci Hagop in 1963. Houses previously owned by Armenians were purchased by Müfit Mazhar Bey, Mustafa Güzelhan, and Müftüzâde Hüseyin Effendi. Houses such as Onnik Boyacian's, Carpenter Hagop's, and others were sold to unnamed private individuals. Before the Aintab War, Armenian houses were located on the local hill. Ice cream sellers Sarkis and Istephan's house was later converted to the Arabacı Inn.

A number of properties were transformed into banks. The building belonging to the notable Leylekian family was assigned to Emlak Kredi Bankası (Estate Credit Bank) in 1952. Adjoining buildings were used at varying times by the Agricultural Bank, Gaziantep Central Bank, and also Estate Credit Bank. Other properties served municipal purposes. The house owned by the Matossian family became the Gaziantep Police Headquarters in 1963. The adjoining buildings at one point housed the Posta Telgraf Teşkilatı (National Post and Telegraph Directorate). One building served as the Gaziantep Directorate of National Education. What had been the Nersessian School and Armenian houses before the Aintab War became a courthouse in 1963. The building previously owned by the Bıchakchian family became the Gaziantep Kültür Derneği (Gaziantep Culture Foundation) and later the offices of lawyer Hulusi Yetkin.

Lausanne Negotiations

The Treaty of Lausanne, signed on 24 July 1923 and enacted on 6 August 1924, officially settled the conflict between the Ottoman Empire and the Allied forces.[114] According to this treaty, Turkey rescinded its claims to the Ottoman Empire, and in return, the Allied powers recognized Turkish sovereignty and its new borders. Directly or indirectly, four different segments can be identified in the Lausanne Treaty as relevant to the abandoned properties question. In the order of the articles of the treaty, first are the provisions of Articles 30 and 36 connected to citizenship in Part I, Political Clauses, Section II, Nationality; second, the provisions of Articles 37–45 in Part I, Political Clauses, Section III, Protection of Minorities; third, the provisions of Articles 65–72 of Part III, Economic Clauses, Section I, Property, Rights and Interests. According to Articles 65–72, it was decided to form a mixed arbitral tribunal. The duties and manner of operation of this tribunal were defined in Articles 92–98 of Part III, Economic Clauses, Section V, titled "Mixed Arbitral Tribunal." The fourth and final segment relevant to abandoned properties is the appendix titled "Notice and Protocol on the Declaration of Amnesty."

The most important issue for Turkey in Lausanne was the return of Christians in general and Armenians in particular. In fact, Turkey's policy concerning this issue was very clear prior to Lausanne. That policy was that any Christians outside of the newly created borders of the Turkish state were not permitted to enter and, if possible, those who remained inside Turkey's borders were to be expelled. Turkey refused the demand for an Armenian land and the mass return of Armenians. Turkey's main argument was one of national security. For Turkey, it was impossible to even discuss the return of the Armenians, since Turkey claimed that the Armenians had caused great harm by participating in revolts and rebellions during World War I and afterward, as well as engaging in activities behind enemy lines.[115]

The result of Turkey's unyielding stance was the closure of the topic without an accord having been reached or, more exactly, the exclusion of the question of mass repatriation of Armenians from the scope of the general amnesty. After succeeding in preventing the establishment of an Armenian homeland or mass repatriation of Armenians, Turkey encountered difficulties in attempting to prohibit the individual return of Armenians. During negotiations on this topic, the Turkish delegation first stated that, according to Turkish law, anybody obtaining foreign citizenship was required to leave Turkey, so that "those who lost Turkish nationality could no longer enter the country of Turkey." However, after objections were lodged, Turkey was forced to soften its stance and accept "the necessity of the consideration of former Turkish citizens [in other countries] as in the situation of other foreigners and this topic being connected to the question of a more general nature of the regime to be applied to foreigners."[116] Turkey, having to agree in principle on repatriation on an individual basis, still wished to reserve for itself the right to determine to whom it would give the right of entry.

İsmet Pasha stated that the Armenians' "return to Turkey, is dependent on the permission of the Turkish government, and this permission only can be given to those who keep to themselves and in the past did not have bad behavior."[117] Turkey pronounced all Armenians, without exception, to be "harmful people" and did not permit them to enter the country.

The Question of the Forsaken Belongings

During the negotiations, Turkey's confiscation of Armenian properties constituted a significant impediment between Turkey and the other signatory countries—France, in particular, since the actual addressees of this issue were primarily Ottoman Armenians who escaped to Syria and Lebanon, both of which were under French control at the time. Furthermore, the French claimed that Turkey was in violation of the Treaty of Ankara. Though Turkey wanted to avoid foreign intervention regarding the confiscated properties, this confrontation was unavoidable because a large number of surviving Ottoman Armenians lived outside of Turkey as foreign citizens, and Turkey did not permit their mass repatriation. Furthermore, Armenians living within the borders of signatory states now benefited from their protection and felt they were in a position to demand their rights in Turkey.[118]

The Turkish position at Lausanne regarding abandoned properties was extremely inconsistent. On the one hand, Turkey was forced to accept the principle of returning these properties to their owners because of the principles evident in the arrangements concerning property, rights and interests, and nationality or citizenship. On the other hand, Turkey used all means possible to prevent the return of Armenians living outside of Turkey and repossession of their properties.

This internal contradiction became evident during the negotiations, and Turkey was accused of preventing the return of the Armenians and the Istanbul Greeks, as well as confiscating their properties. In a telegram of 4 June 1923, İsmet İnönü stressed that it was necessary to make a distinction between those who fled from Istanbul and those who fled from Anatolia and that, in particular, the return of those who left Istanbul will be "imperative sooner or later." According to İnönü, there was no doubt that "we will absolutely be required to reimburse the transactions that we conducted in the past concerning their wealth and real estate."[119]

During the negotiations, the revalidation of the 26 September 1915 Liquidation Law by the 15 April 1923 law was an important point of contention. In fact, even before the proclamation of this law—for example, in December 1922—questions were asked about Abandoned Properties (Liquidation) Laws of the CUP, and information was requested as to "whether the laws are still valid."[120] İsmet Pasha conveyed the protest to Ankara on 22 June and received the following response on 26 June:

> The point of view of our government on the Abandoned Properties Law which the Grand National Assembly of Turkey drew up and placed into practice is only directed toward the protection of the properties and rights of citizens, and concerning the protection of the abandoned properties of those who are fleeing or lost. The amount of their values are registered in their own accounts [at the relevant ministry]; and in this respect, whatever is necessary to do for the preservation of their rights is being assured.[121]

Turkey was not able to say outright that it had confiscated the properties of Armenians and had no intention of returning them to their owners. Instead, the government presented what it did as protection of citizens' properties, registering them in the names of the citizens so that no harm would come to the properties. This claim is farcical, as Turkey at the same time was doing all it could to prevent the return of these citizens and the reparation of their belongings. This deception—the sale of Armenian properties under the facade of protection—was the basis of the complaints and protests of the Allied Powers. İsmet Pasha on 14 July 1923 directly questioned Ankara whether it was true that the properties would be sold: "Is it certain that the immovable properties of those who are lost or runaways are also going to be sold in the 15 April 1923 Abandoned Properties Law? If not, keeping them in the charge of their owners, is the value of their rent going to be preserved in treasury accounts in their names?" The pasha asked that "this information which is essential for responding to the notes known to you immediately" be sent.[122] Right away, the next day, a reply was sent: "In accordance with the special law, the values of the properties of those who flee or are lost are being registered as revenue in their own names, sir."[123]

Putting aside whether this response was communicated to the Allies, it bears significance in that it demonstrates that Turkey repeatedly acknowledged that the "fleeing" Armenians were the true owners of their properties and that the revenues obtained from the latter were being registered in their names in the Treasury.

The Amnesty

There is one final question that resulted from the negotiations: Was the reuniting of families torn apart during the deportations and massacres to continue along with the return of these people's properties? Commencing after the 1918 armistice, the question of reuniting divided families—in particular, small children forcibly removed from their families, and girls and women held in Muslim houses—became an issue as important as the repatriation of the deportees. Through parallel channels, the Allied Powers, the Ottoman government, and the Armenian Patriarchate of Istanbul organized the collection of Armenian women and children from Muslim homes and even attempted to form joint commissions to address the pressing issue, as provided in the Treaty of Sèvres.[124]

During the negotiations, the Allied Powers wished to continue these efforts. The third article of the draft proposal, detailing the protection of minorities, prepared on 15 December 1922, concerned this work:

> The Turkish government, in order to achieve the return to their families or communities of people who were lost or separated from their families from 1 August 1914 until the present, whatever their numbers or religions may be, and return properties to people who were left deprived of them in a lawless manner, confirms that it accepts the results of efforts made from 30 October 1918 until the present. Turkey is going to provide all conveniences so that these efforts are not interrupted.[125]

During the discussions on this topic, the British representative said that "he did not want to return more than necessary to problems belonging to the past,"[126] but he stressed that during the war years, many injustices were carried out, such as the splitting of families and the seizure of properties through the Abandoned Properties Law. After the armistice, some efforts were made to resolve these injustices. He said that commissions were founded, and as the result of the work conducted, many children and women were reunited with their families, and much property was returned to its owners. He declared that these efforts outside of Istanbul were not very successful "due to local conditions."[127] Two things were intended by the article that was being proposed: "to consider what has been done up until now valid, and to not allow an attempt to make its completion impossible due to unfavorable conditions."[128] It was asked that this work be completed under the protection of the League of Nations.

Turkey declared that it "definitely is not going to accept the third article which concerns the past."[129] The Turkish committee "thinks like the other representative committees on the issue of not reopening the debates of the past," and these questions "remained in the past; whereas the conference must struggle with the future."[130] During the negotiations, Turkey made a counterproposal and "informed that it intended not to protest the procedures which took place between 30 October 1918 and 20 November 1922." It would even not obstruct "the procedures under discussion from being reviewed, upon the requests of interested parties," and would accept that "requests for rights concerning properties . . . be concluded by an arbitration commission to be established."[131]

In the end, the issue was formulated in the way Turkey desired, with a minor revision of dates in the sixth article of the amnesty bill:

> The Turkish government, sharing the desire for a general peace felt by all states, with the goal of bringing back together families scattered by war and reuniting legitimate holders of rights with their properties, announces that under the protection of the Allies it intends not to object to procedures conducted between 20 October 1918 and 20 November 1922. [Moreover, it said] requests for rights concerning people and properties will be studied by a commission composed of one representative each from the Red Crescent and the Red Cross.[132]

Some scholars have interpreted this article to mean that Turkey did not accept the return of abandoned properties to their rightful owners after 20 November 1922. In some works, this article has even been interpreted in the sense that the abandoned properties issue appeared on the agenda in Lausanne only within the framework of the discussion on amnesty and that Turkey refused to discuss this topic—which is false.[133] The abandoned properties question directly or indirectly was on the agenda during negotiations concerning many other issues. One result of the understandings reached concerning these issues was that after Lausanne, Turkey would accept the return of confiscated abandoned properties to Armenians. This procedure, however, would remain limited only to those Armenians actually in Turkey, excluding those living abroad. Indeed, the entire fight Turkey waged at Lausanne can be summarized this way.

Lausanne Regulations and the Question of Nationality

The question of the return of the confiscated properties of Armenians was directly connected to the articles concerning nationality. A number of new states were formed from the territory of the Ottoman Empire upon its collapse, making a resolution of the nationality and citizenship question imperative. The question in essence was quite simple: According to the Law on Ottoman Citizenship of 1869, would people who were Ottoman citizens and found themselves for various reasons on the other side of the border when new states were created from previously Ottoman territory compulsorily be citizens of the new states? Would they be given a choice?

The answer to these questions was presented in Articles 30–36 of the Lausanne Peace Treaty under the heading of "Nationality." According to Article 30, "Turkish subjects habitually resident in territory which in accordance with the provisions of the present Treaty is detached from Turkey will become ipso facto, in the conditions laid down by the local law, nationals of the State to which such territory is transferred."[134] Article 31 confirmed that such individuals would automatically lose their citizenship of the Republic of Turkey but allowed them the right to make a choice: "Persons over eighteen years of age, losing their Turkish nationality and obtaining ipso facto a new nationality under Article 30, shall be entitled within a period of two years from the coming into force of the present Treaty to opt for Turkish nationality."[135]

These arrangements concerning nationality also directly pertained to goods and properties, a matter which was clarified in Article 33:

> Persons who have exercised the right to opt in accordance with the provisions of Articles 31 and 32 must, within the succeeding twelve months, transfer their place of residence to the State for which they have opted. They will be entitled to retain their immovable property in the territory of the other State where they had their place of residence before exercising their right to opt. They may carry with them their movable property of every description. No export or import duties may be imposed upon them in connection with the removal of such property.[136]

Accordingly, if somebody who possessed Ottoman nationality and was living in the states outside of Turkey's borders did not apply within a period of two years for that nationality, he would automatically lose it.

However, even in this case, his ownership of immovable properties within Turkey's borders would be preserved.

Turkey clearly trampled on the fundamental principles of Lausanne pertaining to the Armenians. First, it did not permit the return of hundreds of thousands of refugees who had been forced to leave their homes due to war conditions. All efforts made after 1920 by the League of Nations by means of High Commissioner of Refugees Fridtjof Nansen or at Lausanne came to naught. These people were not only cut off from their homes and homeland, but they also lost the right of possession to their belongings.

The first form of Turkey's violation of Lausanne was its failure to annul the Ottoman citizenship of Armenians living in many different countries who were formerly Ottoman citizens. Secondly, it did not recognize the property rights of Armenians who remained outside of Turkey and who, according to the treaty, "will be free to own the immovable properties which they possessed."[137] Instead, it confiscated these properties according to the Abandoned Properties Laws.

Lausanne Regulations on Property, Rights and Interests

The Abandoned Properties Laws and the issue of the return of the properties left behind by Armenians are directly connected to the provisions of Articles 65–72 of the Lausanne Treaty, found in the "Property, Rights and Interests" section. In 1915 and the ensuing years, a majority of the Armenians whose properties had been confiscated found themselves outside of Turkey's borders and became citizens of the new states within whose borders they now lived. Thus, these articles at the very least directly concerned the Abandoned Properties Laws in this sense.

The first paragraph of Article 65 arranged reparations for damages incurred upon individuals who were citizens of the Allied Powers. It declared that "property, rights and interests which still exist and can be identified in territories remaining Turkish at the date of the coming into force of the present Treaty, and which belong to persons who on the 29th October, 1914, were Allied nationals, shall be immediately restored to the owners in their existing state."[138] The second paragraph formulated the principle of reciprocity:

> Property, rights and interests which still exist and can be identified in territories subject to the sovereignty or protectorate of the Allied Powers on the 29th October, 1914, or in territories detached from the Ottoman Empire after the Balkan wars and subject to-day to the sovereignty of any such Power, and which belong to Turkish nationals, shall be immediately restored to the owners in their existing state.[139]

The third paragraph possesses vital importance:

> All property, rights and interests situated in territory detached from the Ottoman Empire under the present Treaty, which, after having been *subjected by the Ottoman Government to an exceptional war measure* are now in the hands of the Contracting Power exercising authority over the said territory, and *which can be identified,* shall be restored to their legitimate owners, in their existing state. The same provision shall apply to immovable property which may have been liquidated by the Contracting Power exercising authority over the said territory. All other claims between individuals shall be submitted to the competent local courts. [Italics added.][140]

Here, the question of whether the expression "subjected by the Ottoman Government to an exceptional war measure" includes the Abandoned Properties Laws is paramount. It is not possible to suggest that this expression excludes these laws because the Ottoman government itself presented and defended these laws as an "extraordinary war measure." Moreover, the mixed arbitral tribunals established through Articles 65–72 in order to address questions of reparations for damages made similar determinations. For example, the British-Turkish Mixed Arbitral Tribunal considered the Abandoned Properties Law as an "exceptional war measure" and decided that it was necessary for reparations to be paid for the confiscated properties of some Armenians who were

British subjects.[141] In other words, the treatment of the Abandoned Properties Laws in the framework of Article 65 of the Lausanne Treaty was recognized under international law.

Article 66 decreed that if property had been liquidated, reparation would be made in the form of payment of its value:

> When at the date of the signature of the present Treaty the property, rights and interests, the restitution of which is provided for in Article 65 have been liquidated by the authorities of one of the High Contracting Parties, that Party shall be discharged from the obligation to restore the said property, rights and interests by payment of the proceeds of the liquidation to the owner.[142]

Articles 65 and 66 also instructed the establishment of a mixed arbitral tribunal to solve any questions that might arise. Articles 92–98 of Part III, Section V, specified how the mixed arbitral tribunals would be founded, the means by which they would operate, and the duration of their operation.

According to these articles, the tribunals would be established within a period of three months after the treaty entered into force with each of the Allied states. Each tribunal would be composed of three people (Article 92). The center of the tribunals would be Istanbul. If their work could not be completed within a period of two years, they could be transferred to another place (Article 93). Decisions would be taken by a majority and would be binding (Article 94). Applications could be made for a period of six months after the tribunals had been established; after this point, no applications would be accepted. However, for "distance and compelling causes," "special permission seen as a justified exception" might be considered (Article 95).[143]

The tribunals were essentially founded in order to solve the issue of reparations between subjects of Allied countries and Turkey. Consequently, problems between Turkey and Armenians who were Turkish citizens were not within the jurisdiction of these tribunals, the justification being that according to the Lausanne Treaty, at least theoretically, the repatriation of Turkish citizens and the restitution of their goods by

Turkey were required. Turkey obstructed these requirements and did not allow these people to enter the country. Even if the Armenians were to have succeeded in applying to the mixed arbitral tribunals, the applications would be considered invalid.

Even when an Armenian was a citizen of any of the signatory countries to the treaty, and thus in a position to apply, Turkey would obstruct the application, by means of two different arguments. First, if the individuals in question had assumed foreign citizenship prior to 1914—and in this sense fit the criteria of the Lausanne Treaty—they had done so without informing the Ottoman government and consequently would still be considered Turkish citizens by Turkish law. Therefore, any payment of reparations was rejected. Second, that some applicants accepted foreign citizenship after 1914 meant that for this very reason it was not possible for their rights to be defended by other countries.

For these reasons, the problem of citizenship was one of the issues with which the mixed arbitral tribunals were most engaged. Turkey did not recognize the Armenians' status as citizens of Allied countries and attempted to prevent the mixed arbitral tribunals from issuing verdicts on this subject. In essence, a competent authority could not be found to advocate the position of the Armenians who remained outside of Turkey, and for this reason they remained unsolved. The Armenians had been abandoned.

A Brief Evaluation of Lausanne

The Lausanne Treaty provisions seemed to guarantee that restitution would be made for the confiscated properties of the Armenians, particularly in the "Nationality" and "Property, Rights and Interests" sections. However, Turkey did not implement these provisions but only returned the properties of Armenians who remained within Turkey's borders or succeeded in entering Turkey unnoticed, while it attempted to confiscate those of Armenians living outside of Turkey.

The Lausanne Treaty—in particular, Articles 65 and 66—was interpreted by Turkey in the sense that if the person whose property was confiscated was at the location of his property at the time that the treaty went into effect, the property would be returned to its owner. If the person was not in Turkey, that person would be considered lost and fleeing, so that the properties of such people would be regulated according to the Liquidation Laws of 26 September 1915 and 15 April 1923. Consequently, people who left Turkey prior to the Lausanne Treaty would be unable to reacquire their properties in any manner.

Since Turkey chose to interpret the Treaty of Lausanne to say that "only if the person is with his property [that is, in Turkey] would it be given to him," Armenians who wanted to return to Turkey in order to be with their properties, prior to or after the date of validity of the treaty, would not be able to enter Turkey. To prevent Armenians abroad from returning to Turkey for claiming their properties, their entry would be prohibited, and those who did manage to enter would be identified and forcibly expelled. Moreover, a regulation (number 2559) issued several weeks before the signing of the treaty, on 28 June 1923, prevented individuals abroad from claiming their properties via proxy statements.

Additionally, Turkey interpreted the articles in the section "Property, Rights and Interests" as concerning reciprocal reparations for the damages of citizens of the Allied states who were in Turkey and of Turkish citizens in other countries.[144] Therefore, it was claimed that these articles did not pertain to Armenians found abroad. During bilateral negotiations on reparations, the desire of signatory countries to defend the rights of Armenians who now were these countries' own citizens was objected to with the justification that the Armenians were Ottoman citizens during the war years. Turkey claimed that only if Armenians had accepted foreign nationality prior to 1914, in accordance with the 1869 Citizenship Law, by obtaining permission from the Ottoman state could providing them reparations be acceptable.

The Abandoned Properties Laws already required that people who had adopted foreign citizenship prior to 1914 not be deported and their properties not be confiscated. However, in practice, this requirement was widely disregarded. Even if Armenians were citizens of foreign countries, they were deported and their properties were confiscated. A telegram dated 8 July 1915 provides evidence of this practice, stating that

American citizens were being deported from Elazığ. The government requested that "if there really are people with American citizenship among those who are being deported, communicating their numbers and the reasons for their deportations" be carried out. If they really were American citizens, "their being set aside from deportation" was desired.[145] The Ottoman government, relying in general on the 1869 citizenship law, recognized the foreign citizenship of such individuals.

Regarding the situation of individuals "who while not citizens of the Allied states, [were under] the de facto protection of these states," Turkey proposed that the signatory states did not have the jurisdiction to defend the rights of these people who were not their citizens.[146] However, this circumstance is a clear violation of the provisions of the Lausanne Treaty, as in the third section of the treaty, addressing economic rights, Article 64 defined "Allied citizens" and clearly stated that they would include individuals "who while not citizens of Allied states, benefited from the de facto protection of these states . . . they [were to be] treated by the Ottoman authorities as if they were Allied citizens."[147]

Turkey, contrary to a principle of the Lausanne Treaty, determined to not return the properties of Armenians who found themselves abroad. This situation can be described as a type of economic plundering, or, as the Turkish finance minister explained during discussions in the Grand National Assembly, the desire to close all deficits by confiscating Armenian and Greek properties.[148] It can be argued that the policies followed by Talat Pasha in 1916 aimed at "completely eliminating the [Armenian] existence" continued in the Republican period. Indeed, Turkey, in the period following Lausanne, enacted a systematic policy of expelling Armenians who remained within Turkish territory.

Final Blocking of Aintab Armenians' Restitution Claims

The properties left behind by the Ottoman Armenians who migrated to Syria and Lebanon continued to constitute a problem between Turkey and France after the Lausanne Treaty. Armenians who became citizens of Syria and Lebanon after the signing of the Lausanne Treaty still maintained rights to their properties in Turkey.[149] It was necessary to either restore their properties or pay their equivalent values. The Turkish government struggled with this issue prior to the enactment of the Lausanne Treaty. Turkish newspapers dated 24 July 1924 reported that "since the Lausanne Treaty is not valid yet, Syrians [were] still retaining Turkish nationality," and "those Syrian people [including Armenians from Aintab] who possess property in Turkey, according to the Abandoned Properties Laws" were to have their real estate confiscated.[150]

Immediately before the Lausanne Treaty went into effect, the Ministry of Treasury, taking this into consideration, asked the Office of the Prime Minister for instruction. As evident from this ministerial exchange of letters, the viewpoint of the Ministry of Foreign Affairs was that the Syrians—including Armenians—who were forced to migrate there during 1921–1922 and immediately thereafter should still be considered Turkish citizens. The ministry felt that even though it might be legal to seize their properties in accordance with the Abandoned Properties Laws, "the treaty will soon be in effect, and thinking of the probability that the real estate in Syria of Turkish citizens could be harmed, the postponement of the application of the procedure" was desired.[151]

According to the newspaper, "the Council of Ministers, examining the matter from both points of view, decided not to consider the properties of the Syrians as abandoned properties, on condition that the Syrians reciprocally act in the same manner."[152] This decision cleared the way for the transfer of these properties. However, the important aspect was who was considered to be Syrian. Logically, the Armenians who survived the 1915 deportations and were still living in Syria would enter into this category. However, Turkey went to great lengths to prevent the Syrian Armenians from benefiting from these rights. The bilateral treaties signed with France were worded to exclude the Armenians of Syria and Lebanon.

The first treaty concerning this issue was signed on 30 May 1926.[153] It included an arrangement pertaining to "people living and present in Turkey" during the signing of the agreement who were over eighteen years old and "among the people of territory separated from the Ottoman Empire and under the authority of the French Republic."[154] These people,

> within a period of six months beginning from the date of effectiveness of the agreement, have the right to choose the citizenship of those countries [in which they now live]. . . . Those who make use of the right of choice must transfer their places of residence outside of Turkey during the following twelve months.[155]

These people in Turkey "will be free to preserve their immovable properties . . . and can take with them all types of movable properties."[156] Since this treaty included only Syrians and Lebanese living in Turkey in 1926, those who were at that time in Syria as well as the Armenians of Aintab were excluded.

In order to make lists of the properties and to estimate their values, French officials located in Syria began to work with the local Armenians at the end of the 1920s. Hoping to at the minimum receive some compensation for their seized properties, Aintab Armenians constituted the main applicants of this process. As Vahé Tachjian indicates, these lists and estimates were prepared for the purpose of future French-Turkish negotiations.[157] Around the same time, Armenians began the process of having their seized properties in Turkey registered with local police stations. The responsibility of compiling these lists was given to the mukhtar of each of Aleppo's districts, who then questioned the local Armenians to ascertain pertinent information.[158]

When the negotiations began in 1927, to exclude the Armenians the Turkish side declared that they opposed using Lausanne as a basis. By legally excluding Armenians from the final agreement, the Turkish government would effectively be able to reject all individual Armenian claims. By the end of 1929, France acquiesced. French ambassador Chambrun asked Paris that the Turkish demands be taken into consideration, since acceding to Armenian requests would have a vastly detrimental influence on Turkish-French relations, which at that point had only recently begun to improve.[159]

An official French document from October 1929 openly stated that "for reasons of appropriateness, the Armenian demands must remain outside the negotiations."[160] One year later, the French minister of foreign affairs put forth that France's responsibility toward native Syrians was greater than toward Armenians. For him, France had already fulfilled its duty to aid Armenians coming to Syria.[161] Ironically, throughout this process, phrases like "Armenian," "Armenians," and "of Armenian origin" were generally absent from most of the official French correspondence regarding seized Armenian properties. Instead, the main concern in these documents were Greek Orthodox properties. By 1929, Armenians' property records were no longer an issue in the eyes of the French government.[162]

In the end, a treaty was signed by both parties on 27 October 1932.[163] The fourth article of the treaty removed all restrictions on immovable property in Turkey of people who left the Ottoman Empire for lands under French administration and became French citizens. These people could regain their properties and the value of the rents obtained from them after this treaty went into effect. The Armenians of Syria and Lebanon, including the Aintab Armenians, were explicitly excluded in this article, as the 1926 treaty concerned the Syrians in Turkey.[164] In practice, Turkey already did not recognize the rights of the Armenians in Syria. According to this treaty, only the Armenians of Aleppo and Antakya would be able to claim rights to their properties.

Articles 7, 8, and 11 of the treaty were also significant. According to Article 7, if the properties in question had been "sequestered, transferred or liquidated," the equivalent value of the property would be paid. Article 8 determined the period of time for all procedures. It stated that the identification of the values of the properties would be conducted within one year, and all liquidation transactions must be completed within eighteen months. Article 11 repeated that the individuals discussed in Articles 1–5 of the treaty would receive either their properties back or their equivalent values, and the article especially stressed that these individuals could seek legal recourse if problems arose during this process. The article decreed that the aforementioned individuals had two years in which they could apply.[165]

Nonetheless, these semantic acrobatics were insufficient. In the signing protocol for the acceptance of the treaty, Turkish Minister of Foreign Affairs Tevfik Rüştü Aras added a restriction to the first paragraph of Article 11: "It will be accepted on condition that it is carried out by them in their country solely in a manner consistent with existing laws and rules."[166] Moreover, Aras, referring to a decision rendered by a Turkish court of appeal, "considers it a duty to declare" that Turkish courts would not accept cases being initiated "concerning the return of movable property left by its owners while they were still Turkish citizens."[167] In other words, if Syrian Armenians attempted to use the provisions of this treaty in their favor to ask for the restitution of their property, this supplementary protocol would obstruct their redress.

Conclusion

The genocidal process is shaped equally by local actors and by the central authorities. Any orders from above are accepted or rejected by local power brokers—the social and political elites.[1] The relationship between the central and local power brokers is symbiotic: the central authorities need the local actors to carry out their orders, while the local actors need the central authorities to "legitimize" their actions, in turn solidifying their social standing. As Uğur Ü. Üngör has aptly observed, some families could mobilize dozens of men into the streets to murder, rape, and pillage; and others could mobilize hundreds, earning them greater favor in the eyes of the central authorities.[2] This reciprocal power dynamic—the locals' needs to secure their power and the central authorities' need for implementers of genocidal policies—is proven capable of manifesting mass murder. The thirst for power, as well as the promise of material gain, is motivation enough to galvanize local actors to commit acts of genocide. The Ottoman district of Aintab also served as a platform for exemplifying and substantiating how these dynamics constituted and shaped the Armenian genocide at the peripheral level.

This book has analyzed the issues of deportation, genocide, and property seizure by concentrating particularly on the city of Aintab, focusing on the local historiography and drawing upon Armenian and Ottoman-Turkish sources, as well as other archival materials. While Aintab's Armenians were not unique and shared the same painful fate of other Armenian communities across Asia Minor, Aintab provides a microcosm that allows us to examine the local forces behind the genocide, to watch how it took place, and to follow its aftereffects in the creation and consolidation of a new Turkish-Muslim bourgeoisie. The case of Aintab presents the complex relations between the center and periphery, while revealing how properties relinquished by Armenians were distributed among local actors. This study offers a description and analysis of the murder and plunder of the Armenians of Aintab and explores the socioeconomic and political hinterlands regionally and nationally, which enabled such events to occur. In this context, this book is a new attempt to write a genuine local historiography of the city in general and that of its Armenians in particular.

This careful journey to the Aintab of this period reveals to what extent massacres in the 1890s already bore elements similar to 1915, if only in terms of the local incentive to use violence as a means of plunder and appropriation. An even more disturbing revelation is that of the continuity the perpetrators have been able to establish between the events of 1915–1916 and the reshaping of the area in the early 1920s by confirming and strengthening the power base and legitimacy of the very elites that had been responsible for the cleansing and spoliation of the Armenian community. This continuity, once against based on the vilest of economic motives, thus links together almost three decades of violence, while at the same time projects into the future the weight of a tacit partnership in crime.

From 1895 until 1915, Muslims and Armenians of Aintab, who had previously coexisted in relative harmony, turned against one another, with the former committing inconceivable acts against the latter. In this study, the lens through which intercommunal and state-minority relations are viewed is primarily an economic one, but in the broad sense of that term, with political economy entailing law, commerce, property relations, and socioeconomic tensions. Economic rivalries were overladen on ethno-religious hierarchies in the late nineteenth century in Aintab. The belief among members of the dominant nation that the normative social order was being gravely upset was shaped by the "nationalization" of the Armenian nation under the modernizing influence of a burgeoning Armenian middle class.[3] International pressure for reforms to ensure the rights of and protection for Armenians seemed to confirm this impression. The 1895 massacres featured extensive plunder of Aintab Armenians, which was an integral step in restoring the hierarchy that the massacres augured. Important members of Aintab's urban Muslim elite, clergy, and local government were implicated in scapegoating Armenians and in cheerleading the killing—more so, it appears, than Abdülhamid II's central regime.

Some of the self-same elites joined the local CUP branch in the second constitutional period, which at once safeguarded their social power, gave them influence in the new ruling regime, and gave the CUP a conduit into local affairs. Although this period at first appeared to create a sense of calm by placing both communities on an equal level, ethnic tensions soon reemerged. The incident of Necmeddin Bey's beating and the case of the severed head demonstrated that different segments of the Muslim community in Aintab were deeply disturbed by their perception that the restoration of the constitution mainly favored the Armenians. As this book has asserted, this so-called equality further exacerbated feelings of resentment toward the Armenians of the city as the Ottoman empire continued to decline politically and economically. In turn, ethno-economic identities became dangerously pronounced and bred more violence, which ultimately erupted in Adana and its outskirts. The Adana massacres proved how fragile the values of the Young Turk Revolution were and consequently created a general atmosphere of insecurity, leading to the general mobilization and ultimately the deportations in Aintab.

In exploring the deportation process in Aintab, the orders and policies of the center constitute only one side of the story; equally important is the implementation of these orders and policies, as there was no absolute accord between the central government and local administrators. In fact, there were disagreements between hard-line and moderate local officials. The central authorities attempted to resolve this conflict by appointing more obedient officers who would carry out the anti-Armenian policies. During the deportations, killings and safekeeping, pillaging and official liquidations were carried out simultaneously. This complexity demonstrates the necessity to look beyond the central government policies and evaluate the ways in which these policies were realized in different localities.[4] While a number of studies examining the central government's orders have contributed to the generally accepted academic view of this process, placing focus on peripheries can help to illuminate the relationship between the dominant narrative and the actual transpired events in a more realistic perspective by providing us with various revisions and substantiations of this historiography.[5]

The slaughter and plunder followed deliberated and declared intent on the part of local perpetrators, who were assisted in their deadly campaign by the Ottoman central authorities. While the pattern of destruction remained locally determined, the central government provided the overall context that allowed for sustained human rights abuses and crimes against humanity. In the case of Aintab, a "suitable" sociopolitical atmosphere was created through the relentless efforts of the Muslim elites to lobby the central authorities to deport the Armenians, whose deportation these elites then facilitated in return for obtaining the Armenians' abandoned material riches. During 1915, these elites propagandized against the Armenians, presenting them spuriously as a rebellious threat, as had been done previously in 1895. The seizure and transfer of Armenian property undergirded popular support for the deportation and ultimate elimination of their fellow citizens. The Armenians had constituted the middle and upper middle class of the Aintab population, and they had predominated in manufacturing, agricultural production, and interregional trade. Thus, their expulsion was a moment for opportunity, for the bandits who robbed Armenians of their personal belongings on the road and especially for Aintab's Muslim elites, who seized the assets and properties the Armenians left behind. These elites had already done their part toward purging their city of its Armenians by lobbying Ottoman authorities in the imperial center for months, charging their unwanted neighbors with rebellion and treason, and demanding their expulsion.

Once the deportations began, Aintab gentry were well positioned to appropriate Armenian goods, properties, and businesses either directly or—via the good offices of the Abandoned Property Commissions and Liquidation Commissions—indirectly through the state. The CUP functionaries of Aintab—including Ali Cenani, district governor Ahmed Faik Bey, and Bulaşıkzâde mufti Arif Effendi—people in good standing with them, and war veterans were those most likely to receive monies, businesses, and properties, or to lease them for nominal fees, in turn transformed those people into capitalists (in the full sense of the word). The mayor, court officials, tax and treasury administrators, title deeds officers, and security forces also obtained immovable and movable assets of Armenians.

By taking up the cause of the CUP and ethnic Turkish nationalism, the leading families of Aintab—including Cenani, Mennazâde, Taşçızâde, Istırapzâde (Barlas), Daizâde, Kethüdazâde Göğüş, Battalzâde (Budak), Fazlızâde, and Haciağazâde—secured their control over the local CUP organization and parliamentary representation for the city. These individuals were far from the only beneficiaries. Direct perpetrators of the massacres often had their own pecuniary motives. Viewing the entirety of the process, the *function* of appropriation was as important as the individual *purposes;* huge numbers of people were bound together in a circle of profit that was at the same time a circle of complicity.

As Thomas Kühne highlights, "Killing and even murdering other people, terrorizing, humiliating, or causing harm to them, is not just destructive. For those who perpetrate violence and terror, it is creative and rewarding. It generates a social dynamic."[6] Perpetrators and bystanders "energized social life and built collective identity through committing genocide. The desire for community, the experience of belonging, and the ethos of collectivity became the basis of mass murder."[7] Another renowned Holocaust historian elucidates how the genocide against the Jews "served as a mechanism for social mobility—for moving into the better houses [of killed or deported Jews], taking over businesses, giving clothes and jewelry to one's wife or mistress or fetching toys for one's children, all facilitated by the shedding of blood."[8] In the same vein, as well as eradicating the Armenian community, deportation was a means of reorienting the Muslim population to a new ideological identity; more than enriching individual perpetrators, plunder was a way of rewarding the "reliable," resourcing immigrants and refugees in order to properly integrate them, and creating a Turkish-Muslim bourgeoisie as a driver of national modernization in a Darwinian world of struggle.

Following the elimination of the Aintab Armenians, the promise of economic power rallied active support for and participation in a macro policy operated by the CUP that aimed to annihilate all of Turkey's Armenians. In fact, it was the drive for material gain that led administrative, political, local, and civil actors to pragmatically engage in the eradication of the Armenians more actively than the central authorities.

More important, property theft and material benefits acquired from the victims were an important means of further binding the beneficiaries to one another and the CUP regime.[9] As early as March 1915, Aintab's provincial notables and landowners as well as municipal officials and other bigwigs were casting covetous eyes on Armenian property, and the Istanbul government was well aware of these desires. In order to fulfill its policy of destruction, the CUP was required to make concessions. Therefore, one could argue that what motivated urban Muslim Aintab notables to join the CUP and take part in its genocidal policies was self-interest rather than a shared ideology; much of the implementation was enacted by local elites and the Muslim population at large out of a base desire to plunder the assets and property of the Armenian community, instead of the generally assumed ideological pressure and encouragements of the political center. This attitude, in turn, greatly widened the scope of complicity—not just in the sense of more people being involved as perpetrators or beneficiaries after the genocide had been initiated, but also in the sense of more sections of society actively encouraging genocide in the first place. In this respect, the general paradigm in the relevant literature, which has approached the localities as passive agents of the Ottoman center, demands revision.

The fate of the abandoned properties in Aintab proves that the transfer of wealth in the form of plunder as well as expropriation was an inextricable part of the genocidal process. The expeditious conversion of the Abandoned Property Commissions to Liquidation Commissions can be understood in the sense that the government sought to utilize the Armenian wealth as tools to maintain the new demographic and economic balance. It is important for us to understand exactly how the liquidation of the Armenian abandoned properties was performed in Aintab. The Aintab Liquidation Commission favored pro-CUP local notables and officials, as well as immigrants and refugees, by selling Armenian properties and assets at a fraction of their real value or giving them away entirely. Specifically, the liquidation of Sarkis Yacoubian's assets offers stark evidence of the operations that were carried out by Aintab's Liquidation Commission. More important, in bringing back the notion of class, which has experienced an eclipse in recent years, his case shows that the economic and political or ideological interests of the perpetrators (the gentry, different sectors of the urban population, and ordinary Muslims) *did* overlap in the process of Armenian persecution and that the intersection of these two interests determined the momentum and intensity of the violence. In this regard, the case of Aintab suggests that foundational history of the Turkish Republic cannot be fully grasped without taking into consideration the importance of class.

After the Ottoman empire was defeated in World War I, many factors affected the restitution process of the surviving Armenians' properties. The attitude of the local authorities, the fickle policies of the British and French occupation forces at the expense of Aintab Armenians, the security issues caused by the rise of the Kemalist resistance movement, and the number of refugees and immigrants who had settled in the properties that had been left behind by Armenians all had tangible impacts. While it appeared that the Ottoman government of the Armistice period favored the restoration of the abandoned properties, the government in Istanbul was not the only authority ruling the Ottoman territories by mid-1919, and this position was short-lived. In the meantime, the nationalist resistance movement gained momentum and rose in power, and various resistance organizations were established, directly affecting this process. As a result, previously appointed officials from the central government in the localities rapidly lost control over their peripheries.

The ties of culpability were an important trigger to resistance against first British and then French occupiers, given the Europeans' desire to punish those who carried out genocide and to restore stolen property to the surviving Aintab Armenians. The legacy of the murder and theft of postwar figures matters. Genocide is, as described by Kühne, a creative as much as a destructive endeavor for the perpetrating polity. Therefore, previously pro-CUP local notables of Aintab began to support the nationalist movement solely out of self-interest born from the fear of losing their newly acquired wealth. To illustrate, a significant segment of the resistance movement was composed of prominent Muslim elites of Aintab who took part in the Armenian deportations and who thus came into possession of their wealth. This work has highlighted that national forces along with the Aintab gentry did not favor restitution. This accumulation of Armenian capital by a new upper class forged from provincial elites, wealthy landowners, state officials, and merchants would in turn finance the nationalist movement that acted not only against postwar European occupiers, but also against the return of the Armenians (as well as the Greeks). This situation catalyzed the flight of the Armenians from Aintab.

The expulsion of the Armenians from Aintab had been accompanied by the seizure of their assets and properties.[10] Armenians had owned not only houses but also fields, inns, schools, shops, and churches, most of which were appropriated by the municipal government for its own purposes. Aintab's CUP leadership was convinced that Armenian communal life on Turkish soil was over forever. The properties that Armenians were forced to abandon were expected to serve, however, yet another patriotic purpose: to strengthen an already *national* bourgeoisie in Aintab. Those in Aintab now in possession of Armenian property, no longer vulnerable to challenge, used their political power during the Republican era to consolidate their hold on these assets. Much of the physical and financial capital of Aintab and its elites was the product of the Armenian genocide.

Official Turkish historiography claims that the Turkish-French war in Aintab was a heroic struggle for national independence, which earned the city glory and its grand title "ghazi" (conqueror). Gaziantep's "heroic epic" was in fact a struggle whose incentive was to wipe out the Armenian presence from the city completely and for good. Its main motive was to ensure that the Armenians of Aintab would never be able to return. Forcibly, or through various administrative measures, the outcome of all of these "struggles" rendered it impossible for Armenian repatriates to remain in their native cities, towns, or villages. Hoping to make these people flee their homeland again, the national warriors continued to terrorize them. When the Armenians left Aintab for good in 1921–1922, their houses, fields, estates, and other properties were sold at bargain prices.

More particularly, Armenian properties were offered at auctions organized at the initiative of local administrators; they were sold especially to members of the Aintab gentry who had participated in the Turkish-French war or supported the national forces financially and logistically. Otherwise the numerous properties once owned by the Armenians of

Aintab were used to house the offices of the civil service of the central government. In yet other cases, properties were handed out free of charge on the orders of the central government and Mustafa Kemal. Upon orders from him, Armenian properties were distributed to Muslim notables, and they thereby formed the foundation of the city's bourgeoisie.[11] Thus, the rich and wealthy Turkish-Muslim class whose foundations were laid in Aintab during the period between 1915 and 1918 consolidated its status in the weeks between December 1921 through January 1922, when the exodus of Aintab Armenians was made irreversible.

With the new administrative and legal regulations coming into effect following the Lausanne Treaty in 1924, and with other bilateral agreements between the republics of France and Turkey in 1926 and 1932 that invalidated the return of properties that had belonged to Armenians throughout Cilicia, all movable and immovable properties of the Armenians who had been forced to leave for Aleppo and Beirut were appropriated. At that time, France was the mandatory power over Syria and Lebanon, and it was easy to imagine that "the mandatory power could act as a defender of the refugee Armenians whose rights had been violated." As Tachjian suggests, "The reality, however, was different. France wanted to establish close ties with the newly-created Turkish state and pursued a policy to that end."[12]

The perpetrators and their families profited from the genocide to the extent that, after 1923, entire generations were educated and provided for by the starting capital of Armenian property acquired in 1915. In other words, the elimination of the Armenians paved the way for the rise of a new upper class in Gaziantep. While the reports published in the 1914 edition of *Annuaire Oriental* clearly show that Armenians from the region controlled all aspects of the economic and business life, the 1925–1928 editions of the *Gaziantep Ticaret Odası Yıllığı* (Gaziantep Chamber of Commerce Yearbook) confirm that no non-Muslim merchants remained in the city.

Until the mid-1940s, the influence of Muslim elites over the city continued. The mayors of the city for the years 1921–1950 all came from the same influential families.[13] These elites entirely dominated the industry and economy of Gaziantep in the 1930s and 1940s. Most of these men, moreover, were members of the Republican People's Party (RPP) and

FIGURE C.1 Aintab citizens, including civil and military officials as well as former members of the Aintab CUP club, pay tribute to Ali Cenani (with walking stick) on his becoming minister of trade, 1924. Courtesy of Gaziantep Kent Arşivi, Gaziantep Photograph and Postcard Collection.

representatives of the party's branch in Aintab.[14] Thus was the Republican regime linked to its CUP predecessor via persecutory economic policy, personnel, and ideology.

Armenian assets such as shops, estates, and houses in the neighborhoods of Kozanlı, İbrahimli, Körkün, Eblehan, Büyükkızılhisar, Şekeroğlu, Sazgın, Isbatrın, Tışlaki, Akyol, Eyüboğlu, Kurb-ı Zincirli, and Tepebaşı began to be sold at rigged auctions to the members of those prominent families for very low prices in post-genocide Turkey.[15] This real estate was auctioned by dealers associated with the Gaziantep Revenue Office. Auctions were preceded by newspaper announcements about the details of the sales in question, listing the approximate location, type, and value in liras of the properties in question and, most important, their previous owners—but with no reference to the state that had acquired the properties and was their current owner.

To sum up, the nouveau riche of Gaziantep were not only influential figures in the national resistance and the Republican period, but also emerged as the new captains of industry in the city. The economic elite of Aintab were being reconstituted along political lines. A new political class, based on such qualifications as previous CUP service, zeal in the Turkish-French war, and political reliability as Republicans, was able, through its acquisition of Armenian wealth, to lay the economic foundations that would sustain its status over generations, long after World War I and its aftermath were only a memory (Figure C.1).

As a native son of Gaziantep, I now fully realize that through having attended the same schools with grandsons and granddaughters of those elites, I myself have witnessed the consequences of Aintab Armenians' physical and material destruction. My account here can offer insight into local history but is only a small step in understanding the complete picture of not only *what* happened but also *how* and *why* these events transpired. Unseen in the archived letters, telegrams, and property lists are the trauma and suffering of Armenian survivors repeatedly subjected to attacks on their lives, culture, assets, and social status. The base motives of their former neighbors left some of the most indelible wounds, which more than a century later remain unhealed.

Appendix

Armenian Merchants in Aintab, 1909

IN MILLET INN		
1	Hagopcan Yaghubian	Coffee and sugar dealer
2	Sahak Bijian	Manusa producer[a]
3	Movses Papazian	Manusa producer
4	Kevork Horomian	Manusa producer
5	Nerses Sulahian and brothers	Lumbering, leather trade, etc.
6	Mateos Yerganian and Serop Keshishian	Manusa producer
7	Hovhannes Bijian	Manusa producer
8	Basmadjian brothers	Manusa producer
9	Mıgırdich Keshkekıan	Manusa producer
10	Cebejian brothers	Lumbering, leather trade
11	Kevork Leylekian	Manusa producer
12	Pilibos Aghdjian	Manusa producer, lumbering
13	Movses Leylekian	Manusa producer, lumbering
14	Hovhannes Khashkhashian	Retailer
15	Misak Nurhanian	Retailer
16	Garabed Barsumian	Moneylender
17	Yeghishe Parseghian	Manusa producer
18	Garuc Mercanian	Manusa producer
19	Markar Cigherdjian	Manusa producer

20	Garabed Kalusdian	Manusa producer
21	Armenak Aydjian	Manusa producer, lumbering
22	Garabed Arusian	Manusa producer, lumbering
23	Garabed Bazikian	Manusa producer
IN NAZAR AGHA INN		
1	Kevork Topbashian	Rug dealer
2	Sarkis Sahakian and Hovsep Sahakian	Moneylenders
3	Bedros Ashjian	Moneylender, landowner
4	Stepan Keshishian	Lumbering, etc.
5	Levon Sahakian	Lumbering, etc.
6	Hovhannes Piranian	Manusa producer
7	Garabet Chakıjian	Lumbering, etc.
8	Krikor Yesaian and Puzant Sukiasian	Fencing, lumbering
9	Hagop Arslanian and son	Copper dealer
10	Krikor Kabakchian and son	Manusa producer
11	Rupen	Clockmaker
IN HACI ÖMER INN		
1	Manuel Topbashian	Soap dealer
2	Garabed Babikian	Manusa producer
3	Toros Sahakian	Moneylender
4	Melkon Kabakchian and brothers	Manusa producer
5	Harutyun Levonian and brothers	Manusa producer
6	Dzerun Dzernikian	Manusa producer
7	Hovhannes Sahatchian	Manusa producer
8	Hovhannes Levonian	Moneylender, pistachio seller
IN SAHAKIAN-GHAZARIAN INN		
1	Kalusd Ghazarian and sons Toros, Garabed, Hagop, and Nazar	Manusa producer
2	Nazaret Manushakian	Custom goods
3	Kevork Tatarian	Manusa producer
4	Sarkis B. Nazarian	Manusa producer
İKI KAPILI INN		
1	Dikran-Rupen Yegavian	Manusa producer
2	Sarkis G. Nazarian	Manusa producer
3	Garabed Kargaian	Manusa producer
4	Kevork Demirdjian	Metal

5	Movses Ammian	Cotton
6	Garabed Hindoian	Oil, etc.
IN YÜKSÜKÇÜ INN		
1	Movses Arslanian	Coppersmith
IN EMIRALI INN		
1	Y. Karamanougian and brothers	Manusa producer
IN BASMAJIAN INN		
1	Harutyun Basmajian	Merchant
MERCHANTS WITH SHOPS BESIDES INNS		
1	Hanna Kurkchuian	Soap producer
2	Garabed Nazaretian	Soap producer, agricultural products
3	Ardashes Adanalian	Soap producer
4	Sarkis Krajian	Embroidery
5	Hovsep Arakelian	Drapery, sheep dealer
6	Garuc Karamanougian	Drapery, embroidery
7	Garabed Yaghsızian	Manusa producer
8	Harutyun Ammian	Manusa producer
9	Melkon Karamanougian	Manusa producer
10	Hagop Bogharian	Manusa producer
11	Kevork Jebejian	Manusa producer
12	Ohan Gurelian	Lumbering
13	Nazar Bireciklian	Moneylender
14	Harutyun Bireciklian	Moneylender
15	Misak Matossian	Dealer of Singer-brand sewing machines and fabric
16	Hırand Sulahian	Rug dealer
17	Hagop Bezjian	Pharmacist
18	Harutyun Kurkchuian	Drapery
19	Hovsep Kendirdjian	Landowner, drapery
20	Minas Kendirdjian	Landowner, drapery
21	Movses Topchuian	Drapery
22	Kevork Loshkhacian	Drapery
23	Hovhannes Bireciklian	Moneylender
24	Apraham Babikian	Moneylender
25	Toros Krajian	Merchant
26	Kevork Krajian	Merchant
27	Hovhannes Jebejian	Large property owner

28	Yeghia Kharajian	Merchant
29	Krikor Jebejian	Merchant
30	L. Nazarian	Merchant

Source: Khachadur Dadaian (ed.), *Dasnhinkerort tare'n minchew 1915: arti T'o'wrqio'h' me'ch' Hah'ero'w Ar'ewdragan ew Dndesagan Ko'rdzo'wne'o'wt'ean masin Dzawalo'wn P'asdat'o'wght'er* [From 15th Century to 1915: Commerce-Economic Activities of Armenians in Today's Turkey, Collected Documents] (Yerevan: Gasprint, 2012). This list is also available at https://hyetert.org/2014/10/21/antep/.

[a] A type of wool woven with cotton.

Economic and Commercial Lists of Aintab before World War I

AINTAB BUREAU OF THE OTTOMAN PUBLIC DEBT ADMINISTRATION	
Mardiros Djanszian	Director
Fadıl Effendi	Secretary
Levon Effendi	Cashier
TOBACCO CONTROLLER	
Yorgi Effendi (Judge)	Director
Levon Kendirdjian	Cashier
CHAMBER OF COMMERCE	
Ahmed Effendi	President
Muzafferzâde Hafız Ahmed	President
Şemseddin Effendi	Secretary
Garabed Yaghsızian	Member
Habib Kurkjian	Member
Hırand Sulahian	Member
Pazarbaşızâde Nuri	Member
Yusuf Babigian	Member
CONSULAR	
Garabed Effendi Nazaretian	Iran Consular
Léon Sahagian	Chief Translator
INSURANCE DEALERS	
Tutundjian	Representative of New York and Russia
Sarkis Sahagian	Representative of Union dé Paris
HOSPITAL	
Taşçızâde Abdullah	Director of Hamidiye Hospital
BANKS	
Léon Maher	Director of Imperial Ottoman
Léon Kevorkian	Controller of Imperial Ottoman
Yervant Stepanian	Cashier of Imperial Ottoman

AGRICULTURAL ADMINISTRATION	
Ahmed Hurşid Effendi	Director
COLLEGES	
John Merrill	Principal of American College
Armenak Chamichian	Director of Cilicia Tchemaran
TOBACCO PAPER	
Hasan Keyf Cigarettes-Egypt-Alexandria	
Artin and Garabed Nazaretian	Owners
Habib Chouha	Aintab Director
LAWYERS	
Dafizâde Mazlum	
Kirkor Der Hagopian	
Hagop Karamanougian	
Ahmedzâde Körükçü	
Artin Kurkjian	
Kirkor Niziblian	
Muhammed Aghazâde Ömer Şevki	
Ohannes Topalian	
BANKERS	
Bedros Ashjian and Corci Ashjian	
Ohannes Beorekdjian	
K. Ghazarian (Kalusd Ghazarian) and sons and partners	
S. Sahakian and sons Hovsep and Toros	
EMBROIDERY EXPORTERS	
Ovaguim Bakkalian	
Artin Shnorokian and sons	
Garuj Karamanougian and sons	
Sarkis Krajian	
Bayan Shepard and Movses Temurdjian	
WOOL-GIRDLE FACTORIES	
Garabed Apanian	
Kevork Arslanian	
A. Pazarbashian	
Tatul Kupelian	
Ohannes Pirimian	
Nerses Sulahian and sons	

COPPERSMITHS
A. Arslanian and G. Arslanian and their sons
Movses Demirdjian
M. Kalemkerian
A. Kinadjian
YELLOW CANDLE EXPORTERS
Geozukian brothers
Mahmut Budeyri
Artin and Garabed Nazaretian
BROKERS
Garabed Arusian
Mahmut Budeyri
Selim Bidjo
Ohannes Bitdjian
Sahag Bitdjian
Naoum Dacho
Mikhayel Farrayet
Kevork Horomian
A. Hougaz and sons
Garabed Kalusdian
Mihran Kavukdjian
Serope Keshishian
Ohan Khachlikhachian
Habib Kurkjian
Mazlum Effendi and Dayızâde Ahmed
Hovahannes Piranian
Vahe Tarpinian
Cosmos Tchopdjian
D. Tchopdjian and brothers
SHOEMAKERS
Movses Arslanian
Hadji Boshgezenian
K. Girboian
H. Kaparikian
Nerses Nalpatian
Artin Parseghian
Avedis Semerdjian
Kevork Sivadjian

COTTON DEALERS
Movses Ammian
Levonian brothers
Manug Topbashian
P. Aghcaian
Selim Bidjo
Jebejian brothers
Kalusd Ghazarian and sons and partners
Melkon and Khatcher Kabakian
Stepan Keshishian
Selim and Naim Khayat
Sarkis Sahagian and sons Toros and Istamboliye
Nerses Sulahian and sons
LEATHER AND WELT (STOUT LEATHER)
Pekmezcizâde Çakır
Jebejian brothers
Haci Osmanzâde Bahab
Mustafa Kafadar
Ali Kimyaoğlu
Eghia Panoian
Salihzâde İbrahim
COPPERSMITHS
Movses Arslanian and brothers
GRAIN AND FOOD SUPPLIES
A. Hougaz and partners
Stepan Keshishian
N.S. Khayat
DENTISTS
Nouridjan Niziblian
Krikor Sarkisian
COGNAC PRODUCERS
Nerses Baronian
Nazaret Bulbulian
Antaki Ilian
IRON MERCHANTS
N. Barsoumian
G. Demirdjian and A. Demirdjian
Kirkor Demirdjian
H. Poladian and sons

FOUNDERS
Hovahannes Boshgezenian
Kevork Hamasian
H. Hagopian
BLACKSMITHS
Toros Bourtaian
Frenk-Garabetian brothers
FRUIT EXPORTERS
Bedros Ashjian
Ahmed Hariri
Nuri Pazarbaşı
Mahmut Budeyri
Selim Bidjo
Habib Kurkjian
Artin and Garabed Nazaretian
OLIVE OIL PRODUCERS
H. Arakelian
Eghia Karadjian
Nazar Karadjian
MANUFACTURERS
Hovsep Ashjian
Rupen Andillian
Arakelian brothers
Abraham Babigian
Garuj Berejiklian
Ohannes Berejiklian
Artin Shnorkian and sons
Garuj Karamanougian and sons
Nouri Karamanougian and Kendirdjian brothers
Nazaret Manushagian
Leon Nazarian
Devlet Simdjian
Zadik Tedjirian
K. Karamanougian
Movses Topdjian

DOCTORS
Kevork Arslanian
Nerses Baghdoian
Hovsep Bezjian
Habib Geozukian
Artin Kalfaian
Yakup Kelleian
Movses Levonian
Habib Nazarian
FURNITURE SELLERS
Amiralian
Mumcuian
Apsi Mahmut
Attar İmam
Avedis Khanzedian
Hovsep Kirlopian
Manuel Panzalian
Salihzâde Mahmut
Salihzâde Ahmet
Ökkeşzâde Timur
Joseph Yemendjian
Avedis Yesaian
STEAM MILLS
Asadur Ekmekdjian
Mahmut Budeyri
Sarkis Sahagian and sons
Simon Serovpian
Hırand Sulahian
FABRIC DYEING
Krikor Esaian
Sarkis Sabundjian and Garabed Geozukian and brothers
MERCHANTS
Bedros Ashjian
Movses Arslanian and brothers
Nazaret Aydjian
Garabed Babigian

Kevork Barsumian and brothers
Habib Chouha and Jebejian brothers
Dikran Egavian
Rupen Egavian
Kalusd Ghazarian and sons[a]
Sarkis Krajian
Hovahannes Levonian
Kevork Leylekian
Misak Leylekian
Nazaret Manushagian
Artin and Garabed Nazaretian
Hovsep Sahagian and sons
Toros Sahagian
Nerses Sulahian and sons
Toros Tahmazian
Kevork Tatarian
Kevork Topbashian
Manuel Topbashian
Sarkis Yacoubian
EXPORTERS OF EGGS
Avram Khayat
Misak Leylekian
JEWELERS
Barsegian brothers
N. Chirikdjian
Daghlian brothers
Artin and Garabed Nazaretian
CIGARETTE PAPER
Setrak Djavian
GASOLINE
P. Aghdjaian
Hacı Osmanzâde
Nazaret Manushagian
Sarkis Sahagian and sons
PHARMACISTS
B. Barsumian
M. Bezjian
K. Demirdjian

A. Geozukian
Nerses Ishakian
Manuel Kendirdjian
PHOTOGRAPHERS
Mihran Haladjian
Artin Muradian
PISTACHIO EXPORTERS
Bedros Ashjian
Kalusd Ghazarian and sons
A. Hougas and sons
Artin Karadjian
Hanna Kurkchuian
Artin and Garabed Nazaretian
K. Topbashian
HARDWAREMEN
Artin Pazarbashian
Abraham Bezirganian
Kevork Boutchakdjian
Said Kaltchindjian
Kamadian brothers
SOAP PRODUCERS
Adanalian
Hayri Muhammed
Hanna and Nazaret Kurkjian
Söylemezzâde Abdülkadir
TAILORS
Hovsep Bulbulian
Dikran Boshgezenian
Ohannes Kazanjian
Khachadour Khachadourian
Misak Matossian
CARPET SELLERS
Arslanian-Melkonian brothers
Krajian brothers
Kevork Topbashian
FABRIC DYERS
Artin Esaian
Minas Bedirian

Nazar Bedirian
Sarkis Gulesserian
Hamid Nigoghosian
Kevork Boyajian
Sarkis Kabadaian
Nerses Tedjirian
H. Balian
Mihran Kavukjian
Hırand Sulahian
Kevork Tahtajian
HANDKERCHIEF PRODUCERS
Artin Ammian
Hovsep Ammian
A. Adaklian
Arakelian brothers
Arslanian
Hasırdjian
Armenak Arslanian
Mikael Arslanian
A. Basmajian and brothers
Garuj Basmajian
Nerses Deghirmendjian
K. Chakmakdjian
K. Jebejian and sons
K. Djoulgian
Movses Hadidian
Agop Hamalian
Avedis Hasirdjian
Bogos Hasirdjian
Adour Kabakian and brothers
Soghomon Kabakian
Yakup Karamanougian and brothers
Levonian brothers
Garoutche Merdjanian
Melkon Manukian
S. G. Nazarian
S. B. Nazarian

Hırand Sulahian
Kevork Temourdjian
Tutundjian brothers
Garabed Yazidjian and sons

Source: Annuaire Oriental Edition 1914: Aintab, 1323–1326.

[a] Licensed since 1882, the Ghazarians ran a full-range import-export business. With branches in Yozgat and Sungurlu, the business provided services to the major cities in Turkey.

The following is the list of those who played a primary role in and bore responsibility for the deportation and destruction of the Aintab Armenians, as well as the seizure of their movable and immovable properties. The individuals on this list fostered the necessary sociopolitical climate to lead the central government to issue deportation orders for the Aintab Armenians from April 1915 until the end of July.

Civil, Military, and Religious Officers

Ahmed Bey	*Mutasarrıf* (district governor) of Aintab
Mustafa Effendi	Mayor of Aintab
Besim Bey	Head of Treasury
Bilal Hilmi	Judge
Kazım Effendi	Officer of Registration Office
Eyüp Sabri Bey	A member of Treasury
Hacı Yusuf Effendi	A member of Treasury
Kemal Bey	Gendarme commander
Bulaşıkzâde Arif Effendi	Mufti and General Secretary of the CUP in Aintab
Bülbül Hoca	Ulema
Muammer Effendi	Ulema
Habibzâde Mustafa	Ulema
Bayramzâde Muammer	Ulema
Fahrettin Hoca	Ulema
Hacı Mahmut Effendi	President of the Court
Kepkepzâde Şakir	Ulema
Bahaeddin Effendizâde Muammer	Ulema
Sheikh Ubeydullah Effendi	Ulema
Major Bekir Bey	Regiment commander of Kızılhisar
Kasım Bey	Military officer
Hakkı Bey	Regiment clerk

Mustafa Effendi	Custodian, depot employee
Hamid Bey	Doctor of the municipal government
Kerim Bey	Member of the Court
Kasım Bey from Urfa	Member of the Court
Emin Effendi	Director of Agriculture Bank
Cemil Effendi	Active member of the Court
Osman Bey	Court clerk
Vahid Effendi Izrabzâde	Pious Foundations clerk
Muammer Effendi	Active member of the Court
Taşir Effendi	First clerk of the municipal government
Mahmut Effendi	Treasurer of the municipal government
Mersinli Hoca's son	Ulema
Zani Hafız	Director of Turkish Orphanage
Rüştü Hoca	Director of news agency
Kurd Muhammed	Ulema
Talibzâde Arif Effendi	District governor's clerk
Fevzi Effendi	Police captain
Körükçü Hafızzâde Mustafa	Police captain
Hacı Sabitzâde Ahmed Effendi	Police officer
Hacı Sabitzâde Said Effendi	Military clerk
Musluzâde Mehmed	Gendarme sergeant
Çubukçu Ali	Gendarme sergeant
Butcher Misdo	Gendarme sergeant
İbrahim Çavuş (Sergeant)	Gendarme sergeant
Hasan Çavuş	Gendarme sergeant
Mehmed Çavuş	Gendarme sergeant
Matağ's son Ali	Gendarme sergeant
Necib Effendi	Doorman
Behzadbaşı Mehmet	Doorman
Mehmet Effendi	Doorman
Ali Effendi	*Tahdidat* (Census) clerk
Emin Effendi	Doorman
Abdullah Agha	Court officer
Hacı Halil Effendi	Gendarme commander
Hacı Halil Effendioğlu	Prison guard
Ömer Şevki	Attorney
Ahmet Effendi	Imam of Kozanlı neighborhood
Sheikh Mustafa Baba	Imam of Alaybeyi neighborhood

Sheikh Mustafa's son	Bandit leader
Hafız Ahmed Effendi	Mukhtar of Alaybeyi neighborhood

Members of the CUP Club and Leading Figures in the Deportation of Armenians and Plunder of Their Properties

Ali Cenani Bey
Ekrem Cenani Bey (Ali Cenani Bey's brother)
Rıza Cenani Bey (Ali Cenani Bey's brother)
Fazlı Ağazâde Nuri Bey
Fazlı Ağazâde Nuri Bey's son Mustafa
Fazlı Ağazâde Nuri Bey's son Kadir
Battal Beyzâde Tahir Bey
Battal Beyzâde Tahir Bey's son Battal
Mısırlızâde Arif Pasha
Arif Pasha's son Necib Bey
Arif Pasha's son Ali Bey
Arif Pasha's brother Ömer Effendi
Arif Pasha's brother Hamza Effendi
Arif Pasha's brother Mehmed Effendi
Obarizâde Kamil Bey
Obarizâde Fadıl Bey
Emin Beyzâde Sadık Bey
Emin Beyzâde Ali Bey
Battal Beyzâde Fazıl Bey
Battal Beyzâde İsmail Bey
Seyyafzâde Abdo Effendi
Seyyafzâde Abdo Effendi's son Nafi
Seyyafzâde Abdo Effendi's son Asaf
Hacı Halil Ağazâde Ahmed Agha
Hacı Halil Ağazâde Zeki Bey
Kethüdazâde Abdülrahman Effendi
Hüseyin Cemil Bey
Hasan Cemal Bey
Mehmet Kemal Bey
Mehmet Bey
Necati Bey
Ahmed Muhtar Bey (Ali Cenani's most reliable man)
Müftüzâde Mehmet Effendi
Müftüzâde Feyzi Effendi

Müftüzâde Abdo Effendi
Kala Ağasızâde Mehmed Effendi
Kala Ağasızâde Osman Effendi
Abbas Hocazâde Ökkeş Effendi
Köylüoğluzâde Ahmed
Kör Hacı Ömerzâde Mehmed Ali Effendi
Kör Hacı Ömerzâde Mahmud Effendi
Hacı Nuhzâde Mahmud
Hacı Halil Ağazâde Sadık
Nazlızâde Sakıb
Grocer Şeyhzâde Mustafa
Kavlakzâde Ali
Marağenoğlu Emin
Marağenoğlu Muammer
Tunaoğlu Mustafa
Tunaoğlu Mustafa's friend Şakir Agha
Amro Ağazâde Ali Agha
Amro Ağazâde Mıstık
Gücelizâde Mahmud Effendi
Musulizâde Ahmed Effendi
'Postman' (former officer of Ahmed Effendi)
Naci Hocazâde Mehmed Effendi
Kafadarzâde Hacı Ali Agha
Kafadarzâde Ali Effendi
Kafadarzâde Hüseyin Effendi
Kafadarzâde Hasan Effendi
Dabbağ Hacı Vehab Effendi
Kepkepzâde Abdülrezzak Effendi
Hacı Koymazâde Abdülkadir Effendi
Hacı Hocazâde Hacı Mehmed
Hacı Hocazâde Mahmud
Diş kören Hocazâde Şakir Effendi
Diş kören Hocazâde Ragıb Effendi
Muzafferzâde Hafız Kadir Effendi
Sadık Kadir Effendi
Timurzâde Ökkeş Effendi
Timurzâde Ökkeş Said Effendi
Arpacızâde Mehmed Effendi

Arpacızâde Ömer
Arpacızâde Mustafa
Küpelizâde Memik Agha
Küpelizâde Mehmed Agha
Küpelizâde Uncu Hurşit
Küpelizâde Uncu Hurşit's brother Ali Veli
Sergeant Hasan
Ibişimzâde Mehmed Emin Agha
Ibişimzâde Mehmed Mustafa
Ibişimzâde Mehmed Abdülkadir
Mollazâde Hacı Muslu
Muammer Effendi
Sıçan Hacı Şakir
Kürdzâde Hamo
Battal Hocazâde Ragıp Effendi
Battal Hocazâde Halil Effendi
Külekçi's son Abdülkadir Effendi
Darağ's son Abdülrahman Effendi
Çitcizâde Mahmut Effendi
Hacı Fazılzâde Hacı Murtaza
Hacı Fazılzâde Hacı Bekir
Hacı Fazılzâde Hacı Mehmed
Savcılı Şıhman Agha
Ömer Ağazâde Ahmet Agha
Ömer Ağazâde Necati Effendi
Ali Rıza
Bazar Başızâde Nuri Effendi
Hacı İbrahimzâde Mustafa Effendi
Salihzâde Hökkeş Effendi
Harputlu Efrayim Effendi
Isa Başızâde Hakkı Effendi
Isa Başızâde Hüseyin
Beyaz Ali Agha
Beyaz Mehmed Agha
Beyaz Ökkeş Agha
Kahraman Süleyman Agha
Kahraman Ahmed Agha
Kahraman Hacı Effendi

Şakir Agha
Güzel Beyzâde Ökkeş Effendi
Jeweler Haşim Effendi
Rüstem's son Ahmed Effendi
Zencir Mustafa
Osman Agha
İbrahim Effendi
Kirişcizâde Abdullah Agha
Kirişcizâde Abdülkadir Effendi
Çavuş İbo's sons
Çilli Bekir's son Abdo Effendi
Çilli Bekir's son Becan
Çilli Bekir's son Ali
Mahmud Bedri Effendi
Karabekirzâde Mehmed Agha
Manavcı Mehmed Said
Innkeeper Osman Agha
Innkeeper Osman Agha's son Hüseyin Effendi
Kilimcizâde Mehmed Effendi
Tuz Hancısı Said Mehmed Effendi
Kendirjian's friend Rasim Agha
Bedestenci Halebli's son
İnco's son Ali
Divrikli Kara Ali and his son
Hacı Mustafa and his brother
Elmacızâde Mehmed Effendi
Hacı Şıh Mehmed's son Ali Effendi
Hacı Şıh Mehmed's son Bekir Effendi
Fazlızâde Tahir Effendi
Çatırdakcızâde Halil Effendi
Butcher Ökkeş
Butcher Ökkeş's son Ökkeş
Grocer Yağcı İbo
Coal dealer Kara Mehmed
Bookseller Hacı Mehmed and his son
Kebab seller Hacı
Kizlizâde Abdülkadir Effendi
Albanian Ahmed and his son

Burnu Kara's son Ahmed
Burnu Kara's son Halil
Bekirci's son Ali
Bekirci's son Ökkeş
Bekirci's son Ali Bayram
Dabbağ Aygır's son Hanifi
Hacı İbrahim's son Mahmud
Haci İbrahim's son Ahmed
Hacı İbrahim' son Ali
Kafadar's son Memo
Zengin Hasan Effendi
Grocer Emin's son Kurd İbrahim
Battalzâde Mehmed Agha
Karslı Sabri Effendi
Karslı Faik Effendi
Ayranzâde Mehmed Effendi
Çakal's son Mehmed
İmamzâde Abdülkadir oğlu Abdülkadir
İmamzâde Ali
İmamzâde Mehmed
Deylibci Çavuş
Butcher Ali
Bostonca Gürcü's sons
Solak's son Ali
Grocer Mehmed
Elbeylizâde Mehmed Ali and sons
Pekmezci Kör Hanifi
Kund Osmanzâde Abdürrahman
Kund Osmanzâde Bekir
Kund Osmanzâde Kara Mehmed
Kavas Ali
Kurd Mahmedo
Bacaksızzâde Mehmed and sons
Seyfeddin Hocazâde Mustafa Effendi
Court crier Süleyman Effendi
Grocer Kuyumcuoğlu İsmail Agha
Hamamcı Süleyman's sons
Grocer Şıho's son Arif Effendi

Wheat Inn's clerk Kör Hasan
Storekeeper Sabri Effendi
Tinner Yirik
Butcher Abuş' son Mehmed
Kurb-ı Zincir's mukhtar Kalender Baba
Kozanlı's Mukhtar Misdo's son Said
Edhem Bey Müseybini Kaimakam
Tekirsinli Salman Agha and sons
Grocer Abdallah Baba's son Ahmed
Salman Beyzâde Ahmed
Salman Beyzâde Ferid
Çıtlo Pıtızâde Yusuf Hoca
Çıtlo Pıtızâde Çavuş
Kumru's son Hacı Hüseyni
Külekci Grocer Saklob in Yeni Çarşı
Grocer Halil's son Mehmed Ali
Grocer Arab Agha
Tılfar village's Imam Mustafa Hoca
Tılfar village's mukhtar Köse Mustafa
Tılfarlı Hazlac Memo's son Hacı İsmail

Source: BNu / Fonds A. Andonian, P.J. 1 / 3, file 4, Aintab, "The Deportation of Armenians in Aintab," 11–17; *Krikor Guerguerian Private Archival Collection*, folder number: 22, file name: Turks (List) Responsible, file no. 46.

Former Presidents of Gaziantep Chamber of Commerce Board

1	Çiftçizâde Hacı Abdullah Effendi	1898–1901
2	Izrapzâde Hamdi Effendi (Barlas)	1901–1904
3	Osmanbey Oğlu Kadir Bey (Battal)	1904–1907
4	Seyyafzâde Abdo Effendi (Ocak)	1907–1907
5	Şıh Mustafa Effendi (Ocak)	1907–1909
6	Salih Effendizâde Ahmet Effendi	1909–1911
7	Mahmut Budeyri	1912–1913
8	Pazarbaşı Nuri Effendi	1914–1917
9	Katip Hocazâde Saadettin Effendi (Özyazıcı)	1917–1921
10	Mahmut Dai	1921–1924
11	Muzafferzâde Hafız Ahmet Effendi	1925–1928
12	Mahmut Ersoy	1947–1951
13	Hacı Muhlis Karslı	1951–1958

14	Necmi Bayram	1959–1960
15	Vehbi Kepkep	1960–1966
16	Kemal Aktan	1966–1968
17	Orhan Sevinç	1968–1969
18	Ahmet Muhtar Açıkkol	1969–1970
19	Reşat Güzelbey	1970–1970
20	Bahattin Kayalı	1971–1971
21	Orhan Sevinç	1971–1978
22	Esat Kaya Turgay	1978–1979
23	Orhan Sevinç	1979–1980
24	Mehmet Batallı	1980–1984
25	Mehmet Ali Zengin	1984–1986
26	Mehmet Batallı	1986–1989
27	Mustafa Geylani	1989–1992
28	Mehmet Aslan	1992–2013

Source: http://www.gto.org.tr/Eski-Yoneticiler-icerik-7.html (accessed 23 October 2014), "Gaziantep Ticaret Odası Geçmiş Dönem Yönetim Kurulu Başkanları"; author and publication date are not available.

Glossary

Askerlik Şubesi Reisi: draft office president

Ayan: Ottoman notables

Başşehbender: chief consul

Batman: an Ottoman unit of measurement (one batman equals 7.7 kilograms)

Bedelat-ı Askeriye: an exemption tax

Chetes: bandits

Defterdarlık: Internal Revenue Office

Emval-i Metruke Kanunları: Abandoned Properties Laws

Evkaf: a rcligious charitable institution

Evkaf Nezareti: Ministry of Pious Foundations

Eytam Mektebi: orphan school

Fatwa: Islamic religious law

Firari: fleeing

Firman: edict

Gayr-ı mübâdil: nonexchanged people (Muslims of Western Thrace who were exempt from the population exchange in 1923)

Gazi: veteran

Heyet: special committee

Heyet-i ihtiyariyye: commission of elders

Hilal-i Ahmer: Turkish Red Crescent

İdadi: high school

İstiklâl Harbi: Turkish War of Independence

Ittihad-ı Anasır: ideology promoting unity among differences

Kadı: Muslim judge

Kaimakam: local prefect governor

Kânûn-ı Esâsî: the first Ottoman Constitution

Katib-i Mesul: responsible secretary

Khan: large commercial building

Khedive: governor

Kıta: a unit of measurement

Kıyye: an Ottoman unit of measurement (one kıyye equals 1.3 kilograms)

Komisyon: commission

Küruh: A unit of measurement

Madrasah: Muslim theological school

Mahalli Maarif İdaresi: Local Administrative Branch of Education Ministry

Mecidiye: five kurush or piasters (kurush is the smallest denomination of Turkish currency)

Milli Emlak: National Estate

Milli İktisat: National Economy

Mübâdil: exchanged people (Muslims who lived in Greece and exchanged with Orthodox Greeks of the Ottoman Empire as a result of the compulsory exchange of populations between Greece and Turkey in January 1923)

Mufti: religious official of the state

Muhacir: immigrant, denoting an individual who had left his or her homeland and settled in the Ottoman Empire

Mukhtar: headman

Mülteci: refugee, denoting an individual forced to migrate to the Ottoman interior because of enemy occupation of the Ottoman lands

Muris: legator

Müsadere: seizure

Mutasarrıf: district governor

Mütegayyip: lost

Nüfus Müdürlüğü: Census Office

Redif Taburu: Military Reserve Battalion

Sadaret: the Grand Vizierate

Sancak-ı Şerif: Banner of the Prophet

Sanjak: Banner

Seferberlik Tahsisatı: Mobilization Allowance

Şer-i Mahkeme: the ecclesiastical court

Sevkiyat Komisyonu: Deportation Committee

Sicil-i ahval: official record

Softa: madrasah student

Tapu İdaresi: Register of Deeds Office

Tapu Sicili Kayıtları: Title Deed Registry

Tapu ve Kadastro: Land Registry and Cadaster

Tarikat: Religious Sect

Tarım Kurulu: Agricultural Assembly

Tebirge: strong gate

Tekalif-i Harbiye: special war taxes

Tekke: convents

Tereke: probate inventory

Teşkilat-i Mahsusa: Special Organization

Ticaret Odası: Chamber of Commerce

Ulema: religious scholar

Vakıflar Dairesi: Pious Foundations Office

Vesika: certificate

Vilayet: province

Ziraat Bankası: Agricultural Bank

Notes

Introduction

1. Raphaël Lemkin, *Axis Rule in Occupied Europe: Laws of Occupation, Analysis of Government, Proposals for Redress* (Washington, DC: Carnegie Endowment for International Peace, 1944), ch. 9, "Genocide," 79. Also see John Docker, "Are Settler-Colonies Inherently Genocidal? Rereading Lemkin," in *Empire, Colony, Genocide: Conquest, Occupation, and Subaltern Resistance in World History,* ed. A. Dirk Moses, (New York, Oxford: Berghahn, 2008), 83.

2. Martin Dean, *Robbing the Jews: The Confiscation of Jewish Property in the Holocaust, 1933–1945* (New York: Cambridge University Press, 2008), 395.

3. Donald Bloxham, *The Great Game of Genocide: Imperialism, Nationalism, and the Destruction of the Ottoman Armenians* (Oxford: Oxford University Press, 2005), 1.

4. Donald Bloxham and Hans-Lukas Kieser, "Genocide," in *The Cambridge History of the First World War,* vol. I, ed. Jay Winter and Charles J. Stille (Cambridge: Cambridge University Press, 2014), 594–596.

5. Fuat Dündar, *Crime of Numbers: The Role of Statistics in the Armenian Question (1878–1918)* (New Brunswick and London: Transaction Publishers, 2010).

6. Matthew Stibbe, "Enemy Aliens, Deportees, Refugees: Internment Practices in the Habsburg Empire, 1914–1918," available from Sheffield Hallam University Research Archive (SHURA) at http://shura.ac.uk/9021/, 1–33 (originally published in *Journal of Modern European History,* 12, no. 4 [2014]: 479–499); Robert Gerwarth and Uğur Ümit Üngör, "The Collapse of the Ottoman and Habsburg Empires and the Brutalisation of the Successor States," *Journal of*

Modern European History 13, no. 2 (2015): 226–248; Donald Bloxham and Dirk Moses, "Genocide and Ethnic Cleansing," in *Political Violence in Twentieth-Century Europe,* ed. Donald Bloxham and Robert Gerwarth (Cambridge: Cambridge University Press, 2011), 11–39.

7. Eric Lohr, *Nationalizing the Russian Empire: The Campaign against Enemy Aliens during World War I* (Cambridge, MA: Harvard University Press, 2003), 1.

8. Stibbe, "Enemy Aliens, Deportees, Refugees," 18. Also see Alan Kramer, *Dynamic of Destruction: Culture and Mass Killing in the First World War* (Oxford: Oxford University Press, 2007), 3, 68.

9. Lohr, *Nationalizing the Russian Empire,* 1.

10. Lohr, *Nationalizing the Russian Empire,* 2.

11. The same process took place in the Russian Empire. The Russians developed the wartime campaign against enemy aliens to expropriate landholdings and transfer them to the Russians and other favored nationalities. For more details, see Lohr, *Nationalizing the Russian Empire,* 66–83, esp. 84.

12. Donald Bloxham, *The Final Solution: A Genocide* (Oxford: Oxford University Press, 2009), 77.

13. Bloxham and Moses, "Genocide and Ethnic Cleansing," 132. For another important work drawing attention to the significance of regional variation in the Armenian genocide, see Üngör, "Explaining Regional Variations in the Armenian Genocide," in *World War I and the End of the Ottomans: From the Balkan Wars to the Armenian Genocide,* ed. Hans-Lukas Kieser, Kerem Öktem, and Maurus Reinkowski (New York: I.B. Tauris, 2015), 241–261.

14. Omer Bartov and Eric D. Weitz (eds.), *Shatterzones of Empires: Coexistence and Violence in the German, Habsburg, Russian, and Ottoman Borderlands* (Bloomington: Indiana University Press, 2013), 12.

15. Frank Bajohr, *"Aryanization" in Hamburg: The Economic Exclusion of Jews and the Confiscation of their Property in Nazi Germany* (New York: Berghahn Books, 2002); Dean, *Robbing the Jews.*

16. Hilmar Kaiser, *The Extermination of Armenians in the Diarbekir Region* (Istanbul: Istanbul Bilgi University Press, 2014); Uğur Ü. Üngör, *The Making of Modern Turkey: Nation and State in Eastern Anatolia, 1913–1950* (Oxford: Oxford University Press, 2011). For another exceptional work in this area of Holocaust studies, see Raz Segal, *Genocide in the Carpathians: War, Social Breakdown, and Mass Violence* (Stanford, CA: Stanford University Press, 2016).

17. Jan T. Gross with Irena Grudzińska Gross, *Golden Harvest: Events at the Periphery of the Holocaust* (New York: Oxford University Press, 2012), 83.

18. For an important discussion with respect to similar questions, see Uğur Ü. Üngör and Mehmet Polatel, *Confiscation and Destruction: The Young*

Turk Seizure of Armenian Property (New York and London: Continuum, 2011), 6–7.

19. There is an enormous amount of literature on the notion of "provincial elites" within the context of the Ottoman Empire. For instance, see Ehud Toledano, "The Emergence of Ottoman-Local Elites (1700–1900): A Framework for Research," in *Middle Eastern Politics and Ideas: A History from Within*, ed. I. Pappy and M. Ma'oz (London and New York: Tauris Academic Studies, 1997); cf. T. Shuval, "The Ottoman Algerian Elite and its Ideology," *International Journal of Middle East Studies* 32, no. 3 (2000): 323–344; Halil İnalcık, "Centralization and Decentralization in Ottoman Administration," in *Studies in Eighteenth Century Islamic History*, ed. T. Naff and R. Owen (Carbondale: Southern Illinois University Press, 1977); J. Haldon, "The Ottoman State and the Question of State Autonomy: Comparative Perspectives," in *New Approaches to State and Peasant in Ottoman History*, ed. Halil Berktay and Sureyya Faroqhi (London: Frank Cass, 1992), 34; Huricihan İslamoğlu-İnan, *State and Peasant in the Ottoman Empire: Agrarian Power Relations and Regional Economic Development in Ottoman Anatolia During the Sixteenth Century* (Leiden: Brill, 1994); Ali Yaycıoğlu, *Partners of the Empire: The Crisis of the Ottoman Order in the Age of Revolutions* (Stanford, CA: Stanford University Press, 2016); and Ali Yaycıoğlu, "Provincial Power-Holders and the Empire in the Late Ottoman World: Conflict or Partnership?," in *The Ottoman World*, ed. Christine Woodhead (London: Routledge Press, 2012), 436–452.

20. Antonis Anastasopoulos (ed.), *Provincial Elites in the Ottoman Empire*. Halcyon Days in Crete V: A Symposium Held in Rethymno, 10–12 January 2003 (Rethymno: Crete University Press, 2005), xi; Yaycıoğlu, "Provincial Power-Holders and the Empire in the Late Ottoman World," 437.

21. Anastasopoulos (ed.), *Provincial Elites in the Ottoman Empire*, xiv, n. 16.

22. Anastasopoulos (ed.), *Provincial Elites in the Ottoman Empire*, xviii. Also see Ariel Salzmann, "An Ancien Régime Revisited: 'Privatization' and Political Economy in the Eighteenth-Century Ottoman Empire," *Politics and Society* 21, no. 4 (1993): 393–423.

23. Hülya Canbakal, *Society and Politics in an Ottoman Town: 'Ayntab in the 17th Century* (Boston: Brill, 2007), 3.

24. Joost Jongerden and Jelle Verheij (eds.), *Social Relations in Ottoman Diyarbekir, 1870–1915* (Boston: Brill, 2012).

25. Jongerden and Verheij (eds.), *Social Relations in Ottoman Diyarbekir*, 3.

26. In the case of Diyarbekir and Adana, Üngör and Polatel also claim that the local perpetrators directly partook in the annihilation of their Armenian neighbors and therefore were rewarded by the central authorities. See Üngör and Polatel, *Confiscation and Destruction*, 13, 107–133, esp. 133, and 133–165,

esp. 163. Yet Kaiser argues quite the opposite. In his analysis, the central authorities were well aware of the potential threat powerful local circles posed to their expropriation program. The CUP aimed to take total control over the expropriation of Armenians properties by not allowing any corruption and personal enrichment; see Kaiser, *The Extermination of Armenians,* 282–283.

27. The same process can be observed in the case of the Holocaust with reference to the 'Aryanization' of Jewish property by the Nazi government. See Frank Bajohr, "Expropriation and Expulsion," in *The Historiography of the Holocaust,* ed. Dan Stone (New York: Palgrave Macmillan, 2004), 52–64, esp. 55. For a comparative analysis of the expropriation and plunder of Armenian and Jewish wealth under the veil of law during the Armenian genocide and the Holocaust, see Ümit Kurt, "Legal and Official Plunder of Armenian and Jewish Properties in Comparative Perspective: the Armenian Genocide and the Holocaust," *Journal of Genocide Research* 17, no. 3 (2015): 305–326.

28. Stephan H. Astourian, "Genocidal Process: Reflections on the Armeno-Turkish Polarization," in *The Armenian Genocide: History, Politics, Ethics,* ed. Richard G. Hovannisian (New York: St. Martin's Press, 1992), 69–71. As Zafer Toprak cautiously explains, "During the war years, political factors played also a role in the fact that some business sectors came into the possession of Turkish-Muslim notables: Muslim-Turkish entrepreneurs filled the voids generated by the 'Armenian deportation.'" *Türkiye'de 'Milli İktisat' (1908–1918)* (Ankara: Yurt Yayınları, 1982), 57.

29. For "Turkification" of the Armenian property and wealth, see Taner Akçam and Ümit Kurt, *The Spirit of the Laws: The Plunder of Wealth in the Armenian Genocide* (New York: Berghahn Books, 2015); Üngör and Polatel, *Confiscation and Destruction;* Nevzat Onaran, *Emval-i Metruke Olayı: Osmanlı'da ve Cumhuriyette Ermeni ve Rum Mallarının Türkleştirilmesi* (Istanbul: Belge, 2010); Nevzat Onaran, *Cumhuriyet'te Ermeni ve Rum Mallarının Türkleştirilmesi (1914–1919) ve (1920–1930): Emval-i Metrukenin Tasfiyesi-I ve II* (Istanbul: Evrensel Basım Yayın, 2013); Stephan H. Astourian, "Testing World-System Theory, Cilicia (1830s–1890s): Armenian-Turkish Polarization and the Ideology of Modern Ottoman Historiography" (unpublished PhD diss., University of California, Los Angeles, 1996), 454.

30. Canbakal, *Society and Politics in an Ottoman Town,* 19.

31. Bloxham, *The Great Game of Genocide,* 4.

32. Bloxham, *The Great Game of Genocide,* 4.

33. For a detailed analysis of this legal-bureaucratic framework, including the Republican era, see Akçam and Kurt, *Spirit of the Laws.*

34. Taner Akçam, *A Shameful Act: The Armenian Genocide and the Question of Turkish Responsibility* (New York: Metropolitan Books, 2006); Bloxham,

The Great Game of Genocide; Vahakn N. Dadrian, *The History of the Armenian Genocide: Ethnic Conflict from the Balkans to Anatolia to the Caucasus* (New York: Berghahn Books, 2004); Ronald G. Suny, *They Can Live in the Desert but Nowhere Else: A History of the Armenian Genocide* (Princeton, NJ: Princeton University Press, 2015); David Gaunt, *Massacres, Resistance, Protectors: Muslim-Christian Relations in Eastern Anatolia During World War I* (Piscataway, NJ: Gorgias Press, 2006); Jacques Sémelin, Claire Andrieu, and Sarah Gensburger (eds.), *Resisting Genocide: The Multiple Forms of Rescue* (London: Hurst, 2010).

35. For some important local studies, see Hilmar Kaiser, *The Extermination of Armenians in the Diarbekir Region;* Hilmar Kaiser, "'A Scene from the Inferno': The Armenians of Erzerum and the Genocide, 1915–1916," in *Der Völkermord an den Armeniern und die Shoah: The Armenian Genocide and the Shoah,* ed. Hans-Lukas Kieser and Dominik J. Schaller (Zurich: Chronos, 2001), 129–186; Uğur Ü. Üngör, *The Making of Modern Turkey;* Üngör, "Diyarbekir (1915–1916): Young Turk Mass Killing at the Provincial Level," Sciences Po: Mass Violence and Resistance-Research Network, 25 March 2009, www.sciencespo.fr/mass-violence-war- massacre-resistance/en/document/diyarbekir-1915–1916-young-turk-mass-killings-provincial-level (accessed 14 July 2014); Üngör, "Center and Periphery in the Armenian Genocide: The Case of Diyarbekir Province," in *Der Genozid an den Armeniern, Die Tü rkei und Europa. The Armenian Genocide, Turkey and Europa,* ed. Hans-Lukas Kieser and Elmar Plozza (Zurich: Chronos 2006), 71–88; Kevork Yeghia Suakjian, *Genocide in Trebizond: A Case Study of Armeno-Turkish Relations during the First World War* (Lincoln: University of Nebraska Press, 1981). The major setback of these studies is the lack of primary and secondary Armenian materials. However, Raymond Kévorkian's work (including Suakjian's book to a certain extent) constitutes an exception in this regard. See Kévorkian, *Le Génocide des Arméniens* (Paris: Odile Jacob, 2006); Kévorkian, *The Armenian Genocide: A Complete History* (London: I.B. Tauris, 2011). In his recently published book, Vahé Tachjian illuminates the story of the Bogharian and Tavukjian families from Aintab, who endured deportation in Hama and Salamiyya, based on their diaries in Armenian. See Tachjian, *Daily Life in the Abyss: Genocide Diaries, 1915–1918* (Oxford and New York: Berghahn Books, 2017). Also, Lerna Ekmekçioğlu's work is the first in-depth study of the post-1915 period, employing Armenian texts and images produced in Istanbul from the close of World War I through the early 1930s; see Ekmekçioğlu, *Recovering Armenia: The Limits of Belonging in Post-Genocide Turkey* (Stanford, CA: Stanford University Press, 2016). Last but not least, employing a number of Armenian materials, Khatchig Mouradian dissects the humanitarian activities of the Armenian Aid Council as a

resistance act in Aleppo throughout the period of deportation; see Mouradian, *The Resistance Network: The Armenian Genocide and Humanitarianism in Ottoman Syria, 1915–1918* (East Lansing: Michigan State University Press, 2021).

36. Lut'fik Kuyumdjian, *Lqeal Ko'h'qero'w Harcy* [The Question of Abandoned Property], *So'wrp P'rgich Hiwantano'c Darekirq* [General Year Book of the National Hospital] (Istanbul, 1928, 1929, 1931, 1932, 1939).

37. K. Haygazn Ghazarian, "Hah'o'c Lqeal Ko'h'qero'w ew Galo'wadznero'w T'alany T'o'wrqero'w Go'ghme'" [The Theft of the Armenian Abandoned Properties by the Turks], *Hayrenik Monthly,* 6–7 October 1964; Ghazarian, *Ceghasban T'o'wrqy* [The Genocidal Turk] (Beirut: Hamazkayin Press, 1968).

38. Levon Vartan, *Hah'gagan Dasnhinky ew Hah'ero'w Lqeal Ko'h'qery: Qnnagan Agnarg ysd T'rqagan Vawerakreri* [The Armenian 1915 and the Abandoned Properties of the Armenians: Critical Commentary According to Turkish Documents] (Beirut: Atlas, 1970).

39. Kevork K. Baghdjian, *La Confiscation, par le Gouvernement Turc, des Biens Arméniens—Dits "Abandonnes"* (Montreal: K. K. Baghdjian, 1987). For an English translation of this book, see *The Confiscation of Armenian Properties by the Turkish Government Said to Be Abandoned,* trans. A. B. Gureghian (Lebanon: Armenian Catholicosate of Cilicia, 2010).

40. Dickran Kouymjian, "Confiscation of Armenian Property and the Destruction of Armenian Historical Monuments as a Manifestation the Genocidal Process," in *Anatomy of Genocide: State-Sponsored Mass-Killings in the Twentieth Century,* ed. Alexandre Kimenyi and Otis L. Scott (Lewiston, NY: Edwin Mellen Press, 2001), 307–319. Also see Üngör and Polatel, *Confiscation and Destruction,* 10.

41. Üngör and Polatel, *Confiscation and Destruction,* 11.

42. Hilmar Kaiser, "Armenian Property, Ottoman Law and Nationality Polices during the Armenian Genocide, 1915–1916," in *The First World War as Remembered in the Countries of the Eastern Mediterranean,* ed. Olaf Farschid, Manfred Kropp, and Stephan Dahne (Beirut: Orient-Institute, 2006), 49–71.

43. Akçam, *'Ermeni Meselesi Hallolunmuştur': Osmanlı Belgelerine göre Savaş Yıllarında Ermenilere Yönelik Politikalar* (Istanbul: İletişim, 2007), 223–236; Akçam, *The Young Turks' Crime Against Humanity: The Armenian Genocide and Ethnic Cleansing in the Ottoman Empire* (Princeton, NJ: Princeton University Press, 2012), 356–371.

44. Bedross Der Matossian, "From Confiscation to Appropriation: Historical Continuity and the Destruction of the 'Armenian Economy' in the Ottoman Empire," *Armenian Weekly,* 24 April 2007, 22–23, cited in Üngör and Polatel, *Confiscation and Destruction,* 11.

45. Der Matossian, "The Taboo within the Taboo: The Fate of 'Armenian Capital' at the End of the Ottoman Empire," *European Journal of Turkish Studies: Social Sciences on Contemporary Turkey,* 2011, 1–38, available at http://ejts.revues.org/4411 (accessed 31 March 2014).

46. Hrayr S. Karagueuzian and Yair Auron, *A Perfect Injustice: Genocide and Theft of Armenian Wealth* (New Brunswick, NJ: Transaction Publishers, 2009).

47. Sait Çetinoğlu, "Ermeni Emval-i Metrukeleri Üzerine," *Birikim,* 2009, available at https://birikimdergisi.com/guncel/746/ermeni-emval-i-metrukeleri-uzerine (accessed 11 March 2014); Çetinoğlu, "Sermayenin 'Türk'leştirilmesi," in *Resmi Tarih Tartışmaları,* vol. II, ed. Fikret Başkaya (Istanbul: Özgür Üniversite Kitaplığı, 2006), 79–152.

48. Onaran, *Emval-i Metruke Olayı;* Onaran, *Cumhuriyet'te Ermeni ve Rum Mallarının Türkleştirilmesi (1914–1919) ve (1920–1930).* See, too, Üngör and Polatel, *Confiscation and Destruction,* 11.

49. Renowned sociologist Çağlar Keyder also demonstrated that the state-orchestrated construction of a Turkish bourgeoisie during World War I and the early 1920s was based on the property of Armenians and Greeks. He depicted their wealth as the "dowry of the state." Çağlar Keyder, "The Consequences of the Exchange of Populations for Turkey," in Renée Hirschon (ed.), *Crossing the Aegean: An Appraisal of the 1923 Compulsory Population Exchange between Greece and Turkey* (New York, Oxford: Berghahn, 2003), 45.

50. Üngör and Polatel, *Confiscation and Destruction.* In the third chapter of this book, Üngör and Polatel analyze the entire legal structure for the confiscation and expropriation of Armenians' properties; however, they misinterpret numerous laws, rules, decrees and regulations concerning the confiscation process. In his article, Taner Akçam critically evaluated this chapter of Üngör and Polatel's book; see Akçam, "Uğur Ümit Üngör and Mehmet Polatel: Confiscation and Destruction: The Young Turk Seizure of Armenian Property," *Armenian Review* 54, no. 1 2 (2013): 51–77. For Üngör and Polatel's response to Akçam's critiques, see Üngör and Polatel, "A Straw Man, a Dead Horse, and a Genocide," *Armenian Review* 54, no. 1–2 (2013): 79–92.

51. *Confiscation and Destruction,* 65. Regarding the construction of the Turkish "national economy," see *Confiscation and Destruction,* 15–41.

52. Esp. ch. 5 and 6 of *Confiscation and Destruction.*

53. Anahid Astoian, *The Pillage of the Century: Expropriation of Armenians in the Ottoman Empire 1914–1923* (Yerevan: Nairi, 2014).

54. Oya Gözel Durmaz, "A City Transformed: War, Demographic Change and Profiteering in Kayseri (1915–1920)" (unpublished PhD diss., Middle East Technical University, 2014), esp. 121–162 (chapter 5).

55. Ellinor Morack, *The Dowry of the State? The Politics of Abandoned Property and the Population Exchange in Turkey, 1921–1945* (Bamberg: University of Bamberg Press, 2017). Also see Murat Koraltürk, *Erken Cumhuriyet Döneminde Ekonominin Türkleştirilmesi* (Istanbul: İletişim, 2011).

56. Akçam and Kurt, *Spirit of the Laws.*

57. Michelle G. Latham, "Economic Motives for Total Genocide: A Comparison of the Armenian, the Holocaust and Rwandan Genocides" (unpublished master's thesis, Boston College, 2000); Aviel Roshwald, *Ethnic Nationalism and the Fall of Empires: Central Europe, Russia and the Middle East, 1914–1923* (London: Routledge, 2001), 108–110; Christian Gerlach, "Nationsbildung im Krieg: Wirtschaftliche Faktoren bei der Vernichtung der Armenier und Beim Mord an den Ungarischen Juden," in *Der Völkermord an den Armeniern und die Shoah,* ed. Hans-Lukas Kieser and Dominik J. Schaller (Zürich: Chronos Verlag, 2002), 347–422; Christian Gerlach, *Extremely Violent Societies: Mass Violence in the Twentieth-Century World* (Cambridge: Cambridge University Press, 2010), 92–119.

58. For studies on the Armenians of Aintab, see Kevork A. Sarafian, *A Briefer History of Aintab: Concise History of the Cultural, Religious, Educational, Political, Industrial and Commercial life of the Armenians of Aintab* (Los Angeles: Union of the Armenians of Aintab, 1957); Sarafian (ed.), *Badmo'wt'iwn Ah'nt'abi Hah'o'c* [History of the Aintab Armenians], vols. I and II (Los Angeles: Union of the Armenians of Aintab, 1953); Yervant Babaian (ed.), *Badmo'wt'iwn Ah'nt'abi Hah'o'c,* vol. III (Los Angeles: Union of the Armenians of Aintab / Abril Publishers, 1994); Alice Shepard Riggs, *Shepard of Aintab* (Princeton, NJ: Gomidas Institute Books / Taderon Press, 2001); Vartan S. Bilezikian, *Apraham Hoja of Aintab* (Winona Lake, Indiana: Light and Life Press, 1952; updated by Thomas and Lila Cosmades, 2008); Stina Katchadourian, *Efronia: An Armenian Love Story* (Princeton, NJ: Gomidas Institute Books, Taderon Press, 2001); Leslie Pierce, *Morality Tales, Law and Gender in the Ottoman Court of Aintab* (Berkeley: University of California Press, 2003); Ramazan Erhan Güllü, *Antep Ermenileri: Sosyal-Siyasi ve Kültürel Hayatı* (Istanbul: IQ Kültür Sanat Yayıncılık, 2010).

59. For a similar and nuanced account dissecting the microdynamics of intercommunal violence in the multiethnic communities of a small town in western Bosnia, Kulen Vakuf, during World War II, see Max Bergholz, *Violence as a Generative Force: Identity, Nationalism, and Memory in a Balkan Community* (Ithaca, NY: Cornell University Press, 2016).

60. Mustafa Aksakal, *The Ottoman Road to War in 1914: The Ottoman Empire and the First World War* (Cambridge: Cambridge University Press, 2010), 9.

61. By "Muslim," I am referring to Turks, Kurds, Circassians, and Arabs living in Aintab at that time.

62. Aksakal, *Ottoman Road to War in 1914*, 9.

63. For a useful overview of the conceptualization of "situational dynamics" within the framework of historical sociology literature, see, for instance, Bennani Chraibi et al., "Towards a Sociology of Revolutionary Situations," *Revue Francaise de Science Politique* 62, no. 5 (2012): 1–29, and Charles Tilly, *From Mobilization to Revolution* (Reading, MA: Addison-Wesley, 1978), 189–222. See also Christopher R. Browning, *Ordinary Men: Reserve Police Battalion 101 and the Final Solution in Poland* (New York: HarperCollins, 2017).

64. Yektan Türkyılmaz, "Rethinking Genocide: Violence and Victimhood in Eastern Anatolia, 1913–1915" (unpublished PhD diss., Duke University, 2011), 18.

65. Türkyılmaz, "Rethinking Genocide: Violence and Victimhood in Eastern Anatolia, 1913–1915," 43.

66. Ali Cenani actively participated in the organization of the Armenians' deportation and confiscation of their properties in Aintab in 1915. Cenani was the president of Aintab's CUP branch after 1908. He was a deputy of Aintab in the Ottoman Parliament during World War I and was expelled to Malta at the end of the war. He played a significant role in forming resistance movements both in Aintab and Adana against French forces between 1919 and 1921. After the introduction of the Turkish Grand National Assembly, he was elected deputy of Aintab in the first, second, and third periods of the Assembly. He served as a minister of commerce in the government of Ali Fethi Okyar and the third governmental period of İsmet İnönü, from 22 November 1924 to 17 May 1926. For detailed information on Ali Cenani and his family, see Cemil Cahit Güzelbey, *Cenaniler* (Istanbul: Ufuk Matbaası, 1984). For Cenani's genocidal activities, see Kurt, "The Curious Case of Ali Cenani Bey: The Story of a Génocidaire," *Patterns of Prejudice* 52, no. 1 (2018): 58–77.

67. Together with Ali Cenani, Ahmed Faik Bey was the main organizer of the deportation of Armenians from Aintab. He played a major role in the liquidation of the movable and immovable properties of Aintab Armenians and made his fortune by acquiring those properties. Bibliothèque armènienne Nubar, Paris [hereafter BNu] / Fonds A. Andonian, P.J. 1 / 3, file 4, Aintab, "The Deportation of Armenians in Aintab," 11–13. He was notoriously known for his harsh and cruel policies against Aintab Armenians. Ahmed Faik Bey was handpicked by Talat to carry out the deportation in Aintab, which he "successfully" fulfilled. After World War I, Ahmed Faik Bey was arrested and handed over to the British Military Authorities to be deported to Malta on 28 May 1919. On Ahmed Faik Bey and his family background, see Nermidil Erner

Binark, *Şakir Paşa Köşkü: Ahmet Bey ve Şakirler* (Istanbul: Remzi Kitapevi, 2000); Erdem Erner, *Davul Sesi: Dışişlerinde 44 Yıl* (Ankara: Bilgi Yayınevi, 1993); İhsan Birinci, "Akan Kan Benimdir," *Hayat Tarih Mecmuası* 2, no. 7 (1966): 63–66.

68. Götz Ally, *Hitler's Beneficiaries: Plunder, Racial War, and the Nazi Welfare State* (New York: Metropolitan Books, 2006); Yitzhak Arad, "Plunder of Jewish Property in the Nazi Occupied Areas of the Soviet Union," *Yad Vashem Studies* 29 (2001): 109–148; A. Barkai, *From Boycott to Annihilation: The Economic Struggle of German Jews 1933–1945* (Hanover, NH: University Press of New England, 1989); Dean, *Robbing the Jews.*

69. Aintab became a district of Aleppo in 1865. Aintab remained a district until 1918, at which point it became a sanjak, which was attached to the Aleppo province. Hale Şıvgın, *19. Yüzyılda Gaziantep* (Ankara: Gaziantep Büyükşehir Belediyesi Yayınları, 1997), 67; Hilmi Bayraktar, "Kurtuluş Harbi Sonrası Ulusal Sınırlarda Meydana Gelen Değişimin Halep ve Gaziantep'e Etkileri," *Tarih ve Toplum Dergisi* 35, no. 206 (2001): 15–21. Aintab gained the status of city in 1924.

70. I accessed relevant primary documents and memoirs housed in the Armenian National Archives and Armenian National Library in Yerevan, Archives of the Haigazian University Library in Beirut, and the Krikor Guerguerian Private Archival Collection at Clark University Library. Sources include Sarafian (ed.), *Badmo'wt'iwn Ah'nt'abi Hah'o'c,* vol. I and II; Babaian (ed.), *Badmo'wt'iwn Ah'nt'abi Hah'o'c,* vol. III; Kevork H. Barsumian, *Badmo'wt'iwn Ah'nt'abi H. H. Tashnagco'wt'iwn 1898–1922* [History of the Aintab Armenian Revolutionary Federation 1898–1922] (Aleppo: Tigris, 1957); A. Gesar, *Ah'nt'abi Ko'h'amardy* [Aintab Self-Defense] (Hayrenik: Boston, 1945); Elie H. Nazarian, *Badmakirq Nazarean Kertasdani (1475–1988)* [History of Nazarian Family] (Beirut: Zartonk Press, 1988); BNu / Fonds A. Andonian, P.J. 1 / 3, file 4, Aintab, "The Deportation of Armenians in Aintab"; Krikor Bogharian, *Orakro'wt'iwn Darakir Geanqis* [Diary of My Life in Exile] in *Ceghasban T'-o'wrqy Vgah'o'wt'iwnner Qagho'wadz Hrashqo'v P'rgo'wadznero'w Zro'h'nere'n* [Genocider Turk: Testimonies Taken from the Accounts of Armenians Who Miraculously Survived] (Beirut: Shirag, 1973); Father Nerses Tavukjian, *Dar'abanqi Orakro'wt'iwn* [Diary of Miserable Days], ed. Toros Toramanian (Beirut: High Type Compugraph—Technopresse, 1991); Sarkis Laleian (ed.), *H'o'wshamadean: No'wiro'wadz Ado'wr H. Lewo'neani, Inqnagensakro'wt'iwn ew Tro'wakner ir Geanqe'n o'w Ko'rdze'n* [Memoir: Dedicated to Adur Levonian, Autobiography and Episodes from His Life and Work] (Beirut: Shirag, 1967); Kersam Aharonian, *H'o'wshamadean Medz Egher'ni* [Memory of Great Crime] (Beirut: Atlas, 1965); Sarkis Balabanian, *Geanqis Daq o'w Bagh Orery:*

Ah'nt'ab, Qe'sab, Hale'b [Hot and Cold Days of My Life: Aintab, Kesap, Aleppo] (Aleppo: Atlas, 1983). I would like to thank Taner Akçam for allowing me to use the Guerguerian archives. These documents were obtained from the Archive of the Armenian Patriarchate of Jerusalem by the priest Krikor Guerguerian. Akçam initiated an archival project to collect numerous materials copied by Guerguerian. He made available the Guerguerian Private Collection through the library database of Clark University in late 2018.

71. *Hürriyet,* 19 September 2006, www.hurriyet.com.tr/gundem/5109117_p.asp, and *Radikal,* 20 September 2006, www.radikal.com.tr/haber.php?haberno=199165; in addition, see http://bianet.org/bianet/bianet/85432-osmanli-arsivleri-acilirsa-resmitez-zayiflar (accessed 8 May 2014). Surprisingly, in his recently published book on documenting the dispossession of Jews, Greeks, and Armenians in Edirne during the 1934 Jewish pogroms and execution of the Wealth Tax in 1941, İlkay Öz managed to access the archives of the Fourteenth Regional Directorate of the Edirne Land Registry and Cadaster after an arduous and long process of vetting and overcoming countless bureaucratic and legal hurdles. Yet this was an exceptional case, perhaps understood when considering that at the time, Öz might have been deemed "harmless" and his work less sensitive by the state authorities, as he did not focus on the genocide period. Previously, records of the Land Registry and Cadaster had not been open to researchers. İlkay Öz, *Mülksüzleştirme ve Türkleştirme: Edirne Örneği* (Istanbul: İletişim, 2020).

1. The 1895 Massacres in Aintab

1. Ussama Makdisi, *Age of Coexistence: The Ecumenical Frame and the Making of the Modern Arab World* (Oakland: University of California Press, 2019), 10; Roderic H. Davison, *Reform in the Ottoman Empire, 1856–1876* (Princeton, NJ: Princeton University Press, 1963).

2. Makdisi, *Age of Coexistence,* 11; Bloxham, *The Great Game of Genocide, Imperialism, Nationalism, and the Destruction of the Ottoman Armenians* (Oxford: Oxford University Press, 2005), 39.

3. Benny Morris and Dror Ze'evi, *The Thirty-Year Genocide: Turkey's Destruction of its Christian Minorities, 1894–1924* (Cambridge, MA: Harvard University Press, 2019), 24.

4. Morris and Ze'evi, *The Thirty-Year Genocide,* 18.

5. David Gutman, *The Politics of Armenian Migration to North America, 1885–1915: Sojourners, Smugglers and Dubious Citizens* (Edinburgh: Edinburgh University Press, 2019), 25.

6. Morris and Ze'evi, *The Thirty-Year Genocide*, 19.

7. Bloxham, *The Great Game of Genocide*, 47; Ryan Gingeras, *Fall of the Sultanate: The Great War and the End of the Ottoman Empire, 1908–1922* (New York: Oxford University Press, 2016), 19–20.

8. Oya Gözel, "The Implementation of the Ottoman Land Code of 1858 in Eastern Anatolia" (unpublished master's thesis, Middle East Technical University, Ankara, 2007); Yücel Terzibaşoğlu, "Landlords, Refugees and Nomads: Struggles for Land around late nineteenth century Ayvalık," *New Perspectives on Turkey* 24 (2001): 51–82.

9. Stephan H. Astourian, "Genocidal Process: Reflections on the Armeno-Turkish Polarization," in *The Armenian Genocide: History, Politics, Ethics*, ed. Richard G. Hovannisian (New York: St. Martin's Press, 1992), 53–79; Bloxham, *The Great Game of Genocide*, 43.

10. Yaşar Tolga Cora, Dzovinar Derderian, and Ali Sipahi (eds.), *The Ottoman East in the Nineteenth Century: Societies, Identities and Politics* (London: I.B. Tauris, 2016).

11. Edip Gölbaşı, "1895–96 Katliamları: Doğu Vilayetlerinde Cemaatler Arası 'Şiddet İklimi' ve Ermeni Karşıtlığı," in *1915: Siyaset, Tehcir ve Soykırım*, ed. Oktay Özel and Fikret Adanır (Istanbul: Tarih Vakfı Yurt Yayınları, 2015), 140; Gölbaşı, "The Official Conceptualization of the Anti-Armenian Riots of 1895–1897: Bureaucratic Terminology, Official Ottoman Narrative, and Discourses of Revolutionary Provocation," *Études arméniennes contemporaines* 10 (2017): 33–63.

12. The most recent and the most nuanced study on Sasun is Owen Miller, "Sasun 1894: Mountains, Missionaries and Massacres at the End of the Ottoman Empire" (unpublished PhD diss., Columbia University, 2015), esp. ch. 4. See also Miller, "Rethinking the Violence in the Sasun Mountains (1893–1894)," *Études arméniennes contemporaines* 10 (2017): 97–125.

13. Selim Deringil, "'The Armenian Question Is Finally Closed': Mass Conversions of Armenians in Anatolia during the Hamidian Massacres of 1895–1897," *Comparative Studies in Society and History* 51, no. 2 (2009): 361.

14. See Jelle Verheij, "'Les Frères de Terre et d'Eau': sur le Rôle des Kurdes dans les Massacres Arméniens de 1894–1896," in *Islam des Kurdes*, ed. M. van Bruinessen and Joyce Blau (Paris: special issue of *Les Annales de l'Autre Islam*, 1998), 225–276; Verheij, "Diyarbekir and the Armenian Crisis of 1895," in *Social Relations in Ottoman Diyarbekir, 1870–1915*, 85–145; Gölbaşı, "1895–96 Katliamları," 140–163; Hans-Lukas Kieser, *Iskalanmış Barış: Doğu Vilayetleri'nde Misyonerlik, Etnik Kimlik ve Devlet, 1839–1938* (Istanbul: İletişim, 2005), 210–220, 332–338, 354–357, 761–766; Edhem Eldem, "26 Ağustos 1896 'Banka Vakası' ve 1896 'Ermeni Olayları,'" *Tarih ve Toplum: Yeni Yaklaşımlar* 5 (2007):

113–146; Robert Melson, "A Theoretical Inquiry into the Armenian Massacres of 1894–1896," *Comparative Studies in Society and History* 24, no. 3 (1982): 481–509; and, for the mass conversion of Armenians during and after the massacres, see Deringil, "The Armenian Question Is Finally Closed," 344–371. See also contributions by Edip Gölbaşı, Ali Sipahi, Owen Miller, Jelle Verheij, Deborah Mayersen, and David Gaunt in "The Massacres of the Hamidian Period (1): Global Narratives and Local Approaches," special issue of *Études arméniennes contemporaines* 10 (2017).

15. İsmail Altınöz, "Dulkadir Eyaletinin Kuruluşunda Antep Şehri (XVI. Yüzyıl)," in *Gaziantep—Cumhuriyetin 75. Yılına Armağan*, ed. Yusuf Küçükdağ (Gaziantep: Gaziantep Üniversitesi Vakfı Kültür Yayınları, 1999), 124.

16. Altınöz, "Dulkadir Eyaletinin Kuruluşunda Antep Şehri," 124–125; see also Yusuf Halaçoğlu, *Ermeni Tehciri ve Gerçekler (1914–1918)* (Ankara: TTK, 2001), 7.

17. Leslie Pierce, *Morality Tales: Law and Gender in the Ottoman Court of Aintab* (Berkeley: University of California Press, 2003), 20.

18. Hülya Canbakal, "Aintab at the End of the 17th Century: A Study of Notables and Urban Politics" (unpublished PhD diss., Harvard University, History and Middle Eastern Studies, 1999), 42.

19. Pierce, *Morality Tales*, 20; Hale Şıvgın, "19. Yüzyılın İlk Yarısında Ayıntap," *OTAM—Ankara Üniversitesi Osmanlı Tarihi Araştırma ve Uygulama Merkezi Dergisi*, no. 11 (2000): 536; Stephan H. Astourian, "Testing World-System Theory, Cilicia (1830s–1890s): Armenian-Turkish Polarization and the Ideology of Modern Ottoman Historiography" (unpublished PhD diss., University of California, Los Angeles, 1996), 151, 206–207.

20. Kevork A. Sarafian, *A Briefer History of Aintab: A Concise History of the Cultural, Religious, Educational, Political, Industrial and Commercial Life of the Armenians of Aintab* (Los Angeles: Union of the Armenians of Aintab, 1957), 8.

21. Şıvgın, "19. Yüzyılın İlk Yarısında Ayıntap," 503–553.

22. Canbakal, "Aintab at the End of the 17th Century," 112.

23. Şıvgın, "19. Yüzyılın İlk Yarısında Ayıntap," 518, 520.

24. Mahmut Oğuz Göğüş, "Gaziantep'in Dününden: 1881'de Antep'te Neler Vardı?" *Gaziantep'i Tanıtıyoruz*, no. 2 (1962): 25.

25. Mehmet Solmaz and Hulusi Yetkin, *Küçük Hafız ve Mustafa Yavuz* (Gaziantep: Gaziantep Kültür Derneği Yayınları, 1965), 8.

26. Kerim Tiryaki, "Gaziantep'teki Ermeniler (1895–1923)" (unpublished master's thesis, Gaziantep Üniversitesi Sosyal Bilimler Enstitüsü, 2003), 40; Celal Pekdoğan, "Antep ve Ermeniler (1895–1922)," *ASAM Ermeni Araştırmaları*

Enstitüsü, Ermeni Araştırmaları 1. Türkiye Kongresi Bildirileri, vol. III, 2003, 144.

27. Bülent Çukurova, "Antep'te Ermeni Ulusçuluğunun Doğuşunda Amerikalılar ve Kolejin Etkisi," *Ankara Üniversitesi Türk İnkılap Tarihi Enstitüsü Atatürk Yolu Dergisi,* no. 40 (2007): 617.

28. Bülent Çukurova, "Antep'te Ermeni Ulusçuluğunun Doğuşunda Amerikalılar ve Kolejin Etkisi," 617. According to Krikor Bogharian, in 1883 the followers of the Armenian Apostolic Church numbered 1,600 families (that is, ten thousand persons), and the number of schoolchildren was 550. In general, the 2,000 Armenian families constituted one-third of the Aintab population at that time. See Krikor Bogharian, "Statistical Notes," in *Badmo'wt'iwn Ah'nt'abi Hah'o'c,* vol. I, 779.

29. *Salname-i Vilayet-i Halep, Ayıntap Kazası,* 1313 / 1895 (Ankara: Global Strateji Enstitüsü, 2007), 187. There were 11,703 Gregorian Armenians, 3,528 Protestants, and 307 Catholics. *Salname-i Vilayet-i Halep, Ayıntap Kazası,* 187.

30. Sarafian, *A Briefer History of Aintab,* 118; Solmaz and Yetkin, *Küçük Hafız ve Mustafa Yavuz,* 55; Hulusi Yetkin, *Gaziantep Tarihi ve Davaları* (Gaziantep: Yeni Matbaa, 1968), 35.

31. *Gaziantep Kültür Envanteri* (Gaziantep: Gaziantep Valiliği Yayını, 2005), 66–68.

32. Cemil Cahit Güzelbey, *Gaziantep Şer'i Mahkeme Sicilleri* (Gaziantep: Gaziantep Kültür Derneği ve Broşürü, 1970); Şakir Sabri Yener, "Gaziantep Şer'iye Mahkemesi Sicillerinden Notlar: I," *Gaziantep Kültür Dergisi* 4, no. 39 (1961): 10–11; Uğurol Barlas, "Halep Salnamelerinin Gaziantep ile İlgili Kısımları," *Gaziantep Kültür Dergisi* 6, no. 61 (1963): 11–12.

33. Mehmet Ali Yıldırım, "1895–1896 İsyanları Sırasında Ayntab'da Ermeniler ve Hınçak Cemiyeti," *Ankara Üniversitesi Dil ve Tarih-Coğrafya Fakültesi Tarih Bölümü Tarih Araştırmaları Dergisi* 27, no. 44 (2008): 170.

34. Hülya Canbakal, "Residential Topography and Social Hierarchy in 17th Century Ayntab," in *Essays in Honor of Aptullah Kuran,* ed. Çiğdem Kafesçioğlu and L. Thys-Şenocak (Istanbul: Yapı Kredi Yayınları, 1999), 161–170.

35. V. Gül Cephanecigil, "Preliminary remarks on the Late Ottoman Churches in Aintab," *A | Z ITU Journal of the Faculty of Architecture* 12, no. 2 (2015): 132.

36. Ali Nadi Ünler, "Gaziantep Ermenileri," *Gaziantep Kültür Dergisi* 13, no. 7 (1972): 151–152; Hulusi Yetkin, *Gaziantep için Söylenenler: Gazianteplilerin Dünya ve Hayat Görüşleri ve Gaziantep'in Geleceği* (Gaziantep: Yeni Matbaa, 1969), 48; Kevork H. Barsumian, *Badmo'wt'iwn Ah'nt'abi H. H. Tashnagco'wt'iwn 1898–1922* (Aleppo: Tigris, 1957), 17; Sarafian, *A Briefer History*

of Aintab, 119; Stina Katchadourian, *The Letters of Theresa Huntington Ziegler, Missionary to Turkey, 1898–1915* (Princeton, NJ: Gomidas Institute Books / Taderon Press, 1999), 19. Interestingly enough, after Armenians left Aintab in 1922, it was almost impossible to identify any people from the aforementioned professions; see Mithat Enç, *Selamlık Sohbetleri* (Istanbul: Ötüken Neşriyat, 2007), 121–123.

37. Ünler, "Gaziantep Ermenileri," 152.

38. Barsumian, *Badmo'wt'iwn Ah'nt'abi H. H. Tashnagco'wt'iwn 1898–1922,* 17.

39. Sarafian, *A Briefer History of Aintab,* 105–112; *Badmo'wt'iwn Ah'nt'abi Hah'o'c* vol. I, 775–791.

40. *Badmo'wt'iwn Ah'nt'abi Hah'o'c,* vol I, 665–670; 740–753.

41. Sarafian, *A Briefer History of Aintab,* 87–91; *Badmo'wt'iwn Ah'nt'abi Hah'o'c,* vol. I, 689–712.

42. Sarafian, *A Briefer History of Aintab,* 81.

43. For example, in 1902, Sarkis Agha and Leylekian Effendis were administrative members of the town council. *Salname-i Vilayet-i Halep, Ayıntab Kazası,* 1320 / 102, 229.

44. Ramazan Erhan Güllü, *Antep Ermenileri: Sosyal-Siyasi ve Kültürel Hayatı* (Ankara: IQ Yayınları, 2010), 72.

45. For more information about the history of the Apostolic Church in Aintab, see *Badmo'wt'iwn Ah'nt'abi Hah'o'c,* vol. I, 335–340. This Gregorian church, the Church of Aintab, was one of the greatest in Turkey. The architect was Sarkis Bey Balian of Istanbul, the royal architect of the sultan. After the Armenians were expelled from and later left Aintab, Saint Mary's Church was used as a prison by the Kemalist government in 1921. Later, it was turned into Kurtuluş Camii (Liberation Mosque) without any change in its architecture. *Gaziantep Kültür Envanteri,* 124–125; see also Chapter 6.

46. The Franciscan monastery was also built in 1884. The Franciscans in 1896 had their own schools for boys and girls. In the Franciscan schools, the French language was taught well. In 1903, the Franciscan church known as Kendirli Church was built. Sarafian, *A Briefer History of Aintab,* 79. After no Armenians were left in Aintab, Kendirli Church was turned into a clubhouse for teachers in Aintab in the Republican period. *Gaziantep Kültür Envanteri,* 145–146; see also Chapter 6.

47. Sarafian, *A Briefer History of Aintab,* 13–14.

48. Sarafian, *A Briefer History of Aintab,* 12–13.

49. Uygur Kocabaşoğlu, *Anadolu'daki Amerika, Kendi Belgeleriyle 19. Yüzyılda Osmanlı İmparatorluğu'ndaki Amerikan Misyoner Okulları* (Ankara: İmge, 2000), 70; Sarafian, *A Briefer History of Aintab,* 46; Frank Andrews

Stone, "The Educational 'Awakening' Among the American Evangelicals of Aintab, Turkey: 1845–1915," *Armenian Review* 35, no. 1 (1982): 30–52.

50. Sarafian, *A Briefer History of Aintab,* 51; Stone, "The Educational 'Awakening' among the American Evangelicals of Aintab, Turkey: 1845–1915," 32; Faruk Taşkın, "Amerikan Misyoner Okullarından 'Merkezi Türkiye Koleji' (1876–1924)" (unpublished PhD diss., Mersin Üniversitesi Sosyal Bilimler Enstitüsü, 2007), 84.

51. Sarafian, *A Briefer History of Aintab,* 51.

52. Sarafian, *A Briefer History of Aintab,* 51.

53. Taşkın, "Amerikan Misyoner Okullarından 'Merkezi Türkiye Koleji' (1876–1924)," 83; Güllü, *Antep Ermenileri,* 91. By the turn of 1913, there were thirty-eight places for worship and 7,580 congregants visiting these places. Taşkın, "Amerikan Misyoner Okullarından 'Merkezi Türkiye Koleji' (1876–1924)," 83. For well-detailed information regarding the history of the religious institutions and churches of the Armenian Protestant community, see Sarafian, *Badmo'wt'iwn Ah'nt'abi Hah'o'c,* vol. I, 500–511.

54. Sarafian, *A Briefer History of Aintab,* 77.

55. Leon Arpee, "A Century of Armenian Protestantism," *Church History* 5, no. 2 (1936): 152, cited in Judd W. Kennedy, "American Missionaries in Turkey and Northern Syria and the Development of Central Turkey and Aleppo Colleges, 1874–1967" (unpublished master's thesis, College of William and Mary, 2008), 31.

56. Emin Baki Adaş, "Antep'in 'Protestan Tarihi': 19. Yüzyıl Osmanlı Taşrasında Din ve Etnisite," in *'Ta Ezelden Taşkındır' . . . Antep* ed. Mehmet Nuri Güntekin (Istanbul: İletişim, 2011), 265.

57. American missionaries arrived in Aintab around 1845–1846 through the leadership of Dr. Azariah Smith. See Sarafian, *A Briefer History of Aintab,* 56, 83; Taşkın, "Amerikan Misyoner Okullarından 'Merkezi Türkiye Koleji' (1876–1924)," 86–92.

58. Turan Baytop, *Antep'in Öncü Hekimleri: Merkezi Türkiye Koleji Tıp Bölümü ve Antep Amerikan Hastanesi* (Istanbul: SEV Yayınları, 2003), 25; Uğurol Barlas, *Gaziantep'in Yakın Tarihi Üzerine Araştırmalar* (Istanbul: Hilmi Barlas Eğitim Vakfı, 2006), 23; Taşkın, "Amerikan Misyoner Okullarından 'Merkezi Türkiye Koleji' (1876–1924)," 116; Faruk Taşkın, "Antep'te Bir Misyoner Üniversitesi: Merkezi Türkiye Koleji," *History Studies* 4, no. 4 (2012): 417.

59. Professor Alexan Bezjian, a senior member of the faculty at the college until his death in 1913, was intimately involved in the founding of the college and was for many years an influential member of its board. *The American Board of Commissioners for Foreign Missions* (hereafter *ABCFM*), Harvard

University, Houghton Library, Boston: 16.9.1.6.1 Central Turkey Mission, Miscellaneous, 1817–1919, unit 5, vol. 1, reel 667–139. He was a native Armenian who studied at Bebek Seminary under Cyrus Hamlin and abroad at Yale, where he taught physics and chemistry. See Stone, "The Educational 'Awakening' among the American Evangelicals of Aintab, Turkey: 1845–1915," 37; Sarafian, *A Briefer History of Aintab,* 52; Baytop, *Antep'in Öncü Hekimleri,* 14.

60. Kennedy, "American Missionaries in Turkey and Northern Syria,"; Adaş, "Antep'in 'Protestan Tarihi'," 263–293; Taşkın, "Amerikan Misyoner Okullarından 'Merkezi Türkiye Koleji' (1876–1924)"; Stone, "The Educational 'Awakening' among the American Evangelicals of Aintab, Turkey: 1845–1915," 30–52.

61. Kennedy, "American Missionaries in Turkey and Northern Syria"; Stone, "The Educational 'Awakening' among the American Evangelicals of Aintab, Turkey: 1845–1915"; *ABCFM,* "The Missionary Herald," *APS Online* 70, no. 3 (1874): 73; Nazarian, *Badmakirq Nazarean Kertasdani (1475–1988),* 115–127, 207–208; *Badmo'wt'iwn Ah'nt'abi Hah'o'c,* vol. I, 637–897; Sarafian, *A Briefer History of Aintab,* 81–112; Barsumian, *Badmo'wt'iwn Ah'nt'abi H. H. Tashnagco'wt'iwn 1898–1922,* 18–19; A. Gesar, *Ah'nt'abi Ko'h'amardy,* 20–25.

62. BOA. İ.HUS. 7 / 1310.C / 26 (16 Kânûnıevvel 1308–8. C.1310–28 December 1892); BOA.A.MKT.MHM. No. 749 / lef 6, Sadaret [the Grand Vezirate] to Ministry of Education 17 Kânûnıevvel 1308 (29 December 1892).

63. BOA.Y.PRK.DH. No. 5 / 83 lef 26, Abidin Pasha, governor of Ankara, to Mâbeyn Baş Kitâbet, 9 Kânûnısâni 1308 (21 January 1893).

64. Sarkis Y. Karaian, "On the Number of Armenians in Aintab in 1914," in *Badmo'wt'iwn Ah'nt'abi Hah'o'c,* vol. III, 15; Hulusi Yetkin (ed.), *Gençlere Başarı Yolu: Cemil Alevli'nin Hayatı ve Hayat Görüşü* (Gaziantep: Işık Matbaası, 1963), 16.

65. Şıvgın, *19. Yüzyılda Antep,* 70–71; Solmaz Yetkin, *Küçük Hafız ve Mustafa Yavuz,* 55; Yetkin, *Gaziantep Tarihi ve Davaları,* 35–36.

66. Bülent Çukurova, "1922 Yılında Ermenilerin Antep'ten Suriye'ye Göçlerinde Sosyo-Ekonomik Faktörler," *ASAM Ermeni Araştırmaları Enstitüsü, Ermeni Araştırmaları 1. Türkiye Kongresi Bildirileri,* vol. III, 2003, 167.

67. Rev. Edwin Munsell Bliss, *Turkey and the Armenian Atrocities* (Philadelphia: Edgewood Publishing Company, 1896), 41.

68. Donald Bloxham and Fatma Müge Göçek, "The Armenian Genocide," in *The Historiography of Genocide,* ed. Dan Stone (New York: Palgrave-Macmillan, 2008), 365.

69. The quote appears in Bekir Sıtkı Baykal, *Şark Buhranı ve Sabah Gazetesi* (Ankara: Ankara Üniversitesi, 1948), cited in Çetin Yetkin, *Türk Halk Hareketleri ve Devrimleri Tarihi* (Istanbul: Say Yayınları, 1984), 303.

70. Mark Levene, "The Changing Face of Mass Murder: Massacre, Genocide, and Postgenocide," *International Social Science Journal* 54, no. 174 (2002): 444.

71. Yves Ternon, *The Armenians: History of a Genocide* (Ann Arbor, MI: Caravan Books, 1990), 51; Kieser, *Iskalanmış Barış,* 166.

72. Arman J. Kirakossian, *British Diplomacy and the Armenian Question from the 1830s to 1914* (Princeton, NJ: Gomidas Institute Books, 2003), xii.

73. Miller, "Sasun 1894," 154–230.

74. Verheij, "Diyarbekir and the Armenian Crisis of 1895," 94. Also see Bloxham, *The Great Game of Genocide,* 51–52.

75. Christopher J. Walker, *Armenia the Survival of a Nation* (London: Routledge, 1990), 136–151; Verheij, "'Les Frères de Terre et d'Eau,'" 238–246; Verheij, "Die armenischen Massaker von 1894–1896: Anatomie und Hintergründe eine Krise," in *Die Armenische Frage und die Schweiz (1896–1923),* ed. Hans-Lukas Kieser (Zurich: Chronos Verlag, 1999), 81–84; Verheij, "Diyarbekir and the Armenian Crisis of 1895," 94.

76. In April 1895, Great Britain prepared a reform proposed for Western Armenia "which provided de facto autonomy of the region under the auspices of the European powers"; see Arman J. Kirakossian, *The Armenian Massacres 1894–1896: U.S. Media Testimony* (Detroit: Wayne State University Press, 2004), 25.

77. Mehmet Cebeci, *Die deutsch-türkischen Beziehungen in der Epoche Abdülhamids II. (1876–1908): Die Rolle Deutschlands in der türkischen Aussenpolitik* (Marburg, Germany: Tectum, 2010), 308.

78. Manug Pancardjian, "Ah'nt'abi Ch'arti" [The Aintab Massacre], in *Badmo'wt'iwn Ah'nt'abi Hah'o'c,* vol. I, 906; Sarkis Balabanian, *Geanqis Daq o'w Bagh Orery: Ah'nt'ab, Qe'sab, Hale'b* [Hot and Cold Days of My Life: Aintab, Kesap, Halep] (Aleppo: Atlas, 1983), 30.

79. Vahakn Dadrian, *The History of Armenian Genocide: Ethnic Conflict from the Balkans and Anatolia to the Caucasus* (Oxford: Berghahn Books, 2004), 61–110; Raymond Kévorkian, *The Armenian Genocide: A Complete History* (London: I.B. Tauris, 2011), 10–11; Richard Hovannisian, "The Historical Dimensions of the Armenian Question, 1878–1923," in *The Armenian Genocide in Perspective,* ed. Richard Hovannisian (New Brunswick, NJ: Transaction Books, 1986), 24. For a detailed study on the role of British diplomacy and policies on the Armenian question and reforms, see Kirakossian, *British Diplomacy and the Armenian Question from the 1830s to 1914.*

80. Walker, *Armenia the Survival of a Nation,* 136–151; Ternon, *The Armenians,* 61.

81. See the extensive bibliography in George N. Shirinian, "The Armenian Massacres of 1894–1897: A Bibliography," *Armenian Review* 47, no. 1–2 (2001): 113–164.

82. Kieser, *Iskalanmış Barış*, 200; Bloxham, *The Great Game of Genocide*, 55.

83. Bloxham, *The Great Game of Genocide*, 55; Kieser, *Der verpasste Friede: Mission, Ethnie und Staat in den Ostprovinzen der Tü rkei 1839–1938* (Zurich: Chronos, 2000), 243–247.

84. Bloxham, *The Great Game of Genocide*, 55.

85. Barsumian, *Badmo'wt'iwn Ah'nt'abi H. H. Tashnagco'wt'iwn 1898–1922*, 20; *Badmo'wt'iwn Ah'nt'abi Hah'o'c*, vol. I, 936.

86. Barsumian, *Badmo'wt'iwn Ah'nt'abi H. H. Tashnagco'wt'iwn 1898–1922*, 20.

87. *Badmo'wt'iwn Ah'nt'abi Hah'o'c*, vol. I, 937.

88. Dadrian, *The History of Armenian Genocide*, 128.

89. Verheij, "Diyarbekir and the Armenian Crisis of 1895," 96. Also see Cebeci, *Die deutsch-türkischen Beziehungen*, 313, and Stefan Ihrig, *Justifying Genocide: German and the Armenians from Bismarck to Hitler* (Cambridge, MA: Harvard University Press, 2016), 38.

90. *Blue Book* in Turkey No. 8 (1896), Doc. No. 10, enclosure, 13, and Aleppo Consul Henry Barnham's lengthy report, 212–222, cited in Dadrian, *History of Armenian Genocide*, 129.

91. Dadrian, *The History of Armenian Genocide*, 129.

92. Dadrian, *The History of Armenian Genocide*, 129.

93. *Badmo'wt'iwn Ah'nt'abi Hah'o'c*, vol. I, 934.

94. Soghomon B. Bastadjian, "Zĕyt'uni Absdamput'iwnĕ ew Hnch'agean Gusagts'ut'iwnĕ [Zeitun Revolt and Hunchakian Party]," in *Badmo'wt'iwn Ah'nt'abi Hah'o'c*, vol. I, 936.

95. Nazarian, *Badmakirq Nazarean Kertasdani (1475–1988)*, 140, 145; Barsumian, *Badmo'wt'iwn Ah'nt'abi H. H. Tashnagco'wt'iwn 1898–1922*, 33; *Badmo'wt'iwn Ah'nt'abi Hah'o'c*, vol. I, 934.

96. *Badmo'wt'iwn Ah'nt'abi Hah'o'c*, vol. I, 936. Nazarian, *Badmakirq Nazarean Kertasdani (1475 1988)*, 162.

97. FO 195 / 1883, Barnham to Currie, November 1895.

98. Rev. Fuller, Aintab, to Chas. E. Swett, 9 May 1895, *ABCFM* 16.9.5, unit 5, vol. 12, reel 655; Morris and Ze'evi, *The Thirty-Year Genocide*, 93.

99. Balabanian, *Geanqis Daq o'w Bagh Orery*, 32.

100. *Badmo'wt'iwn Ah'nt'abi Hah'o'c*, vol. I, 907.

101. Balabanian, *Geanqis Daq o'w Bagh Orery*, 30.

102. F. D. Shepard to James Barton, 9 October 1895, *ABCFM* 16.9.5, unit 5, vol. 14, reel 659.

103. FO 195 / 1883, Barnham to Currie, November 1895; and Poche to Terrell, 2 November 1895, *FRUS* 1895, vol. II, 1346–1347.

104. Fuller to Smith, 5 November 1895, *ABCFM* 16.9.5, unit 5, vol. 21, reel 667; Morris and Ze'evi, *The Thirty-Year Genocide*, 93.

105. Fuller to Clark, 23 November 1895 and Fuller to Lord Bryce, 5 March 1896, both in *ABCFM* 16.9.5, unit 5, vol. 12, reel 655. See also Rev. George H. Filian, *Armenia and Her People* (Hartford, CT: American Publishing Company, 1896), 286–287.

106. FO 195 / 1883, Barnham to Currie, November 1895. BOA.A.MKT.MHM 647 / 9 and BOA.Y.PRK.ASK 108 / 55 5 Teşrinisânî 1311 (17 November 1895).

107. Fuller to Clark, 23 November 1895, *ABCFM* 16.9.5, unit 5, vol. 12, reel 655; see also Filian, *Armenia and Her People,* 287.

108. FO 195 / 1932, Barnham to Currie, 21 January 1896.

109. FO 195 / 1932, Barnham to Currie, 21 January 1896.

110. To be deployed in every district of the Empire, Sultan Mahmud II introduced redif battalions in 1834. For detailed information about the history of these battalions, see Musa Çadırcı, "Anadolu'da Redif Askeri Teşkilatının Kuruluşu," *Ankara Üniversitesi Dil Tarih Coğrafya Fakültesi Tarih Araştırmaları Dergisi* 8, no. 14 (1963): 63–75.

111. BOA.A.MKT.MHM 648 / 10, 31 Teşrinevvel 1311 (12 November 1895).

112. BOA.A.MKT.MHM 646 / 33; 648 / 10, 2 Teşrinisânî 1311 (14 November 1895).

113. *Badmo'wt'iwn Ah'nt'abi Hah'o'c,* vol. I, 915.

114. *Badmo'wt'iwn Ah'nt'abi Hah'o'c,* vol. I, 912; Avedis Nakashian, *A Man Who Found a Country* (New York: Crowell, 1940), 160–161. Avedis Nakashian was born in Aintab and finished medical school in the College. During the massacres in 1895, he was a doctor in Urfa and paid a visit to Aintab, where his entire family resided. As opposed to firsthand testimonial accounts of Sarafian and Nakashian, in his report to Mr. Terrell (US minister in Istanbul), the missionary Rev. Saunders stated that the majority of the Muslim notables had always been friendly to them. In the same report, Saunders also expressed gratitude to the Aintab soldiers by saying that "what they did or did not in the city is not our affair. They certainly protected us well on Saturday, the 16th." See Saunders to Terrell, 27 November 1895, *FRUS* 1895, vol. II, 1389. Saunders also offered his special gratitude to the Beridjik (Birecik) contingent, so as to protect missionaries in the Central Turkey College and the American Hospital on Saturday the 16th and Sunday the 17th (Saunders to Terrell, 27 November 1895, 1390).

115. Mihran Der Melkonian, *Geanqi ew Maho'wan Mich'ew* [Between Life and Death] (Beirut: Aravot Press, 1939), 4; Khatchadourian, *Efronia: An Armenian Love Story,* 27.

116. FO 195 / 1883, Barnham to Currie, November 1895.

117. BOA.A.MKT.MHM 648 / 10, 4 Teşrinisânî 1311 (16 November 1895).

118. FO 195 / 1883, Sanders to Barnham, 11 December 1895.

119. Terrell to Olney, 17 November 1895, *FRUS* 1895, vol. II, 1341; Saunders to Terrell, 27 November 1895, *FRUS* 1895, vol. II, 1388.

120. Filian, *Armenia and Her People,* 289.

121. Nakashian, *A Man Who Found a Country,* 160; Filian, *Armenia and Her People,* 289.

122. Emre Barlas, *Doktor Mecid Barlas'ın Anıları* (Istanbul: Cinius Yayınları, 2010), 12.

123. *Badmo'wt'iwn Ah'nt'abi Hah'o'c,* vol. I, 907.

124. *Badmo'wt'iwn Ah'nt'abi Hah'o'c,* vol. I, 907; Melkonian, *Geanqi ew Maho'wan Mich'ew,* 4.

125. Fred D. Shepard, "Personal Experience in Turkish Massacres and Relief Work," *The Journal of Race Development* 1, no. 3 (1911): 319; Kirakossian, *Armenian Massacres 1894–1896,* 119.

126. Fuller to Clark, 23 November 1895, *ABCFM* 16.9.5, unit 5, vol. 12, reel 655; Shepard, "Personal Experience in Turkish Massacres and Relief Work," 319; Bliss, *Turkey and the Armenian Atrocities,* 451; Riggs, *Shepard of Aintab,* 109; Filian, *Armenia and Her People,* 289.

127. *Badmo'wt'iwn Ah'nt'abi Hah'o'c,* vol. I, 915–916.

128. *Badmo'wt'iwn Ah'nt'abi Hah'o'c,* vol. I, 909.

129. "Pasha" was the title of a man of high rank or office in the Ottoman Empire, given to soldiers and high civil officials. Peasants from the surrounding villages of Aintab referred to members of Aintab's wealthy families, such as the Babigians and Niziblians, as "Pasha" when talking about them.

130. *Badmo'wt'iwn Ah'nt'abi Hah'o'c,* vol. I, 909.

131. FO 195 / 1932, Barnham to Currie, 21 January 1896.

132. FO 195 / 1932, Barnham to Currie, 21 January 1896.

133. *Badmo'wt'iwn Ah'nt'abi Hah'o'c,* vol. I, 910; Melkonian, *Geanqi ew Maho'wan Mich'ew,* 3; Filian, *Armenia and Her People,* 289.

134. BOA.A.MKT.MHM 647 / 9, 5 Teşrinisânî 1311 (17 November 1895).

135. BOA.A.MKT.MHM 647 / 9, 4 Teşrinisânî 1311 (16 November 1895).

136. F.D. Shepard to Alice Shepard, 18 November 1895; Fuller to Clark, 23 November 1895, *ABCFM* 16.9.5, unit 5, vol. 12, reel 655; Bliss, *Turkey and the Armenian Atrocities,* 452.

137. Bliss, *Turkey and the Armenian Atrocities,* 452.

138. Bliss, *Turkey and the Armenian Atrocities,* 452.

139. Shepard, "Personal Experience in Turkish Massacres and Relief Work," 320.

140. Nazarian, *Badmakirq Nazarean Kertasdani (1475–1988),* 127.

141. Shepard, "Personal Experience in Turkish Massacres and Relief Work," 320.

142. Bliss, *Turkey and the Armenian Atrocities,* 452.

143. *Badmo'wt'iwn Ah'nt'abi Hah'o'c,* vol. I, 916.

144. BOA.A.MKT.MHM 647 / 15, 7 Teşrinisânî 1311 (19 November 1895).

145. BOA.Y.A.HUS 304 / 44, 7 Teşrinisânî 1311 (19 November 1895).

146. Kirakossian, *The Armenian Massacres 1894–1896, U.S. Media Testimony,* 121.

147. Fuller to Smith, 25 December 1895, *ABCFM* 16.9.5.

148. *Badmo'wt'iwn Ah'nt'abi Hah'o'c* vol. I, 908; J. Rendel Harris & Helen Harris, *Letters from the Scenes of the Recent Massacres in Armenia* (London: James Nisbet, 1897), 32.

149. *Badmo'wt'iwn Ah'nt'abi Hah'o'c,* vol. I, 913.

150. For a short biography of Dayızâde Ahmed Agha, see Şakir Sabri Yener, *Gaziantep'in Yakın Tarihinden Notlar, Gaziantep Vilayet Merkezinin 76 Sene Evveline Kadar Olan Mahalli Maarif Hareketlerinin Kısa Bir Tarihçesi* (Gaziantep: Gaziyurt Matbaası, 1968), 54–68. Dayızâde Ahmed Agha also actively participated in the deportation of Aintab Armenians and the depredation process of their properties, wealth, and assets in 1915–1917. He even founded a school on an Armenian property in the Akyol district.

151. F. D. Shepard to Alice Shepard, 18 November 1895, *ABCFM* 16.9.5, unit 5, vol. 14, reel 659; Bliss, *Turkey and the Armenian Atrocities,* 453.

152. Bliss, *Turkey and the Armenian Atrocities,* 451.

153. Bliss, *Turkey and the Armenian Atrocities,* 451.

154. Barlas, *Doktor Mecid Barlas'ın Anıları,* 12–13; Yervant Kuchukian, *Hariwr Zham Ah'nt'abi: H'o'wsher ew Dbawo'ro'wt'iwnner* [100 Hours in Aintab: Memories and Impressions] (Beirut: Aravot, 1958), 27.

155. FO 195 / 1883, Barnham to Currie, November 1895.

156. *Badmo'wt'iwn Ah'nt'abi Hah'o'c* vol. I, 912.

157. Balabanian, *Geanqis Daq o'w Bagh Orery,* 33.

158. *Badmo'wt'iwn Ah'nt'abi Hah'o'c,* vol. I, 913.

159. *Badmo'wt'iwn Ah'nt'abi Hah'o'c,* vol. I, 913. The same Mazlum Effendi also helped numerous Armenians during the 1915 Armenian deportation.

160. *Badmo'wt'iwn Ah'nt'abi Hah'o'c,* vol. I, 913.

161. *Badmo'wt'iwn Ah'nt'abi Hah'o'c,* vol. I, 901.

162. *Badmo'wt'iwn Ah'nt'abi Hah'o'c,* vol. I, 908.

163. *Badmo'wt'iwn Ah'nt'abi Hah'o'c,* vol. I, 908.

164. Barlas, *Doktor Mecid Barlas'ın Anıları,* 12–13; Kuchukian, *Hariwr Zham Ah'nt'abi: H'o'wsher ew Dbawo'ro'wt'iwnner,* 27. Interestingly enough, the same Patpatzâde (both Nuri and Bahtiyar Beys) became one of the major perpetrators during the deportation and destruction of the Armenians, as well as one of the main profiteers of plunder of their wealth in 1915.

165. *Badmo'wt'iwn Ah'nt'abi Hah'o'c,* vol. I, 909.

166. *Badmo'wt'iwn Ah'nt'abi Hah'o'c,* vol. I, 910.

167. Bliss, *Turkey and the Armenian Atrocities,* 453.

168. Bliss, *Turkey and the Armenian Atrocities,* 453.

169. Filian, *Armenia and Her People,* 290.

170. Melkonian, *Geanqi ew Maho'wan Mich'ew,* 3.

171. Saunders to Terrell, 27 November 1895, *FRUS,* 1895, vol. II, 1388–1390.

172. For instance, on 16 November 1895, the exact date when the Armenian pogroms began in the marketplace of Aintab, Sadaret sent a ciphered telegraph to Aleppo Province ordering the protection of the Americans and taking every single precaution, so as to maintain security and order in Aintab; see BOA.A.MKT.MHM 647 / 5 lef 4, 4 Teşrinisânî 1311 (16 November 1895). Moreover, Aleppo governor Hasan Pasha asked Sadaret to send reinforcement military units to protect American schools, consulates, and other foreign houses; see BOA.A.MKT.MHM 647 / 9, lef 5, 8 Teşrinisânî 1311 (20 November 1895). Also see BOA.HR.SYS 73 / 49, 29 December 1895.

173. Terrell to Tevfik Pasha, 11 December 1895, *FRUS* 1895, vol. II, 1390; BOA.HR.SYS 73 / 44, 5 December 1895; BOA.HR.SYS 73 / 46, 12 December 1895.

174. FO 195 / 1932, Barnham to Currie, 21 January 1896.

175. Shepard, "Personal Experience in Turkish Massacres and Relief Work," 320.

176. *Badmo'wt'iwn Ah'nt'abi Hah'o'c* vol. I, 932; Riggs, *Shepard of Aintab,* 110; Saunders to Terrell, 27 November 1895, *FRUS* 1895, vol. II, 1389; Filian, *Armenia and Her People,* 290.

177. Shepard, "Personal Experience in Turkish Massacres and Relief Work," 320; Bliss, *Turkey and the Armenian Atrocities,* 451.

178. Shepard, "Personal Experience in Turkish Massacres and Relief Work," 320; Riggs, *Shepard of Aintab,* 109; Bliss, *Turkey and the Armenian Atrocities,* 451; Harris & Harris, *Letters from the Scenes of the Recent Massacres in Armenia,* 36; Kirakossian, *The Armenian Massacres 1894–1896, U.S. Media Testimony,* 120. Also, see telegraphs of American and Belgium Consulates in Istanbul regarding security of the lives and properties of Americans in Aintab, BOA.A.MKT.MHM 647 / 5 lef 2–3, American Embassy to Ministry of Foreign Affairs, BOA.HR.SYS 73 / 15, 5 Teşrinisânî 1311 (17 November 1895).

179. Terrell to Tevfik Pasha, 11 December 1895, *FRUS* 1895, vol. II, 1390; BOA.HR.SYS 73 / 44, 5 December 1895; BOA.HR.SYS 73 / 46, 12 December 1895.

180. Bliss, *Turkey and the Armenian Atrocities,* 451; Saunders to Terrell, 27 November 1895, *FRUS* 1895, vol. II, 1388.

181. Barlas, *Doktor Mecid Barlas'ın Anıları,* 12; Göğüş, *İlk İnsanlardan Bugüne Çeşitli Yönleriyle Gaziantep;* Yener, *Gaziantep Yakın Tarihinden Notlar,* 368;

Bliss, *Turkey and the Armenian Atrocities,* 455; Harris & Harris. *Letters from the Scenes of the Recent Massacres in Armenia,* 32.

182. *Badmo'wt'iwn Ah'nt'abi Hah'o'c* vol. I, 923; Bliss, *Turkey and the Armenian Atrocities,* 455–456; 553; F.D. Shepard to Alice Shepard, 18 November 1895 and Fuller to Smith, 25 December 1895, *ABCFM* 16.9.5, unit 5, vol. 14, reel 659; Harris & Harris, *Letters from the Scenes of the Recent Massacres in Armenia,* 32; Saunders to Terrell, 27 November 1895, *FRUS* 1895, vol. II, 1390; Filian, *Armenian and Her People,* 295; M. S. Gabrielian, *Armenia: A Martyr Nation. A Historical Sketch of the Armenian People from Tradition Times to the Present Tragic Days* (New York: Fleming H. Revell Company, 1918), 257–258; Turkey, No. 2, 1896, 318–337; Shadid Bey, *Islam, Turkey and Armenia and How They Happened* (St. Louis: Press of C. B. Woodward Company, 1898), 201; E. Antoine, *Les Massacres d'Armenie* (Bruxelles: Société belge de librairie, 1897), 72–79; Kirakossian, *British Diplomacy and the Armenian Question from the 1830s to 1914,* 261.

183. BOA.DH.ŞFR 184 / 30, 5 Teşrinisânî 1311 (17 November 1895); BOA. DH.ŞFR 184 / 44, 7 Teşrinisânî 1311 (19 November 1895). According to the records of Hüseyin Nazım Pasha, fifty-one Muslim men and eight Muslim women, and 103 Armenian men and eight Armenian women, lost their lives, while 110 Muslims and ninety-seven Armenians were injured. Hüseyin Nazım Paşa, *Ermeni Olayları Tarihi,* vol. I (Ankara: Başbakanlık Osmanlı Arşivleri, 1998), 131.

184. *Badmo'wt'iwn Ah'nt'abi Hah'o'c,* vol. I, 914; *Hah Ah'nt'ab* 10, no. 5 (1969): 20–21; Filian, *Armenian and Her People,* 295; Barsumian, *Badmo'wt'iwn Ah'nt'abi H. H. Tashnagco'wt'iwn 1898–1922,* 30; A. Gesar, *Ah'nt'abi Ko'h'amardy,* 25.

185. Fuller to Smith, 19 March 1896, *ABCFM* 16.9.5, unit 5 vol. 12, reel 655; Morris and Ze'evi, *The Thirty-Year Genocide,* 95.

186. *Badmo'wt'iwn Ah'nt'abi Hah'o'c,* vol. I, 916.

187. BOA.MKT.MHM 651 / 28, 31 May 1312 (12 June 1896); Morris and Ze'evi, *The Thirty-Year Genocide,* 95.

188. FO 195 / 1932, Catoni to Herbert, 1 July 1896.

189. FO 195 / 1932, Barnham to Currie, 21 January 1896; Morris and Ze'evi, *The Thirty-Year Genocide,* 95.

190. *Badmo'wt'iwn Ah'nt'abi Hah'o'c,* vol. I, 911.

191. Bliss, *Turkey and the Armenian Atrocities,* 456; Shepard, "Personal Experience in Turkish Massacres and Relief Work," 323.

192. Balabanian, *Geanqis Daq o'w Bagh Orery,* 35.

193. Filian, *Armenian and Her People,* 291.

194. Fuller to Lord Bryce, 5 March 1896, *ABCFM* 16.9.5, unit 5, vol. 12, reel 655. Frank D. Shepard also pointed out that some sixty leading men of the Armenian community in Aintab were arrested on "false charges of murder,

arson, treason, etc.," and kept in prison in Aleppo for six months. They were finally released only on "the payment of heavy bribes"; see Shepard, "Personal Experience in Turkish Massacres and Relief Work," 323.

195. Güllü, *Antep Ermenileri,* 229.

196. BOA.A.MKT.MHM 650 / 13 lef 3, 20 February 1312 (3 March 1896) and for another telegraph as such, BOA.A.MKT.MHM 649 / 9 lef 16, 7 March 1312 (19 March 1896).

197. BOA.A.MKT.MHM 650 / 13 lef 2, 22 February 1312 (5 March 1896).

198. Fuller to Smith, 6 February 1896; and Hovannes Krikorian to his sister, 5 February 1896, *ABCFM* 16.9.5, unit 5, vol. 14, reel 659.

199. FO 195 / 1883, Barnham to Currie, November 1895; Morris and Ze'evi, *The Thirty-Year Genocide,* 95. On the other hand, Aleppo governor Hasan Pasha telegrammed the Ministry of Interior about the number of Armenians who were arrested and imprisoned during the supposed Armenian insurgency, describing what occurred in Aintab as an "Armenian insurrection" and claiming that 700 Armenians had been arrested and another 65 interned temporarily in inns and government buildings. See BOA.DH.ŞFR 184 / 49, 7 Teşrinisânî 1311 (19 November 1895).

200. FO 195 / 1932, Barnham to Currie, 21 January 1896.

201. FO 195 / 1949, "Notes on the Situation at Aintab (Province of Aleppo)," 6 February 1896, unsigned, attached to Dwight to Currie, 19 February 1896; Shepard, "Personal Experience in Turkish Massacres and Relief Work," 323; Morris and Ze'evi, *The Thirty-Year Genocide,* 95.

202. BOA.A.MKT.MHM 649 / 9 lef 14; BOA.HR.SYS.2859/18, 24 February 1896.

203. BOA. A.MKT.MHM 651 / 12, Aleppo Governor Raif Pasha to Sadaret, 15 May 1896.

204. BOA.HR.SYS 2791 / 29, 24 February 1896.

205. Fuller to Smith, 25 December 1895, *ABCFM* 16.9.5, unit 5; Morris and Ze'evi, *The Thirty-Year Genocide,* 95.

206. Güllü, *Antep Ermenileri,* 143; Halil Özşavlı, "1895 Antep Ermeni Olayları," *The Journal of Academic Social Science Studies* 5, no. 8 (2012): 951–969; Yıldırım, "1895–1896 İsyanları Sırasında Ayntab'da Ermeniler ve Hınçak Cemiyeti," 167–179; BOA.A.MKT.MHM 648 / 10 lef 11, 4 Teşrinisânî 1311 (16 November 1895); BOA.A.MKT.MHM 649 / 10 lef 3, Aleppo Province to Istanbul Vizierate, 26 Teşrinievvel 1311 (7 November 1895).

207. Peter Balakian, *The Burning Tigris: The Armenian Genocide and America's Response* (New York: HarperCollins, 2004), 51; Raymond Kévorkian and Paul B. Paboudjian, "Les massacres de Cilicie d'avril 1909," in *La Cilicie (1909–1921) de Massacres d'Adana au Mandat Français,* ed. Raymond Kévorkian

(Paris: Revue d'Histoire Armenienne Contemporaine Tome III, 1999), 7–248; Simon Payaslian, *The History of Armenia: From the Origins to the Present* (New York: Palgrave, 2007), 120; Dadrian, "The Role of the Turkish Military in the Destruction of the Ottoman Armenians: A Study in Historical Continuities," *Journal of Political and Military Sociology* 20, no. 2 (1992): 262; Levene, "Creating a Modern 'Zone of Genocide': The Impact of Nation-and State-Formation on Eastern Anatolia, 1878–1923," *Journal of Holocaust and Genocide Studies* 12, no. 3 (1998): 396. On the Hamidiye, see Stephen Duguid, "The Politics of Unity: Hamidian Policy in Eastern Anatolia," *Middle Eastern Studies* 9, no. 2 (1973): 139–156; Bayram Kodaman, *Sultan II. Abdülhamid Devri Doğu Anadolu Politikası* (Ankara: Türk Kültürünü Araştırma Enstitüsü, 1987); Janet Klein, *The Margins of Empire. Kurdish Militias in the Ottoman Tribal Zone* (Stanford, CA: Stanford University Press, 2011); Bloxham, *The Great Game of Genocide*, 47, 55.

208. Hovannisian, "The Historical Dimensions of the Armenian Question, 1878–1923," in *The Armenian Genocide in Perspective*, ed. Richard G. Hovannisian (New Brunswick, NJ: Transaction Books, 1986), 5–26; Ronald G. Suny, *Looking toward Ararat: Armenian in Modern History* (Bloomington: Indiana University Press, 1993), 99. Dragoman of the British Embassy Fitzmaurice was certain that the massacres came into existence at a signal from the sultan: "No direct orders had been issued . . . but clear hints had come down from Yıldız that 'it would be desirable to give the Armenians a good lesson.' In an Oriental country, he said, this was all that was needed." See G. R. Berridge, *Gerald Fitzmaurice (1865–1939): Chief Dragoman of the British Embassy in Turkey* (Leiden: Martinus Nijhoff Publishers, 2007), 25, cited in Deringil, "'The Armenian Question Is Finally Closed,'" 368.

209. Norman M. Naimark, *Fires of Hatred: Ethnic Cleansing in Twentieth Century Europe* (Cambridge, MA: Harvard University Press, 2001), 23.

210. Johannes Lepsius, *Armenia and Europe* (London: Hodder and Stoughton, 1897), 76–77; Levene, "The Changing Face of Mass Murder," 449.

211. Deringil, "'The Armenian Question Is Finally Closed,'" 368.

212. According to Mr. Terrell, this reform program contained "absolutely nothing new of practical values for the future security of life or property," and only announced "the order to enforce existing laws, or as regulations in harmony with them." Terrell to Olney, 24 October 1895, *FRUS 1895*, vol. II, 1325–1326; Verheij, "Diyarbekir and the Armenian Crisis of 1895," 95–96.

213. Dadrian, *A History of Armenian Genocide*, 151–154; Levene, "The Changing Face of Mass Murder," 445; Verheij, "Diyarbekir and the Armenian Crisis of 1895," 96; Jelle Verheij, "Die armenischen Massaker von 1894–1896:

Anatomie und Hintergründe eine Krise," in *Die Armenische Frage und die Schweiz (1896–1923)*, ed. Hans-Lukas Kieser (Zurich: Chronos, 1999), 85.

214. Verheij, "Diyarbekir and the Armenian Crisis of 1895," 97; the same argument appears in Gölbaşı, "1895–96 Katliamları," 140–163. As a matter of fact, this is not entirely a recent development, as Jelle Verheij in his 1999 article had demanded caution with regard to the Sultan's role in the 1895 massacres; see Verheij, "Die armenischen Massaker von 1894–1896," 81–91. On the other hand, according to Selim Deringil, "there is substantial evidence, albeit circumstantial, that points in the direction of his [Abdülhamid II] benign neglect, if not actual covert support for the perpetrators of the massacres and forced conversions." Deringil, "'The Armenian Question Is Finally Closed,'" 351.

215. Omer Bartov and Eric D. Weitz (eds.), *Shatterzones of Empires: Coexistence and Violence in the German, Habsburg, Russian, and Ottoman Borderlands* (Bloomington: Indiana University Press, 2013), 4.

216. Bloxham, *The Great Game of Genocide*, 55.

217. Bloxham, *The Great Game of Genocide*, 55; Bloxham and Göçek, "The Armenian Genocide," 361.

218. Edip Gölbaşı, "Hamidiye Alayları: Bir Değerlendirme" in *1915: Siyaset, Tehcir, Soykırım*, ed. Oktay Özel and Fikret Adanır (Istanbul: Tarih Vakfı Yurt Yayınları, 2015), 164–175; Verheij, "Diyarbekir and the Armenian Crisis of 1895"; Verheij, "'Les Frères de Terre et d'Eau': Sur le rôle des Kurdes dans les massacres arméniens de 1894–1896," 225–276.

219. Verheij, "Diyarbekir and the Armenian Crisis of 1895," 135, 138. Verheij notes that there is not much evidence regarding Hamidiye involvement in the rural areas generally, "notwithstanding the fact that Kurds featured much more heavily as identifiable perpetrators there than in urban environments" in the province of Diyarbekir. Verheij, "Diyarbekir and the Armenian Crisis of 1895," 138.

220. Verheij, "Diyarbekir and the Armenian Crisis of 1895," 136.

221. Gölbaşı, "Hamidiye Alayları: Bir Değerlendirme"; Verheij, "Diyarbekir and the Armenian Crisis of 1895," 136.

222. Gölbaşı, "1895–96 Katliamları," 156; Bloxham, *The Great Game of Genocide*, 56.

223. Astourian, "Testing World-System Theory, Cilicia (1830s–1890s)," 459–460. For the impact of resentment on motivating individuals to participate in ethnic violence, see Roger D. Petersen, *Understanding Ethnic Violence: Fear, Hatred, and Resentment in Twentieth-Century Eastern Europe* (Cambridge: Cambridge University Press, 2002), 53–56; Donald L. Horowitz, *Ethnic Groups in Conflict* (Berkeley: University of California Press, 1985), 40.

224. Verheij, "Diyarbekir and the Armenian Crisis of 1895," 138. See too Gölbaşı, "1895–96 Katliamları," 162.

2. Ethnic Politics after the Young Turk Revolution

1. Studies regarding the Young Turk Revolution of 1908: Şerif Mardin, *Jön Türklerin Siyasi Fikirleri, 1895–1908* (Ankara: Türkiye İş Bankası, 1964); Şükrü Hanioğlu, *Bir Siyasal Örgüt Olarak Osmanlı İttihad ve Terakki Cemiyeti ve Jön Türklük* (Istanbul: İletişim, 1986); Aykut Kansu, *1908 Devrimi* (Istanbul: İletişim, 2006); Sina Akşin, *Jön Türkler ve İttihat ve Terakki* (Ankara: İmge Kitapevi, 2001); Ali Birinci, *Hürriyet ve İtilaf Fırkası: II. Meşrutiyet Devrinde İttihat ve Terakki'ye Karşı Çıkanlar* (Istanbul: Dergah Yayınları, 1990); Ernest Edmondson Ramsaur, *The Young Turks: Prelude to the Revolution of 1908* (New York: Russell and Russell, 1957); Hanioğlu, *The Young Turks in Opposition* (New York: Oxford University Press, 1995); Bernard Lewis, *The Emergence of Modern Turkey* (Oxford: Oxford University Press, 1968); Feroz Ahmad, *The Young Turks: The Committee of Union and Progress in Turkish Politics, 1908–1914* (Oxford: Clarendon Press, 1969); Eric J. Zürcher, *Unionist Factor: The Role of the Committee of Union and Progress in the Turkish National Movement, 1905–1926* (Leiden: E.J. Brill, 1984); Naim Turfan, *Rise of the Young Turks: Politics, the Military and Ottoman Collapse* (London: I.B. Tauris, 2000); Hasan Kayalı, *Arabs and Young Turks: Ottomanism, Arabism, and Islamism in the Ottoman Empire, 1908–1918* (Berkeley: University of California Press, 1997); Nader Sohrabi, *Revolution and Constitutionalism in the Ottoman Empire and Iran* (Cambridge: Cambridge University Press, 2011); Michelle U. Campos, *Ottoman Brothers: Muslims, Christians, and Jews in Early Twentieth-Century Palestine* (Stanford, CA: Stanford University Press, 2011); Bedross Der Matossian, *Shattered Dreams of Revolution* (Stanford, CA: Stanford University Press, 2014).

2. Nerses (Mahdesian) Hagopian, "Hay Yeghap'okhagan Tashnagts'ut'iwně Aynt'abi měch ew Yaragits' Těbk'er" [Armenian Revolutionary Federation in Aintab and Following Events] in *Badmo'wt'iwn Ah'nt'abi Hah'o'c,* vol. I, 971.

3. Hagopian, "Hay Yeghap'okhagan Tashnagts'ut'iwně Aynt'abi měch ew Yaragits' Těbk'er," 972.

4. Hagopian, "Hay Yeghap'okhagan Tashnagts'ut'iwně Aynt'abi měch ew Yaragits' Těbk'er," 538. Rev. Fred Field Goodsell, "Shepard of Aintab: The Beloved Physician," *Envelope Series* 19, no. 2 (1916): 10. Despite the general positive reception of the revolution, there was a different situation in some places in the eastern provinces. In those areas, the ancien régime continued to rule. For example, the declaration of the constitution brought no reform in Mush.

On the contrary, the Hamidiye regiments and the Kurdish tribes continued to oppress the population. In Bitlis, the announcement of the constitution was followed by a violent reaction. Sir G. Lowther to Sir Edward Grey (received September 26), *Therapia,* 20 September 1908, in "Correspondence respecting the Constitutional Movement in Turkey, 1908," *Parliamentary Papers,* 1909, 88, cited in Der Matossian, "Ethnic Politics in Post-Revolutionary Ottoman Empire: Armenians, Arabs, and Jews during the Second Constitutional Period (1908–1909)" (unpublished PhD diss., Columbia University, 2008), 213–214.

5. Attendees included Cenanizâde Ali Bey (a deputy from Aintab), Taşçızâde Abdullah Efendi, Tuzcuzâde Hafız Ahmet Efendi, Ahmet Muhtar Bey, Kethüdazâde Hüseyin Cemil Bey, Bulaşıkzâde mufti Hacı Arif Efendi, Mahmut Çitçi, Rüştü Attaroğlu, Hacı Hanifizâde Abdullah Efendi, Iztırapzâde Şefik Bey, Cenanizâde Rıza Bey, Nizipli Hacı Mehmet Efendi, Battal Beyzâde Tahir Bey, Mennazâde Mustafa, Iztırapzâde Celal Kadri Bey, and Daizâde Hasan Sadık Bey. See "Celal Kadri Barlas'ın Dilinden, İttihat ve Terakki Cemiyeti Nasıl Kuruldu?" *Gaziantep'i Tanıtıyoruz* 2, no. 2 (1963): 16–17. Celal Kadri Barlas took charge of the administrative boarding of the club, see Şakir Sabri Yener, "Celal Kadri Barlas'ı Kaybettik," *Gaziantep Kültür Dergisi* 6, no. 68 (1963): 177. All those named as members of the Aintab CUP branch played pivotal roles in the mass deportation of Armenians, organized plunder, confiscation, and despoliation of their properties in 1915–1917. They were the main profiteers of destruction of the city's Armenians. For the full list of names who were responsible for deportations and plunder in Aintab in 1915, see BNu / Fonds A. Andonian, P.J.1 / 3, file 4, Aintab, 11–17. This list and those names will be elaborated in a detailed manner in Chapter 3.

6. "Celal Kadri Barlas'ın Dilinden, İttihat ve Terakki Cemiyeti Nasıl Kuruldu?," 16. Upon Ali Cenani Bey's election as the deputy of Aleppo, Taşçızâde Abdullah Effendi became the president of the Aintab CUP branch. Ömer Asım Aksoy, "Arkadaşım Faik Taşçıoğlu," *Gaziantep Kültür Dergisi* 5, no. 56 (1962): 173. BNu / Fonds A. Andonian, P.J.1 / 3, file 4, Aintab, 11–17.

7. "Çitçi ve Arsan ailelerinden yetişen On Fikir ve İş adamı," *Gaziantep Kültür Dergisi* 8, no. 88 / 89 (1965): 16–17; *Gaziantep Kültür Dergisi* 2, no. 20 (1959): 181. Mahmut Çitçi was previously an honorary director of the CUP's *Türktepe Birinci Ana Mektebi* (Türktepe Primary School) during World War I. "Çitçi ve Arsan ailelerinden yetişen On Fikir ve İş adamı," 18.

8. *Gaziantep'i Tanıtıyoruz* 3, no. 2 (1968): 3. During the British occupation of the city started in December 1918, Bulaşıkzâde, along with other Unionists Bahtiyar Patpat and Muhtar Ahmet Agha, was arrested at Central Turkey College and then sent to Aleppo. After the British left, he returned to Aintab. BNu / Fonds A. Andonian, P.J.1 / 3, file 4, Aintab, f 10v.

9. BNu / Fonds A. Andonian, P.J.1 / 3, file 4, Aintab, 16.

10. Hırand Effendi Sulahian was born in Aintab on 21 January 1871. He was a member of a wealthy family and was well educated. He greatly contributed to the foundation of educational institutions. He was one of the founding fathers of the Cilicia College in 1912. Sulahian constituted a "self-defence organization" in 1909 to defend the Aintab Armenians so that a counterpart to the Adana massacres would not take place in the district. He was deported together with his whole family to Damascus in October 1915. Sulahian was arrested and brought to Aintab in March 1916. After being imprisoned for four months in Aintab, he was set free and returned to Damascus with his family. He was put on trial and sentenced to death by the military court for his alleged involvement with and engagement in "revolutionary and nationalist activities." Through the intercession of Cemal Pasha, he was saved from being hanged and was then again set free. He immigrated to America on 27 December 1939 and died in Boston in 1949; see "Hırand K. Sulahian 1871–1949," *Nor Ah'nt'ab* 3, no. 50–51 (1972): 11–14; BNu / Fonds A. Andonian, P.J. 1 / 3, file 4, Aintab, 11–12; Kevork A. Sarafian, *A Briefer History of Aintab: A Concise History of the Cultural, Religious, Educational, Political, Industrial and Commercial Life of the Armenians of Aintab* (Los Angeles: Union of the Armenians of Aintab, 1957), 290.

11. BNu / Fonds A. Andonian, P.J. 1 / 3, file 4, Aintab, 1. *Turkish Homeland* was the pioneering attempt to promote Turkish nationalism in the Ottoman Empire, founded on 31 August 1911. It aimed to defend the rights of the Turkish people within the Empire, expand Turkish nationalism, deliver the news—negative or positive—from every corner of the Turkish world, and promote Turkish interests. For a comprehensive study on this institution and its role in forming early modern Turkish nationalism, see Ümit Kurt, *'Türk'ün Büyük, Biçare Irkı': Türk Yurdu'nda Milliyetçiliği Esasları (1911–1916)* (Istanbul: İletişim, 2012); Kurt and Doğan Gürpınar, "The Balkan Wars and the Rise of the Reactionary Modernist Utopia in Young Turk Thought and Turkish Homeland," *Nations and Nationalism* 21, no. 2 (2015): 348–368. On the eve of World War I, the main task of these two organizations was to orchestrate the harassment of Armenian institutions, urge confiscation of farms on various pretexts, and generally foster Turkism.

12. Şükrü Hanioğlu, *Preparation for a Revolution: The Young Turks 1902–1908* (Oxford: Oxford University Press, 2001), 191–209; Hans-Lukas Kieser, "The Ottoman Road to Total War (1913–15)," in *World War I and the End of the Ottomans*, ed. Hans-Lukas Kieser, Kerem Öktem, and Maurus Reinkowski (New York: I.B. Tauris, 2015), 30; Houri Berberian, *Roving Revolutionaries: Armenians the Connected Revolutions in the Russian, Iranian, and Ottoman Worlds* (Oakland, CA: University of California Press, 2019), 277–279.

13. For a detailed history of Aintab Dashnaksutiun, see Kevork H. Barsumian, *Badmo'wt'iwn Ah'nt'abi H. H. Tashnagco'wt'iwn 1898–1922* (Halep: Tigris, 1957).

14. Sarafian, *A Briefer History of Aintab,* 135; Barsumian, *Badmo'wt'iwn Ah'nt'abi H. H. Tashnagco'wt'iwn 1898–1922,* 23.

15. Sarafian, *A Briefer History of Aintab,* 135; Hovhannes Araradian, "H. H. Dashnaktsutyun Ah'nt'abi mĕch 1908–1915" [Dashnaksutiun in Aintab 1908–1915], in *Badmo'wt'iwn Ah'nt'abi Hah'o'c,* vol. I, 985.

16. Barsumian, *Badmo'wt'iwn Ah'nt'abi H. H. Tashnagco'wt'iwn 1898–1922,* 23.

17. Halep Vilayet Salnamesi [Aleppo Yearbook] dated 1324 (1908), 250, cited in *Osmanlı Vilayet Salnamelerinde Halep,* Cengiz Eroğlu et al., 196.

18. Halep Vilayet Salnamesi, cited in *Osmanlı Vilayet Salnamelerinde Halep,* 196.

19. V. N. Gulesserian, "Dasnmeg Egheragan Dariner Ah'nt'abi mĕch 1908–1919" [11 Brutal Years in Aintab 1908–1919], in *Badmo'wt'iwn Ah'nt'abi Hah'o'c,* vol. I, 1003. This kind of revolutionary festival seemed to be a crucial aspect of the creation of Ottoman patriotism. In these celebrations, symbolism was rather significant in terms of providing solidarity and uniting all the ethnic groups under one identity: Ottomanism; see Der Matossian, "Ethnic Politics in Post-Revolutionary Ottoman Empire," 120.

20. Nerses (Mahdesian) Hagopian, "Hay Yeghap'okhagan Tashnagts'ut'iwnĕ Aynt'abi mĕch ew Yaragits' Tĕbk'er," in *Badmo'wt'iwn Ah'nt'abi Hah'o'c,* vol. I, 972, and vol. II, 491. Indeed, when the restoration of the constitution was officially announced on 23 July 1908, the reactions that most surprised observers were the scenes of great celebration by the broad masses of the people, as well as demonstrations of fraternization that could be discerned not only in the capital but also in the provinces. For the anatomy of the revolutionary festivities and celebrations of the 1908 revolution within different provinces, see Der Matossian, "Ethnic Politics in Post-Revolutionary Ottoman Empire," 69–87.

21. *Badmo'wt'iwn Ah'nt'abi Hah'o'c,* vol. I, 972.

22. Barsumian, *Badmo'wt'iwn Ah'nt'abi H. H. Tashnagco'wt'iwn 1898–1922,* 35.

23. *Badmo'wt'iwn Ah'nt'abi Hah'o'c,* vol. I, 972, 974–975.

24. *Badmo'wt'iwn Ah'nt'abi Hah'o'c,* vol. I, 975.

25. *Badmo'wt'iwn Ah'nt'abi Hah'o'c,* vol. I, 972–973.

26. The list that was prepared by Khachadur Dadaian clearly indicates how powerful and influential the Armenians were in Aintab's economy and trade. For this list, see Khachadur Dadaian (ed.), *Dasnhinkerort tare'n minchew 1915: arti T'o'wrqio'h' me'ch' Hah'ero'w Ar'ewdragan ew Dndesagan Ko'rdzo'wne'-o'wt'ean masin Dzawalo'wn P'asdat'o'wght'er* [From 15th Century to 1915:

Commerce-Economic Activities of Armenians in Today's Turkey, Collected Documents] (Yerevan: Gasprint, 2012). This list is also available at https://hyetert.org/2014/10/21/antep/.

27. *Gençlere Başarı Yolu: Cemil Alevli'nin Hayatı ve Hayat Görüşü*, 15.

28. Ali Nadi Ünler, *Gaziantep Savunması* (Istanbul: Kardeşler Matbaacılık, 1969), 12–13. The same accusatory, exclusionist, and discriminatory discourse and narratives were used to legitimize violence against the Jews in Eastern Europe during the Holocaust; see Jan Grabowski, *Hunt for the Jews: Betrayal and Murder in German-Occupied Poland* (Bloomington, Indiana: Indiana University Press, 2013); Bartov, *Anatomy of a Genocide: The Life and Death of a Town Called Buczacz* (New York: Simon & Schuster, 2018).

29. Astourian, "Testing World-System Theory, Cilicia (1830s–1890s)," 403. According to Şükrü Hanioğlu, the 24 July 1908 declaration of the constitution and *Ittihad-ı Anasır*, Ottomanism, and Ottoman citizenship state the obvious—that it is taken for granted that the Turkish-Muslim identity is superior to other non-Muslim identities and accepted in its dominance. Şükrü Hanioğlu, *A Brief History of the Late Ottoman Empire* (Princeton, NJ: Princeton University Press, 2010).

30. *Badmo'wt'iwn Ah'nt'abi Hah'o'c*, vol. I, 976.

31. *Badmo'wt'iwn Ah'nt'abi Hah'o'c*, vol. I, 973.

32. Ahmad, *The Young Turks*, 14.

33. Abdülhamit Kırmızı, "Meşrutiyette İstibdat Kadroları: 1908 İhtilalinin Bürokraside Tasfiye ve İkame Kabiliyeti," 1908–2008 Jön Türk Devrimi'nin 100. Yılı, Uluslararası Kongre 28–30 May 2008, Ankara Üniversitesi Siyasal Bilgiler Fakültesi, 3.

34. Hanioğlu, *Preparation for a Revolution*, 282.

35. *Maşrık-ı İrfan*, no. 129, 17 June 1326 (30 June 1910), 1, cited in Birinci, *Hürriyet ve İtilaf Fırkası*, 28n94.

36. Hanioğlu, *Preparation for a Revolution*, 282. Enver Karal stated that Unionist clubs in provinces openly interfered with the administration, dismissing unwanted governors and administrators from their duties and mentoring the ones supported by Unionists. According to him, these people had the administrators in their pocket. Enver Ziya Karal, *Osmanlı Tarihi*, vol. IX (Ankara: TTK, 1996), 58.

37. Necmeddin Bey was born in Baalbek, Beirut, and came from an Arabic family. An educated, farsighted official, he was appointed district governor of Aintab on 31 December 1907. Before then, he served as district governor of Diyadin. BOA.BEO 3221 / 241518, 20 Kanunuevvel 1323 (2 January 1908). For his *sicil-i ahval* (official record), see BOA.İ.DH 1461 / 33, 18 Kanunuevvel 1323 (31 December 1907).

38. Kudret Emiroğlu, *Anadolu'da Devrim Günleri: II. Meşrutiyet'in İlanı* (Ankara: İmge, 1999), 125–126; Ahmed Djemal Pasha, *Memories of a Turkish Statesman, 1913–1919* (Miami: HardPress Publishing, 2010), 256.

39. Şakir Sabri Yener, "Antep Tarihinde 1908 Yılı Ayaklanması," *Gaziantep Kültür Dergisi* 5, no. 201 (1962): 9; *Badmo'wt'iwn Ah'nt'abi Hah'o'c,* vol. I, 973.

40. Sera was where Aintab's municipality and district governorate were located at the time.

41. Whereas Kevork A. Sarafian gave September 1908 as the date of this meeting, according to Şakir Sabri Yener, it took place right after the day of the Young Turk Revolution. *Badmo'wt'iwn Ah'nt'abi Hah'o'c* vol. I, 973; Yener, "Antep Tarihinde 1908 Yılı Ayaklanması," 9.

42. Born in 1888, Şakir Sabri Yener was a regular contributor to *Gaziantep Kültür Dergisi.* The magazine, founded in 1957, examined Aintab's history and other aspects, as well as presented an intensive official historiography on a micro scale from a nationalist point of view. Yener witnessed the beating of Necmeddin Bey and published his experiences and opinions concerning this incident in *Gaziantep Kültür Dergisi.*

43. Yener describes lawyer Ali Rıza Bey as an ardent, dark, and bearded preacher and states that his face resembled Namık Kemal's face. Yener, "Antep Tarihinde 1908 Yılı Ayaklanması," 9.

44. Yener, "Antep Tarihinde 1908 Yılı Ayaklanması," 9. Mennanzâde Mustafa Bey was a member of one of the prominent and wealthy Aintab families at the time. As the president of the CUP branch in Aintab during the war, he played a critical role in the creation of the "necessary" sociopolitical environment for the decision-making process of Armenians' deportation in late July 1915. He also appropriated a part of the immovable properties left by the Armenian deportees.

45. *Badmo'wt'iwn Ah'nt'abi Hah'o'c,* vol. I, 974.

46. Yener, *Gaziantep'in Yakın Tarihinden Notlar ve Hatıralar,* 31 32; Bar sumian, *Badmo'wt'iwn Ah'nt'abi H. H. Tashnagco'wt'iwn 1898–1922,* 34.

47. BOA.DH.MKT 2646 / 92, 18 Teşrinievvel (31 October 1908); BOA. DH.MKT 2646 / 92 and 2647 / 5, 22 Teşrinievvel 1324 (4 November 1908).

48. *Badmo'wt'iwn Ah'nt'abi Hah'o'c,* vol. I, 976; Yener, "Antep Tarihinde 1908 Yılı Ayaklanması," 9–10.

49. BOA.DH.MKT 2687 / 3, 5 Kanunuevvel 324 (18 December 1908).

50. BOA.DH.MKT 2687 / 3, 6 Kanunuevvel (19 December 1908); BOA. DH.MKT 2753 / 70, 8 February 1324 (21 February 1909).

51. *Badmo'wt'iwn Ah'nt'abi Hah'o'c,* vol. I, 977.

52. *Badmo'wt'iwn Ah'nt'abi Hah'o'c,* vol. I, 977; Yener, "Antep Tarihinde 1908 Yılı Ayaklanması," 10; Barsumian, *Badmo'wt'iwn Ah'nt'abi H. H. Tashnagco'wt'iwn 1898–1922,* 34.

53. After Aintab, Necmeddin Bey was first appointed to Kilis in December 1908. Then, he was assigned to Çölemerik, a town of Van Province, as the kaimakam in August 1909. BOA.DH.MKT 2900 / 66, 1 August 1325 (14 August 1909); BOA.DH.MKT 2909 / 82, 12 August 1325 (25 August 1909); BOA.BEO 3622 / 271648, 9 August 1325 (22 August 1909). However, he was removed from his post in July 1912 and appointed to the district governorship of Merc-i Uyun. BOA.İ.DH 1494 / 31, 28 June 1328 (11 July 1912); BOA.BEO 4061 / 304569, 28 June 1328 (11 July 1912); BOA.BEO 4182 / 313608, 30 May 1329 (12 June 1913). It seems that there were several complaints about him in Çölemerik as well, for another investigation was conducted in Merc-i Uyun. BOA.DH.MTV 22-2 / 47, 21 Teşrinievvel 1328 (3 November 1912); BOA.ŞD 1898 / 21, 1 Kanunuevvel 1328 (14 December 1912). By the time World War I started, he was the district governor of Nebk.

54. Necmeddin Bey himself came to Hama on 6 October 1915 and identified the artisans among the deportees in order to relocate them to Salamiyya. He registered more than 110 Armenian families (the majority of whom were Aintab Armenians) as craftsmen and artisans and resettled them to Salamiyya. These activities of Necmeddin in Hama and Salamiyya were emphasized in the diaries of two genocide survivors from Aintab, Krikor Bogharian and Nerses Tavukjian; see Krikor Bogharian, *Orakro'wt'iwn Darakir Geanqis* [Diary of My Life in Exile] in *Ceghasban T'o'wrqy Vgah'o'wt'iwnner Qagho'wadz Hrashqo'v P'rgo'wadznero'w Zro'h'nere'n* [Genocider Turk: Testimonies Taken from the Accounts of Armenians Who Miraculously Survived] (Beirut: Shirag, 1973), 138, 140–142, 154–157; Father Nerses Tavukjian, *Dar'abanqi Orakro'wt'iwn* [Diary of Miserable Days], ed. Toros Toramanian (Beirut: High Type Compugraph—Technopresse, 1991), 91, 93, 115.

55. Birinci, *Hürriyet ve İtilaf Fırkası*, 28.

56. Selim Sırrı Tarcan, *Hatıralarım* (Istanbul: Türkiye Yayınevi, 1946), 29. Dr. Bahaeddin Şakir and Dr. Nazım, as members of the central CUP, started a massive reorganization process in Anatolia. From July 1908 until March 1910, governors from twenty-nine provinces were replaced. Additionally, 93 percent of the local telegram offices, 93 percent of education administrators in the provinces, all ambassadors of the Empire, and 94 percent of those serving as public officials were dismissed and replaced by officials who were loyal to the new regime. Being one of the prominent figures of the central committee of the party, Bahaeddin Şakir declared that toward the end of 1909, the CUP had 360 branches with more than 850,000 members within the Empire. See Hanioğlu, *Preparation for a Revolution*, 287–288.

57. Hanioğlu, *Preparation for a Revolution*, 283; Djemal Pasha, *Memories of a Turkish Statesman, 1913–1919*, 256.

58. The Reorganization Law (Tensikat Kanunu) was enacted by the Young Turks on 30 June 1909 to eliminate the old regime officials, under pressure from the rising provincial civil and military functionaries unwilling to work with the elders. The full name of the *tensikat* law was "Devâir ve Mehâkimde İcra Edilecek Teşkilat ve Tensikat Cihetiyle Açıkda Kalacak Olanlarla Evvelce Memuriyetlerinden Birer Suretle İnfisal Veya İnfikak Eden Memurîn ve Hükkâm ile Ketebe Hakkında Kanun," *Mecmua-i Kavanin-i Cedide-i Osmani* (Istanbul: Matbaa-i Kütübhane-i Cihan, 1327). BOA. İ.KAN 1327 C / 5. On the *tensikat,* see Kırmızı, "Meşrutiyette İstibdat Kadroları," and Erkan Tural, *Son Dönem Osmanlı Bürokrasisi: İkinci Meşrutiyet Döneminde Bürokratlar, İttihatçılar ve Parlamenterler* (Ankara: TODAİE, 2009).

59. Şükrü Hanioğlu, in a similar fashion, underlines the fact that the CUP refrained from forming a government with a grand vizier from its own cadres until June 1913. However, he also points out that the party did not hesitate to manipulate ruling governments in various ways before that date. *Preparation for a Revolution,* 285.

60. Sina Akşin, *Jön Türkler ve İttihat ve Terakki* (Istanbul: Remzi, 1987), 250–308.

61. "Report of Central Turkey College," Aintab, for 1908–1909, #52, *ABCFM* 16.9.5, Central Turkey Mission, vol. 16, Reports, Documents (M661); *ABCFM* 16.9.5, Letter from Fred F. Goodsell to William W. Peet, 3 March 1909.

62. Vartanants commemorates the Battle of Avararyr in 451 A.D. Armenians, under the leadership of Vartan Mamigonian, fought against the Persians, who wanted to force them into Mazdaism, or Zoroastrianism. Vastly outnumbered, the Armenians lost the war. Yet their determination and guerilla wars won them the right to freedom of worship; see Shusan Yeni-Komshian Teager, *The Krajians of Aintab* (Belmont, MA, 2007), 53.

63. Barsumian, *Badmo'wt'iwn Ah'nt'abi H. H. Tashnagco'wt'iwn 1898 1922,* 36, 145, 150–151; A. Gesar, *Ah'nt'abi Ko'h'amardy* [Aintab Self-Defense] (Boston: Hayrenik, 1945), 26–29. Krikor Baghdasarian, a first-year student of the college in late February 1909 and also one of the Dashnak sympathizers, accused seven Armenian members of the faculty administration of collaborating with the college's American missionaries to ban students from commemorating Vartanants Day. Krikor Baghdasarian, "Erp Vartanants'ĕ G'arkilen" [When Vartanants Were Prohibited], in Barsumian, *Badmo'wt'iwn Ah'nt'abi H. H. Tashnagco'wt'iwn 1898–1922,* 150. In fact, in an article that appeared in the Armenian newspaper *Harach* (*Forward*) in 1951, those Armenian professors were depicted as sycophants of the missionaries at the college. Baghdasarian, "Erp Vartanants'ĕ G'arkilen," 153.

64. Baghdasarian, "Erp Vartanants'ĕ G'arkilen,"146.

65. Baghdasarian, "Erp Vartanants'ĕ G'arkilen,"146; Goodsell, "Statement," Central Turkey College, March 1909, #192, *ABCFM* 16.9.5, Central Turkey Mission, vol. 18 (M663).

66. "Brief Report," Aintab, for 1908–1909, #52, *ABCFM* 16.9.5, Letter from Fred F. Goodsell to William W. Peet, 3 March 1909.

67. "Brief Report," Aintab, for 1908–1909, #52, *ABCFM* 16.9.5, Letter from Fred F. Goodsell to William W. Peet, 3 March 1909; Barsumian, *Badmo'wt'iwn Ah'nt'abi H. H. Tashnagco'wt'iwn 1898–1922*, 147. Baghdasarian, "Erp Vartanants'ĕ G'arkilen," 152–153. After thorough investigation of each student, the faculty administration sent official letters to families regarding the fate of their sons in the college. There were two types of letters. One said, "Your son will be permitted to continue his education in the college, provided that he shall not take part in any political party, shall not use any weapon, shall not sing revolutionary songs, and shall accept all other rules of the college"; the other said, "Your son will no longer be permitted to continue his education in the college." Krikor Baghdasarian noted that there were students from Adana in the college who were forced to return to Adana following their dismissal. By the time they returned to Adana, they faced the Adana massacres and were killed. Baghdasarian, "Erp Vartanants'ĕ G'arkilen," 153.

68. On the Adana pogroms: Raymond Kévorkian, *The Armenian Genocide: A Complete History* (London: I.B. Tauris, 2011), 74–96; Kévorkian and Paul B. Paboudjian, "Les massacres de Cilicie d'avril 1909," in *La Cilicie (1909–1921) de Massacres d'Adana au Mandat Français*, ed. Raymond Kévorkian (Paris: Revue d'Histoire Armenienne Contemporaine Tome III, 1999), 7–248; Kévorkian, "The Cilician Massacres, April 1909," in *Armenian Cilicia*, ed. Richard G. Hovannisian and Simon Payaslian (Costa Mesa, CA: Mazda Publishers, 2008), 339–370; Vahakn Dadrian, *The History of Armenian Genocide: Ethnic Conflict from the Balkans and Anatolia to the Caucasus* (Oxford: Berghahn Books, 2004), 179–184; Dadrian, "The Circumstances Surrounding the 1909 Adana Holocaust," *Armenian Review* 41, no. 4 (1988): 1–16; Der Matossian, "Ethnic Politics in Post-Revolutionary Ottoman Empire," 423–488; Der Matossian, "From Bloodless Revolution to Bloody Counterrevolution: The Adana Massacres of 1909," *Genocide Studies and Prevention* 6, no. 2 (2011): 152–173; Der Matossian, *Shattered Dreams of Revolution*, 163–170. For a well-detailed analysis on the Adana massacres on the basis of missionary reports, see Barbara Merguerian, "Adana 1909: The American Response" (paper presented at the international workshop Adana 1909: History, Memory, and Identity from a Hundred Year Perspective, Sabancı University, November 6–7, 2009); Richard Hovannisian, "The Historical Dimensions of the Armenian Question, 1878–1923," in *The Armenian Genocide in Perspective*, ed. Richard Hovannisian (New

Brunswick, NJ: Transaction Books, 1986), 27. For some firsthand accounts of the Adana massacres, see Hrachik Simonian, *The Destruction of Armenians in Cilicia, April 1909* (London: Gomidas Institute, 2012) and Hagop H. Terzian, *Cilicia 1909: The Massacres of Armenians* (London: Gomidas Institute, 2009).

69. Meltem Toksöz, "Adana Ermenileri ve 1909 'iğtişâşı'", *Tarih ve Toplum Yeni Yaklaşımlar* 5, no. 245 (2007): 150; Der Matossian, "From Bloodless Revolution to Bloody Counterrevolution," 156.

70. Aram Arkun, "Les Relations armé no-turques et les massacres de Cilicie de 1909," in Comité de Défense de la Cause Arménienne (ed.), *L'Actualité du Génocide des Arméniens* (Paris: Edipol, 1999), 60–64.

71. Der Matossian, "From Bloodless Revolution to Bloody Counterrevolution," 152.

72. For a detailed analysis of counterrevolution and its aftermath, see that Sohrabi, *Revolution and Constitutionalism in the Ottoman Empire and Iran,* 224–287.

73. Der Matossian, "From Bloodless Revolution to Bloody Counterrevolution," 153. Also see Eric J. Zürcher, "The Ideas of April: A Fundamentalist Uprising in Istanbul in 1909," in *State and Islam,* ed. Cees van Dijk and Alexander H. de Groot (Leiden: CNWS, 1996), 64–76; David Farhi, "The Seriat as a Political Slogan—or the 'Incident of the 31st of Mart,'" *Middle Eastern Studies* 7, no. 3 (1971): 275–299. On the counterrevolution, see Sina Akşin, *31 Mart Olayı* (Ankara: Sevinç Matbaası, 1970); Talat Fuat, *31 Mart İrtica* (Istanbul: Türk Matbaası, 1911); Cemal Kutay, *31 Mart İhtilalinde Abdülhamit* (Istanbul: Cemal Kutay Kitaplığı ve Tarih Sevenler Kulübü, 1977); Ecevit Güresin, *31 Mart İsyanı* (Istanbul: Habora Kitabevi, 1969); Mustafa Baydar, *31 Mart Vak'ası* (Istanbul: Amil Matbaası, 1955); Sadık Albayrak, *31 Mart Gerici Bir Hareket mi?* (Istanbul: Bilim-Araştırma Yayınları, 1987); Süleyman Kani İrtem, *31 Mart İsyanı ve Hareket Ordusu: Abdülhamid'in Selanik Sürgünü* (Istanbul: Temel, 2003); Mustafa Eski, *31 Mart Olayı'nın Kastamonu'daki Yankıları* (Ankara: Ayyıldız Matbaası A.S, 1991).

74. Der Matossian, "From Bloodless Revolution to Bloody Counterrevolution," 163–164.

75. Vartan S. Bilezikian, *Apraham Hoja of Aintab* (Winona Lake, Indiana: Light and Life Press, 1952; updated by Thomas and Lila Cosmades, 2008), 44; *ABCFM* 16.9.1, unit 5, vol. 1, reel 668–463, 1817–1919, January 1911.

76. *Badmo'wt'iwn Ah'nt'abi Hah'o'c* vol. I, 538; Bilezikian, *Abraham Hoja of Aintab,* 42–44; Frank Andrews Stone, "The Educational 'Awakening' Among the American Evangelicals of Aintab, Turkey: 1845–1915," *Armenian Review* 35, no. 1 (1982): 42; Letter from John Merrill to the Trustees of Central Turkey College, May 18, 1909, *ABCFM* 16.9.1, unit 5, vol. 1, reel 673, 1817–1919, no. 1324;

Alice Shepard Riggs, *Shepard of Aintab* (Princeton, NJ: Gomidas Institute Books/Taderon Press, 2001), 117–118; Abraham H. Hartunian, *Neither to Laugh Nor to Weep: A Memoir of the Armenian Genocide,* translated by Vartan Hartunian (Cambridge, MA: Armenian Heritage Press, NAASR, 1986), 45.

77. For the critical role of rumor in mass violence, see Horowitz, *The Deadly Ethnic Riot* (Berkeley: University of California Press, 2001), 74–89.

78. Shepard, "Personal Experience in Turkish Massacres and Relief Work," 329; Riggs, *Shepard of Aintab*, 118.

79. *Badmo'wt'iwn Ah'nt'abi Hah'o'c,* vol. I, 979. It is very interesting to see that the same kind of conversation happened early in August 1908 between Ömer Naci Bey, a member of the Ittihad's Central Committee, responsible for inspecting the local CUP branches, and ARF representatives in Van. In this conversation, Ömer Naci declared in a humorous tone: "We Turks are lagging far behind European civilization, whereas you [Armenians] have made considerable progress. If it is true that it is indispensable to move forward together and live together as brothers, you will have to pause for a while and wait for us to catch up. If you don't, we shall have to latch on to your skirts to prevent you from advancing." See Vahan Papazian, *H'o'ws'h'er* [Memoirs], vol. II (Boston: Hayrenik, 1952), 225, cited in Kévorkian, *The Armenian Genocide,* 60.

80. This meeting of Dashnaksutiun took place in the house of Kalusd Agha Ghazarian. Other Dashnak participants in the meeting were Hagop and Nazar Ghazarian, B. B. Armenag, Nazaretian, and Yenavik Sulahian. *Badmo'wt'iwn Ah'nt'abi Hah'o'c,* vol. I, 978.

81. *Badmo'wt'iwn Ah'nt'abi Hah'o'c,* vol. I, 978; Araradian, "H. H' Tashnagco'wt'iwn Ah'nt'abi měch 1908–1915," in *Badmo'wt'iwn Ah'nt'abi Hah'o'c,* vol. I, 988, vol. II, 491; Barsumian, *Badmo'wt'iwn Ah'nt'abi H. H. Tashnagco'wt'iwn 1898–1922,* 37.

82. *Badmo'wt'iwn Ah'nt'abi Hah'o'c,* vol. I, 978.

83. Kévorkian, *The Armenian Genocide,* 74; Dikran Mesrob Kaligian, *Armenian Organization and Ideology Under Ottoman Rule: 1908–1914* (New Brunswick, NJ: Transaction Publishers, 2009), 43–47.

84. Gulesserian, "Dasnmeg ew Egheragan Dariner Ah'nt'abi měch 1908–1919," in *Badmo'wt'iwn Ah'nt'abi Hah'o'c,* vol. I, 1004. Although there was support for and involvement of ARF in the Young Turk Revolution, this involvement did not bring mutual trust between the two political forces. As Hanioğlu pointedly noted, "The CUP papers and available Ottoman documents reveal that the joint CUP-Dashnaksutiun revolutionary activities were very insignificant and that the CUP never trusted the Dashnaksutiun." This comment demonstrates the level of distrust between the CUP and the ARF, the only Armenian party cooperating with the CUP. *Preparation for a Revolu-*

tion, 207. For a more nuanced analysis of disrupted relations between the ARF and CUP after the 1909 Adana massacres, see Kaligian, *Armenian Organization and Ideology Under Ottoman Rule,* 13–81; Gadiz F. Minassian-Arsen Avagyan, *Ermeniler ve İttihat ve Terakki: İşbirliğinden Çatışmaya* (Istanbul: Aras Yayıncılık, 2013).

85. *Badmo'wt'iwn Ah'nt'abi Hah'o'c,* vol. I., 979.

86. *Badmo'wt'iwn Ah'nt'abi Hah'o'c,* vol. I, 538; Stone, "The Educational 'Awakening' among the American Evangelicals of Aintab, Turkey: 1845–1915," 43.

87. Hanioğlu, *A Brief History of the Late Ottoman Empire,* 154.

88. Der Matossian, "From Bloodless Revolution to Bloody Counterrevolution," 161–164.

89. *Badmo'wt'iwn Ah'nt'abi Hah'o'c,* vol. I, 979, Barsumian, *Badmo'wt'iwn Ah'nt'abi H. H. Tashnagco'wt'iwn 1898–1922,* 36.

90. *Badmo'wt'iwn Ah'nt'abi Hah'o'c,* vol. I, 979; 1005; *Hah Ah'nt'ab* 10, no. 6 (1969): 12.

91. *Badmo'wt'iwn Ah'nt'abi Hah'o'c,* vol. I, 979; 1005; *Hah Ah'nt'ab* 10, no. 6 (1969): 12.

92. *Badmo'wt'iwn Ah'nt'abi Hah'o'c,* vol. I, 979–980; Barsumian, *Badmo'wt'iwn Ah'nt'abi H. H. Tashnagco'wt'iwn 1898–1922,* 37.

93. Barsumian, *Badmo'wt'iwn Ah'nt'abi H. H. Tashnagco'wt'iwn 1898–1922,* 36; Goodsell, "What Might Have Happened," *Missionary Herald, 1909,* 139.

94. "Ayıntab İslamları ne kadar amal-i insaniyyet-perverane ile mütehali olduklarını bi-l-fi'il dahi isbat eylemişlerdir [Muslims of Aintab in fact proved how philanthropist they were]." A telegraph wired to the *Tanin* newspaper by Doctor Avedis Nakashian. *Tanin,* no. 263, 27 May 1909, cited in Güllü, *Antep Ermenileri,* 256. This telegraph demonstrates that Armenian community in the city also appreciated the Muslims' efforts to maintain quiescence and peace.

95. *Badmo'wt'iwn Ah'nt'abi Hah'o'c,* vol. I, 980; 1005; *Hah Ah'nt'ab* 10, no. 6 (1969): 12.

96. *Badmo'wt'iwn Ah'nt'abi Hah'o'c,* vol. I, 980; 1005; *Hah Ah'nt'ab* 10, no. 6 (1969): 12.

97. BNu / Fonds A. Andonian, P.J.1 / 3, liasse 9, *Aintab,* ff? Ali Kemal Bey was a former district governor of Duma appointed to Aintab to replace Necmeddin Bey on 7 December 1908; see BOA.DH.MKT 2677 / 47, 1326 Za 13 (7 December 1908); Barsumian, *Badmo'wt'iwn Ah'nt'abi H. H. Tashnagco'wt'iwn 1898–1922,* 37.

98. *Badmo'wt'iwn Ah'nt'abi Hah'o'c,* vol. I, 980.

99. BOA.DH.MKT 2861 / 50, 1327 C 11 (30 June 1909). Interestingly enough, the same Ali Kemal Bey was dismissed from his post because of a complaint lodged against him from when he was a district governor in Duma, alleging

that he was involved in corrupt activities at that time. Since an investigation was opened to investigate these accusations, he was discharged from his post as Aintab district governor. See DH.MKT 2906 / 10, 1327 Ş 3 (20 August 1909) and DH.MKT 2910 / 20, 1327 Ş 8 (25 August 1909).

100. *Tanin* newspaper, no. 263, 27 May 1909; *Tasvir-i Efkâr,* no. 5, 4 June 1909.

101. *Yeni Tasvir-i Efkâr* newspaper, no. 207, 28 December 1909.

102. Suny, *They Can Live in the Desert but Nowhere Else,* 363.

103. Hanioğlu, *A Brief History of the Late Ottoman Empire,* 155.

104. Bloxham, *The Great Game of Genocide,* 60.

105. Bloxham, *The Great Game of Genocide,* 60.

106. Yusuf Doğan Çetinkaya, *The Young Turks and the Boycott Movement: Nationalism, Protest and the Working Classes in the Formation of Modern Turkey* (London: I.B. Tauris, 2014), 39–159; Çetinkaya, "Revenge! Revenge! Revenge! 'Awakening a Nation' through Propaganda in the Ottoman Empire during the Balkan War (1912–1913)," in *World War I and the End of the Ottomans,* 77–103.

107. For the historical account of the concept of "atrocity propaganda," see James Morgan Reed, *Atrocity Propaganda 1914–1919* (New York: Arno Press, 1941); Reed, "Atrocity Propaganda and the Irish Rebellion," *Public Opinion Quarterly* 2, no. 2 (1948): 229–244.

108. Çetinkaya, "'Revenge! Revenge! Revenge!,'" 87–88; Yusuf Doğan Çetinkaya, "Atrocity Propaganda and the Nationalization of the Masses in the Ottoman Empire during the Balkan Wars (1912–1913)," *International Journal of Middle Eastern Studies* 46, no. 4 (2014): 759–778; Yusuf Doğan Çetinkaya, "Illustrated Atrocity: Stigmatization of Non-Muslims through Images in the Ottoman Empire during the Balkan War," *Journal of Modern European History* 12, no. 4 (2014): 460–478. Also see Uğur Ü. Üngör and Mehmet Polatel, *Confiscation and Destruction: The Young Turk Seizure of Armenian Property* (New York and London: Continuum, 2011), 61–63.

109. FO 195 / 2458, no. 84, 11 July 1914, 470 quoted and cited in Çetinkaya, "'Revenge! Revenge! Revenge!,'" 86–87.

110. Çetinkaya, "'Revenge! Revenge! Revenge!,'" 88; Toprak, "Balkan Harbi, İntikam ve Ötekileştirme Süreci," *Toplumsal Tarih,* no. 228, December 2012, 42–53, cited in Çetinkaya, "'Revenge! Revenge! Revenge!,'" 88; Üngör and Polatel, *Confiscation and Destruction,* 62.

111. Mehmed Emin, "Genç Türk," *Türk Yurdu* 2, no. 1 (1912): 391.

112. Yusuf Akçuraoğlu, "Türklük Şuûnu: 1328 Seferi (Maba'd)" *Türk Yurdu* 2, no. 26 (1912): 45.

113. Bloxham, *The Great Game of Genocide,* 64.

114. Kieser, Polatel, and Thomas Schmutz, "Reform or Cataclysm? The Agreement of 8 February 1914 regarding the Ottoman Eastern Provinces," *Journal of Genocide Research* 17, no. 3 (2015): 285–304; Morris and Ze'evi, *The Thirty-Year Genocide,* 146; Suny, *They Can Live in the Desert,* 204; Kieser, *Talaat Pasha: Father of Modern Turkey, Architect of Genocide* (Princeton, NJ: Princeton University Press, 2018), 164–165.

115. Zaven Der Yeghiayan, *My Patriarchal Memoirs* (Barrington, RI: Mayreni Publications, 2002), 33.

116. Bloxham, *The Great Game of Genocide,* 65.

117. Hans-Lukas Kieser, Kerem Öktem, and Maurus Reinkowski (eds.), *World War I and the End of the Ottomans,* 9–10. Hagop Kabbejian, a native of Aintab, recorded that the responsible party for the deportation of the Armenians was the Unionist government. Having overthrown the tyranny of sultan Abdülhamid II in 1908, the CUP's motto was "Liberty, Justice, and Equality." However, he claimed, "massacres that occurred in Cilicia clearly show that the constitutional government of 'Comrade' Talat and the tyranny of Abdülhamid II were both of the exact same mindset." For Kabbejian, Unionists revived "the Red sultan spirit, which was surely evil: Looking down on this organization called Union, which fed on himself, the Red sultan was joyfully watching his own competence and legacy." See *Badmo'wt'iwn Ah'nt'abi Hah'o'c,* vol. I, 927.

3. Wartime Deportation and Destruction of the Aintab Armenians

1. Şükrü Hanioğlu, *A Brief History of the Late Ottoman Empire* (Princeton, NJ: Princeton University Press, 2010), 175; Omer Bartov and Eric D. Weitz (eds.), *Shatterzones of Empires: Coexistence and Violence in the German, Habsburg, Russian, and Ottoman Borderlands* (Bloomington: Indiana University Press, 2013), 163.

2. Hanioğlu, *A Brief History of the Late Ottoman Empire,* 174–175; Mustafa Aksakal, *The Ottoman Road to War in 1914: The Ottoman Empire and the First World War* (Cambridge: Cambridge University Press, 2010), 60; Uğur Ü. Üngör, *The Making of Modern Turkey: Nation and State in Eastern Anatolia, 1913–1950* (Oxford: Oxford University Press, 2011), 55–56.

3. Aksakal, *Ottoman Road to War;* Mete Tunçay, *Cihat ve Tehcir* (Ankara: Salyangoz Yayınları, 2007), 102–104.

4. Hans-Lukas Kieser, "The Ottoman Road to Total War (1913–15)," in *World War I and the End of the Ottomans,* ed. Hans-Lukas Kieser, Kerem Öktem, and Maurus Reinkowski (New York: I.B. Tauris, 2015), 36; Kieser, *Talaat Pasha:*

Father of Modern Turkey, Architect of Genocide (Princeton, NJ: Princeton University Press, 2018), 189. Also see Yücel Yanıkdağ, *Healing the Nation: Prisoners of War, Medicine and Nationalism in Turkey, 1914–1939* (Edinburgh: Edinburgh University Press, 2013), 16–20.

5. Yiğit Akın, "Seferberlik: Building up the Ottoman Home Front," in *World War I and the End the Ottomans,* ed. Hans-Lukas Kieser, Kerem Öktem, and Maurus Reinkowski (New York: I.B. Tauris, 2015), 59; Akın, *When the War Came Home: The Ottomans' Great War and the Devastation of an Empire* (Stanford, CA: Stanford University Press, 2018); Eugene Rogan, *Frontiers of the State in the Late Ottoman Empire: Transjordan, 1850–1921* (Cambridge: Cambridge University Press, 1999), 220; Frances E. Newton, *Fifty Years in Palestine* (London: Coldharbour Press, 1948), 105.

6. Kevork A. Sarafian (ed.), *Badmo'wt'iwn Ah'nt'abi Hah'o'c* [History of Aintab Armenians], (Los Angeles: Union of the Armenians of Aintab, 1953), vol. I, 1011.

7. Stina Katchadourian, *Efronia, An Armenian Love Story* (Princeton, NJ: Gomidas Institute Books), 128.

8. Sarafian, *Badmo'wt'iwn Ah'nt'abi Hah'o'c,* vol. I, 1011.

9. Sarafian, *Badmo'wt'iwn Ah'nt'abi Hah'o'c,* vol. I, 1011.

10. Donald Bloxham, *The Great Game of Genocide: Imperialism, Nationalism, and the Destruction of the Ottoman Armenians* (Oxford: Oxford University Press, 2005), 72; Kieser, *Talaat Pasha,* 190.

11. BOA.DH.ŞFR 44 / 200, 6 September 1914, cited in Taner Akçam, *Young Turks' Crime against Humanity: The Armenian Genocide and Ethnic Cleansing in the Ottoman Empire* (Princeton, NJ: Princeton University Press, 2012), 152.

12. Eric J. Zürcher, "Introduction: The Ottoman Jihad, the German Jihad and the Sacralization of War," in *Jihad and Islam in World War I,* ed. Eric J. Zürcher (Leiden: Leiden University Press, 2016), 14. Also see Aksakal, *Ottoman Road to War,* esp. ch. 5.

13. Zürcher, "Introduction: The Ottoman Jihad, the German Jihad and the Sacralization of War," 14; Mustafa Aksakal, "The Ottoman Proclamation of Jihad," in *Jihad and Islam in World War I,* 53–71; John Keegan, *The First World War* (New York: Vintage, 1998), 217; Kieser, *Talaat Pasha,* 206.

14. Kieser, "The Ottoman Road to Total War (1913–15)," 40.

15. In June 1909, the Law on the Conscription of Non-Muslim Communities passed through Parliament and was adopted on 21 July 1909. *Meclisi Mebusan Zabıt Ceridesi,* 475–486, in Taner Akçam, *Shameful Act: The Armenian Genocide and the Question of Turkish Responsibility* (New York: Metropolitan Books, 2006), 73; Ufuk Gülsoy, *Osmanlı Gayrimüslimlerinin Askerlik Serüveni* (Istanbul: Simurg Yayınları, 2000); Mehmed Hacısalihoğlu, "Inclusion and

Exclusion: Conscription in the Ottoman Empire," *Journal of Modern European History* 5, no. 2 (2007): 266–283; Eric J. Zürcher, "The Ottoman Conscription System in Theory and Practice, 1844–1918," in Eric J. Zürcher (ed.), *Arming the State: Military Conscription in the Middle East and Central Asia, 1775–1925* (New York: I.B. Tauris, 1999), 87–90.

16. Akın, "Seferberlik: Building up the Ottoman Home Front," 56, 62–63.

17. The articles included socks, bags, sacks, cottons, clothes, and so on. This monthly practice later became permanent and continued until the deportation. Sarafian, *Badmo'wt'iwn Ah'nt'abi Hah'o'c,* vol. I, 1010.

18. Sarafian, *Badmo'wt'iwn Ah'nt'abi Hah'o'c,* vol. I, 1013.

19. Kieser, "The Ottoman Road to Total War (1913–15)," 42; Michael A. Reynolds, *Shattering Empires: The Clash and Collapse of the Ottoman and Russian Empires, 1908–1918* (Cambridge: Cambridge University Press, 2011), 124–127.

20. Edward J. Erickson, *Ordered to Die: A History of the Ottoman Army in the First World War* (Westport, CT: Greenwood Press, 2000), 51–74; Üngör, *The Making of Modern Turkey,* 59; Ryan Gingeras, *Fall of the Sultanate: The Great War and the End of the Ottoman Empire, 1908–1922* (New York: Oxford University Press, 2016), 119–120.

21. Karekin Pastermadjian, *Why Armenia Should Be Free: Armenia's Role in the Present War* (Boston: Hairenik Publishing Company, 1918), 21; Bloxham, *The Great Game of Genocide,* 75; Üngör, *The Making of Modern Turkey,* 59; Kieser, *Talaat Pasha,* 222–223.

22. BOA.DH.ŞFR 48 / 166, Talat to the provinces of Erzurum, Bitlis, and Van, 26 December 1914, cited in Üngör, *The Making of Modern Turkey,* 59.

23. Edward J. Erickson, "The Armenians and Ottoman Military Policy, 1915," *War in History* 15, no. 2 (2008): 152; Mehmet Beşikçi, *The Ottoman Mobilization of Manpower in the First World War: Between Voluntarism and Resistance* (Boston: Brill, 2012).

24. While Cemal Pasha concerned himself with the Ottoman campaigns in the Suez Canal area, Fahri Pasha was charged with the coastal defenses of Syria and Cilicia, as well as internal security of these areas; see Hilmar Kaiser (ed.), *Eberhard Count Wolffskeel Von Reichenberg, Zeitun, Mousa Dagh, Ourfa: Letters on the Armenian Genocide,* Letter to his wife, 24 April 1915 (London: Gomidas Institute, 2004), xiii.

25. *Badmo'wt'iwn Ah'nt'abi Hah'o'c,* vol. I, 1015.

26. *Badmo'wt'iwn Ah'nt'abi Hah'o'c,* vol. I, 1016.

27. BNu / Fonds A. Andonian, P.J. 1 / 3, file 4, Aintab, "The Deportation of Armenians in Aintab," 2.

28. Akçam, *Young Turks' Crime,* 83; Henry Morgenthau, *Ambassador Morgenthau's Story* (Detroit: Wayne State University Press, 2003), 222–223; Taner

Akçam, *From Empire to Republic: Turkish Nationalism and the Armenian Genocide* (New York: Zed Books, 2004), 147; Arnold Toynbee, *The Western Question in Greece and Turkey* (London: Constable, 1922), 140; A. A. Pallis, "Racial Migrations in the Balkans during the Years 1912–1924," *Geographical Journal* 66, no. 4 (1925): 318; Yusuf Doğan Çetinkaya, "Muslim Merchants and Working Class in Action: Nationalism, Social Mobilization and Boycott Movement in the Ottoman Empire 1908–1914" (unpublished PhD diss., Leiden University, 2010), 218.

29. Matthias Bjørnlund, "The 1914 Cleansing of Aegean Greeks as a Case of Violent Turkification," *Journal of Genocide Research* 10, no. 1 (2008): 45; Akçam, *Young Turks' Crime,* 55, 63; Gingeras, *Sorrowful Shores: Violence, Ethnicity, and the End of the Ottoman Empire 1912–1923* (New York: Oxford University Press, 2011), 39–40.

30. Yusuf Doğan Çetinkaya, "Muslim Merchants and Working Class in Action: Nationalism, Social Mobilization and Boycott Movement in the Ottoman Empire 1908–1914" (unpublished PhD. diss., Leiden University, 2010), 193.

31. BNu / Fonds A. Andonian, P.J. 1 / 3, file 4, Aintab, "The Deportation of Armenians in Aintab," 2–3.

32. Papken Gulesserian, "Hah'er'en ew Turk Lez'o'w" [The Armenian and Turkish Language], *Datev,* 1929, 32. Datev is a religious yearbook, published in Aleppo, Syria; Sarkis Y. Karaian, "On the Number of Armenians in Aintab in 1914," in *Badmo'wt'iwn Ah'nt'abi Hah'o'c,* vol. III, 11–12, and *Nor Ah'nt'ab* 13, no. 50–51 (1972): 33–35; Archbishop Ormanian, *Ha'h'o'c Egeghecin* [The Armenian Church] (Beirut: Antilias, 1952), 210; Bogharian, "Ah'nt'ab Hah'o'c T'iwē: Nakh Kan Hamashkharhayin A. Baderazmē" [The Number of Aintab Armenians: Before the World War], *Hah Ah'nt'ab* 10, no. 6 (1969): 59–61; Krikor Bogharian, *Orakro'wt'iwn Darakir Geanqis* [Diary of My Life in Exile] in *Ceghasban T'o'wrqy Vgah'o'wt'iwnner Qagho'wadz Hrashqo'v P'rgo'wadznero'w Zro'h'nere'n* [Genocider Turk: Testimonies Taken from the Accounts of Armenians Who Miraculously Survived] (Beirut: Shirag, 1973), 122; Kevork A. Sarafian, *A Briefer History of Aintab: A Concise History of the Cultural, Religious, Educational, Political, Industrial and Commercial Life of the Armenians of Aintab* (Los Angeles: Union of the Armenians of Aintab, 1957), 11. According to Rössler, the German Consul in Aleppo, as of 30 July 1915, Aintab had 32,000 Armenian inhabitants; see 1915-07-30-DE-011 in Wolfang Gust (ed.), *The Armenian Genocide: Evidence from the German Foreign Office Archives, 1915–1916* (New York: Berghahn Books, 2014), 275. Armenian author Yeghia Dolbakian also gives 30,000 as the number of Armenians in Aintab before the deportation; see Yeghia H. Dolbakian, *Aynt'abn u Aynt'abahayē* [Aintab and Aintab Armenians] (Yerevan 1992; Halep, 1994), 40; A. Gesar, *Ah'nt'abi*

Ko'h'amardy [Aintab Self-Defense] (Hayrenik: Boston, 1945), 18; Kévorkian and Paul B. Paboudjian, "Les massacres de Cilicie d'avril 1909," in *La Cilicie (1909–1921) de Massacres d'Adana au Mandat Français,* ed. Raymond Kévorkian (Paris: Revue d'Histoire Armenienne Contemporaine Tome III, 1999), 318–323; M. Abadi, *Türk Verdünü Antep'in Dört Muhasarası* (Gaziantep: Gaziantep Kültür Derneği Yayınları, 1959), 11; FO 608 / 77, *British High Commission in Istanbul,* 28 May 1919. On the other hand, Kevork Barsumian, another Armenian author, reports that the general population of Aintab in 1913 was closer to 80,000, with Armenians comprising 36,000. The information on the 1915 population Barsumian provides—based on Necati Bey, who held an official position at the General Registration Office—is extremely dramatic. Barsumian claims that in 1915, 42,000 Armenians were deported from Aintab. If we add the number of those not deported, the total would be around 47,000. Kevork H. Barsumian, *Badmo'wt'iwn Ah'nt'abi H. H. Tashnagco'wt'iwn 1898–1922* [History of the Aintab Armenian Revolutionary Federation 1898–1922] (Aleppo: Tigris, 1957), 16.

33. Kemal Karpat, *Ottoman Population (1830–1914): Demographic and Social Character* (Madison: University of Wisconsin Press, 1985), 176. Stanford Shaw has also given the same population statistics with regard to the 1914 population in Aintab. However, with regard to the number of Armenians, Shaw has estimated the number as 14,466, only by taking into consideration the number of Gregorian Armenians. He did not mention the number of Catholic and Protestant Armenians. Stanford Shaw, "Ottoman Population Movement during the Last Years of the Empire, 1885–1914: Some Preliminary Remarks," *Journal of Ottoman Studies* 1 (1980): 205; Genelkurmay Başkanlığı, *Arşiv Belgeleriyle Ermeni Faaliyetleri 1914–1918,* vol. 1 (Ankara: Genelkurmay Basımevi, 2005), 655; Uğurol Barlas, *Gaziantep Tıp Fakültesi Tarihi ve Azınlık Okulları* (Gaziantep: Gaziantep Kültür Derneği, 1971), 13; Yetkin, *Gaziantep Tarihi ve Davaları,* 39. According to an Ottoman document, by December 1915, the total Aintab population was around 120,000, with approximately 100,000 being Muslim and around 19,000 Armenian. See BOA.DH.EUM.II.Şube 73 / 69, 17 Kanunuevvel 1331 (30 December 1915).

34. BNu / Fonds A. Andonian, P.J. 1 / 3, file 4, Aintab, "The Deportation of Armenians in Aintab," 1.

35. Bloxham, *The Great Game of Genocide,* 80–82. In fact, disturbances in Zeitun started shortly after the declaration of general mobilization in early August 1914; see BOA.DH.ŞFR 438 / 80, 13 August 1330 (26 August 1914) and BOA.DH.ŞFR 442 / 80, 17 September 1330 (30 September 1914).

36. Kévorkian, *The Armenian Genocide,* 589; also see Gust (ed.), *The Armenian Genocide,* 61; Fuat Dündar, *Crime of Numbers: The Role of Statistics in*

the Armenian Question (1878–1918) (New Brunswick and London: Transaction Publishers, 2010), 72.

37. Report by a witness, 12 March, annexed to a letter from the Dr. Eugen Büge, German consul in Adana, to Wangenheim, 13 March 1915: Lepsius (ed.), *Archives du génocide des Arméniens: recueil des documents diplomatiques allemands* (Paris: Fayard, 1986), doc. 19, 74–76; Raymond Kévorkian, *The Armenian Genocide: A Complete History* (London: I.B. Tauris, 2011), 590; Kévorkian, "The Extermination of Ottoman Armenians by the Young Turk Regime (1915–1916)," *Online Encyclopedia of Mass Violence* (3 June 2008), http://www.massviolence.org/The-Extermination-of-Ottoman-Armenians-by-the-Young-Turk-Regime (accessed 14 July 2014).

38. Genelkurmay Başkanlığı, *Arşiv Belgeleriyle Ermeni Faaliyetleri 1914–1918,* vol. 1 (Ankara: Genelkurmay Basımevi, 2005), 55.

39. Genelkurmay Başkanlığı, *Arşiv Belgeleriyle Ermeni Faaliyetleri 1914–1918,* vol. 1, 55–56; Kévorkian, *The Armenian Genocide,* 590.

40. BOA.DH.ŞFR 50 / 141, Ministry of Interior / Public Security Directorate (EUM) to Adana, 2 March 1915; Akçam, *Young Turks' Crime,* 175. For a broader discussion of the February 1915 deportations from Dörtyol, İskenderun and the later ones from Zeitun and Marash that occurred in March and April, see Akçam, *Shameful Act,* 146–147; 159–161.

41. James Bryce and Arnold Toynbee, *The Treatment of Armenians in the Ottoman Empire, 1915–1916: Document Presented to Viscount Grey of Falloden by Viscount Bryce* (Princeton, NJ: Gomidas Institute / Taderon Press, 2000), 636.

42. BOA.DH.ŞFR 467 / 29, 26 March 1331 (8 April 1915).

43. BOA.DH.ŞFR 467 / 29, 26 March 1331 (8 April 1915).

44. For the 9 April 1915 coded telegram, see the Archive of Turkish General Staff Directorate of Military History and Strategic Studies (ATASE) cl.2287, ds.32–12, n.1–37 cited in Dündar, *Crime of Numbers,* 71–72.

45. *Askeri Tarih Belgeleri Dergisi,* no. 81, 1982, doc. 1823, Cemal Pasha to Enver Pasha, Jerusalem, 10 April 1915, telegram 3108, cited in Hilmar Kaiser, "Regional Resistance to Central Government Policies: Ahmed Cemal Pasha, the Governors of Aleppo, and Armenian Deportees in the Spring and Summer of 1915," *Journal of Genocide Research* 12, no. 3–4 (2010): 180; NA / RG 59 / 867.00 / 761, Report from United States Consul in Aleppo, J. B. Jackson, to Ambassador Morgenthau, dated 21 April 1915, in *United States Official Records on the Armenian Genocide, 1915–1917,* ed. Ara Sarafian (Princeton, NJ: Gomidas Institute, 2004), 10; Gulesserian, "Dasnmeg Egheragan Dariner Ah'nt'abi mĕch, 1908–1919," [11 Brutal Years in Aintab 1908–1919], in *Badmo'wt'iwn Ah'nt'abi Hah'o'c,* vol. I, 1019. Vahe N. Gulesserian was born in Aintab on 2 March 1894. He graduated from Vartanian High School and at-

tended Cilicia College until 1915. During the deportation period, he was allowed to stay in Aintab with his father and family, as his father was a coppersmith and was needed in the city. He entered the United States on 1 November 1939; see Sarafian, *A Briefer History of Aintab,* 251.

46. Bloxham, *The Great Game of Genocide,* 80–82.

47. Kévorkian and Paboudjian, *Le Génocide des Arméniens,* 304, 393, 394–395, 408.

48. Dündar, *Crime of Numbers,* 75.

49. BOA.DH.ŞFR 52 / 93, EUM to Cemal Pasha, 24 April 1915.

50. BOA.DH.ŞFR 52 / 95, EUM to all governors, 24 April 1915. Two days later, Enver Pasha gave orders to the commanders that all Armenian organizations were to be closed; see ATASE cl. 2287, ds.32-12, f. 12-1, cited in Dündar, *Crime of Numbers,* 74n42.

51. BOA.DH.ŞFR 52 / 286 coded telegram from EUM to the Provincial District of Marash, 9 May 1915 and also see NA / RG59 / 867.4016 / 95 from Henry Morgenthau, American Ambassador, Istanbul, to the Secretary of State, 20 July 1915, in *United States Official Records on the Armenian Genocide 1915–1917,* 98; for the number of Armenians deported from places like Hacin and Dörtyol, see BOA.DH.ŞFR 52 / 338, EUM to Adana, 12 May 1915.

52. Bryce and Toynbee, *The Treatment of Armenians in the Ottoman Empire, 1915–1916,* 100.

53. Bloxham, *The Great Game of Genocide,* 94; Donald Bloxham, "The Armenian Genocide of 1915–1916: Cumulative Radicalization and the Development of a Destruction Policy," *Past and Present* 181, no. 1 (2003): 188.

54. Bloxham, *The Great Game of Genocide,* 95; Bloxham, "The Armenian Genocide of 1915–1916," 189.

55. Yektan Türkyılmaz, "Rethinking Genocide: Violence and Victimhood in Eastern Anatolia, 1913–1915" (unpublished PhD diss., Duke University, 2011), 23.

56. Bloxham, "Armenian Genocide of 1915–1916," 190 191.

57. Bloxham, "Armenian Genocide of 1915–1916," 191; Bloxham, *The Great Game of Genocide,* 96.

58. BOA.DH.ŞFR 53 / 91, 53 / 92, 53 / 93, and 53 / 94 coded telegrams from minister of Interior Talat Pasha to the commander of the Imperial Fourth Army, 23 May 1915. Also see Akçam, *Young Turks' Crime,* 192.

59. BOA.DH.ŞFR 53 / 85, Talat to Cemal, 23 May 1915, cited in Üngör, *The Making of Modern Turkey,* 70.

60. Üngör, "Diyarbekir (1915–1916): Young Turk Mass Killing at the Provincial Level," Sciences Po: Mass Violence and Resistance-Research Network, 25 March 2009, www.sciencespo.fr/mass-violence-war-massacre-resistance/en/

document/diyarbekir-1915-1916-young-turk-mass-killings-provincial-level (accessed 14 July 2014).

61. Vahakn Dadrian, *The History of Armenian Genocide: Ethnic Conflict from the Balkans and Anatolia to the Caucasus* (New York: Berghahn Books, 2004), 239; Bloxham, *The Great Game of Genocide,* 85, 136–137; Bloxham, "Armenian Genocide of 1915–1916," 179–180.

62. *Takvim-i Vekayi* no. 2189, 19 May 1331 (1 June 1915). The precise name of the law is "Vakt-i Seferde İcraat-ı Hükûmete Karşı Gelenler İçin Cihet-i Askeriyece İttihâz Olunacak Tedâbir Hakkında Muvakkat Kanun" (Provisional Law on Steps to be Taken Militarily Concerning Those Who During Campaigns Oppose the Actions of the Government). Also see Üngör, *Making of Modern Turkey,* 71.

63. Üngör, *Making of Modern Turkey,* 71.

64. BOA.DH.ŞFR 54 / 87, EUM to Trabzon, Ma'muretü'l-aziz, Sivas, Diyarbekir and Canik, 21 June 1915; BOA.DH.ŞFR 54-A / 97, coded telegram from EUM to the Province of Trebziond and the Provincial District of Canik, 24 June 1915; BOA.DH.ŞFR 54-A / 100, coded telegram from EUM to the Provinces of Erzurum, Adana, Bitlis, Aleppo, Diyarbekir, Sivas, Trebziond, Ma'muretü'l-aziz, and Van, and to the Provincial Districts of Urfa and Marash, 25 June 1915. Also see 1915-06-30-DE-001 in Gust (ed.), *The Armenian Genocide,* 70; Dündar, *Crime of Numbers,* 90–91; and Akçam, *Young Turks' Crime,* 232.

65. *Arşiv Belgeleriyle Ermeni Faaliyetleri 1914–1918,* vol. 1, 152; Azmi Süslü, *Ermeniler ve 1915 Tehcir Olayı* (Ankara: Yüzüncü Yıl Üniversitesi Yayınları, 1990), 112.

66. BOA.DH.ŞFR 53 / 94, coded telegram from Minister of Interior to Fourth Army Commander, 23 May 1915; *Arşiv Belgeleriyle Ermeni Faaliyetleri,* vol. 8 (Ankara: Genelkurmay ATASE ve Genelkurmay Denetleme Başkanlığı Yayınları, 2008), 3.

67. BOA.DH.ŞFR 54-A / 51, 21 July 1915. In the well-known "Black Book of Talat Pasha," Talat provided detailed figures for cities in every province and provincial district on the numbers of Armenians. This book was published by Turkish journalist Murat Bardakçı in 2008; see Murat Bardakçı, *Talat Paşa'nın Evrak-ı Metrukesi: Sadrazam Talat Paşa'nın Özel Arşivinde Bulunan Ermeni Tehciri Konusundaki Belgeler ve Hususi Yazışmalar* (Istanbul: Everest Yayınları, 2008), 76–77, 89–94, 101–104, and 108–145.

68. BOA.DH.EUM.II.Şube 68 / 34, Celal to Ministry of Interior, 29 March 1915; BOA.DH.ŞFR 466 / 92, Celal to Ministry of Interior, Aleppo, 29 March 1915.

69. After the war, Aram Andonian remained in Aleppo, staying for a while at the Baron Hotel. He received numerous letters, personal papers, diaries,

notes, and other documents from genocide survivors regarding their experiences, which he collected and classified by province and district, including for Aintab. He also produced one of the first analytical publications on the Armenian massacres. He later became the first curator of the Nubarian Library of the Armenian General Benevolent Union (AGBU) in Paris, where his files are. After the war, he obtained telegrams from a Turkish official named Naim Bey (who worked in an office in Aleppo on issues connected with the settlement of Armenians) that included orders concerning the killing of Armenians. They were first published in French as *Documents Officiels Concernant les Massacres Armeniens,* trans. M. S. David-Beg (Paris: Imprimerie H. Turabian, 1920), and subsequently in English as *The Memoirs of Naim Bey* (London, 1920; 2nd repr., Newton Square, PA: Armenian Historical Research Association, 1965). The Armenian translation was published in 1921; see *Medz O'jiry* [The Great Crime] (Boston: Bahag Printing House, 1921). See also Taner Akçam's recent publication on the Andonian and Naim Bey documents: *Killing Orders: Talat Pasha's Telegrams and the Armenian Genocide* (Basingstoke: Palgrave Macmillan, 2018).

70. BNu / Fonds A. Andonian, P.J. 1 / 3, file 4, Aintab, "The Deportation of Armenians in Aintab," 3; Johannes Lepsius, *Der Todesgang des armenische Volkes: Bericht über das Schicksal des armenischen Volkes in der Türkei wahrend des Weltkrieges* (Potsdam: Der Tempelverlag, 1919), 27–28, 35–37.

71. BNu / Fonds A. Andonian, P.J. 1 / 3, file 4, Aintab, "The Deportation of Armenians in Aintab," 3. Krikor Bogharian (1897–1975) was deported to Aleppo, then Hama, and finally to Salamiyya alongside his entire family and also kept a diary about his life from 29 July 1915 to 6 December 1916. Bogharian, *Orakro'wt'iwn Darakir Geanqis,* 121–122. Sebouh Aguni, *Milion my Hah'ero'w Ch'arti Badmo'wt'iwny* [History of the Massacre of One Million Armenians] (Istanbul: H. Asaduryan Vortik, 1920), 310. Sebouh Aguni was the former editor of the daily *Zhamanag.* He was the first to publish a global study of the massacres, basing his work on a large number of documents at the disposal of the Patriarchate.

72. It was clear that, as Eberhard Graf von Wolffskeel, chief of staff to Fahri Pasha, had confirmed, certain circles in Marash sent a blatantly "made up telegram" to Istanbul in which they affirmed that the Armenians "occupied a mosque" and "began to kill the Muslims." Kaiser (ed.), *Eberhard Count Wolffskeel Von Reichenberg, Zeitun, Mousa Dagh, Ourfa,* 14.

73. BNu / Fonds A. Andonian, P.J. 1 / 3, file 4, Aintab, "The Deportation of Armenians in Aintab," 4.

74. BNu / Fonds A. Andonian, P.J. 1 / 3, file 4, Aintab, "The Deportation of Armenians in Aintab," 4.

75. BOA.DH.ŞFR 52 / 48, Ministry of Interior to Aleppo Province, 20 April 1915; BOA.DH.ŞFR 468 / 54; BOA.DH.ŞFR.II.Şube, 10 / 89, 21 April 1915.

76. When Rössler arrived in Aintab late on the evening of 8 April, he reported later, "I learned that General Fakhri Pasha was in town, accompanied by the German Major Count Wolffskeel, in order to go on a tour of inspection of Marash, Zeytun and elsewhere." 1915-10-25-DE-011 and 1915-04-12-DE-001 in Gust (ed.), *The Armenian Genocide,* 99, 166.

77. BNu / Fonds A. Andonian, P.J. 1 / 3, file 4, Aintab, "The Deportation of Armenians in Aintab," 4.

78. NA / RG 59, 867.00 / 761, Report from United States consul in Aleppo, J. B. Jackson, to Ambassador Morgenthau, 21 April 1915, in *United States Official Records on the Armenian Genocide, 1915–1917,* 12; "Miss Frearson's Experiences and Observations in Turkey," *ABCFM* 16.9.6.1, unit 5, vol. 2, part 1, reel 670-7.1.20, 1817–1919, 10.

79. 1915-07-17-DE-002 in Gust (ed.), *The Armenian Genocide,* 99–100.

80. ATASE, First World War Collection (FWW); file (F): 1846, dossier (D): 79, index (I): 13 / 4 cited in Polat Safi, "History in the Trench: The Ottoman Special Organization–Teşkilat-ı Mahsusa Literature," *Middle Eastern Studies* 48, no. 1 (2012): 89.

81. Ryan Gingeras, *Heroin, Organized Crime, and the Making of Modern Turkey* (New York: Oxford University Press, 2014), 38–39; Vahakn Dadrian and Taner Akçam, *Judgment at Istanbul: The Armenian Genocide Trials* (New York: Berghahn Books, 2011).

82. BNu / Fonds A. Andonian, P.J. 1 / 3, file 4, Aintab, "The Deportation of Armenians in Aintab," 5; Kévorkian, *The Armenian Genocide,* 606.

83. BNu / Fonds A. Andonian, P.J. 1 / 3, file 4, Aintab, "The Deportation of Armenians in Aintab," 5; Aguni, *Milion my Hah'ero'w Ch'arti Badmo'wt'iwny,* 310.

84. BNu / Fonds A. Andonian, P.J. 1 / 3, file 4, Aintab, "The Deportation of Armenians in Aintab," 5.

85. Gulesserian, "Dasnmeg Egheragan Dariner Ah'nt'abi měch, 1908–1919," in *Badmo'wt'iwn Ah'nt'abi Hah'o'c,* vol. I, 465, 1020; Bogharian, *Orakro'wt'iwn Darakir Geanqis,* 121–122; BNu / Fonds A. Andonian, P.J. 1 / 3, file 4, Aintab, "The Deportation of Armenians in Aintab," 4; Father Nerses Tavukjian, *Dar'abanqi Orakro'wt'iwn* [Diary of Miserable Days], ed. Toros Toramanian (Beirut: High Type Compugraph—Technopresse, 1991), 66, 69; Aguni, *Milion my Hah'ero'w Ch'arti Badmo'wt'iwny,* 310; Barsumian, *Badmo'wt'iwn Ah'nt'abi H. H. Tashnagco'wt'iwn 1898–1922,* 49; "Hırant K. Sulahian 1871–1949," *Nor Ah'nt'abi* 13, no. 50–51 (1972): 11; Kévorkian, *The Armenian Genocide,* 606.

86. Bogharian, *Orakro'wt'iwn Darakir Geanqis,* 122; NA / RG59 / 867.4016 / 95, from Henry Morgenthau American Ambassador, Istanbul to the Secretary of State, 20 July 1915, in *United States Official Records on the Armenian Genocide 1915–1917,* 98.

87. Gulesserian, "Dasnmeg Egheragan Dariner Ah'nt'abi měch, 1908–1919," 1020; Bogharian, *Orakro'wt'iwn Darakir Geanqis,* 121.

88. BNu / Fonds A. Andonian, P.J. 1 / 3, file 4, Aintab, "The Deportation of Armenians in Aintab," 6.

89. Gulesserian, "Dasnmeg Egheragan Dariner Ah'nt'abi měch, 1908–1919," 1019; Sarkis Balabanian, *Geanqis Daq o'w Bagh Orery: Ah'nt'ab, Qe'sab, Hale'b* [Hot and Cold Days of My Life: Aintab, Kesap, Halep] (Aleppo: Atlas, 1983), 54; Kévorkian, *The Armenian Genocide,* 606.

90. Balabanian, *Geanqis Daq o'w Bagh Orery,* 54–55; Bogharian, *Orakro'wt'iwn Darakir Geanqis,* 122; Katchadourian, *Efronia: An Armenian Love Story,* 126.

91. Report by Miss Frearson, a missionary in Aintab, written in September 1915 after her departure from Turkey in Bryce and Toynbee, *The Treatment of Armenians in the Ottoman Empire, 1915–1916,* 541–550; James L. Barton, *Turkish Atrocities: Statements of American Missionaries on the Destruction of Christian Communities in Ottoman Turkey, 1915–1917* (Ann Arbor, MI: Gomidas Institute, 1998), 107; Kévorkian, *The Armenian Genocide,* 606.

92. NA / RG59 / 867.4016 / 72, Jackson to Morgenthau, Aleppo, 12 May 1915, No 276, in *United States Official Records on the Armenian Genocide 1915–1917,* 41.

93. Bogharian, *Orakro'wt'iwn Darakir Geanqis,* 122; Tavukjian, *Dar'abanqi Orakro'wt'iwn,* 65; Balabanian, *Geanqis Daq o'w Bagh Orery,* 63; Gulesserian, "Dasnmeg Egheragan Dariner Ah'nt'abi měch, 1908–1919," 1019–1020.

94. BNu / Fonds A. Andonian, P.J. 1 / 3, file 4, Aintab, "The Deportation of Armenians in Aintab," 9; Balabanian, *Geanqis Daq o'w Bagh Orery,* 63; Karnig Panian, *Goodbye, Antoura: A Memoir of the Armenia Genocide* (Stanford, CA: Stanford University Press, 2015), 39; *Germany, Turkey and Armenia, A Selection of Documentary Evidence Relating to the Armenian Atrocities from German and Other Sources* (London: J. J. Keliher and Co., 1917), 71; NA / RG5 9 / 867.4016 / 80, from Henry Morgenthau American Ambassador, Istanbul to the Secretary of State, June 26, 1915, in *United States Official Records on the Armenian Genocide 1915–1917,* 68–69.

95. BNu / Fonds A. Andonian, P.J. 1 / 3, file 4, Aintab, "The Deportation of Armenians in Aintab," 9; Balabanian, *Geanqis Daq o'w Bagh Orery,* 55–56; Kévorkian, *The Armenian Genocide,* 606.

96. Gulesserian, "Dasnmeg Egheragan Dariner Ah'nt'abi měch, 1908–1919," 1020; Balabanian, *Geanqis Daq o'w Bagh Orery,* 56; Harutyun H. Nazarian,

Eghernēn Verabrogh H'o'wsher [Memoires of a Genocide Survivor], ed. Toros Toronian (Halep, 2009), 13.

97. Gulesserian, "Dasnmeg Egheragan Dariner Ah'nt'abi mĕch, 1908–1919," 1020.

98. BNu / Fonds A. Andonian, P.J. 1 / 3, file 4, Aintab, "The Deportation of Armenians in Aintab," 7.

99. Cemal Bey was the absolute master of the entire Aleppo province, higher than the governor-general, for civil administrative affairs. He could not intervene in military affairs, but in civil affairs—such as the deportation and massacre—everything was submitted to his authority. See Krikor Guerguerian Private Archival Collection, folder number: 22, file name: Technical Analysis Dossier, file no: 59.

100. AA-PA, Konsulat Aleppo, Paket 1, vol. 1, J. no 1311, Rössler to Embassy, Aleppo, 21 June 1915, telegram 9, cited in Kaiser, "Regional Resistance to Central Government Policies," 193; Rössler to Embassy, Aleppo, 21 June 1915 J. no. 3790 AA-PA Konstantinopel 169 telegram 9; Rössler to Embassy, Aleppo, 21 June 1915 J. no. 3799 AA-PA Konstantinopel 169 telegram 10 cited in Kaiser, in collaboration with Luther and Nancy Eskijian, *At the Crossroads of Der Zor: Death, Survival, and Humanitarian Resistance in Aleppo, 1915–1917* (Princeton, NJ: Gomidas Institute Books / Taderon Press, 2001), 15.

101. Kaiser, "Regional Resistance to Central Government Policies," 193.

102. BNu / Fonds A. Andonian, P.J. 1 / 3, file 4, Aintab, "The Deportation of Armenians in Aintab," 8.

103. BOA.DH.ŞFR 480 / 53, 17 July 1915.

104. BOA.DH.ŞFR 54A / 113, 26 July 1915. Mehmed Şükrü Bey was appointed to district governorship of Çankırı on 27 July 1915. BOA.İ.DH 1515 / 1333, 27 July 1915. His official appointment decree was promulgated in *Takvim-i Vekayi* on 21 August 1915. *Takvim-i Vekayi,* no. 2266, 1.

105. According to Aguni and Andonian, the mutasarrıf Mehmed Şükrü and military commander Hilmi resigned so as not to have to carry out the deportation order as a final blow to the Aintab Armenians. Aguni, *Milion my Hah'ero'w Ch'arti Badmo'wt'iwny,* 310; BNu / Fonds A. Andonian, P.J. 1 / 3, file 4, Aintab, "The Deportation of Armenians in Aintab," 4.

106. BNu / Fonds A. Andonian, P.J. 1 / 3, file 4, Aintab, "The Deportation of Armenians in Aintab," 7.

107. BNu / Fonds A. Andonian, P.J. 1 / 3, file 4, Aintab, "The Deportation of Armenians in Aintab," 7.

108. 1915-07-31-DE-002 in Gust (ed.), *The Armenian Genocide,* 276.

109. Telegram from the German consul in Aleppo, Walter Rössler, to the embassy in Istanbul, 30 July 1915 in Lepsius (ed.), *Archives du Génocide des*

Arméniens, doc. 125, 119–120, cited in Kévorkian, *The Armenian Genocide,* 606–607.

110. Letter from the consul Jackson to Morgenthau, 3 August 1915 in *United States Official Records on the Armenian Genocide, 1915–1917,* 169 cited in Kévorkian, *The Armenian Genocide,* 607.

111. 1915-09-03-DE-002 in Gust (ed.), *The Armenian Genocide,* 351.

112. 1915-09-03-DE-002 in Gust (ed.), *The Armenian Genocide,* 351.

113. Barsumian, *Badmo'wt'iwn Ah'nt'abi H. H. Tashnagco'wt'iwn 1898–1922,* 49; 204–206. Vahe N. Gulesserian (ed.), *H'o'wshamadean Awedis Kalemqereani* [Memoir of Avedis Kalemkerian] (Beirut: Dıbaran Der Sahagyan, 1965), 58. In his memoirs, Avedis Kalemkerian, who was one of the participants of this meeting, gave 28 July as the date of this meeting.

114. Dikran Sebouh Tchakmakdjian (1894–1964) was deported first to Hama and then Lebanon, where he painted Cemal Pasha's portrait and gave it to him as a present. Thanks to the gift, Cemal Pasha protected him. *Badmo'wt'iwn Ah'nt'abi Hah'o'c,* vol. III, 933; Raymond Kévorkian et al. (eds.), *Les Arméniens de Cilicie: Habitat, Mémoire et Identé* (Paris: Presses de L'université Saint-Joseph, 2012), 154; Sarafian, *A Briefer History of Aintab,* 299; Ümit Kurt, "A Rescuer, an Enigma and a Génocidaire: Cemal Pasha," in *The End of the Ottomans: The Genocide of 1915 and the Politics of Turkish Nationalism,* ed. Hans-Lukas Kieser et al. (New York: I.B. Tauris / Bloomsbury, 2019), 234.

115. Given *vesika* (certificate) by Cemal Pasha's order, Avedis Kalemkerian and his family were safely sent to Damascus. Cemal Pasha personally knew Avedis's father and protected him. On 1 December 1917, Avedis Kalemkerian was hired at a construction factory in Damascus by Cemal Pasha's order again. He obtained a "military certificate" and worked in this factory until the British occupation of Damascus. In his memoirs, Avedis himself gave credit to Cemal Pasha for his effort to protect his family from being sent to Deir ez-Zor. Barsumian, *Badmo'wt'iwn Ah'nt'abi H. H. Tashnagco'wt'iwn 1898 1922,* 49; *H'o'wshamadean Awedis Kalemqereani,* 58–63, 70.

116. Barsumian, *Badmo'wt'iwn Ah'nt'abi H. H. Tashnagco'wt'iwn 1898–1922,* 49–50; 204–206. Balabanian attended this meeting, and he attested to Barsumian's remarks; see Balabanian, *Geanqis Daq o'w Bagh Orery,* 58.

117. Gulesserian, "Dasnmeg Egheragan Dariner Ah'nt'abi měch, 1908–1919," 1022; Tavukjian, *Dar'abanqi Orakro'wt'iwn,* 70; Katchadourian, *Efronia: An Armenian Love Story,* 126; BNu / Fonds A. Andonian, P.J. 1 / 3, file 4, Aintab, "The Deportation of Armenians in Aintab," 7; *H'o'wshamadean Awedis Kalemqereani,* 56; Barsumian, *Badmo'wt'iwn Ah'nt'abi H. H. Tashnagco'wt'iwn 1898–1922,* 49; Balabanian, *Geanqis Daq o'w Bagh Orery,* 58.

118. Different dates are given in memoirs regarding the exact beginning of deportations of Aintab Armenians; see BNu / Fonds A. Andonian, P.J. 1 / 3, file 4, Aintab, "The Deportation of Armenians in Aintab," 7; Bogharian, *Orakro'wt'iwn Darakir Geanqis,* 122, 126–129; Elie H. Nazarian, *Badmakirq Nazarean Kertasdani (1475–1988)* [History of Nazarian Family, 1475–1988] (Beirut: Zartonk Press, 1988), 184; Katchadourian, *Efronia: An Armenian Love Story,* 137; Kersam Aharonian, *H'o'wshamadean Medz Egher'ni* [Memoir of the Great Crime] (Beirut: Atlas, 1965), 46; Barsumian, *Badmo'wt'iwn Ah'nt'abi H. H. Tashnagco'wt'iwn 1898–1922,* 204; Aguni, *Milion my Hah'ero'w Ch'arti Badmo'wt'iwny,* 311; M. Arzumian, *Ha'hasdan, 1914–1917* [Armenia, 1914–1917] (Yerevan: Hayasdan 1969), 438.

119. Bogharian, *Orakro'wt'iwn Darakir Geanqis,* 123; Tavukjian, *Dar'abanqi Orakro'wt'iwn,* 71. As opposed to Bogharian's and Tavukjian's accounts, Gulesserian gave the number of thirteen affluent and well-known families and other people from the Gregorian community who formed the first convoy of deportees. Gulesserian, "Dasnmeg Egheragan Dariner Ah'nt'abi měch, 1908–1919," 1023. Additionally, according to Miss Frearson's accounts, the first convoy of Aintab Armenians was sent away on 30 or 31 July 1915. "Miss Frearson's Experiences and Observations in Turkey," *ABCFM* 16.9.6.1, unit 5, vol. 2, part 1, reel 670-7.1.14, 1817–1919, 4.

120. Gulesserian, "Dasnmeg Egheragan Dariner Ah'nt'abi měch, 1908–1919," 1023.

121. Sarafian, *Badmo'wt'iwn Ah'nt'abi Hah'o'c,* vol. I, 924.

122. Interview conducted with Yervant Derentz, *USC Shoah Foundation,* Visual History Archive Online, Armenian Film Foundation.

123. Gulesserian, "Dasnmeg Egheragan Dariner Ah'nt'abi měch, 1908–1919," 1023; Bogharian, *Orakro'wt'iwn Darakir Geanqis,* 122.

124. Like the other families mentioned, the Leylekians were a rich and prominent family of textile manufacturers. They lost everything during the genocide. Shusan Yeni-Komshian Teager, *The Krajians of Aintab* (Belmont, MA, 2007), 51.

125. Report by Miss Frearson, written on 11 April 1918, in Bryce and Toynbee, *The Treatment of Armenians in the Ottoman Empire,* doc. 137, 543–544; Bogharian, *Orakro'wt'iwn Darakir Geanqis,* 136.

126. Gulesserian, "Dasnmeg Egheragan Dariner Ah'nt'abi měch, 1908–1919," 1026.

127. In his diary, Bogharian describes Yasin Effendi (Mehmet Yasin Sani Kutluğ, 1889–1973) as a man who seemed kind but sometimes treated deportees cruelly and punished them with the whip he carried. Bogharian, *Orakro'wt'iwn Darakir Geanqis,* 127. After the war, Yasin escaped to Ankara, joined Kemalist-

national forces (*kuvayı milliye*) in Halfeti, a town of Urfa, and became a deputy for Aintab in April 1920. He played an active role in the war between the Aintab national forces and the French military units in 1920–1921. Yasin Kutluğ, "İstiklal Savaşı'ndan Hatıralar," *Gaziantep Halkevi Mecmuası,* no. 25 (1940): 12; *Başpınar Aylık Edebiyat ve Kültür Mecmuası,* no. 16–17 (1940): 11; no. 25, no. 28, no. 30–31, March, June, July-August 1941; 7, 8, 13.

128. *Krikor Guerguerian Private Archival Collection,* folder number: 22, file name: Turks (List) Responsible, file no: 46.

129. BNu / Fonds A. Andonian, P.J. 1 / 3, file 4, Aintab, "The Deportation of Armenians in Aintab," 8; Tavukjian, *Dar'abanqi Orakro'wt'iwn,* 71.

130. Gulesserian, "Dasnmeg Egheragan Dariner Ah'nt'abi měch, 1908–1919," 1023.

131. FO 371 / 4241, 170751, Code No: 25, 5 August 1915. It is important to point out that at the bottom of this message is the name Hilmi Bey, district governor of Aintab.

132. Gulesserian, "Dasnmeg Egheragan Dariner Ah'nt'abi měch, 1908–1919," 1023. Meanwhile, Krikor Bogharian gives the date of 4 August 1915 as the departure of the second convoy of Armenian deportees from Aintab. Bogharian, *Orakro'wt'iwn Darakir Geanqis,* 123. Also, Bogharian mentions that the second convoy was composed of approximately eighty Armenian families. Bogharian, *Orakro'wt'iwn Darakir Geanqis,* 123. In addition, according to Tavukjian's diary, the second convoy comprised fifty-five families. Tavukjian, *Dar'abanqi Orakro'wt'iwn,* 72.

133. BNu / Fonds A. Andonian, P.J. 1 / 3, file 4, Aintab, "The Deportation of Armenians in Aintab," 8; Bogharian, *Orakro'wt'iwn Darakir Geanqis,* 123.

134. BNu / Fonds A. Andonian, P.J. 1 / 3, file 4, Aintab, "The Deportation of Armenians in Aintab," 8; Tavukjian, *Dar'abanqi Orakro'wt'iwn,* 72; Balabanian, *Geanqis Daq o'w Bagh Orery,* 57; NA / RG59 / 867.4016 / 148, Letter from the Consul Jackson to Morgenthau, 19 August 1915 in *United States Official Records on the Armenian Genocide, 1915–1917,* 207. In another report to Morgenthau on 3 August 1915, Jackson notes: "Now all Armenians have been ordered deported from the cities of Aintab, Mardin, Kilis, Antioch, Alexandretta, Kesab, and all the smaller towns in Aleppo province, estimated at 60,000 persons." NA / RG59 / 867.4016 / 126, Letter from the Consul Jackson to Morgenthau, 3 August 1915, in *United States Official Records on the Armenian Genocide, 1915–1917,* 169.

135. BNu / Fonds A. Andonian, P.J. 1 / 3, file 4, Aintab, "The Deportation of Armenians in Aintab," 8; Bogharian, *Orakro'wt'iwn Darakir Geanqis,* 123; Tavukjian, *Dar'abanqi Orakro'wt'iwn,* 72.

136. BNu / Fonds A. Andonian, P.J. 1 / 3, file 4, Aintab, "The Deportation of Armenians in Aintab," 8.

137. BNu / Fonds A. Andonian, P.J. 1 / 3, file 4, Aintab, "The Deportation of Armenians in Aintab," 9.

138. BNu / Fonds A. Andonian, P.J. 1 / 3, file 4, Aintab, "The Deportation of Armenians in Aintab," 9.

139. Gulesserian, "Dasnmeg Egheragan Dariner Ah'nt'abi mĕch, 1908–1919," 1025; Tavukjian, *Dar'abanqi Orakro'wt'iwn,* 72. Kayacık and Akyol were two neighborhoods where the majority of the Armenian population resided. Even today, the neighborhoods' original features have been preserved, including the architecture as well as Armenian schools and churches, which are now used for other purposes or have become private property.

140. Bogharian, *Orakro'wt'iwn Darakir Geanqis,* 123.

141. Bogharian, *Orakro'wt'iwn Darakir Geanqis,* 124.

142. These were neighborhoods where most of the Aintab Armenians resided.

143. Bogharian, *Orakro'wt'iwn Darakir Geanqis,* 123. Nerses Tavukjian was born in 1873 in Aintab and received his early education at the National Armenian Schools of Aintab. He was the most prominent clergyman in Aintab. He was deported to Hama in 1915. Like Bogharian, he noted his daily experiences of the deportation in his diary, published as *Dar'abanqi Orakro'wt'iwn.* He died in Aleppo in 1934. Armenag Chamichian was a graduate of Vartanian High School. He earned degrees in history and philosophy at Harvard in 1912. Chamichian became the president of Cilicia College on 27 August 1912. He passed away in Hama from typhus on 25 December 1915. Sarafian, *A Briefer History of Aintab,* 39; 275; Bogharian, *Orakro'wt'iwn Darakir Geanqis,* 153; Tavukjian, *Dar'abanqi Orakro'wt'iwn,* 105.

144. Bogharian, *Orakro'wt'iwn Darakir Geanqis,* 124.

145. As in Eblahan, Armenians and Muslims resided together in Akyol. However, the Armenian population was higher in number in this neighborhood.

146. Bogharian, *Orakro'wt'iwn Darakir Geanqis,* 124–125.

147. 1915-09-03-DE-002, the Consul in Aleppo to the Imperial Chancellor, in Gust (ed.), *The Armenian Genocide,* 344.

148. Bogharian, *Orakro'wt'iwn Darakir Geanqis,* 128.

149. NA / RG59 / 867.4016 / 148, Letter from the Consul Jackson to Morgenthau, 19 August 1915 in *United States Official Records on the Armenian Genocide, 1915–1917,* 207.

150. Gulesserian, "Dasnmeg Egheragan Dariner Ah'nt'abi mĕch, 1908–1919," 1026; BNu / Fonds A. Andonian, P.J. 1 / 3, file 4, Aintab, "The Deportation of Armenians in Aintab," 9. In late August 1915, Rössler reported that since the government decided to have Marash, Aintab, Tarsus, Adana, Mersin, and the coastal strip of Aleppo cleared of Armenians, the figures for those affected

by the deportation within the area of the Fourth Army "must be estimated at 120,000 to 150,000; of these, 15,000 are in Deir ez-Zor, and about 10,000 are here in Aleppo." See 1915-09-03-DE-002, in Gust (ed.), *The Armenian Genocide,* 348.

151. BOA.DH.ŞFR 486 / 7, 29 August 1915. Also see Kaiser, "Regional Resistance to Central Government Policies," 193.

152. FO 371 / 4241, Governor of Aleppo to the district governor of Aintab dated 21 August 1915, No: 4410, Code No: 25.

153. *Osmanlı Belgelerinde Ermeniler (1915–1920)* (Ankara: Başbakanlık Devlet Arşivleri Genel Müdürlüğü Yayınları, 1994), 72.

154. Kaiser, "Regional Resistance to Central Government Policies," 200.

155. Bloxham, *The Great Game of Genocide,* 89. Akçam noted that orders to the provinces that "they [Catholic and Protestant Armenians] not be touched were produced for German consumption and quickly rescinded by follow-up cables." *Young Turks' Crime,* 375.

156. BOA.DH.ŞFR 55-A / 23, EUM to Adana, 2 September 1915. See also BOA.DH.EUM.V.Şube. 15 / 19, 14 July 1915 and BOA.DH.ŞFR 55 / 92 coded telegram from EUM to the Provinces of Hüdavendigar (Bursa), Ankara, Konya, Izmit, Adana, Marash, Urfa, Aleppo, (Der) Zor, Sivas, Kütahya, Karesi (Balıkesir), Niğde, Ma'muretü'l-aziz, Diyarbekir, Karahisar-ı Sahib (Afyon Karahisar), Erzurum, and Kayseri, 29 August 1915. This telegram reports "Protestant and Catholic Armenians are not to be deported."

157. This was the case in Erzurum, where Catholic and Protestant Armenians were also deported soon after the main body of Apostolic Armenians were sent away. See BOA.DH.EUM.II.Şube 10 / 23, 6 L 1333 (18 August 1915).

158. BOA.DH.ŞFR 485 / 48 and BOA.DH.EUM.II.Şube 73 / 18, 11, Aleppo Governor Bekir Sami Bey to Ministry of Interior, 24 August 1915; BOA.DH. EUM.II.Şube 73 / 69, 17 Kanunuevvel 1331 (30 December 1915).

159. Gulesesrian, "Dasnmeg Egheragan Dariner Ah'nt'abi mĕch, 1908 1919," 1026; BOA.DH.EUM.II.Şube 73 / 69, 17 Kanunuevvel 1331 (30 December 1915).

160. Katchadourian, *Efronia: An Armenian Love Story,* 131; BNu / Fonds A. Andonian, P.J. 1 / 3, file 4, Aintab, "The Deportation of Armenians in Aintab," 9.

161. Bogharian, *Orakro'wt'iwn Darakir Geanqis,* 125; BNu / Fonds A. Andonian, P.J. 1 / 3, file 4, Aintab, "The Deportation of Armenians in Aintab," 5.

162. BOA.DH.ŞFR 488 / 33, Aleppo Governor Bekir Sami Bey to Ministry of Interior, 8 September 1915.

163. BOA.DH.ŞFR 55-A / 174, 9 September 1915.

164. Gulesserian, "Dasnmeg Egheragan Dariner Ah'nt'abi mĕch, 1908–1919," 1026.

165. Gulesserian, "Dasnmeg Egheragan Dariner Ah'nt'abi mĕch, 1908–1919," 1026–1027; Sarafian, *Badmo'wt'iwn Ah'nt'abi Hah'o'c,* vol. I, 491, 573; A. Gesar,

Ah'nt'abi Ko'h'amardy, 26–29; Bogharian, *Orakro'wt'iwn Darakir Geanqis,* 125; Aguni, *Milion my Hah'ero'w Ch'arti Badmo'wt'iwny,* 311.

166. NA / RG59 / 867.4016 / 219, 29 September 1915 in *United States Official Records on the Armenian Genocide 1915–1917,* 314.

167. Gulesserian, "Dasnmeg Egheragan Dariner Ah'nt'abi měch, 1908–1919," 1027; Kévorkian, *The Armenian Genocide,* 607.

168. On 15 August 1915, the Ministry of Interior requested data on the number of deported and remaining Armenian Protestants. *Osmanlı Belgelerinde Ermeniler (1915–1920),* 75–76; BOA.DH.ŞFR 55 / 20, EUM to Erzurum, Adana, Angora, Bitlis, Aleppo, Bursa, Diyarbekir, Sivas, Trabzon, Konya, Harput, Van provinces, Urfa, İzmit, Canik, Karesi, Afyon, Marash, Niğde, Eskişehir districts, 15 August 1915.

169. "Miss Frearson's Experiences and Observations in Turkey," *ABCFM* 16.9.6.1, unit 5, vol. 2, part 1, reel 670-7.1.17, 1817–1919, 7.

170. Gulesserian, "Dasnmeg Egheragan Dariner Ah'nt'abi měch, 1908–1919," 1028; Bogharian, *Orakro'wt'iwn Darakir Geanqis,* 125. Prof. Lutfi Levonian, Babikian Badveli Kharalambos, Mihran Halladjian, Dokmeci Nerses (a famous Hunchak), the Protestant priest of Kayacık Church, Hovhannes Hasırdjian, Manase Andonian, Abraham Hoca Levonian, and Sarkis Balabanian were among the Protestants who were arrested. Balabanian, *Geanqis Daq o'w Bagh Orery,* 66.

171. Gulesserian, "Dasnmeg Egheragan Dariner Ah'nt'abi měch, 1908–1919," 1028; Kévorkian, *The Armenian Genocide,* 608.

172. Nazarian, *Eghernēn Verabrogh H'o'wsher,* 14.

173. Bedros Ashjian was a brilliant merchant, the owner of a vast acreage of pistachio groves, who amassed enormous wealth. He greatly supported the church, schools, and charities. On 21 November 1915, he was settled in Aleppo. This was arranged through the mediary of Aintab Deputy Artin Boshgezenian, who had close ties with Talat Pasha. Bogharian, *Orakro'wt'iwn Darakir Geanqis,* 148. Bedros Ashjian died in Alexandria, Egypt, and lost all his wealth because of the Armenian genocide. Sarafian, *A Briefer History of Aintab,* 289. Artin Boshgezenian also fruitfully intervened on behalf of many Aintab natives who were settled in Salamiyya. Sarkis Krajian, Hırand Sulahian, Hagop Karamanugian, and the Basmajian, Ghazarian, and Ashjian families were given the right to settle in Aleppo through Boshgezenian's personal efforts. *Archives of the Haigazian University Library, Krikor Bogharian's Collection,* "The Natives of Ayntab in Syria" (unpublished manuscript) by Krikor Bogharian, 3. Hagop Karamanougian (1863–1939), in *Ayntabiana,* vol. 2 in *Mahartzan: Mahakro'wt'iwnner, Tampanaganner ew Gensakragan Not'er* [Funeral Monument: Necrologies, Funeral Orations and Biographical Notes] (Beirut:

Atlas, 1974), 422; BOA.DH.EUM.II.Şube 35 / 11, 25 Teşrinisâni 1331 (8 December 1915); 2 Kânunisani 1331 (15 January 1916); 10 Kânunisani 1331 (23 January 1916); 24 March 1332 (6 April 1916); BOA.DH.ŞFR 60 / 38, 3 Kânunuevvel 1331 (16 December 1915); BOA.DH.ŞFR 59 / 203, 22 Kânunuevvel 1331 (4 January 1916); BOA.DH.ŞFR 71 / 27, 5 Kânunievvel 1332 (18 December 1916); Vahé Tachjian, "Gender, Nationalism, Exclusion: The Reintegration Process of Female Survivors of the Armenian Genocide," *Nations and Nationalism* 15, no. 1 (2009): 61.

174. Sarkis Effendi Krajian (1872–1929) was a leading citizen of Aintab who greatly contributed to charity and public service. A highly educated, intelligent, and successful businessman, he was very active in Armenian civic affairs and a member of both the Municipal and National Provincial Councils. He was one of the founders of the Atenagan School, serving on its board for many years, and a member of the Judicial Court. In 1904, Sarkis Effendi married Zarman Nazaretian, the daughter of Garabed Nazaretian, from one of the most notable families in the city. He had two villages, Küçük and Büyük Kızılhisar, and owned extensive pistachio groves. His other pursuit, Krajian and Co., Manufacturers of Embroidered Handkerchiefs, founded in 1896, was a philanthropic venture to help destitute women who were victims of the 1895 massacres. *Badmo'wt'iwn Ah'nt'abi Hah'o'c* vol. II, 763; Teager, *The Krajians of Aintab*, 21, 55, 57.

175. BOA.DH.EUM.KLH 5 / 48, 19 October 1915; BOA.DH.EUM.KLH 5 / 48, 21 October 1915. The same Ali Cenani Bey seized the entire supply of fat in Aintab in November 1915. This situation led to extreme difficulties in procuring fat for the military unit in the district. Thereupon, the Aintab district governor bought a certain amount of fat from Ali Cenani to meet the needs of the military and informed the governor-general of Aleppo Province. The governor-general also informed the Ministry of Interior about this situation. BOA.DH.İ.UM 16–63 / 40-3, 15 November 1915.

176. *Hah Ah'nt'ab* 7, no. 21 (1966): 32.

177. Gulesserian, "Dasnmeg Egheragan Dariner Ah'nt'abi mĕch, 1908–1919," 1030.

178. *Hah Ah'nt'ab* 7, no. 21 (1966): 32.

179. Balabanian, *Geanqis Daq o'w Bagh Orery*, 73.

180. *Hah Ah'nt'ab* 7, no. 21 (1966): 32.

181. Gulesserian, "Dasnmeg Egheragan Dariner Ah'nt'abi mĕch, 1908–1919," 1033; Balabanian, *Geanqis Daq o'w Bagh Orery*, 73.

182. Gulesserian, "Dasnmeg Egheragan Dariner Ah'nt'abi mĕch, 1908–1919," 1033.

183. *Hah Ah'nt'ab* 7, no. 21 (1966): 32.

184. Gulesserian, "Dasnmeg Egheragan Dariner Ah'nt'abi mĕch, 1908–1919," 1035; Balabanian, *Geanqis Daq o'w Bagh Orery,* 73. The report by Elvesta T. Leslie, an assistant to the American vice-consul in Urfa (report by 11 April 1918) in Barton, *Turkish Atrocities,* 107, gives 14 December as the first convoy's departure date.

185. *Hah Ah'nt'ab* 7, no. 21 (1966): 35.

186. Report by Miss Frearson, written on 11 April 1918, in Bryce and Toynbee, *The Treatment of Armenians in the Ottoman Empire,* 546–549.

187. *Hah Ah'nt'ab* 7, no. 21 (1966): 35.

188. Yervant Kuchukian, *Hariwr Zham Ah'nt'abi: H'o'wsher ew Dbawo'ro'wt'iwnner* [100 Hours in Aintab: Memories and Impressions] (Beirut: Aravot, 1958), 21.

189. *Badmo'wt'iwn Ah'nt'abi Hah'o'c,* vol. I, 552. Sarafian stated that out of 5,500 Protestants in Aintab, 2,450 survived. *Badmo'wt'iwn Ah'nt'abi Hah'o'c,* vol. I, 552.

190. *Badmo'wt'iwn Ah'nt'abi Hah'o'c,* vol. I, 548.

191. BOA.DH.EUM.II.Şube 73 / 73, Governor-General of Aleppo Mustafa Abdülhalik Bey to the Ministry of Interior, 10 January 1916. According to a report sent to the Ministry of Interior on 28 February 1916, 14,006 of 18,610 Orthodox Armenians, 215 of 6,450 Protestant Armenians, and 650 of 699 Catholic Armenians were deported from Aintab. Based on this data, the total Armenian population was 25,759, and the number of deported Armenians was 14,871. For these figures, see *Krikor Guerguerian Private Archival Collection,* folder number: 22, file name: Modern Turkish Documents, file number: 11. These figures provided by Ottoman state officials contradict those from Armenian sources.

192. Andonian, *Medz O'jiry,* 104; Aharonian, *H'o'wshamadean Medz Egher'ni,* 104; Andonian, *The Memoirs of Naim Bey,* 56.

193. FO 371 / 6500; also see "British Foreign Office Dossiers on Turkish War Criminals" in *British Foreign Office Dossiers on Turkish War Criminals,* ed. Vartkes Yeghiayan (La Verne, CA: American Armenian International College, 1991), 111; *The Memoirs of Naim Bey,* 56.

194. The district of Rumkale was inhabited by 1,500 Armenians. They mostly lived in Ehnesh, Cibin, and Rumkale. Kévorkian and Paboudjian, *Les Arméniens dans l'Empire Ottoman à La Veille Du Génocide,* 337–340. The Armenians of Ehnesh, Cibin, and Rumkale were also deported in mid-August 1915 by the direction of the district governor, Midhat Bey, who held this post from 22 August 1913 to 24 February 1916. BNu / Fonds A. Andonian, P.J.1 / 3, file 4, Aintab, 26–30ff.

195. FO 371 / 6500, also see "British Foreign Office Dossiers on Turkish War Criminals," 110; Andonian, *Medz O'jiry,* 105; Aharonian, *H'o'wshamadean Medz Egher'ni,* 531; *The Memoirs of Naim Bey,* 56.

196. Levon Vartan, *Zhamanagakro'wt'iwn Hah'gagan Dasnhinki 1915–1923* [Chronology of the Armenian 1915–1923] (Beirut: Aravot, 1975), 131n9.

197. BOA.DH.EUM.II.Şube. 69 / 6, 7 February 1916; *Osmanlı Belgelerinde Ermeniler (1915–1920),* 122.

198. BOA.DH.ŞFR 508 / 36, 6 February 1916; BOA.DH.EUM.II.Şube 69 / 7, 8 February 1916; *Osmanlı Belgelerinde Ermeniler (1915–1920),* 123.

199. Jesse B. Jackson to Henry Morgenthau, report dated Aleppo, 8 February 1916 in *United States Official Documents on the Armenian Genocide,* document number 117; Ara Sarafian, "The Absorption of Armenian Women and Children into Muslim Households as a Structural Component of the Armenian Genocide," in *Genocide and Religion in the Twentieth Century,* ed. Omer Bartov and Phylis Mack (New York: Berghahn, 2001), 211.

200. *Hah Ah'nt'ab* 7, no. 21 (1966): 37.

201. *Hah Ah'nt'ab* 7, no. 21 (1966): 38.

202. BOA.DH.ŞFR 520 / 18, 17 May 1916; According to the memoirs of Naim Bey, Ahmed Bey became the chief of police of Istanbul on 14 May 1916; see FO 371 / 6500, "Ahmet Bey," Malta no. 2724, Interned 02 / 06 / 1919, Native of Bursa, Appointments; "British Foreign Office Dossiers on Turkish War Criminals," 110. Actually, before being appointed to Istanbul, Ahmed Bey was recommended to Cemal Pasha by Talat for the position of Assistant Governor of the Syria province. BOA.DH.ŞFR 62 / 190 and 62 / 194, 1 April 1916.

203. Gulesserian, "Dasnmeg Egheragan Dariner Ah'nt'abi mĕch, 1908–1919," 1036–1037; Kévorkian, *The Armenian Genocide,* 608.

204. Pharmacists in Aintab were nearly all Armenians: Manuk Kendirjian, Eczacı (Pharmacist) Nerses, Eczacı Puzant, Hagop Bezjian, Topal Asadour, Eczacı Samuel, Eczacı Annikian, Eczacı Dikran, and Eczacı Sabis; see Göğüş, *İlk İnsanlardan Bugüne Çeşitli Yönleriyle Gaziantep,* 301.

205. Gulesserian, "Dasnmeg Egheragan Dariner Aynt'abi mēch, 1908–1919," 1038; Bogharian, *Orakro'wt'iwn Darakir Geanqis,* 125; Nazarian, *Eghernēn Verabrogh H'o'wsher,* 10.

206. *Osmanlı Belgelerinde Ermenilerin Sevk ve İskanı* (1878–1920) (Ankara: Devlet Arşivleri Genel Müdürlüğü, 2007), 215; BOA.DH.ŞFR 55 / 18, the Ministry of Interior to Erzurum, Adana, Angora, Bitlis, Aleppo, Bursa, Diyarbekir, Sivas, Trabzon, Konya, and Van provinces, and Urfa, Izmit, Karesi, Afyon, Kayseri, Marash, Niğde, and Eskişehir districts, 15 August 1915; Bogharian, *Orakro'wt'iwn Darakir Geanqis,* 125. There were Armenian military physicians

from Aintab who served in the Ottoman Army—exempting their families from deportation—such as Hovsep Hahdessian, Vartan Piranian, Albert Apelian, Aram Der Boghossian, Hovsep Yenikomshouian, Movses Kupelian, Avedis Nakashian, Avedis Jebejian, Yervant H. Khrlopian, and Movses Babigian; see *ABCFM* 16.9.6.1, unit 5, vol. 2, part 1, reel 667, 1817–1919, no 288.

207. Gulesserian, "Dasnmeg Egheragan Dariner Ah'nt'abi mĕch, 1908–1919," 1039; Kévorkian, *The Armenian Genocide,* 608.

208. For his diary of 1914–1918, see Avedis Jebejian, *Osmanean Gah'seragan Panagi Sbah': Pzhishg Awedis Je'be'jeani Orakiry 1914–1918* [An Officer in the Army of the Ottoman Empire: Doctor Avedis Jebejian's Diary 1914–1918] (Beirut: Zartonk, 1986), and for his short biography, see *Badmo'wt'iwn Ah'nt'abi Hah'o'c,* vol. III, 796. For a detailed biography of Avedis Nakashian, another Armenian military physician, see "Doctor Avedis Nakashian," *Hah Ah'nt'ab* 10, no. 3–4 (1969): 8–12.

209. BOA.DH.EUM.II.Şube 35 / 34, 27 October 1916; 5 November 1916; 30 November 1916; 12 December 1916; 14 January 1917 and 14 February 1917.

210. BOA.DH.EUM.II.Şube 49 / 2, 12 February 1918.

211. Bogharian, *Orakro'wt'iwn Darakir Geanqis,* 125; Kévorkian, *The Armenian Genocide,* 608.

212. Aguni, *Milion my Hah'ero'w Ch'arti Badmo'wt'iwny,* 311.

213. BOA.DH.ŞFR 86 / 45, 3 April 1918; BOA.DH.ŞFR 87 / 259, 23 May 1918.

214. The term "muhacir" (immigrant) denoted an individual who had left his / her homeland and settled in the Ottoman Empire, while "mülteci" (refugee) was used for anyone forced to migrate to the interior because of enemy occupation of Ottoman lands. For the difference between the terms in the Ottoman context during World War I, see Nedim İpek, *İmparatorluktan Ulus Devlete Göçler* (Trabzon: Serander, 2006), 18.

215. BOA.DH.ŞFR 63 / 87 coded telegram from Ministry of Interior to Aleppo Province, 24 April 1916; BOA.DH.ŞFR 63 / 144, 30 April 1916.

216. BOA.DH.ŞFR 61 / 121, 26 February 1916; BOA.DH.ŞFR 511 / 62, 29 February 1916; BOA.DH.ŞFR 61 / 237, 1 March 1916; BOA.DH.İ.UM.EK 13 / 34, 19 March 1916.

217. BOA.DH.ŞFR 521 / 64, 31 March 1916; BOA.DH.ŞFR 527 / 54, 5 April 1916; BOA.DH.ŞFR 522 / 74, 8 April 1916; BOA.DH.ŞFR 522 / 91, 10 April 1916; BOA.DH.ŞFR 523 / 8, 12 April 1916; BOA.DH.ŞFR 523 / 19, 13 April 1916.

218. BOA.DH.ŞFR 63 / 187, 4 May 1916.

219. BOA.DH.ŞFR 667 / 71, 4 June 1916.

220. BOA.DH.ŞFR 539 / 59, 7 July 1916.

221. BOA.DH.ŞFR 526 / 34, 24 July 1916.

222. BOA.DH.ŞFR 558 / 58, coded telegram from Urfa district governor to the Ministry of Interior, 3 July 1917; BOA.DH.ŞFR 559 / 99, 16 July 1917. According to the cipher telegram sent from the Ministry of Interior to the provincial district of Urfa on 29 March 1917, one thousand refugees were sent to Aintab by train. BOA.DH.ŞFR 74 / 294, 22 March 1917.

223. For a well-detailed study on the migration and settlement policies of the CUP applied during 1913–1918, see Dündar, *Modern Türkiye'nin Şifresi: İttihat Terakki'nin Etnisite Mühendisliği* (Istanbul: İletişim, 2008).

224. For the full list of names who were responsible for deportations and plunder in Aintab in 1915–1917, see BNu / Fonds A. Andonian, P.J. 1 / 3, file 4, Aintab, "The Deportation of Armenians in Aintab," 11–17 and *Krikor Guerguerian Private Archival Collection,* folder number: 22, file name: Turks (List) Responsible, file no: 46. Also see Aguni, *Milion my Hah'ero'w Ch'arti Badmo'wt'iwny,* 312; Kévorkian, *The Armenian Genocide,* 609. Aram Andonian and Krikor Guerguerian provided the full list of those who played a primary role in the deportation and destruction of Aintab Armenians as well as enabling the seizure of their movable and immovable properties. The entire list of names is in the appendix.

225. Yervant Babaian, *Pages from My Diary / Archpriest Der Nerses Babaian* (Los Angeles: Abril Publisher, 2000), vi; Babaian, *Badmo'wt'iwn Ah'nt'abi Hah'o'c,* vol. III, 18. For an interesting work on contextualization of the Syrian desert as both suffering and survival space for Armenians, see Sam Dolbee, "The Desert at the End of Empire: An Environmental History of the Armenian Genocide," *Past & Present* 247, no. 1 (2020): 197–233.

226. BNu / Fonds A. Andonian, P.J. 1 / 3, file 4, Aintab, 20. According to a report prepared and sent by Admiral Bristol to the United States secretary of state immediately after the war, the number of Armenians who were not deported from Aintab was twelve thousand. NARA 860J.01 / 341 cited in Kemal Çiçek, *Ermenilerin Zorunlu Göçü (1915–1917)* (Ankara: TTK, 2000), 194.

227. BNu / Fonds A. Andonian, P.J. 1 / 3, file 4, Aintab, 10; Kévorkian, *The Armenian Genocide,* 609.

228. *Bogharian, Orakro'wt'iwn Darakir Geanqis,* 154–155. For more information about Necmeddin Bey, see Chapter 2.

229. Sarafian, *A Briefer History of Aintab,* 141; Bogharian, *Orakro'wt'iwn Darakir Geanqis,* 131–136, 157, 182; Tavukjian, *Dar'abanqi Orakro'wt'iwn,* 83–88.

230. *Badmo'wt'iwn Ah'nt'abi Hah'o'c,* vol. I, 1026; 1052.

231. Sarafian, *A Briefer History of Aintab,* 141–142.

232. Sarafian, *A Briefer History of Aintab,* 142.

233. DE / PA-AA / R14094, DE-001, Consul Rössler in Aleppo to Bethmann Hollweg, 5 November 1916, cited in Wolfang Gust, http://www.armenocide.net/ (accessed 23 March 2015). Also see Gust (ed.), *The Armenian Genocide,* 37.

234. DE / PA-AA / R14094, DE-001, Consul Rössler in Aleppo to Bethmann Hollweg, 5 November 1916, cited in Wolfang Gust, http://www.armenocide.net/ (accessed 23 March 2015). Also see Gust (ed.), *The Armenian Genocide,* 37.

4. Confiscation and Plunder under the Abandoned Properties Laws

1. Nüket Alevli Ersoy and Haşim Akman, *Türk Tekstil ve Eğitim Sektöründe Gaziantepli Bir Öncü: Cemil Alevli* (Istanbul: Doğan Kitap, 2020), 221.

2. The term used at the time, "abandoned properties," is employed here for ease of reference. But note that it unequivocally embodies a falsehood; deportees did not willingly "abandon" their properties but were forced to leave them behind. During the war, the Russian Empire also introduced extraordinary measures such as outright confiscation and sequestration of properties of its own Jewish, Polish, and German subjects who were business owners, investors, managers, private landowners, store owners, white-collar employees, engineers, foremen, and skilled workers. Through a set of decrees in 1915–1916, the Russian state identified and categorized large populations of its Jewish, Polish, and German citizens as enemy aliens. In doing so, it applied the extreme requisition and expropriation policies applied to enemy subject lands. Both the government and the army played an active role in the mass deportations of enemy-alien citizens, confiscating and transferring enemy-alien properties by means of a number of decrees and temporary laws in this time period. Thus, there are a number of similar patterns between the Ottoman and the Russian Empires in terms of using "legal" mechanisms to confiscate, expropriate, and transfer the properties, wealth, and assets of their own subjects during the war. For a comprehensive study on wartime expropriation and confiscation of the properties of Jewish, Polish, and German subjects of the Russian Empire, see Eric Lohr, *Nationalizing the Russian Empire: The Campaign against Enemy Aliens during World War I* (Cambridge, MA: Harvard University Press, 2003), esp. 62–120.

3. *Takvim-i Vekayi* no. 2189, 19 May 1331 (1 June 1915). The precise name of the law is "Vakt-i Seferde İcraat-ı Hükûmete Karşı Gelenler İçin Cihet-i Askeriyece İttihâz Olunacak Tedâbir Hakkında Muvakkat Kanun" (Provisional Law on Steps to Be Taken Militarily Concerning Those Who During Campaigns Oppose the Actions of the Government).

4. BOA.BEO 4355 / 326591, Private Secretariat of the Office of the Prime Minister, confidential, to the Ministry of War, 4 May 1331 (17 May 1915).

5. BOA.DH.ŞFR 53 / 94-1, coded telegram EUM to Fourth Army Command, 10 May 1331 (23 May 1915).

6. BOA, Minutes of the Council of Ministers (henceforth MV) 198 / 163 17 May 1331 (30 May 1915), quoted in Süslü, *Ermeniler ve 1915 Tehcir Olayı*, 112, 115; Genelkurmay Başkanlığı, *Arşiv Belgeleriyle Ermeni Faaliyetleri, 1914–1918*, vol. I, 131–133, 427–438.

7. *Arşiv Belgeleriyle Ermeni Faaliyetleri, 1914–1918*, vol. 1, 131.

8. *Arşiv Belgeleriyle Ermeni Faaliyetleri, 1914–1918*, vol. 1, 131–132.

9. *Arşiv Belgeleriyle Ermeni Faaliyetleri, 1914–1918*, vol. 1, 132.

10. *Arşiv Belgeleriyle Ermeni Faaliyetleri, 1914–1918*, vol. 1, 132.

11. See *Arşiv Belgeleriyle Ermeni Faaliyetleri, 1914–1918*, vol. 1, 139–142, for the text of this regulation, formally known as "Ahval-i Harbiye ve Zaruret-i Fevkalade-i Siyasiye Dolayısıyla Mahall-i Ahire Nakilleri İcra Edilen Ermenilere Ait Emval ve Emlâk ve Arazinin Keyfiyet-i İdaresi Hakkında Talimatname" (Regulation on the Condition of Administration of Property, Possessions, and Land Belonging to Armenians Whose Transportation to Other Places is Being Conducted Due to the Conditions of War and Extraordinary Political Exigencies).

12. *Arşiv Belgeleriyle Ermeni Faaliyetleri, 1914–1918*, vol. 1, 141.

13. *Takvim-i Vekayi* no. 2303, 14 September 1331 (27 September 1915). The full name of the law was "Âher Mahallere Nakledilen Eşhâsın Emvâl ve Düyûn ve Matlûbât-ı Metrûkesi Hakkında Kanun-ı Muvakkat" (Temporary Law on the Abandoned Possessions and Debts and Abandoned Debts of Persons Transported to Other Places). *Takvim-i Vekayi* no. 2343, 28 Teşrinievvel 1331 (10 November 1915). The full name of the decree was "Âher Mahallere Nakledilen Eşhâsın Emvâl ve Düyûn ve Matlûbât-ı Metrûkesine Mütedair 18 Zilkade 1333 Tarihli Kanun-ı Muvakkatin Suver-i İcraiyesi Hakkında Talimatname" (Regulation on the Manners of Execution of the Temporary Law Dated 18 Zilkade 1333 [27 September 1915] Concerning the Possessions and Debts and Abandoned Debts of Persons Transported to Other Places). For the original texts of some laws and decrees relevant to the topic of the present volume, see also T. C. Maliye Vekâleti Milli Emlak Müdürlüğü, *Milli Emlak Muamelelerine Müteallik Mevzuat* (Ankara: Başvekâlet Matbaası, 1937); Salâhaddin Kardeş, *"Tehcir" ve Emval-i Metruke Mevzuatı* (Ankara: T. C. Maliye Bakanlığı Strateji Geliştirme Başkanlığı, 2008).

14. The differentiation between the committee and commission was made in a separate decree.

15. *Takvim-i Vekayi* no. 2343, 28 Teşrinievvel 1331 (10 November 1915). The full name of the decree was "Âher Mahallere Nakledilen Eşhâsın Emvâl ve Düyûn ve Matlûbât-ı Metrûkesine Mütedair 18 Zilkade 1333 Tarihli Kanun-ı Muvakkatin Suver-i İcraiyesi Hakkında Talimatname" (Regulation on the Manners of Execution of the Temporary Law Dated 18 Zilkade 1333 [27 September 1915]). See also T. C. Maliye Vekâleti Milli Emlak Müdürlüğü, *Milli Emlak Muamelelerine Müteallik Mevzuat;* Kardeş, *"Tehcir" ve Emval-i Metruke Mevzuatı.*

16. *Takvim-i Vekayi* no. 2343, 28 Teşrinievvel 1331 (10 November 1915).

17. Internal correspondence of the Ministry of Interior dated 6 November 1915 reveals that these commissions were called Abandoned Properties Commissions, while the commissions to be established through the new regulation were to be called Liquidation Commissions (BOA / Legal Counsel Office of the Ministry of Interior [henceforth DH.HMŞ]) 12 / 31, Note dated 24 Teşrinievvel 1331 (6 November 1915) written by the Vice Undersecretary in the name of the Minister of Interior.

18. Orders were issued in various telegrams sent to the provinces in accordance with this regulation for the creation of a commission composed of officials from the Treasury and civil service. For one example, see BOA.DH.ŞFR 54 / 226, coded telegram IAMM Interior Ministry to Kayseri provincial district government, 15 June 1331 (28 June 1915).

19. Ephraim K. Jernazian, *Judgment unto Truth: Witnessing the Armenian Genocide,* trans. Alice Haig (New Brunswick, NJ: Transaction Publishers, 1990), 94.

20. On the commissions that were to be established and their regions of authority, see BOA / Record Office of the Public Security Directorate of the Ministry of Interior 73 / 43. List prepared by Ministry of Interior dated 19 Kanunuevvel 1331 (1 January 1916) showing where the Abandoned Properties Liquidation Commissions were located. According to it, in Istanbul the commission was in the capital of the province. In Edirne, the commission was in Tekfurdağı. In Adana province, including Adana and Mersin, the commission was in Adana. In Cebel-i Bereket, the commission was in the provincial district center. In Kozan, the commission was in the provincial district center. In Erzurum, the commission was in the provincial capital. In Hüdâvendigâr (Bursa) province: [one entry is illegible]; for Karacabey, the commission was in Bursa; for Kirmastı, the commission was in Bursa; for Gemlik and Orhangazi, the commission was in Gemlik; for Ertuğrul and its surrounding areas, the commission was in Bilecik. In Ankara province: for Yozgat, Kırşehir, and Boğazlıyan, the commission was in Yozgat; for Ankara, Keskin, and Çorum, the commission was in Ankara. In Trabzon province: for Bafra, Termen, and Çarşamba, the commission was in Samsun; for Ünye, Fatsa and Tirebolu, the

commission was in Ordu; for Trabzon, the commission was in the capital of the province. In Sivas province: for Amasya and Gümüşhacıköy, the commission was in Sivas; for Merzifon and Havza, the commission was in Merzifon; for Tokat, it was in Tokat. In the İzmit provincial district: for Izmit, Karamürsel, and Yalova, the commission was in Izmit; for Adapazarı, Kandıra, and Gemlik, the commission was in Adapazarı. In the Eskişehir provincial district: for Sivrihisar and Mihalıççık, the commission was in the provincial district capital; for Eskişehir, the commission was in the provincial district capital. In the Kayseri provincial district: for Kayseri, the commission was in the provincial district capital; for Develi, the commission was in the county center. In Aleppo province: for Aleppo, the commission was in the provincial capital; for Marash, it was in the provincial district capital; for Antakya, it was in the provincial district capital. In Konya, Bitlis, Ma'muretü'l-aziz, and Diyarbekir, the commissions were in the respective provincial capitals. In Niğde, Karahisar-ı Sahib, Urfa, and Karesi, the commissions were in the respective provincial district capitals.

21. Kardeş, *"Tehcir" ve Emval-i Metruke Mevzuatı*, 37. The full name of the law is *13 Eylül 1331* (26 September 1915) *Tarihli Kanunun İkinci Maddesinin Birinci Fıkrasına Ek İbare Hakkında Kanun* (Law on the Supplemental Phase to the First Paragraph of the Second Article of the Law Dated 13 September 1331).

22. BOA / Foreign Affairs Ministry Political Division (henceforth HR.SYS.), 2873 / 3–35, AMMU to the Foreign Affairs Ministry 30 April 1332 (13 May 1916). On the procedure of transference as of 23 May 1916, see BOA. DH.HMŞ.1-1/6–26, HMŞ communication dated 20 July 1333 (20 July 1917).

23. *Takvim-i Vekayi*, no. 2303, 14 September 1331 (27 September 1915).

24. *Takvim-i Vekayi*, no. 2343, 28 October 1331 (10 November 1915).

25. BOA.DH.ŞFR 54 / 393, coded telegram IAMM to Trabzon provincial government, 29 June 1331 (11 July 1915)

26. BOA.DH.ŞFR 54-A / 368, coded telegram IAMM to Erzurum, Adana, Ankara, Aydın, Bitlis, Aleppo, Hüdâvendigâr (Bursa), Diyarbekir, Suriye, Sivas, Trabzon, Ma'muretü'l-aziz, Musul, and Van provinces, and Urfa, Izmit, Canik, Zor, Karesi, Kayseri, Karahisar-ı Sahib, Marash, Eskişehir, and Niğde provincial district governments, 28 July 1331 (10 August 1915).

27. BOA.DH.ŞFR 54-A / 388, coded telegram IAMM to the Erzurum, Adana, Ankara, Aydın, Bitlis, Aleppo, Hüdâvendigâr (Bursa), Diyarbekir, Suriye, Sivas, Trabzon, Ma'muretü'l-aziz, Musul, and Van provinces; the Urfa, Izmit, Canik, Zor, Karesi, Kayseri, Karahisar-ı Sahib, Marash, Eskişehir, and Niğde provincial district governments; and the Adana, Aleppo, Marash, Diyarbekir, Sivas, Trabzon, Ma'muretü'l-aziz, Erzurum, and Izmit Abandoned Properties Commission Chairmanships, 29 July 1331 (11 August 1915).

28. BOA.DH.ŞFR 55 / 280, coded telegram IAMM to the Erzurum, Adana, Ankara, Bitlis, Aleppo, Hüdâvendigâr (Bursa), Diyarbekir, Sivas, Trabzon, Ma'muretü'l-aziz, Van, and Konya provinces; Urfa, Izmit, Canik, Karesi, Kayseri, Karahisar-ı sâhib, Marash, Eskişehir, and Niğde provincial district governments; and the chairmanship of the Aleppo, Adana, Sivas and Trabzon Abandoned Properties Administrative Commissions, 15 August 1331 (28 August 1915).

29. Yervant Kuchukian, *Hariwr Zham Ah'nt'abi: H'o'wsher ew Dbawo'ro'wt'iwnner* [100 Hours in Aintab: Memories and Impressions] (Beirut: Aravot, 1958), 24.

30. *Badmo'wt'iwn Ah'nt'abi Hah'o'c,* vol. II, 275–303. The 1914 edition of *Annuairé Oriéntal du Commerce* also indicated how Armenians controlled most aspects of economic and business life in Aintab; see *Annuaire Oriental: Commerce, Industrié, Administration, Magistraturé de l'Oriént, Edition 1914: Aintab,* 1323–1326. A comprehensive economic and commercial list of Aintab can be found in this edition. This list should suffice to demonstrate the economic and commercial power of the Armenians in Aintab before World War I. For the whole list, see Karaian, "On the Number of Armenians in Aintab in 1914," in *Badmo'wt'iwn Ah'nt'abi Hah'o'c,* vol. III, 16.

31. *H'o'wshamadean Awedis Kalemqereani,* 56; Krikor Bogharian, *Orakro'wt'iwn Darakir Geanqis* [Diary of My Life in Exile] in *Ceghasban T'-o'wrqy Vgah'o'wt'iwnner Qagho'wadz Hrashqo'v P'rgo'wadznero'w Zro'h'nere'n* [Genocider Turk: Testimonies Taken from the Accounts of Armenians Who Miraculously Survived] (Beirut: Shirag, 1973), 122; Sarkis Balabanian, *Geanqis Daq o'w Bagh Orery: Ah'nt'ab, Qe'sab, Hale'b* [Hot and Cold Days of My Life: Aintab, Kesap, Halep] (Halep: Atlas, 1983), 79; interview with Yevnige Berejiklian-Koundakjian, *Zoryan Institute Oral History Project.* I would like to thank Perla Kotoian-Nazarian for sharing this interview with me. Also, in *Meşveret,* the official organ of the government published in Trabzon, it was stated that deportation of the Armenians was a temporary arrangement; see BOA.DH.ŞFR 54-A / 163, 16 July 1331 (29 July 1915), and NA / RG59 / 867.4016 / 105 in *United States Official Records on the Armenian Genocide,* 129–136.

32. *H'o'wshamadean Awedis Kalemqereani,* 56; Bogharian, *Orakro'wt'iwn Darakir Geanqis,* 122; Balabanian, *Geanqis Daq o'w Bagh Orery,* 79; interview with Yevnige Berejiklian-Koundakjian, *Zoryan Institute Oral History Project.*

33. "Miss Frearson's Experiences and Observations in Turkey." *ABCFM,* 16.9.6.1, unit 5, vol. 2, part 1, reel 670-7.1.11, 1817–1919, 8. Alice Kazazian, a genocide survivor from Aintab who reached Aleppo by bribing Kurdish escorts, was interviewed by Richard Hovannisian in 1986 about her experience. Of the seizure, plunder, and confiscation of Armenian properties, Alice Kaza-

zian stated that "a few days before our deportation, the local government told us to lock your houses' doors; either take your keys with you or hand them over to the government." Interview with Alice Kazazian, 1986, Philadelphia, 19. I am grateful to late Pakrad Kazazian, a son of Alice Kazazian, for sharing the transcription of his mother's interview.

34. BNu / Fonds A. Andonian, P.J. 1 / 3, file 4, Aintab, "The Deportation of Armenians in Aintab," 7; Gulesserian, "Dasnmeg Egheragan Dariner Ah'nt'abi mēch, 1908–1919," 1025; Aguni, *Milion my Hah'ero'w Ch'arti Badmo'wt'iwny,* 311; "Miss Frearson's Experiences and Observations in Turkey." *ABCFM,* 16.9.6.1, unit 5, vol. 2, part 1, reel 670-7.1.11, 1817–1919, 6.

35. Nazarian, *Eghernēn Verabrogh H'o'wsher,* 9.

36. Gulesserian, "Dasnmeg Egheragan Dariner Ah'nt'abi mēch, 1908–1919," 1025.

37. Nazarian, *Eghernēn Verabrogh H'o'wsher,* 7; Bogharian, *Orakro'wt'iwn Darakir Geanqis,* 124.

38. *Badmo'wt'iwn Ah'nt'abi Hah'o'c,* vol. I, 924–925.

39. Nazarian, *Eghernēn Verabrogh H'o'wsher,* 7; "Political Diary (20 November 1915 to 21 April 1916)," *Hah Ah'nt'ab* 7, no. 21 (1966): 34; Katchadourian, *Efronia: An Armenian Love Story,* 126. The same process took place in Kharpert. According to Henry Riggs, an American missionary in Kharpert during the genocide, dissatisfied with buying at ridiculously low prices at the public auctions, "many of the Muslims went to the homes of the Armenians and often frightened the poor women into parting with their property for a song in order to get rid of their truculent customers"; see Henry H. Riggs, *Days of Tragedy in Armenia: Personal Experiences in Harpoot, 1915–1917* (Ann Arbor, Michigan: Gomidas Institute, 1997), 85.

40. Gulesserian, "Dasnmeg Egheragan Dariner Ah'nt'abi mēch, 1908–1919," 1025. In his memoir, Hagop Arsenian, a pharmacist from Izmit witnessed the same process: "On Saturday, July 25 [1915], all the goods and furniture of the Armenians were displayed on the sidewalks for sale. But who was going to buy? All of them knew that they would be able to lay their hands on these items for free the next day, without paying a piaster." Hagop Arsenian, *Towards Golgotha: The Memoirs of Hagop Arsenian, a Genocide Survivor,* trans. and annotated by Arda Arsenian Ekmekji (Beirut: Haigazian University Press, 2011), 55.

41. From Consul J. B. Jackson, Aleppo, Syria to Henry Morgenthau American Ambassador, Istanbul, 19 August 1915, NA / RG59 / 867.4016 / 148 in *United States Official Records on the Armenian Genocide 1915–1917,* 207.

42. BOA.DH.ŞFR 55-A / 259 coded telegram IAMM to the provinces of Adana, Edirne, Erzurum, Bitlis, Diyarbekir, Aleppo, Hüdâvendigâr (Bursa),

Sivas, Trabzon, Ma'muretü'l-aziz, and Van; to the provincial districts of Izmit, Canik, Çatalca, Kayseri, Karesi (Balıkesir), Marash, Kale-i Sultaniye (Çanakkale), and Deir ez-Zor; and to the presidents of the Abandoned Properties Commissions in Adana, Erzurum, Aleppo, Marash, Trabzon, Canik, Sivas, Ma'muretü'l-aziz, and Diyarbekir, 3 August 1915; BOA.DH.ŞFR 54A / 259, 22 July 1331 (4 August 1915).

43. BOA.DH.ŞFR 54 / 381 coded telegram IAMM to the provinces of Erzurum, Adana, Ankara, Aydın, Bitlis, Aleppo, Hüdâvendigâr (Bursa), Diyarbekir, Suriye, Sivas, Trabzon, Ma'muretü'l-aziz, Musul; to the provincial districts of Urfa, Izmit, Canik, Zor, Karesi, Kayseri, Karahisâr-ı Sâhib, Marash, Eskişehir, Niğde, and to the presidents of the Abandoned Properties Commissions in Adana, Aleppo, Marash, Diyarbekir, Sivas, Trabzon, Ma'muretü'l-aziz, Erzurum, and Izmit, 30 N 1333 (11 August 1915); *Osmanlı Belgelerinde Ermeniler (1915–1920)* (Ankara: Başbakanlık Basımevi, 1995), 73–77; BOA.DH.ŞFR 54-A / 388 coded telegram IAMM to the provinces of Erzurum, Adana, Ankara, Aydın, Bitlis, Aleppo, Hüdâvendigâr (Bursa), Diyarbekir, Damascus, Sivas, Trabzon, Ma'muretü'l-aziz, Mosul, and Van; to the provincial districts of Urfa, Izmit, Canik, Zor, Karesi (Balıkesir), Kayseri, Karahisar-i Sahib (Afyon Karahisar), Marash, Eskişehir, and Niğde; and to the presidents of the Abandoned Properties Commissions in Aleppo, Adana, Marash, Diyarbekir, Sivas, and Trabzon, Ma'muretü'l-aziz, Erzurum, Izmit, 11 August 1915.

44. Riggs, *Days of Tragedy in Armenia*, 89.

45. Kuchukian, *Hariwr Zham Ah'nt'abi*, 10.

46. *Badmo'wt'iwn Ah'nt'abi Hah'o'c*, vol. I, 928.

47. Some Armenians who fell under this category were Hanna Kurkchuian and his children; brothers Nigoghos, Harutyun, and Garabed Nazaretian; Hovsep and Minas Kendirdjian; Garabed Barsumian and his children; Adour Niziblian; and Bedros Ashjian. *Badmo'wt'iwn Ah'nt'abi Hah'o'c*, vol. I, 927–928.

48. In the second category, there were Kalusd Ghazarian and his sons, Avedis Parseghian, Hovhannes Jebejian, Sarkis Krajian, Garuj Karamanougian and his sons, the Matossian brothers, the Khachaturian brothers, and the Birecikliian brothers. *Badmo'wt'iwn Ah'nt'abi Hah'o'c*, vol. I, 927–928.

49. *Badmo'wt'iwn Ah'nt'abi Hah'o'c*, vol. I, 928–929.

50. *Badmo'wt'iwn Ah'nt'abi Hah'o'c*, vol. I, 929.

51. For more detailed information, see Cemal Avcı, "Tekalif-i Harbiye ile Tekalif-Milliye Vergilerinin Karşılaştırmalı Tanımı," *Atatürk Araştırma Merkezi (ATAM)*, 11 no. 31 (1995): 223–237. During World War I, the Russian army also carried out broad powers to requisition "(demand goods or properties with payment) and sequester (take properties for state or army use without

formally changing ownership)"; see RGVIA-Russian State Military-Historical Archive, f. 2005, op. 1, cited in Lohr, *Nationalizing the Russian Empire*, 18n31.

52. Avcı, "Tekalif-i Harbiye ile Tekalif- Milliye Vergilerinin Karşılaştırmalı Tanımı"; Hilmar Kaiser, *The Extermination of Armenians in the Diyarbekir Region* (Istanbul: Istanbul Bilgi University Press, 2014), 116; Artem Ohandjanian, *Der verschwiegene Völkermord* (Cologne: Böhlau, 1989), 81–82.

53. BOA.DH.İ.UM 93–4 / 38-1, 20 March 1916.

54. *Alaja* was a wine-red or dark-blue cotton cloth with yellow stripes that was woven in many parts of Anatolia. In Aintab, it was prized for its beauty and strength, for two-thirds of it was made of silk and one-third of cotton with golden threads. Mehmet Zeki Pakalın, *Osmanlı Tarihi Deyimleri ve Terimleri Sözlüğü*, vol. I (Istanbul: Milli Eğitim Basımevi, 1971), 43–44.

55. BOA.DH.İ.UM 21 / 85, 25 July 1916.

56. BOA.DH.İ.UM 21 / 85, 24 September 1916.

57. BNu / Fonds A. Andonian, P.J. 1 / 3, file 4, Aintab, "The Deportation of Armenians in Aintab," 11–17.

58. BNu / Fonds A. Andonian, P.J. 1 / 3, file 4, Aintab, "The Deportation of Armenians in Aintab," 10–11; Kévorkian, *The Armenian Genocide*, 608.

59. BNu / Fonds A. Andonian, P.J. 1 / 3, file 4, Aintab, "The Deportation of Armenians in Aintab," 16–17.

60. FO 371 / 5089, 664, A letter from Ali Cenani Bey, former deputy for Aintab, sent from Malta, 9 June 1920.

61. FO 371 / 5089, 664, A letter from Ali Cenani Bey, former deputy for Aintab, sent from Malta, 9 June 1920. In his letter to the British High Commissioner dated 7 July 1920, this statement of Cenani was also corroborated by former Aleppo governor Celal Bey. He also noted that "when orders were given to Shukri Bey for the deportations, he tried to take more humane-measures than any other governor." See FO 371 / E. 11188 / 37 / 44, A letter to British High Commissioner, Chichli Djadessi, Pera, 07 / 07 / 1920.

62. Dikran Ammian, "Inch'bēs Goghobdets'i [How I Plundered]," *Hah Ah'nt'ab* 1 (1996): 8–10.

63. BNu / Fonds A. Andonian, P.J. 1 / 3, file 4, Aintab, "The Deportation of Armenians in Aintab," 14.

64. BNu / Fonds A. Andonian, P.J. 1 / 3, file 4, Aintab, "The Deportation of Armenians in Aintab," 15–16; *Krikor Guerguerian Private Archival Collection*, folder number: 22, file name: Turks (List) Responsible, file no: 46.

65. BNu / Fonds A. Andonian, P.J. 1 / 3, file 4, Aintab, "The Deportation of Armenians in Aintab," 16–17; *Krikor Guerguerian Private Archival Collection*, folder number: 22, file name: Turks (List) Responsible, file no: 46.

66. BNu / Fonds A. Andonian, P.J. 1 / 3, file 4, Aintab, "The Deportation of Armenians in Aintab," 14; Kévorkian, *The Armenian Genocide*, 608.

67. FO 371 / 5089, 664, A letter from Ali Cenani Bey, former deputy for Aintab sent from Malta, 9 June 1920. In the same letter, Cenani also claimed that both the director of the Ottoman Bank, M. Tahir, and his Armenian secretary knew the names of all those who purchased any of these goods.

68. BNu / Fonds A. Andonian, P.J. 1 / 3, file 4, Aintab, "The Deportation of Armenians in Aintab," 15.

69. In a telegram sent from the Ministry of Foreign Affairs to the Ministry of Treasury on 1 July 1920, it was explained why the Commissariat confiscated the gold in question. According to the telegram, General Allenby prohibited the exportation of gold and money from occupied lands, and the punishment for that was confiscation of the asset in question, thus warranting the fate of the gold Besim Bey claimed to own. BOA.HR.SYS 2271 / 10, 1 July 1920.

70. BOA.HR.SYS 2271 / 10, 1 July 1920.

71. "Political Diary (20 November 1915 to 21 April 1916)," *Hah Ah'nt'ab* 7, no. 21 (1966): 34.

72. "Political Diary (20 November 1915 to 21 April 1916)," *Hah Ah'nt'ab* 7, no. 21 (1966): 37.

73. "Political Diary (20 November 1915 to 21 April 1916)," *Hah Ah'nt'ab* 7 no. 21 (1966): 37. These Armenians were sent to those places to meet the needs of the Muslim community.

74. "Political Diary (20 November 1915 to 21 April 1916)," *Hah Ah'nt'ab* 7, no. 21 (1966): 38.

75. BOA.DH.ŞFR 667 / 66, 23 May 1916.

76. BOA.MF.MKT 1221 / 47, 11 December 1916.

77. BOA.MF.MKT 1219 / 48, 5 October 1916. It is worth noting that these books were confiscated not for use or resale but as a means of eradicating the Armenian culture.

78. BCA / TİGMA 272.65 / 6.1.9, 5 June 1332 (18 June 1916). On 29 July 1917, the Ministry of Interior sent the same telegram to various provinces and districts including Aintab. BOA.DH.ŞFR 78 / 225, 29 July 1333 (29 July 1917).

79. Tebaiyet-i Osmaniye Kanunnamesi (Law on Ottoman Citizenship), *Düstur*, series 1, vol. 1 (Istanbul: Matbaa-ı Amire, 1289); see also BOA / Yıldız Palace Collection (henceforth Y.EE). 41 / 133. The relevant articles in English translation are:

Article 5. People adopting foreign citizenship from citizenship of the exalted dominion [namely, the Ottoman Empire] with permission are, from the date they change citizenship, considered foreigners and are treated in this manner. However, if he [such a person] adopts foreign citizenship without permission from the Sublime State [the Ottoman state], this new citizenship is considered void and he is considered a citizenship of the Sublime State as before, in all matters he will be treated in the same manner as citizens of the Sublime State. In any case, the abandonment of a person of his citizenship of the Sublime State will depend upon a certificate to be given as a result of an exalted decree [of the Ottoman state].

Article 6. If the Sublime State desires, it can cast out from its citizenship a person who changes his citizenship status in a foreign land without permission from the exalted dominion [the Ottoman Empire], or serves for the military service of a foreign state; and the return to the imperial domains of this category of people whose citizenship has been rejected is prohibited.

80. For detailed information on the different concepts of citizenship of the two countries according to international law, see Leland J. Gordon, "The Turkish American Controversy over Nationality," *American Journal of International Law* 25, no. 4 (1931): 658–669.

81. BOA.DH.ŞFR 62 / 45, 16 March 1916.

82. BOA.DH.ŞFR 514 / 18, coded telegram the Province of Aleppo to the Ministry of Interior, 21 March 1916.

83. BOA.DH.ŞFR 514 / 18, coded telegram, the Province of Aleppo to the Ministry of Interior, 21 March 1916.

84. BOA.DH.ŞFR 514 / 18, coded telegram, the Province of Aleppo to the Ministry of Interior, 21 March 1916.

85. BOA.DH.ŞFR 92 / 240, 24 October 1918; BOA.HR.HMŞ.İŞO 214 / 40, 29 March 1919.

86. BOA.HR.SYS 2875 / 7, 23 May 1916.

87. BOA.HR.SYS 2875 / 7, 23 May 1916.

88. BOA.HR.SYS 2875 / 7, 15 August 1916.

89. BOA.HR.SYS 2875 / 7, 14 November 1916.

90. BOA.HR.SYS 2875 / 7, 19 December 1916.

91. BOA.HR.SYS 2875 / 7, 29 January 1917; BOA.HR.SYS 2875 / 7, 6 March 1917.

92. BOA.DH.ŞFR 55 / 210, 12 August 1915.

93. BOA.DH.HMŞ 12 / 32, 12 August 1915.

94. BNu / Fonds A. Andonian, P.J. 1 / 3, file 4, Aintab, "The Deportation of Armenians in Aintab," 11; Gulesserian, "Dasnmeg Egheragan Dariner Ah'nt'abi mĕch, 1908–1919," 1031; "Miss Frearson's Experiences and Observations in Turkey," *ABCFM*, 16.9.6.1, unit 5, vol. 2, part 1, reel 670-7.1.11, 1817–1919, 6; Kévorkian, *The Armenian Genocide*, 608.

95. BNu / Fonds A. Andonian, P.J. 1 / 3, file 4, Aintab, "The Deportation of Armenians in Aintab," 11–13; Gulesserian, "Dasnmeg Egheragan Dariner Ah'nt'abi mĕch, 1908–1919," 1031; "Miss Frearson's Experiences and Observations

in Turkey," *ABCFM*, 16.9.6.1, unit 5, vol. 2, part 1, reel 670-7.1.11, 1817–1919, 6, 8; Bogharian, *Orakro'wt'iwn Darakir Geanqis*, 156; "Political Diary (20 November 1915 to 21 April 1916)," *Hah Ah'nt'ab* 7, no. 21 (1966): 34; *Badmo'wt'iwn Ah'nt'abi Hah'o'c*, vol. II, 549; M. Abdülhalik Renda, *Hatırat* (Istanbul: Yapı Kredi Yayınları, 2018), 175.

96. "Miss Frearson's Experiences and Observations in Turkey," *ABCFM*, 16.9.6.1, unit 5, vol. 2, part 1, reel 670-7.1.11, 1817–1919, 7.

97. Nazarian, *Eghernēn Verabrogh H'o'wsher*, 10; "Political Diary (20 November 1915 to 21 April 1916)," *Hah Ah'nt'ab* 7, no. 21 (1966): 34.

98. Bogharian, *Orakro'wt'iwn Darakir Geanqis*, 156.

99. Gulesserian, "Dasnmeg Egheragan Dariner Ah'nt'abi měch, 1908–1919," 1050.

100. Nazarian, *Eghernēn Verabrogh H'o'wsher*, 11; "Political Diary (20 November 1915 to 21 April 1916)," *Hah Ah'nt'ab* 7, no. 21 (1966): 34; "Miss Frearson's Experiences and Observations in Turkey," *ABCFM*, 16.9.6.1, unit 5, vol. 2, part 1, reel 670-7.1.11, 1817–1919, 8.

101. Nazarian, *Eghernēn Verabrogh H'o'wsher*, 12.

102. Bogharian, *Orakro'wt'iwn Darakir Geanqis*, 137.

103. BOA.DH.ŞFR 12 / 28, 25 October 1915.

104. Gulesserian, "Dasnmeg Egheragan Dariner Ah'nt'abi měch, 1908–1919," 1042–1043. As an eyewitness, Alice Kazazian said that both Turks and the local government occupied houses of wealthy Armenians. Also, the local government used other assets, tools, and shops of the deported Armenians. Later, Muslim refugees from Erzurum were settled in the houses by the local government. An interview with Alice Kazaian, 1986, Philadelphia, 20–21.

105. BOA.DH.ŞFR 57 / 261, 20 Teşrinievvel 1331 (2 November 1915).

106. BOA.DH.ŞFR 61 / 121, 26 February 1916.

107. BOA.DH.ŞFR 71 / 86, 26 December 1916.

108. Kuchukian, *Hariwr Zham Ah'nt'abi*, 10.

109. I obtained these title deeds from relatives of the Nazaretian and Danielian families, living in Boston and Los Angeles, respectively.

110. I obtained this document from Sarkis Yacoubian's grandchildren living in Los Angeles. Sarkis Yacoubian was born in Aintab. He escaped from the genocide to Aleppo. He died from tuberculosis in Aleppo in 1924.

111. BCA / TİGMA 272.00.00.10.1.1.18.1, 22 Kânunuevvel 1331 (4 January 1916); BCA / TİGMA 272.00.00.10.1.2.18.1, 19 Kânunuevvel 331 (1 January 1916); BCA / TİGMA 272.00.00.10.1.1.20, 23 Kânunuevvel 1331 (5 January 1916); BCA / TİGMA 272.00.00.10.1.2.18, 22 Kânunuevvel 1331 (4 January 1916).

112. Kurt, "Emval-i Metruke ve Tasfiye Komisyonlarının Yapısı ve İşlevi," *Toplumsal Tarih*, no. 259, June 2015, 23.

113. Teager, *The Krajians of Aintab,* 11.

114. BCA / TİGMA 272.00.00.11.8.7.2, 5 May 1916.

115. BCA / TİGMA 272.00.00.11.8.7.2, 17 May 1916.

116. BOA.HR.İM 40 / 18, 5 February 1923; Teager, *The Krajians of Aintab,* 105; Nilhan Aras, *Gaziantep Deyince* (Istanbul: Metro Kültür Yayınları, 2008), 87.

117. Taner Akçam and Ümit Kurt, *Kanunların Ruhu: Emval-i Metruke Kanunlarında Soykırımın İzini Sürmek* (Istanbul: İletişim, 2012), 31–44; Kurt, "The Plunder of Wealth through Abandoned Properties Laws in the Armenian Genocide," *Genocide Studies International* 10, no. 1 (2016): 37–51; Kurt, "Legal and Official Plunder of Armenian and Jewish Properties in Comparative Perspective: The Armenian Genocide and the Holocaust," *Journal of Genocide Research* 17, no. 3 (2015): 305–326; Kurt, "Varlık ve Yokluk Kıskacında Ermeniler: 1915 Ermeni Kırımı'nın Ekonomik Şiddet Boyutu," in *Türkiye'de Siyasal Şiddetin Boyutları,* ed. Güney Çeğin and İbrahim Şirin (Istanbul: İletişim, 2014), 79–127; Fuat Dündar, *Modern Türkiye'nin Şifresi: İttihat Terakki'nin Etnisite Mühendisliği* (Istanbul: İletişim, 2008), 293–296; Dündar, *Kahir Ekseriyet: Ermeni Nüfus Meselesi (1878–1923)* (Istanbul: Tarih Vakfı Yayınları, 2013), 145–147.

5. The Flawed Restitution Process for Armenians

1. In its place, Teceddüt Fırkası (the Renovation Party) was founded by the Unionists present at the final CUP party congress on 11 November. Although the party officially denied that it was continuation of the CUP, its takeover of CUP assets, such as organizational networks, real estate (the clubs), and cash undermined the credibility of this claim. Eric J. Zürcher, *The Young Turk Legacy and Nation Building: From the Ottoman Empire to Atatürk's Turkey* (New York: I.B.Tauris, 2010), 198; Zürcher, *The Unionist Factor: The Role of the Committee of Union and Progress in the Turkish National Movement 1905–1926* (Leiden: E.J. Brill, 1984), 72–73. The party was closed and its members banned from politics.

2. On the rule of these governments, established by seven different grand viziers, see Tarık Zafer Tunaya, *Türkiye'de Siyasi Partiler, Cilt II, Mütareke Dönemi* (Istanbul: Hürriyet Vakfı Yayınları, 1986), 37.

3. From 1919 to 1922, the court-martial active in Istanbul tried sixty-three cases in total and prosecuted approximately 200 defendants. For more detailed information on this topic, see Vahakn Dadrian and Taner Akçam, *Judgment at Istanbul: The Armenian Genocide Trials* (New York: Berghahn Books, 2011).

4. *Osmanlı Belgelerinde Ermenilerin Sevk ve İskanı (1878–1920),* 396.

5. *Osmanlı Belgelerinde Ermenilerin Sevk ve İskanı (1878–1920),* 397–398; BOA.DH.ŞFR 92 / 235, a coded telegram sent by the IAMM to the provinces of Edirne, Aleppo, and Sivas, as well as the provincial districts of Urfa, Izmid, Bolu, and so on, dated 23 October 1918.

6. On the communications of 28 October and 5 and 23 November 1918, see *Osmanlı Belgelerinde Ermenilerin Sevk ve İskânı,* 399–403.

7. *Meclis-i Mebusan Zabıt Ceridesi,* Period 3, Assembly Year 5, vol. 1 (Ankara: TBMM Basımevi, 1992), 114–116.

8. *Osmanlı Belgelerinde Ermenilerin Sevk ve İskanı (1878–1920),* 402. For a more detailed work on the returnees, see İbrahim Ethem Atnur, "Tehcirden Dönen Rum ve Ermenilerin İskânı" (unpublished master's thesis, Erzurum University, 1991).

9. *Meclis-i Mebusan Zabıt Ceridesi,* Period 3, Assembly Year 5, vol. 1, 362.

10. *Osmanlı Belgelerinde Ermeniler (1915–1920)* (Ankara: Başbakanlık Basımevi, 1995), 230.

11. *Memleket* newspaper, 12 March 1335 (1919).

12. *Osmanlı Belgelerinde Ermeniler (1915–1920),* 246.

13. *Ati* newspaper, 3 February 1336 (1920), and *İleri* newspaper, 3 February 1336 (1920).

14. *İleri* newspaper, 28 Teşrinievvel 1335 (28 October 1919); *Tarik* newspaper, 22 Teşrinievvel 1335 (22 October 1919); *Alemdar* newspaper, 27 Kanunuevvel 1334 (27 December 1918); Adem Günaydın, "The Return and Resettlement of the Relocated Armenians 1918–1920" (unpublished master's thesis, Middle East Technical University, 2007), 2; Tayfun Eroğlu, "Tehcirden Milli Mücadeleye Ermeni Malları (1915–1922)" (unpublished master's thesis, Dokuz Eylül University, 2008), 134–135.

15. Günaydın, "The Return and Resettlement of the Relocated Armenians 1918–1920," 2. Also see Eroğlu, "Tehcirden Milli Mücadeleye Ermeni Malları (1915–1922)," 157; Hacer Çelik, "Ermeni Tehciri ve Tehcirden Dönen Ermenilerin İskan Sorunu," *ÇTTAD* 7, no. 16–17 (2008): 151–152; Atnur, "Tehcirden Dönen Rum ve Ermenilerin İskanı," 136; *Tasvir-i Efkâr,* 17 Teşrinievvel 1334 (17 October 1918).

16. BOA.DH.ŞFR 92 / 285, 28 October 1918. Also see Oya Gözel Durmaz, "A City Transformed: War, Demographic Change and Profiteering in Kayseri (1915–1920)" (PhD diss., METU, Ankara, 2014), 203.

17. BOA.DH.ŞFR 93 / 108, 9 November 1918; BOA.HR.SYS 2569 / 1 in *Osmanlı Belgelerinde Ermenilerin Sevk ve İskânı,* 402; *Tasvir-i Efkâr,* 3 Teşrinisâni 1334 (3 November 1918); Durmaz, "A City Transformed," 203.

18. *Osmanlı Belgelerinde Ermenilerin Sevk ve İskânı,* 412–417; BOA.DH.ŞFR 92 / 238; *Osmanlı Belgelerinde Ermeniler,* 178; İbrahim Ethem Atnur,

"Osmanlı Hükümetleri ve Tehcir Edilen Rum ve Ermenilerin Yeniden İskânı Meselesi," *Atatürk Yolu* 4, no. 14 (1994): 126. Also see Durmaz, "A City Transformed," 204.

19. BOA.BEO 341055, 18 and 22 December 1918, in *Osmanlı Belgelerinde Ermenilerin Sevk ve İskânı,* 412–417; Durmaz, "A City Transformed," 205.

20. BOA.BEO 341055, 18 and 22 December 1918, in *Osmanlı Belgelerinde Ermenilerin Sevk ve İskânı,* 412–417; Durmaz, "A City Transformed," 205.

21. BOA.DH.ŞFR 94 / 231 in *Osmanlı Belgelerinde Ermenilerin Sevk ve İskânı,* 414, 417. This temporary law of 22 September 1916 stipulated that the property of the deported would be subject to liquidation. BOA.DH.ŞFR 94 / 231 in *Osmanlı Belgelerinde Ermenilerin Sevk ve İskânı,* 414, 417.

22. *İkdam* newspaper, 25 Kanunuevvel 1334 (25 December 1918); Eroğlu, "Tehcirden Milli Mücadeleye Ermeni Malları (1915–1922)," 142–143.

23. BCA / TİGMA 272.11.14.50.4, 21 July 1919; BCA / TİGMA 272.10.2.12.1, 3 January 1921. Also see Günaydın, "The Return and Resettlement of the Relocated Armenians 1918–1920," 54.

24. Günaydın, "The Return and Resettlement of the Relocated Armenians 1918–1920," 56.

25. BOA.DH.HMŞ 4-2 / 11–20, 25 January 1919.

26. *Turkish—Armenian Conflict,* document no: 53, 154–156 cited in Günaydın, "The Return and Resettlement of the Relocated Armenians 1918–1920," 58.

27. BCA / TİGMA 272.10.1.6.9, 21 October 1919.

28. BCA / TİGMA 272.11.13.42.18, 3 December 1918. Also see Günaydın, "The Return and Resettlement of the Relocated Armenians 1918–1920," 57.

29. Günaydın, "The Return and Resettlement of the Relocated Armenians 1918–1920," 57.

30. BCA / TİGMA 272.11.13.45.16, 2 April 1919; Günaydın, "The Return and Resettlement of the Relocated Armenians 1918–1920," 57. This punishment process accelerated immediately after promulgation of the regulation of 12 January 1920, which annulled the confiscation and liquidation laws enacted during the CUP government; see BOA.ŞD 1885 / 2, 29 April 1920 and BOA. ŞD 2252 / 45, 26 April 1921.

31. Vahé Tachjian, "The Cilician Armenians and French Policy, 1919–1921," in *Armenian Cilicia,* ed. Richard G. Hovannisian and Simon Payaslian (Costa Mesa, CA: Mazda Publishers, 2008), 544–545.

32. Tachjian, "Cilician Armenians and French Policy, 1919–1921," 545.

33. Tachjian, "Cilician Armenians and French Policy, 1919–1921," 545–556.

34. BNu / Fonds M.S.C. / 1-V, Cilicia-Adana. 227: 10 and 12 April 1919, Annotation sent by military governor of the sanjak of Cebel-i Bereket, Second

Lieutenant Andrea to military governor of the province of Adana Colonel Brémond; Ümit Kurt, "The Political Micro-Economy of the Armenian Genocide, 1915–1922," *Journal of Balkan and Near Eastern Studies* 20, no. 6 (2018): 618–638; Kurt, "I. Cihan Harbi Sonrası Ermeni Mallarının İadesi: Cebel-i Bereket Örneği," *Toplumsal Tarih,* no. 254 (November 2014): 22–28.

35. For the entire list, see BNu / Fonds M.S.C. / 1-V, Cilicia-Adana. 227: 10 and 12 April 1919, Annotation sent by military governor of the sanjak of Cebel-i Bereket, Second Lieutenant Andrea to military governor of the province of Adana Colonel Brémond; and Kurt, "The Political Micro-Economy of the Armenian Genocide," 636–638; Kurt, "I. Cihan Harbi Sonrası Ermeni Mallarının İadesi," 26–28. Following the withdrawal of French troops from the region in 1921, the process of returning properties to their Armenian owners was aborted, and the properties were seized once again by reverting to the laws on abandoned and liquidated properties issued in 1915.

36. Durmaz, "A City Transformed," esp. 203–231.

37. Durmaz, "A City Transformed," 204.

38. Günaydın, "The Return and Resettlement of the Relocated Armenians 1918–1920," 57–58.

39. BOA.ML.EEM 132-1 / 17-1a, 10 July 1919.

40. BOA.ML.EEM 132-1 / 33–2, 27 April 1920.

41. Günaydın, "The Return and Resettlement of the Relocated Armenians 1918–1920," 58. Also see BOA.ML.EEM 132-1 / 18–1a and 1b, 16 July 1919; BOA.ML.VZN, 1 / 45–1b, 1 June 1920.

42. Günaydın, "The Return and Resettlement of the Relocated Armenians 1918–1920," 58. There are certain examples to demonstrate that the Commission for the Administration of Abandoned Properties restituted the money that had been gained through sale of the abandoned properties to their returning owners in Edirne, Milas, and Canik. BCA / TİGMA 272.10.2.11.3, 15 March 1920; BCA / TİGMA 272.74.68.39.9, 30 March 1918; BCA / TİGMA 272.10.2.10.14, 13 March 1920; BCA / TİGMA 272.10.2.11.11, 22 April 1920. In the case of Aintab, I could not find similar documents.

43. Günaydın, "The Return and Resettlement of the Relocated Armenians 1918–1920," 59.

44. Günaydın, "The Return and Resettlement of the Relocated Armenians 1918–1920," 60.

45. BOA.ŞD 1885 / 2, 29 April 1920.

46. BOA.ŞD 2252 / 45, 26 April 1921.

47. Günaydın, "The Return and Resettlement of the Relocated Armenians 1918–1920," 62.

48. BOA.ŞD 50 / 14, March 1919. Article 31 of Sicil-i Nüfus Kanunu (the Law of Civil Registry), 27 August 1914: "Vefat vukuunda müteveffanın ve pederinin ismini ve müteehhil olup olmadığını ve müteehhil ise kimin zevci veya zevcesi olduğunu ve sinnini ve san'atını ve maskatı re'isini ve sebebi vefatını ve vefatının yevm ve kabil ise saatini mübeyyin iki şahit huzurunda vefiyat vukuatına ait usul dairesi'nde bir ilmühaber tanzimile mahalli nüfus idaresine vermeğe muhtaran mecburdur." Cited in Durmaz, "A City Transformed," 207–208n625.

49. BOA.DH.ŞFR 96 / 230, 19 February 1919; Durmaz, "A City Transformed," 206.

50. Günaydın, "The Return and Resettlement of the Relocated Armenians 1918–1920," 63; Durmaz, "A City Transformed," 215.

51. Günaydın, "The Return and Resettlement of the Relocated Armenians 1918–1920," 65. Also see Selahattin Tansel, *Mondros'tan Mudanya'ya Kadar* (Istanbul: Milli Eğitim Bakanlığı, 1991), 63; Eroğlu, "Tehcirden Milli Mücadeleye Ermeni Malları (1915–1922)," 151. Immediately after signing the Mudros Armistice on 30 October 1918, the Armenian Patriarchate, under the presidency of Zaven Der Yeghiayan, founded a unique commission. This commission was presided over by Arakel Chakrian; see Zaven Der Yeghiayan, *My Patriarchal Memoirs* (Barrington, RI: Mayreni Publications, 2002), 181–182. The most important task of this commission was to find children and women who were orphaned, adopted, and widowed during the Armenian deportation and genocide; deliver them to their families and relatives; and provide restitution of movable and immovable assets and properties of deported Armenians to their original owners. For a detailed analysis of the situation of Armenian orphans and widowed women, see Lerna Ekmekçioğlu, "A Climate for Abduction, a Climate for Redemption: The Politics of Inclusion during and after the Armenian Genocide," *Comparative Studies in Society and History* 55, no. 3 (2013): 522–553; Ekmekçioğlu, "Kız Kaçırma, Kız Kurtarma: Birinci Dünya Savaşı sırasında ve Mütareke yıllarında İstanbul'da Ermenilik ve Müslümanlık," *Toplum ve Bilim*, no. 129 (2014): 225–256. This commission worked in cooperation with the Armenian-Greek section of the commission. For reports of this section, see Yeghian (ed.), *British Reports on Ethnic Cleansing in Anatolia, 1919–1922: The Armenian-Greek Section* (Glendale, CA: Center for Armenian Remembrance, 2007).

52. For the full text of "Âher Mahallere Nakledilmiş Olan Eşhâsın 17 Zilkade 1733 (26 Eylül 1915) Tarihli Kararname Mucibince Tasfiyeye Tâbi Tutulan Emvâli Hakkında Kararname" (Regulation on Properties of People Transported to Other Places Subject to Liquidation According to the 17

Zilkade 1733 [26 September 1915] Dated Regulation), *Düstur,* Tertip. 2, vol. 11 (Istanbul: Evkaf Matbaası, 1928), 553–561, and *Takvim-i Vekayi,* no: 2747, 12 Kanunisani 1336 (12 January 1920). See also Salâhaddin Kardeş, *"Tehcir" ve Emval-i Metruke Mevzuatı* (Ankara: T. C. Maliye Bakanlığı Strateji Geliştirme Başkanlığı, 2008), 69–91, and Taner Akçam and Ümit Kurt, *The Spirit of the Laws: The Plunder of Wealth in the Armenian Genocide* (New York: Berghahn Books, 2015), 38–39.

53. *Takvim-i Vekayi,* no: 2747, 12 Kanunisani 1336 (12 January 1920); Akçam and Kurt, *The Spirit of Laws,* 39.

54. *Takvim-i Vekayi,* no: 2747, 12 Kanunisani 1336 (12 January 1920).

55. *Badmo'wt'iwn Ah'nt'abi Hah'o'c,* vol. II, 45.

56. BOA.DH.ŞFR 608 / 20, 28 December 1918.

57. BOA.DH.ŞFR 608 / 20, 28 December 1918.

58. "Antep Savunması," *Gaziantep Kültür Dergisi* 10, no. 109 (1967): 4; *Badmo'wt'iwn Ah'nt'abi Hah'o'c,* vol. II, 45; Abadi, *Türk Verdün'ü Gaziantep: Antep'in Dört Muhasarası* (Gaziantep: Osman Nuri Tuzcu Eğitim ve Kültür Vakfı, 1999), 26; Ali Nadi Ünler, "Antep Savunması," *Gaziantep Kültür Dergisi* 1, no. 1 (1957): 10. According to some sources, Aintab was occupied by British forces on 17 December 1918; see Ahmet Hulki Saral, *Türk İstiklal Harbi,* vol. 4, *Güney Cephesi* (Ankara: Genelkurmay Harp Tarihi Başkanlığı, 1966), 50; Eyüp Sabri (Akgöl), *Esaret Hatıraları (Bir Esirin Hatıraları, Gaziantep'te İngiliz Tecavüzünün Başlangıcı ve Türk Üserasına Zulüm ve İşkenceler),* ed. Nejat Sefercioğlu (Istanbul: Tercüman, 1978), 13; Ramazan Erhan Güllü, *Antep Ermenileri: Sosyal-Siyasi ve Kültürel Hayatı* (Ankara: IQ Yayınları, 2010), 296; Stanley E. Kerr, *The Lions of Marash: Personal Experience with American Near East Relief, 1919–1922* (Albany: State University of New York Press, 1973), 35; Ali Fuat Türkgeldi, *Mondros ve Mudanya Mütarekelerinin Tarihi* (Ankara: Güney Matbaacılık ve Gazetecilik, 1948), 67; Zeki Sarıhan, *Kurtuluş Savaşı Günlüğü,* vol. 1 (Ankara: Öğretmen Dünyası, 1982), 79.

59. *Badmo'wt'iwn Ah'nt'abi Hah'o'c,* vol. I, 1071.

60. Lutfi Levonian used to be a member of the faculty at Central Turkey College. He and his family members were exempted from deportation. He served as the head of the government Commercial High School in Aintab. His brother, Adour Levonian, served in the Ottoman army during the war; and his two sisters, Mari and Nuritsa, were teachers in the Turkish schools; see *ABCFM* 16.9.6.1, unit 5, vol. 2, part 1, reel 674, no. 369, 1817–1919; H. Harutyun Nazarian, *Eghernēn Verabrogh H'o'wsher* [Memoirs of a Genocide Survivor], ed. Toros Toronian (Aleppo, 2009), 15.

61. *Badmo'wt'iwn Ah'nt'abi Hah'o'c,* vol. I, 1071.

62. CAB 24 / 145, *Eastern Report,* 26 December 1918, 170.

63. *Badmo'wt'iwn Ah'nt'abi Hah'o'c.* vol. I, 1072. The Indian Cavalry Corps served under General Allenby in his successful advance from Egypt to Aleppo. There were three squadrons of the Indian Cavalry lodged at Central Turkey College in December 1918. *Missionary Herald* 116, no. 1 (1919): 159.

64. Stina Katchadourian, *Efronia: An Armenian Love Story* (Princeton, NJ: Gomidas Institute Books, Taderon Press, 2001), 159.

65. Sarkis Laleian (ed.), *H'o'wshamadean: No'wiro'wadz Ado'wr H. Lewo'neani, Inqnagensakro'wt'iwn ew Tro'wakner ir Geanqe'n o'w Ko'rdze'n* [Memoir: Dedicated to Adour Levonian, Autobiography and Episodes from His Life and Work] (Beirut: Shirag, 1967), 37.

66. Eyüp Sabri (Akgöl), *Bir Esirin Hatıraları,* 30.

67. FO 371 / 4174, no. 102551 and FO 10991 / M.1159 from the high commissioner in Istanbul, Arthur Calthorpe, to Lord Curzon, Istanbul, 27 June 1919, concerning official documents in the possession of the mutasarrıf of Aintab seized by the British military authorities on 4 February 1919.

68. ATASE, Arş 1 / 105, Dosya No: (6)-2, K1 255, Fihrist: 5 / 1 cited in Ayhan Öztürk, *Milli Mücadele'de Gaziantep* (Kayseri: Geçit Yayınları, 1994), 31; Mustafa Nurettin Lohanizade, *Gazi Antep Savunması* (Istanbul: Kastaş Yayınları, 1989), 18.

69. ATASE, Arş 1 / 105, Dosya No: (6)-2, K1 255, Fihrist: 5 / 1 cited in Öztürk, *Milli Mücadele'de Gaziantep,* 31.

70. *Badmo'wt'iwn Ah'nt'abi Hah'o'c,* vol. I, 1075.

71. FO 608 / 95, *General Headquarter Intelligence Summary,* 4 March 1919, 15.

72. FO 608 / 95, *General Headquarter Intelligence Summary,* 4 March 1919, 15; *Supplement to General Headquarter Intelligence Summary,* 1 April 1919; *Badmo'wt'iwn Ah'nt'abi Hah'o'c,* vol. I, 1075; Sarkis Balabanian, *Geanqis Daq o'w Bagh Orery: Ah'nt'ab, Qe'sab, Hale'b* [Hot and Cold Days of My Life: Aintab, Kesap, Halep] (Aleppo: Atlas, 1983), 149; *H'o'wshamadean: No'wiro'wadz Ado'wr H. Lewo'neani,* 41.

73. BOA.DH.ŞFR 609 / 14, 1 January 1919.

74. BOA.DH.ŞFR 609 / 14, 1 January 1919.

75. Daizâde Ahmed Hurşid Effendi was involved in the *kuvayı milliye* (national forces) and provided financial support for the forces of national struggle. He was also one of the prominent local notables who seized a number of Armenian properties during the deportation; see Chapter 4.

76. Eyüp Sabri (Akgöl), *Bir Esirin Hatıraları,* 15.

77. Eyüp Sabri (Akgöl), *Bir Esirin Hatıraları,* 24. This newspaper was raided and shut down again by the French during their occupation in November 1919. Even though the newspaper continued to be published intermittently after

April 1920, it was dismantled following the surrender of Aintab to the French as a result of starvation. Uğurol Barlas, *Gaziantep Basın Tarihi, 100. Yıl* (Karabük: Özer Matbaası, 1972), 25; Barlas, "Gaziantep'te Gazetecilik," *Gaziantep Kültür-Aylık Fikir ve Bilgi Dergisi* 1, no. 8 (1958): 8.

78. *Badmo'wt'iwn Ah'nt'abi Hah'o'c,* vol. II, 52; Celal Pekdoğan, "Acı Zerdali Çekirdeği Ekmeğinden Uvralı Buğday Ekmeğine," in *Gaziantep 'Dört Yanı Dağlar Bağlar',* ed. Refik Duru (Istanbul: Yapı Kredi Yayınları, 2007), 126.

79. *Badmo'wt'iwn Ah'nt'abi Hah'o'c,* vol. I, 1074; Katchadourian, *Efronia: An Armenian Love Story,* 159; *H'o'wshamadean: No'wiro'wadz Ado'wr H. Lewo'neani,* 45; Balabanian, *Geanqis Daq o'w Bagh Orery,* 149.

80. *Badmo'wt'iwn Ah'nt'abi Hah'o'c,* vol. I, 1074; Eyüp Sabri (Akgöl), *Bir Esirin Hatıraları,* 24–25; Hüseyin Beyaz, *Antep Savunması Günlüğü* (Istanbul: Engin Matbaası, 1994), 124.

81. Eyüp Sabri (Akgöl), *Bir Esirin Hatıraları,* 27.

82. Eyüp Sabri (Akgöl), *Bir Esirin Hatıraları,* 28–29.

83. Eyüp Sabri (Akgöl), *Bir Esirin Hatıraları,* 14, 24–25; *Badmo'wt'iwn Ah'nt'abi Hah'o'c,* vol. I, 1074; "Celal Kadri Barlas'ın Dilinden, İttihat ve Terakki Cemiyeti Nasıl Kuruldu?," 16–17, and Şakir Sabri Yener, "Celal Kadri Barlas'ı Kaybettik," *Gaziantep Kültür Dergisi* 6, no. 68 (1963): 177.

84. BOA.DH.ŞFR 613 / 100, 5 February 1919; BOA.HR.HU 43 / 61, 15 C 1337 (18 March 1919), *Osmanlı Belgelerinde Ermeniler (1915–1920),* 222–224; M. Oğuz Göğüş, "General Faik Taşçıoğlu'nu Kaybettik," *Gaziantep'i Tanıtıyoruz* 1, no. 2 (1952): 17.

85. Sedat Bey was a teacher at a CUP *idadi* (high school) in Aintab.

86. Hüseyin Bey was a retired major.

87. Eyüp Sabri (Akgöl), *Bir Esirin Hatıraları,* 19, 41; BEO 4595 / 344573, 14 and 24 Teşrinievvel 1335 (14 and 24 October 1919); DH.İ.UM 19–9 / 1–35, 1338 M 27 (22 October 1919).

88. Eyüp Sabri (Akgöl), *Bir Esirin Hatıraları,* 45.

89. Enver Behnan Şapolyo, *Kemal Atatürk ve Milli Mücadele Tarihi* (Ankara: Berkalp Kitapevi, 1944), 224; Ümit Kurt, "The Curious Case of Ali Cenani Bey: The Story of a Génocidaire," *Patterns of Prejudice* 52, no. 1 (2018): 58–77.

90. BOA.HR.SYS 2704 / 11, 31 December 1918 and BOA.DH.EUM.AYŞ 32 / 16, 11 February 1920; Edouard Brémond, "La Cilicie en 1919–1920," *Revue des Etudes Arméniennes* 1, no. 3 (1921): 309, 311; Du Véou, *La Passion de la Cilicie,* 66, 90–91, cited in Vahram L. Shemmassian, "Repatriation of Armenian Refugees from the Arab Middle East, 1918–1920," in *Armenian Cilicia,* ed. Richard G. Hovannisian and Simon Payaslian (Costa Mesa, CA: Mazda Pub-

lishers, 2008): 432; Zaven Der Yeghiayan, *My Patriarchal Memoirs,* 191; Doğan Avcıoğlu, *Milli Kurtuluş Tarihi,* vol. I (Istanbul: Tekin Yayınevi, 1977), 115.

91. Brémond, "La Cilicie en 1919–1920," 309, 311; Du Véou, *La Passion de la Cilicie,* 66, 90–91, cited in Shemmassian, "Repatriation of Armenian Refugees from the Arab Middle East," 432.

92. *Times* newspaper (London), 16 January 1919, cited in Shemmassian, "Repatriation of Armenian Refugees from the Arab Middle East," 425.

93. FO 371 / 3405, 199352 / 55708 / 44, Sykes to FO for Boghos Nubar's information, 2 December 1918, cited in Shemmassian, "Repatriation of Armenian Refugees from the Arab Middle East," 425.

94. FO 371 / 3405, 199352 / 55708 / 44, Sykes to FO for Boghos Nubar's information, 2 December 1918, cited in Shemmassian, "Repatriation of Armenian Refugees from the Arab Middle East," 425.

95. *Darakir* (Deportees), Aleppo, 25 December 1918. Detailed lists of potential repatriates originating from various localities are found in France, *Archives du Ministére des Affaires Etrangéres,* Nantes, Beyrouth: Cilicie 1919–1921, Cilicie-Alep, cartons 319–331; APA, Files 42, 46–52, cited in Shemmassian, "Repatriation of Armenian Refugees from the Arab Middle East," 429. Kilis was a district of Aintab in 1918.

96. The French in Cilicia and the British in Syria recognized the need of interlocutors "who could fairly claim to represent the diverse components of Armenian society." As soon as the Mudros Armistice was signed, both Allenby, commander of the Allied forces in the Near East, and François Georges-Picot, the French commissioner, encouraged "the formation of the branches of the ANU in all of the Allied-occupied areas where there was an Armenian population." In Cilicia, the ANU, along with the representative of the Paris-based Armenian National Delegation, Mihran Damadian, were quasi-official spokesmen for Armenian interests. Tachjian, "The Cilician Armenians and French Policy, 1919–1921" in *Armenian Cilicia,* 542n4.

97. BCA / TİGMA 272.00.00.74.68.37.5, 9 January 1919.

98. Archives of the Armenian Patriarchate of Jerusalem (hereafter APC / APJ), PCI Bureau, 367, list of the regions where the Armenians and the Greeks were repatriated, cited in Raymond Kévorkian, *The Armenian Genocide: A Complete History* (London: I.B. Tauris, 2011), 748.

99. Barsamian and Gedzvanian on behalf of Ehnesh refugees to Aleppo ANU chairman and members, 16 January 1919; Barsamian on behalf of twenty-five Ehnesh refugees to Aleppo ANU chairman and members, 13 February 1919, in Shemmassian, "Repatriation of Armenian Refugees from the Arab Middle East," 424n19. Colonel Clouscard (director of the Central Service

of Armenian Repatriation), announcement in Armenian regarding repatriation of Armenians to Aintab and Marash, 12 May 1919. See also Colonel Cousscard to President of Inter-Provincial Committee of Aleppo, 8 June 1919, in Shemmassian, "Repatriation of Armenian Refugees from the Arab Middle East," 424n19.

100. NARA / RG 84, Vol. 83, *Correspondence, American Consulate, Aleppo, 1919,* Jackson, Political and Economic Conditions, May 31, 1919; NARA / RG59 / 867.00 / 897. See also Shemmassian, "Repatriation of Armenian Refugees from the Arab Middle East," 440.

101. NARA / RG59 / 867.48 / 1316, Jackson to Secretary of State, 23 August 1919; Harutyun Simonian (ed.), *H'awelo'wazd: Ah'nt'abi Hah'o'c Badmo'wt'iwn* [Collected: History of Aintab Armenians] (Waltham: Mayreni, 1997), 105.

102. Barlas, *Gaziantep Tıp Fakültesi Tarihi ve Azınlık Okulları,* 14; M. Oğuz Göğüş, *İlk İnsanlardan Bugüne Çeşitli Yönleriyle Gaziantep* (Ankara: Cihan Ofset, 1997), 69; 306; Sahir Üzel, *Gaziantep Savaşının İç Yüzü* (Ankara: Doğuş Matbaası, 1952), 7. Another local source claims that fifty thousand Armenians gathered in Aintab after the British occupation of Aintab. *Gaziantep Kültür Dergisi* 3, no. 28 (1960): 89.

103. This number includes 4,000 Aintab Armenians who were already exempted from deportation and had never left the city. Kevork H. Barsumian, *Badmo'wt'iwn Ah'nt'abi H. H. Tashnagco'wt'iwn 1898–1922* [History of the Aintab Armenian Revolutionary Federation 1898–1922] (Aleppo: Tigris, 1957), 331. Archpriest Nerses Babaian, who reached Aintab on 21 November 1919 from exile, estimated the Armenian population there at 17,000–18,000; see *Pages from My Diary / Archpriest Der Nerses Babaian,* ed. Yervant Babaian (Los Angeles: Abril Publisher, 2000), 31.

104. Barsumian, *Badmo'wt'iwn Ah'nt'abi H. H. Tashnagco'wt'iwn 1898–1922,* 51.

105. Karaian, "On the Number of Armenians in Aintab in 1914," in *Badmo'wt'iwn Ah'nt'abi Hah'o'c,* vol. III, 17. An administrative body named the Armenian National Union Committee of Aintab was formed in early 1919. It was composed of seven elected members: Dr. Hovsep Bezjian, chairman (Armenian Protestant); Yeghiazan Benlian, secretary (Armenian Orthodox); Dr. Kevork Arslanian, treasurer (Armenian Catholic); Mushegh Hadidian, consultant (Armenian Protestant); Nerses Ishkhanian, consultant (Armenian Protestant); Kevork Leyleguian, consultant (Armenian Orthodox); Bedros Merjenian, consultant (Armenian Orthodox). The Armenian National Union was founded for the purpose of managing community and religious affairs in Aintab; see *Badmo'wt'iwn Ah'nt'abi Hah'o'c,* vol. I, 1080.

106. *Badmo'wt'iwn Ah'nt'abi Hah'o'c,* vol. I, 1067.

107. *Badmo'wt'iwn Ah'nt'abi Hah'o'c,* vol. I, 1067; vol. II, 45; FO 608 / 95, *General Headquarter Intelligence Summary,* 5 February 1919, 20.

108. BCA / TİGMA 272.00.00.11.14.51.15, the Ministry of Interior to the governorship of Aintab, 1 September 1919.

109. BNu / M.S.L., 1.v., Cilicia-Adana, 168, "Compte Rendu d'une Tournes a Aintab et Marache," a report of Aintab-Marash tour dated 14 August 1919, and Nazarian, *Eghernēn Verabrogh H'o'wsher,* 14, 17. Kevork Agha Demirdjian was the owner of one of those ruined and looted houses; see Nazarian, *Eghernēn Verabrogh H'o'wsher,* 17. Der Nerses Tavukjian also mentioned the Armenian demands for the reparations of two thousand ruined houses; see Tavukjian, *Dar'abanqi Orakro'wt'iwn,* 195.

110. For example, compensation was made for Aleks Balutian's properties, which were sold during the deportation in Izmit. BCA / TİGMA 272.11 / 15.58.5, 13 May 1920. In the same way, in March 1920, Armenak Kurkchuian from Edirne also received compensation from the government for the liquidation of his properties by the Commission; see BCA / TİGMA 272.11 / 15.57.2, 11 March 1920. Also, Dikran Frinkian from Kayseri, whose mansion had been turned into a school after his deportation, applied for compensation for his loss; see BOA.DH.İ.UM.EK, 50 / 45, 14 April 1919.

111. BCA / TİGMA 272.11 / 15.54.3, 12 January 1920.

112. *H'o'wshamadean: No'wiro'wadz Ado'wr H. Lewo'neani,* 41.

113. On 16 January 1919, the former residents of Ehnesh village near Rum-Kale in the Aintab region asked for measures to stop "the destruction of their homes and pistachio groves by Muslim refugee occupants and wished to reclaim their only source of income once repatriation took place"; see Barsamian and Gedzvanian on behalf of Ehnesh refugees to ANU chairman and members, 16 January 1919; Barsamian on behalf of twenty-five Ehnesh refugees to Aleppo ANU chairman and members, 13 February 1919, in Shemmassian, "Repatriation of Armenian Refugees from the Arab Middle East," 424n19.

114. Nazarian, *Eghernēn Verabrogh H'o'wsher,* 19.

115. *ABCFM,* 16.9.6.1, unit 5, reel 670–10.52.5, 1817–1919, American Mission, Adana, Turkey, from Nesbit Chambers to James Barton, recorded 22 November 1919.

116. Karnig Panian, *Goodbye, Antoura: A Memoir of the Armenia Genocide* (Stanford, CA: Stanford University Press, 2015), 170.

117. *Badmo'wt'iwn Ah'nt'abi Hah'o'c,* vol. I, 550, 1078; Balabanian, *Geanqis Daq o'w Bagh Orery,* 148; Nazarian, *Eghernēn Verabrogh H'o'wsher,* 65. The first Protestant church, known as Hajik Church, suffered damage during the deportation and was reopened on 4 April 1919; see *Badmo'wt'iwn Ah'nt'abi Hah'o'c,* vol. I, 550.

118. *Badmo'wt'iwn Ah'nt'abi Hah'o'c,* vol. I, 1078. With British support, schools that belonged to Protestant Armenians were reopened on 15 January 1919; see *Badmo'wt'iwn Ah'nt'abi Hah'o'c,* vol. I, 551.

119. BCA / TİGMA 272.00.00.11.14.50.4, 15 May 1919.

120. BCA / TİGMA 272.00.00.11.14.50.4, 13 July 1919.

121. BCA / TİGMA 272.00.00.11.14.50.7, 20 July 1919.

122. BCA / TİGMA 272.00.00.74.68.45.3, 21 December 1919.

123. FO 861 / 69, "Statutory Declaration," 16 April 1920.

124. FO 861 / 69, "Statutory Declaration," 16 April 1920.

125. FO 861 / 69, "Statutory Declaration," 16 April 1920.

126. CAB 24 / 96 / 4, 15 November 1919, Dispatch from Civil Commissioner, Mesopotamia, to Secretary of State for India, 21.

127. "T'urk'erun Zēnk Gē pazhnui: K'ilisēn Gē kren" [Arms Were Distributed to the Turks: They Are Writing from Kilis], *Chagadamard* newspaper, G. Bolis (Istanbul), 16 July 1919.

128. "T'urk'erun Zēnk Gē pazhnui: K'ilisēn Gē kren" [Arms Were Distributed to the Turks: They Are Writing from Kilis], *Chagadamard* newspaper, G. Bolis (Istanbul), 16 July 1919.

129. Ünler, *Gaziantep Savunması,* 15; Ömer Asım Aksoy, *Türkçe Bir Hayat* (Istanbul: Yapı Kredi Yayınları, 1999), 36.

130. *Badmo'wt'iwn Ah'nt'abi Hah'o'c,* vol. II, 51.

131. Yaşar Akbıyık, *Milli Mücadele'de Güney Cephesi (Maraş)* (Ankara: Kültür Bakanlığı, 1990), 48–52; Gotthard Jaeschke, *Kurtuluş Savaşı ile İlgili İngiliz Belgeleri* (Ankara: TTK, 1991), 46.

132. *Badmo'wt'iwn Ah'nt'abi Hah'o'c* vol. I, 1080; Mustafa Budak, *İdealden Gerçeğe, Misak-ı Milli'den Lozan'a Dış Politika* (Istanbul: ATAM Yayınları, 2003), 116–121.

133. BOA.DH.ŞFR 648 / 44, 11 October 1919.

134. *Badmo'wt'iwn Ah'nt'abi Hah'o'c,* vol. I, 553; Tavukjian, *Dar'abanqi Orakro'wt'iwn,* 195; M. Abadie (Lieut.-Colonel Br.), *Les Quatre Sièges d'Aintab (1920–1921)* (Paris: Charles Lavauzelle, 1922), 30; Zekai Güner, "Antep Savunması ve Ali Şefik Özdemir Bey'in Faaliyetleri," *Zonguldak Karaelmas Üniversitesi Sosyal Bilimler Dergisi* 3, no. 6 (2007): 51.

135. *Badmo'wt'iwn Ah'nt'abi Hah'o'c,* vol. I., 1080; Balabanian, *Geanqis Daq o'w Bagh Orery,* 150; Nazarian, *Eghernēn Verabrogh H'o'wsher,* 21; Hah'asdani Azkah'in Arxiw (National Archives of Armenia), catalogue no: 430 / 1 / 824, 28 April 1920.

136. *Badmo'wt'iwn Ah'nt'abi Hah'o'c,* vol. II, 52–53; M. Abadi, *Türk Verdün'ü Gaziantep: Antep'in Dört Muhasarası* (Gaziantep: Osman Nuri Tuzcu Kültür ve Eğitim Vakfı, 1999), 30; Sarafian, *A Briefer History of Aintab,*

152. The Legion had been formed in Egypt as the Légion d'Orient (Eastern Legion) on 15 November 1916, under the command of Allied officers, to assist in the war efforts against the Ottoman armies. It was the Armenian Legion that first entered in Cilicia in late 1918. For a detailed history of Armenian Legion, see *Tenth Anniversary Booklet of the Armenian Legionnaires* (Cairo, 1928); Dickran H. Boyajian, *Armenian Legion: Historical Memoirs* (Watertown, MA: Baikar Press, 1965); Krikor Ajemian, *Pages from the Battles of Marash* (Cairo, 1928); Aram Karamanoukian, *Les Etrangers et le Service Militaire* (Paris: Padena, 1978); Manoug Baghdasarian, *Memoirs from the Days of the Cilician Legionnaire Movement* (Boston, 1943); Kerr, *The Lions of Marash;* Susan P. Pattie, *The Armenian Legionnaires: Sacrifice and Betrayal in World War I* (New York: I.B. Tauris, 2018).

137. BOA.DH.ŞFR 649 / 89, 1 November 1919; *Badmo'wt'iwn Ah'nt'abi Hah'o'c,* vol. II, 54.

138. *Badmo'wt'iwn Ah'nt'abi Hah'o'c,* vol. III, 553; WO 32 / 5730, 9 November 1919; BOA.DH.ŞFR 648 / 44, 6 November 1919; Ünler, "Antep Savunması," 10; Dolbakian, *Aynt'abn u Aynt'abahayē*, 40.

139. *Badmo'wt'iwn Ah'nt'abi Hah'o'c,* vol. I, 1080; Balabanian, *Geanqis Daq o'w Bagh Orery,* 150; Hah'asdani Azkah'in Arxiw (Armenian National Archives, HAA), catalogue no: 430 / 1 / 824, 28 April 1920.

140. ATASE, İSHK, Box: 48, File: 151, No. 3562. Indignation of the Local Populace to the French Occupation of Marash, 25 November 1919, cited in Yücel Güçlü, *Armenians and the Allies in Cilicia 1914–1923* (Salt Lake City: University of Utah Press, 2010), 116.

141. *Eghernēn Verabrogh H'o'wsher,* 21.

142. John E. Merrill, "Pen Pictures of the Siege of Aintab," *Envelope Series* 23, no.3 (1920): 3; *Badmo'wt'iwn Ah'nt'abi Hah'o'c* vol. III, 52; "Gaziantep Savunması," *Gaziantep Kültür Dergisi* 10, no. 109 (1967): 22; Fatma Ülgen, "Reading Mustafa Kemal Atatürk on the Armenian genocide of 1915," *Patterns of Prejudice* 44, no. 4 (2010): 377.

143. Sabahattin Selek, *Anadolu İhtilali,* vol. II (Istanbul: Kastaş, 2000), 702. See also Avcıoğlu, *Milli Kurtuluş Tarihi,* vol. 4 (Istanbul: Tekin Yayınları, 1997), 1382–1383; İlhan Tekeli, "Osmanlı İmparatorluğu'ndan Günümüze Nüfusun Zorunlu Yer Değiştirmesi ve İskân Sorunu," *Toplum ve Bilim,* no. 50 (1990): 62; Keyder, "İmparatorluk'tan Cumhuriyet'e Geçişte Kayıp Burjuvazi Aranıyor," *Toplumsal Tarih* 12, no. 68 (1999): 4–11.

144. Tachjian, "Cilician Armenians and French Policy," 545.

145. Ünler, *Gaziantep Savunması,* 18.

146. Ünler, *Gaziantep Savunması,* 17–21; Üzel, *Gaziantep Savaşı'nın İçyüzü,* 253–255; Ünler, "Gaziantep Müdafaası," *Gaziantep Halkevi Broşürü* (Gaziantep:

Halk Fırkası Matbaası, 1935), 94; "Ahmet Muhtar Göğüş," *Gaziantep'i Tanıtıyoruz* 3, no. 4 (1968): 20; Pamuk, *Bir Şehrin Direnişi: Antep Savunması,* 136; *Badmo'wt'iwn Ah'nt'abi Hah'o'c,* vol. II, 52. Other members were Dr. Hamid, Dr. Mecid, Bülbülzâde Hacı Abdullah, Kepkepzâde Şakir, Hasan Sadık, Bulaşıkzâde mufti Hacı Arif, Fahreddin Hoca, Mısrizâde Nuri, Hoca Abdullah Edib, Fazlı Ağazâde Nuri, Izrapzâde Şefik, Zaafizâde Mazlum, Şeyh Ubeydullah, Müftüzâde Hayri, Mevlevi Şeyhi Mustafa, Dai Ahmed Agha, Hacı Hanefizâde Abdullah, Ahmed Muhtar and Celal Kadri Hacı Ömerzâde, Mehmet Ali, Mahmut Budeyri, Pazarbaşı Nuri, Sadık Effendi, Kahramanzâde Hacı Mehmed, İncozâde Hüseyin, Timurzâde Rıfat, Kepkepzâde Abdürrezzak, Hacı Hilmi, Hacı Hüseyin Ağazâde, Körükçüzâde Mustafa, Mehmet Hayri, Mutafzâde Abdülkadir, Attarzâde Abdullah, Sait Ağazâde Mustafa, Musa Kazım, and vice mayor of Aintab Refik Bey.

147. "Gaziantep'i Tanıtıyoruz," *Gaziantep Kültür Dergisi* 3, no. 2 (1968): 3.

148. There is an enormous amount of Turkish and Armenian literature on the Turkish-French War in Aintab. See Ünler, *Gaziantep Savunması;* Ali Sancar, *Gaziantep Muharebeleri* (Istanbul: Harp Akademileri Basımevi, 1962); Üzer, *Gaziantep Savaşının İç Yüzü 1 (Kılıç Ali Devri)* (Kayseri: Sümer Matbaası, 1949); Üzer, *Gaziantep Savaşının İç Yüzü 2 (Özdemir Devri)* (Ankara: Doğuş Matbaası, 1952); Yetkin, *Gaziantep Savaşı Hatıralarından Derlemeler* (Gaziantep: Işık Matbaası, 1962); Yetkin, *Kurtuluş Destanı* (Gaziantep: Mürüvvet Matbaası, 1959); Yetkin and Solmaz, *Şehit Şahin* (Gaziantep: Güneş Matbaası, 1965); M. Abadie, *Gaziantep Fedaileri; Gazi Ayıntab'ın Dört Muhasarası* (Istanbul: Yeni Kültür Yayın, 1970); Beyaz, *Antep Savunması Günlüğü;* Burhan Bozgeyik, *İstiklal Harbinde Gaziantep* (Gaziantep: Şehitkamil Belediyesi, 1998); Adil Dai, *Harbin Kahraman Çocukları* (Gaziantep: Gaziantep Üniversitesi Vakfı Yayını, 2000); Adil Dai, *Olaylarla Gaziantep Savaşı* (Gaziantep: Gaziyurt Matbaası, 1992); Göğüş, *Gaziantep Savaşı* (Gaziantep: Gaziyurt Matbaası, 1971); Lohanizade Nurettin Mustafa, *Gaziantep Savunması;* Öztürk, *Milli Mücadele'de Gaziantep;* Pamuk, *Bir Şehrin Direnişi;* Göğüş, *İlk İnsanlardan Bugüne Çeşitli Yönleriyle Gaziantep;* Barsumian, *Badmo'wt'iwn Ah'nt'abi H. H. Tashnagco'wt'iwn 1898–1922; Badmo'wt'iwn Ah'nt'abi Hah'o'c,* vol. I, II, and III; A. Gesar, *Ah'nt'abi Ko'h'amardy;* Tavukjian, *Dar'abanqi Orakro'wt'iwn; H'o'wshamadean: No'wiro'wadz Ado'wr H. Lewo'neani; Ah'nt'abi Or: Ethnic Day of Aintab* (Armenian Apostolic Church of America, 1992); *Pages from My Diary;* Kevork A. Sarafian, *A Briefer History of Aintab: A Concise History of the Cultural, Religious, Educational, Political, Industrial and Commercial Life of the Armenians of Aintab, California* (Los Angeles, CA: Union of the Armenians of Aintab, 1957); Shusan Yeni-Komshian Teager, *The Krajians of Aintab* (Belmont, MA, 2007).

149. Ha'h'asdani Azkah'in Arxiw (National Archives of Armenia), *A Letter from Catholicate Deputy Der Nerses Tavukjian to Arshak Chobanian,* 14 November 1921, catalogue no: 430 / 1 / 842; *A Letter from Catholicate Deputy Der Nerses Tavukjian to Monsieur Briand, President of the French Republic Council in Paris,* 16 November 1921, catalogue no: 430 / 1 / 844; FO 608 / 278, British Armenian Committee, Cilicia, 8 June 1921, 181–182; Balabanian, *Geanqis Daq o'w Bagh Orery,* 151; *Badmo'wt'iwn Ah'nt'abi Hah'o'c,* vol. II, 308.

150. Cited in Güçlü, *Armenians and the Allies in Cilicia 1914–1923,* 144.

151. Göğüş, *İlk İnsanlardan Bugüne Çeşitli Yönleriyle Gaziantep,* 69, 306; Şakir Sabri Yener, *Gaziantep'in Yakın Tarihinden Notlar, Gaziantep Vilayet Merkezinin 76 Sene Evveline Kadar Olan Mahalli Maarif Hareketlerinin Kısa bir Tarihçesi* (Gaziantep: Gaziyurt Matbaası, 1968), 42.

152. FO 608 / 95, *General Headquarters Intelligence Summary,* 4 March 1919, 17; Bloxham, *The Great Game of Genocide,* 152.

153. *Zhamanag* newspaper, 11 December 1918, no: 3381.

154. BOA.DH.ŞFR 96 / 195, 15 February 1919, cited in Durmaz, "A City Transformed," 212.

155. Eyüp Sabri (Akgöl), *Bir Esirin Hatıraları;* Göğüş, *İlk İnsanlardan Bugüne Çeşitli Yönleriyle Gaziantep;* Yener, *Gaziantep Yakın Tarihinden Notlar.*

156. Durmaz, "A City Transformed," 221.

157. Ali Nadi Ünler, a native of Aintab, joined the Aintab war between French and Kemalist forces in 1920–1921 as a senior military officer and later wrote his memoirs about the war, claiming that a commission named "Muhafaza-i Emval Komisyonu" (Commission for the Protection of Properties) was formed in June 1920 in order to protect the assets of Armenians who were residents of Aintab's Turkish quarters. See Ali Nadi Ünler, *Türk'ün Kurtuluş Savaşı'nda Gaziantep Savunması* (Istanbul: Kardeşler Matbaası, 1969), 48–49. During my extensive research in various archives, including Gaziantep's local libraries, I could not find reports and records of this commission.

158. For realization of the same process in Adana, see Damar Arıkoğlu, *Hatıralarım* (Istanbul: Tan Matbaası, 1961), 100.

6. The End of the Armenian Community in Aintab

1. BNu / Fonds, *Notes Sur La Cilicie,* 3; Ha'h'asdani Azkah'in Arxiw, catalogue no: 340 / 1 / 716, 19 April 1921; Tavukjian, *Dar'abanqi Orakro'wt'iwn,* 352–353; Harutyun Nazarian, *Eghernēn Verabrogh H'o'wsher* [Memoirs of a Genocide Survivor], ed. Toros Toronian (Aleppo, 2009), 67.

2. BNu / Fonds, *Notes Sur La Cilicie,* 1; Ha'h'asdani Azkah'in Arxiw, *A Letter from Catholicate Deputy Der Nerses Tavukjian to Arshak Chobanian,*

catalogue no: 430 / 1 / 842, 14 November 1921, 6. Tavukjian asked French authorities to facilitate their exodus from Aintab under French protection, to settle them in places designated for Armenians, and also to take the proceeds from the sale of Armenian houses and give the moneys to their former owners. For a similar letter, written by Tavukjian to the president of the French Republic, see Ha'h'asdani Azkah'in Arxiw, *A Letter from the Catholicate Deputy Nerses Tavukjian to the President of French Republic Council,* catalogue no: 430 / 1 / 844, 16 November 1921.

3. BNu / Fonds, *Notes Sur La Cilicie,* 1. As of 14 November 1921, according to Father Nerses Tavukjian, there were 8,500 Armenians in Aintab; see Ha'h'asdani Azkah'in Arxiw, *A Letter from Catholicate Deputy Der Nerses Tavukjian to Arshak Chobanian,* catalogue no: 430 / 1 / 842, 14 November 1921, 9.

4. *Pages from My Diary / Archpriest Der Nerses Babaian,* ed. Yervant Babaian (Los Angeles: Abril Publisher, 2000), 58.

5. Ha'h'asdani Azkah'in Arxiw, *A Letter from Catholicate Deputy Der Nerses Tavukjian to Arshak Chobanian,* catalogue no: 430 / 1 / 842, 14 November 1921, 6.

6. BNu / Fonds, *Notes Sur La Cilicie,* a report from the president of the Commission of Immigrant dated 12 February 1922, Larnaka.

7. *Badmo'wt'iwn Ah'nt'abi Hah'o'c,* vol. III, 307; Vahé Tachjian, "The Expulsion of Non-Turkish Ethnic and Religious Groups from Turkey to Syria during the 1920s and early 1930s," in Jacques Semelin (ed.), *Online Encyclopedia of Mass Violence,* http://www.massviolence.org/IMG/article_PDF/The-expulsion-of-non-Turkish-ethnic-and-religious-groups.pdf, 6. According to the report of the British Consulate in Aleppo, as of November 1922, there were still three thousand Armenians living in Aintab. See FO 371, "Diplomatic Records: Report on the forced exile of the remaining Armenians from Aintab and Marash," 15 November 1922; Ha'h'asdani Azkah'in Arxiw, catalogue no: 430 / 1 / 838, 1922; ATASE, İSHK, box: 1706, file: 72, no. 1440. French Plans for Evacuation, 29 November 1921, cited in Güçlü, *Armenians and the Allies in Cilicia 1914–1923,* 145.

8. Tachjian, "The Expulsion of Non-Turkish Ethnic and Religious Groups," 6. In the 1927 population census, there were fifty-five Christians living in Gaziantep. The number of Armenians was forty to forty-five. *1927 Yılı Umumi Nüfus Tahriri,* Türkiye Cumhuriyeti Başvekalet İstatistik Umum Müdürlüğü, 28 October 1927, Fascicule 1–2, Ankara 1929. The last Armenian, Sarkis Tutundjian, left Aintab for Aleppo in 1936. *Badmo'wt'iwn Ah'nt'abi Hah'o'c,* vol. III, 307.

9. Hulusi Yetkin, *Gaziantep için Söylenenler: Gazianteplilerin Dünya ve Hayat Görüşleri ve Gaziantep'in Geleceği* (Gaziantep: Yeni Matbaa, 1969), 46;

Mithat Enç, *Selamlık Sohbetleri* (Istanbul: Ötüken Neşriyat, 2007), 70; "Gaziantep Savunması," *Gaziantep Kültür Dergisi* 10, no. 118 (1967): 234.

10. Indeed, the homes "abandoned" by the Armenians in Cilicia were put into the hands of a Turkish committee appointed by Hamit Bey, undersecretary of the Ministry of Interior and a former governor of Trabzon and Diyarbekir, to be kept for them. This arrangement was to continue for a year, in the event any Armenians returned. By the time these homes were confiscated by the Kemalist government in 1922, the Armenians of Aintab had already crowded into the three enormous camps at İskenderun, Aleppo, and Beirut; see Service Historique de VArmee de Terre (hereafter SHAT), Armée du Levant, 4H 175, Dossier I, *Rapports et correspondance relatifs a l'évacuation de Cilicie* (March 1921–April 1922); Clair Price, *The Rebirth of Turkey* (New York: Thomas Seltzer, 1923), 192.

11. Salâhaddin Kardeş, *'Tehcir' ve Emval-i Metruke Mevzuatı* (Ankara: T. C. Maliye Bakanlığı Strateji Geliştirme Başkanlığı, 2008), 95–98.

12. Kardeş, *'Tehcir' ve Emval-i Metruke Mevzuatı,* 98.

13. T. C. Maliye Vekâleti Milli Emlak Müdürlüğü, *Milli Emlak Muamelelerine Müteallik Mevzuat* (Ankara: Başvekalet Matbaası, 1937), 158.

14. T. C. Maliye Vekâleti Milli Emlak Müdürlüğü, *Milli Emlak Muamelelerine Müteallik Mevzuat,* 158.

15. BCA / 30.10.218.472.11.2, Chief of the General Staff to the Presidency of the Council of Ministers, 27 September 1338 (1922).

16. BCA / 30.10.218.472.11.2, Chief of the General Staff to the Presidency of the Council of Ministers, 27 September 1338 (1922).

17. BCA / 30.10.218.472.11.2, Chief of the General Staff to the Presidency of the Council of Ministers, 27 September 1338 (1922).

18. BCA / 30.10.218.406.6.1.2, Hüseyin Rıfat in the name of the President of the Council of Ministers to the Presidency of the Council of Ministers, 28 September 1338 (1922).

19. Kardeş, *'Tehcir' ve Emval-i Metruke Mevzuatı,* 122. The full name of the decree is "Âher Mahallere Nakledilmiş Eşhâsın Tasfiyeye Tâbi Emvâli Hakkında Mevcut Kararnamenin Reddine Dair Heyet-i Umumiye Kararı" (Decree of the General Assembly on the Abrogation of the Existing Regulation on Assets Subject to Liquidation of People Who Were Transported to Other Places).

20. Kardeş, *'Tehcir' ve Emval-i Metruke Mevzuatı,* 126. The full name of this regulation is "Mahall-i Ahara Nakledilen Eşhâsın Emvâl-i Metrukesi Hakkında 17 Zilkade 1333 Tarihli Kanun-u Muvakkatin Suver-i İcraiyesine Mütedair 26 Teşrinievvel 1331 Tarihli Nizamnamenin Bazı Mevaddını Muaddil Kararname" (Regulation Modifying Some Articles of the Regulation Dated 26 Teşrinievvel 1331 [8 November 1915] concerning Manners of Execution of the Temporary Law

Dated 17 Zilkade 1333 [26 September 1915] on Abandoned Properties of People Who Were Transported to Other Places).

21. Kardeş, *'Tehcir' ve Emval-i Metruke Mevzuatı,* 127.

22. Kardeş, *'Tehcir' ve Emval-i Metruke Mevzuatı,* 127–128.

23. *TBMM Gizli Celse Zabıtları,* Period 1, Assembly Year III, vol. 3, 769.

24. *TBMM Gizli Celse Zabıtları,* Period 1, Assembly Year III, vol. 3, 769.

25. *TBMM Gizli Celse Zabıtları,* Period 1, Assembly Year III, vol. 3, 776.

26. *TBMM Gizli Celse Zabıtları,* Period 1, Assembly Year III, vol. 3, 773.

27. T. C. Maliye Vekâleti Milli Emlak Müdürlüğü, *Milli Emlak Muamelelerine Müteallik Mevzuat,* 159–161; in addition, see Kardeş, *'Tehcir' ve Emval-i Metruke Mevzuatı,* 100–104. The full name of the law is "Âher Mahallere Nakledilen Eşhâsın Emvâl ve Düyûn ve Matlûbât-ı Metrûkesi Hakkındaki 17 Zilkade 1333 ve 13 Eylül 1331 Tarihli Kanun-ı Muvakkatin Bazı Mevaddı ile 20 Nisan 1338 Tarihli Emvâl-i Metruke Kanununu Muaddil Kanun" (Law Modifying the 20 April 1338 Dated Abandoned Properties Law and Several Articles of the 17 Zilkade 1333 [26 September 1915] Dated Temporary Law on the Possessions and Debts and Abandoned Debts of People Transported to Other Places).

28. For the full text, see Kardeş, *'Tehcir' ve Emval-i Metruke Mevzuatı,* 100–104.

29. Kardeş, *'Tehcir' ve Emval-i Metruke Mevzuatı,* 101.

30. Kardeş, *'Tehcir' ve Emval-i Metruke Mevzuatı,* 154–164. Its full name was "13 Eylül 1331 Tarihli Kanun-ı Muvakkat ile İşbu Kanunun Bazı Mevaddını Muaddil 15 Nisan 1339 Tarihli Kanunun Suver-i Tatbikiyesini Mübeyyin Talimatname" (Regulation That Explains the Manners of Application of the 15 April 1339 [15 April 1923] Law Modifying the 26 September 1915 Dated Temporary Law and Some Articles of This Law).

31. Kardeş, *'Tehcir' ve Emval-i Metruke Mevzuatı,* 154–156.

32. Kardeş, *'Tehcir' ve Emval-i Metruke Mevzuatı,* 163.

33. As the archives are closed, I walked Gaziantep's old Armenian neighborhood street by street and interviewed the inhabitants of the city as well as relatives of Aintab Armenians from the diaspora. I also tried to obtain title deeds from Armenians in the diaspora in order to determine which buildings they used to own, as well as the previous and present-day Muslim owners. A list of these properties and their locations, along with their previous and present-day owners, can be seen on Map 2.

34. *Badmo'wt'iwn Ah'nt'abi Hah'o'c,* vol. I, 442.

35. Lütfiye Aydın, *Anka Kentim Antep'im* (Istanbul: Heyamola Yayınları, 2008), 301; M. Oğuz Göğüş, *İlk İnsanlardan Bugüne Çeşitli Yönleriyle Gaziantep* (Ankara: Cihan Ofset, 1997), 203; Enç, *Selamlık Sohbetleri,* 70; interview with

Aykut Tuzcu on 12 March 2014 in Gaziantep. It is important to note that the same policy was also applied by the Nazi government to Jewish movable and immovable properties during the Holocaust. Many of the goods, assets, and properties of the Jews were given to Germans who had lost their possessions in bombing raids during World War II. Martin Dean, *Robbing the Jews: The Confiscation of Jewish Property in the Holocaust, 1933–1945* (New York: Cambridge University Press, 2008), 224.

36. An interview with Cemil Aslan on 17 November 2014 in Gaziantep.

37. Nazarian, *Eghernēn Verabrogh H'o'wsher,* 40.

38. BCA / TİGMA 272.00.00.11.19.91.17, 17 August 1924.

39. BCA / TİGMA 272.00.00.12.46.82.8, 3 November 1925.

40. BCA / TİGMA 272.00.00.12.46.82.8, 7 November 1925.

41. BCA / TİGMA 272.00.00.12.52.117.27, 10 February 1927 and BCA / TİGMA 272.00.00.12.52.117.27, 5 March 1927.

42. BCA / TİGMA 272.00.00.12.52.117.27, 5 March 1927.

43. BCA / TİGMA 272.00.00.12.47.87.9, 27 December 1925.

44. BCA / TİGMA 272.00.00.12.47.87.9, 27 December 1925.

45. BCA / TİGMA 272.00.00.12.47.87.9, 27 December 1925; BCA / TİGMA 272.00.00.12.47.87.9, 31 December 1925.

46. BCA / TİGMA 272.00.00.12.55.136.13, 11 November 1926. Among those settled in Gaziantep, twenty exchanged and five nonexchanged people as well as nineteen Syrian refugees were given land but not houses.

47. BCA / TİGMA 272.00.00.11.23.122.12, 25 December 1927.

48. BCA / TİGMA 272.00.00.11.23.122.12, 28 January 1928.

49. BCA / TİGMA 272.00.00.12.44.71.14, Settlement Directorate of Gaziantep Province to the Ministry of Interior, 3 January 1925.

50. BCA / TİGMA 272.00.00.12.44.71.14, General Directorate of the Settlement of the Ministry of Interior to Gaziantep Province, 21 May 1925.

51. BCA / TİGMA 272.00.00.12.58.153.11, 12 March 1928. On 7 February 1928, the Revenue Office of Gaziantep Province informed the Ministry of Interior that the immigrants of Crete and Kesriye—who, pursuant to the Code of Obligations, were assigned immovable properties that they would pay for over twenty years, in equal installments—had settled in Gaziantep and applied to the office to demand that tax should not be accrued on their behalf as long as these properties that they were assigned were not bound to them in the land office. BCA / TİGMA 272.00.00.12.58.153.11, 7 February 1928.

52. Interview with Murad Uçaner and Aykut Tuzcu on 28 March 2014 in Gaziantep.

53. Interview with Murad Uçaner, Aykut Tuzcu, and Mehmet Nuri Güntekin on 28 March 2014 in Gaziantep. Also see "Hasan Süzer Etnoğrafya Müzesi,"

http://www.kulturvarliklari.gov.tr/TR,43815/gaziantep—hasan-suzer-etnografya-muzesi.html (accessed 18 March 2015).

54. Interview with Murad Uçaner, Aykut Tuzcu, and Kamil Gereççi on 14 March 2014 in Gaziantep.

55. Yervant Kuchukian, *Hariwr Zham Ah'nt'abi: H'o'wsher ew Dbawo'ro'wt'-iwnner* [100 Hours in Aintab: Memories and Impressions] (Beirut: Aravot, 1958), 21. As mentioned in Chapter 5 of this book, Nuri Patpatzâde was one of the perpetrators responsible for the deportation of Armenians and the despoliation of their properties during the 1915 genocide. He was also one of the founding and permanent members of Aintab's CUP branch; see BNu / Fonds A. Andonian, P.J. 1 / 3, file 4, Aintab, "The Deportation of Armenians in Aintab," 11–17. Nuri Patpatzâde was also a member of Antep Heyet-i Merkeziye, which was founded as a resistance movement, acting in conjunction with the Kemalist forces against the French occupation and the presence of the Armenians.

56. *Gaziantep Gazetesi,* no. 296, 297, 302, 304, 305 dated 1934; no. 334, 335, 337, 342, 343, 367 dated 1935.

57. *Gaziantep Gazetesi,* no. 296 dated 1934, 4.

58. *Gaziantep Gazetesi,* no. 334 dated 1935, 3.

59. *Gaziantep Kültür Derneği Dergisi* 4, no. 48 (1961): 268.

60. Kuchukian, *Hariwr Zham Ah'nt'abi,* 16.

61. For the complete list of names of chairmen of the Chamber of Commerce in Aintab, see http://www.gto.org.tr/Eski-Yoneticiler-icerik-7.html (accessed 12 November 2015). You may also find the same list in the appendix.

62. BOA.HR.İM 40 / 18, 5 February 1923.

63. Hasan Mahir, *Gaziantep: Gezi Notları* (Gaziantep: Prizma Basım, 2008), 38; Nilhan Aras, *Gaziantep Deyince* (Istanbul: Metro Kültür Yayınları, 2008), 87.

64. Aras, *Gaziantep Deyince,* 88–92; Shusan Yeni-Komshian Teager, *The Krajians of Aintab* (Belmont, MA, 2007), 105.

65. BNu / Fonds A. Andonian, P.J. 1 / 3, file 4, Aintab, "The Deportation of Armenians in Aintab," 11–17; *Krikor Guerguerian Private Archival Collection,* folder number: 22, file name: Turks (List) Responsible, file no: 46.

66. "Çaycı Mıstık ve Nazar Ağa Davası," *Gaziantep Kültür Dergisi* 4, no. 38 (1961): 41.

67. See "Gaziantep Büyükşehir Belediyesi Gaziantep Atatürk Anı Müzesi," http://www.ataturkanimuzesi.org/hakkimizda.html (accessed 18 September 2015).

68. Interview with Kevork Arslanian on 9 January 2015 in Beirut.

69. Göğüş, *İlk İnsanlardan Bugüne Çeşitli Yönleriyle Gaziantep,* 192.

70. *Gaziantep Kültür Envanteri,* 101–102.

71. *Gaziantep Kültür Envanteri,* 102.

72. Göğüş, *İlk İnsanlardan Bugüne Çeşitli Yönleriyle Gaziantep,* 193; interview with Aykut Tuzcu on 12 March 2014 in Gaziantep. Mustafa Humanızlı purchased numerous other abandoned properties at low prices at auctions in the early 1930s. Interview with Murad Uçaner on 12 March 2014 in Gaziantep.

73. *Gaziantep Kültür Envanteri,* 66–68.

74. Interview with Murad Uçaner, Aykut Tuzcu, and Kamil Gereççi on 18 April 2014 in Gaziantep.

75. Göğüş, *İlk İnsanlardan Bugüne Çeşitli Yönleriyle Gaziantep,* 203; Enç, *Selamlık Sohbetleri,* 70.

76. For the entire list of district commandants, see Ali Nadi Ünler, *Gaziantep Savunması* (Istanbul: Kardeşler Matbaası, 1969), 20–21; Hulusi Yetkin, *Gaziantep Savaşı Hatıralarından Derlemeler* (Gaziantep: Işık Matbaası, 1962), 20–21; Gaziantep Savaşı Müzesi; Şahinbey Belediyesi Fotoğraf Arşivi; Mahmut Oğuz Göğüş Arşivi.

77. BCA / TİGMA 272.00.00.12.43.59.32, 14 December 1924.

78. BCA / TİGMA 272.00.00.12.43.59.32, the Ministry of Population Exchange, Development, and Settlement to the Ministry of Finance, 23 December 1924.

79. BCA / TİGMA 272.00.00.12.47.88.2, Settlement Secretary of Gaziantep Province to the Ministry of Interior, 16 January 1926.

80. BCA / TİGMA 272.00.00.12.47.88.2, General Directorate of Settlement of the Ministry of Interior to Gaziantep Province, 3 February 1926.

81. Sahir Üzel, *Gaziantep Savaşı'nın İçyüzü 2 (Özdemir Devri)* (Ankara: Doğuş Matbaası, 1952), 253.

82. Interview with İclal İncioğlu on 20 December 2014 in Gaziantep. The İnco family adopted İncioğlu as a last name in 1934. İncozâde Hüseyin was the paternal grandfather of İclal İncioğlu.

83. Nüket Alevli Ersoy and Haşim Akman, *Türk Tekstil ve Eğitim Sektöründe Gaziantepli Bir Öncü: Cemil Alevli* (Istanbul: Doğan Kitap, 2020), 91–95; Kuchukian, *Hariwr Zham Ah'nt'abi,* 10.

84. *Gençlere Başarı Yolu,* 20; Şakir Sabri Yener, *Gaziantep'in Yakın Tarihinden Notlar, Gaziantep Vilayet Merkezinin 76 Sene Evveline Kadar Olan Mahalli Maarif Hareketlerinin Kısa bir Tarihçesi* (Gaziantep: Gaziyurt Matbaası, 1968), 38; for a long biography of Cemil Alevli, see "Kurucumuz Cemil Alevli," available at http://www.gkv.k12.tr/kurucumuz.asp (accessed 26 October 2014).

85. *Gençlere Başarı Yolu,* 10. Born in Aintab in 1901, Cemil Alevli witnessed the city's economic, political, and cultural improvement and personally

contributed to this development. As a literati resident of Aintab, who had received a good education abroad and had a Western worldview, Alevli was also a significant representative of the rural bourgeoisie in the city, which had played an active role in Aintab's primitive capital accumulation. Doubtless, behind this primitive capital accumulation lay the movable and immobile [real estate] properties of Armenians who had left Aintab in 1921–1922. Alevli, who was a prominent representative of Aintab's local bourgeoisie, was a product of this process. See *Gençlere Başarı Yolu,* 20; "Kurucumuz Cemil Alevli," available at http://www.gkv.k12.tr/kurucumuz.asp (accessed 26 October 2014).

86. "Kurucumuz Cemil Alevli," available at http://www.gkv.k12.tr/kurucumuz.

87. V. Gül Cephanecigil, "Preliminary Remarks on the Late Ottoman Churches in Aintab," *A-Z ITU Journal of the Faculty of Architecture* 12, no. 2 (2015): 134.

88. Ersoy and Akman, *Türk Tekstil ve Eğitim Sektöründe Gaziantepli Bir Öncü,* 215. The son of Ömer Ersoy, Celal Ersoy, and the daughter of Cemil Alevli, Nüket Alevli also married. It was the very first intra-capitalist family marriage in Gaziantep.

89. Göğüş, *İlk İnsanlardan Bugüne Çeşitli Yönleriyle Gaziantep,* 203. The same information was attested to by an anonymous person in Gaziantep; interview with a native of Aintab on 3 March 2014 in Gaziantep.

90. Ersoy and Akman, *Türk Tekstil ve Eğitim Sektöründe Gaziantepli Bir Öncü,* 47.

91. Ünler, *Gaziantep Savunması,* 22, 47, 65–66, 71.

92. M. Oğuz Göğüş, "Broşüre Başlarken," *Gaziantep'i Tanıtıyoruz* 1, no. 2 (1962): 2–3; Yetkin, *Gaziantep Tarihi ve Davaları,* 65–66.

93. Göğüş, *İlk İnsanlardan Bugüne Çeşitli Yönleriyle Gaziantep,* 203; "Sakarya Ortaokulu Tarihçesi," available at http://sahinbeysakaryaortaokulu.meb.k12.tr /meb_iys_dosyalar/27/08/716339/icerikler/sakarya-ortaokulu-tarihcesi_1568726 .html?CHK=88765129affaa4c938af1732dd3f9df8 (accessed 16 December 2014).

94. Mehmet Solmaz, *Gaziantep'de Gazi Mustafa Kemal* (Gaziantep: Gaziyurt Matbaası, 1968); "Gaziantep Büyükşehir Belediyesi Gaziantep Atatürk Anı Müzesi," http://www.ataturkanimuzesi.org/hakkimizda.html (accessed 18 September 2015).

95. BCA / Secretariat of the Prime Ministry, 030.0.18.01.01.014.41.18.001, 22 June 1925.

96. BCA / Secretariat of the Prime Ministry, 030.0.18.01.01.015.49.19.001, 9 August 1925.

97. BCA / Secretariat of the Prime Ministry, 030.0.18.01.01.021.67.010, 3 November 1926.

98. BCA / Secretariat of the Prime Ministry, 030.0.18.01.01.025.49.018, 30 August 1927.

99. *Gaziantep Kültür Envanteri,* 124–125; E. Tavacıgil and Ö. Tavacıgil, *Kurtuluş Camii Rölöve, Restitüsyon, Restorasyon Projesi Raporu* (Gaziantep: Gaziantep Vakıflar Müdürlüğü Arşivi, 2012).

100. *Gaziantep Halkevi Broşürü* (Gaziantep: Gaziantep Halk Fırkası Matbaası, 1935), 10–55, esp. 12–15.

101. *Gaziantep Halkevi Broşürü,* 14. Halkevleri (People's Houses) was an enlightenment project introduced by Mustafa Kemal aimed at generating support for the Kemalist reforms from the city's populace. On 17 February 1932, branches of the People's Houses were opened in seventeen cities and soon thereafter spread to other cities. On People's Houses, see Neşe Gürallar Yeşilkaya, *Halkevleri: İdeoloji ve Mimarlık* (Istanbul: İletişim, 1999).

102. Kuchukian, *Hariwr Zham Ah'nt'abi,* 9.

103. Kuchukian, *Hariwr Zham Ah'nt'abi,* 9.

104. *Gaziantep Kültür Envanteri,* 145–146.

105. For all of this information, see "Kendirli Kilisesi Kültür Merkezi Oldu," available at http://www.gaziantep27.net/guncel-kendirli-kilisesi-kultur-merkezi-oldu-462885.html (accessed 16 July 2015).

106. Kuchukian, *Hariwr Zham Ah'nt'abi,* 13. The Democrat Party, a right-wing political party and Turkey's third legal opposition party, was founded and led by Celal Bayar and Adnan Menderes in 1945. The party came into power during the national elections of 1950 and ended Turkey's one-party era by unseating the RPP.

107. Kuchukian, *Hariwr Zham Ah'nt'abi,* 16.

108. Kuchukian, *Hariwr Zham Ah'nt'abi,* 16–17.

109. Kuchukian, *Hariwr Zham Ah'nt'abi,* 17–18.

110. Kuchukian, *Hariwr Zham Ah'nt'abi,* 18.

111. I acquired this information as a result of interviews with local residents during field research in Gaziantep. Map 2 contains the most thorough list of present-day owners of immovable Armenian properties I was able to obtain.

112. Mustafa Güzelhan, "Dünkü ve Bugünkü: Çukurbostan," *Gaziantep Kültür Dergisi* 6, no. 68 (1963): 187.

113. Güzelhan, "Dünkü ve Bugünkü: Çukurbostan," 185.

114. The minutes of the Lausanne Conference and texts of the agreements signed at Lausanne are in *Conference de Lausanne sur les affaires du Proche-Orient (1922–1923), Recueil des actes de la Conférence* (Paris: Imprimerie Nationale, 1923). The records of the first phase of the conference, not including the minutes of the subcommittees, were published by the British Government in

Great Britain, Parliamentary Papers, Cmd. 1814, *Turkey no. 1 (1923): Lausanne Conference on Near Eastern Affairs, 1922–1923: Records of Proceedings and Draft Terms of Peace* (London: His Majesty's Stationery Office, 1923), http://archive.org/details/recordsofproceedooconfuoft (accessed 18 May 2013). For quotations from the actual Treaty of Lausanne, I used the English version of the text published in Lawrence Martin, compiler, *The Treaties of Peace 1919–1923, vol. II: Containing the Treaties of Neuilly and Sè vres, the Treaties between the United States and Germany, Austria and Hungary Respectively, and the Treaty of Lausanne, the Convention Respecting the Regime of the Straits and Other Instruments Signed at Lausanne* (New York: Carnegie Endowment for International Peace, 1924), which is available online at http://wwi.lib.byu.edu/index.php/Treaty_of_Lausanne, in the World War I Document Archive, ed. Richard Hacken, 2010, Brigham Young University Library (accessed 18 May 2013).

115. Taner Akçam and Ümit Kurt, *The Spirit of the Laws: The Plunder of Wealth in the Armenian Genocide* (New York: Berghahn Books, 2015), 82.

116. For some arguments made on the topic, see Seha L. Meray, *Lozan Barış Konferansı Tutanaklar-Belgeler*, vol. 3 (Istanbul: Yapı Kredi Yayınları, 2001), 88–89, 186, 189–190.

117. Meray, *Lozan Barış Konferansı Tutanaklar-Belgeler*, vol. 6, 192.

118. On this topic, it is necessary to distinguish between two groups of Armenians. The first were Armenians who prior to 1914 became citizens of signatory states, such as the United States. The second were Armenians who became citizens of France or Great Britain or came under their protection through their protectorate regimes in places such as Iraq, Syria, Lebanon, or Jordan.

119. Bilal Şimşir, *Lozan Telgrafları II (Şubat–Ağustos 1923)* (Ankara: TTK, 1994), 396.

120. On Venizelos asking this question during the meetings of the Minorities Subcommission, see Meray, *Lozan Barış Konferansı, Tutanaklar-Belgeler*, vol. 2, 205.

121. Şimşir, *Lozan Telgrafları II (Şubat–Ağustos 1923)*, 473–474, 494.

122. Şimşir, *Lozan Telgrafları II (Şubat–Ağustos 1923)*, 570.

123. Şimşir, *Lozan Telgrafları II (Şubat–Ağustos 1923)*, 575.

124. For more information on Armenian children and women who converted religions and were dispersed among Muslim families, see Akçam, *İnsan Hakları ve Ermeni Sorunu: İttihat ve Terakki'den Kurtuluş Savaşına* (Ankara: İmge, 1999), 430–445; İbrahim Ethem Atnur, *Türkiye'de Ermeni Kadınları ve Çocukları Meselesi (1915–1923)* (Ankara: Babil Yayıncılık, 2005), 113–235. On the Armenian-Greek Section created within the framework of the English High

Commission, see Yeghiayan (ed.), *British Reports on Ethnic Cleansing in Anatolia, 1919–1922.*

125. Meray, *Lozan Barış Konferansı, Tutanaklar-Belgeler,* vol. 2, 161.

126. Meray, *Lozan Barış Konferansı, Tutanaklar-Belgeler,* vol. 2, 183.

127. Meray, *Lozan Barış Konferansı, Tutanaklar-Belgeler,* vol. 2, 183–184.

128. Meray, *Lozan Barış Konferansı, Tutanaklar-Belgeler,* vol. 2, 183–184.

129. Meray, *Lozan Barış Konferansı, Tutanaklar-Belgeler,* vol. 2, 184.

130. Meray, *Lozan Barış Konferansı, Tutanaklar-Belgeler,* vol. 2, 161, 204.

131. Meray, *Lozan Barış Konferansı, Tutanaklar-Belgeler,* vol. 2, 238, 254.

132. Meray, *Lozan Barış Konferansı, Tutanaklar-Belgeler,* vol. 8, 93. The commission discussed here should not be confused with the mixed arbitral tribunal, discussed in the section of the treaty titled "Property, Rights and Interests."

133. Two examples are Üngör and Polatel, *Confiscation and Destruction,* 54; and Eroğlu, "Tehcirden Milli Mücadeleye Ermeni Malları (1915–1922)," 181–182.

134. Treaty of Lausanne, http://wwi.lib.byu.edu/index.php/Treaty_of_Lausanne.

135. Treaty of Lausanne. The right of people to choose their citizenship did not exist only between Turkey and other states; Article 32 confirmed this right to exist between all separating states.

136. Treaty of Lausanne.

137. Treaty of Lausanne.

138. Treaty of Lausanne.

139. Treaty of Lausanne.

140. Treaty of Lausanne.

141. W. H. Hill, "The Anglo-Turkish Mixed Arbitral Tribunal," *Juridical Review* 47, no. 3 (1935): 247.

142. Treaty of Lausanne, http://wwi.lib.byu.edu/index.php/Treaty_of_Lausanne.

143. Treaty of Lausanne.

144. For example, for İsmet İnönü's report to Istanbul on the negotiations on the founding of the mixed arbitral tribunals and their powers, see Şimşir, *Lozan Telgrafları II (Şubat–Ağustos 1923),* 375–376.

145. BOA / DH. ŞFR 54 / 356, EUM cipher telegram to Ma'muretü'l-aziz Province, 25 June 1331 (8 July 1915).

146. Meray, *Lozan Barış Konferansı, Tutanaklar-Belgeler,* vol. 8, 22–23.

147. Meray, *Lozan Barış Konferansı, Tutanaklar-Belgeler,* vol. 8, 22–23.

148. *TBMM Gizli Celse Zabıtları,* Period 1, Assembly Year III, vol. 3, 1131.

149. Armenians who were Ottoman citizens until the signing of the Lausanne Treaty lost their Turkish citizenship through the August 1924 and January 1925 regulations issued by France and became Syrian or Lebanese citizens. The Turkish government did not automatically denaturalize these

Armenians until 1964. On Lebanon, see Nicola Migliorino, *(Re)constructing Armenia in Lebanon and Syria: Ethno-Cultural Diversity and the State in the Aftermath of a Refugee Crisis* (New York: Berghahn Books / Oxford, 2008), 55; on Syria, see Uri Davis, "Citizenship Legislation in the Syrian Arab Republic," *Arab Studies Quarterly* 18, no. 1 (1996): 35.

150. *Tevhid-i Efkâr,* 24 July 1340 (1924). Also see *Cumhuriyet* newspaper, 22 July 1340 (1924).

151. *Tevhid-i Efkâr,* 24 July 1340 (1924).

152. *Tevhid-i Efkâr,* 24 July 1340 (1924).

153. İsmail Soysal, *Tarihçeleri ve Açıklamaları ile Birlikte Türkiye'nin Siyasal Antlaşmaları, 1. Cilt (1920–1945)* (Ankara: TTK, 2000), 293–311.

154. Soysal, *Tarihçeleri ve Açıklamaları ile Birlikte Türkiye'nin Siyasal Antlaşmaları,* 294.

155. Soysal, *Tarihçeleri ve Açıklamaları ile Birlikte Türkiye'nin Siyasal Antlaşmaları,* 294.

156. Soysal, *Tarihçeleri ve Açıklamaları ile Birlikte Türkiye'nin Siyasal Antlaşmaları,* 294.

157. Vahé Tachjian, "An Attempt to Recover Armenian Properties in Turkey through the French Authorities in Syria and Lebanon in the 1920s," *International Criminal Law Review* 14, no. 2 (2014): 349.

158. The question of the registration of property abandoned by the Armenians, *Yeprad,* no. 70, 10 March 1928, 2, cited in Tachjian, "An Attempt to Recover Armenian Properties in Turkey through the French Authorities in Syria and Lebanon in the 1920s," 349n13.

159. Tachjian, "An Attempt to Recover Armenian Properties in Turkey through the French Authorities in Syria and Lebanon in the 1920s," 351. Tachjian gave the following source for the ambassador's letter: France, Ministère des Affaires Étrangères (Ministry of Foreign Affairs; henceforth MAE), Levant 1918–1940, Turquie, vol. 260, Letter of Charles de Chambrun, Ambassador of France to Turquie at Locquin, Deputy, Vice-President of the Commission of Finances, Chamber of Deputies, 10 July 1929, Istanbul, f° 27.

160. MAE, Levant 1918–1940, Turquie, vol. 260, Secrétariat Général, Bureau Fiplomatique, "Négociations Relatives aux biens Syriens et Libanais en Turquie: Etat de la Question du 21 Octobre 1929" (Negotiations Concerning Syrian and Lebanese Property in Turkey: The State of the Question on 21 October 1929), 22 October 1929, Beyrouth, f° 231. The original French is as follows: "*La Question des Réclamations Arméniennes, Pour des Raisons D'opportunité, Doit être Maintenue Hors du Débat,*" quoted and cited in Tachjian, "An Attempt to Recover Armenian Properties in Turkey through the French Authorities in Syria and Lebanon in the 1920s," 352.

161. France, Centre des Archives Diplomatiques de Nantes (henceforth CADN), Record Group Ankara, no. 129, Minister of Foreign Affairs Aristide Briand, Letter no. 281, to Charles de Chambrun, 15 December 1930, 3. The original French quotation follows: "Nos obligations sont incontestablement moins impératives à leur égard (des Arméniens) que vis-à-vis des Syriens d'origine . . . depuis leur arrivée (des Arméniens) en Syrie, nous avons largement rempli vis-à-vis d'eux notre devoir d'assistance." (Our obligations are unquestionably less imperative for them [Armenians] and vis-à-vis the original. Since they arrived [the Armenians] in Syria, we have largely fulfilled vis-à-vis our duty to assist.) Quoted and cited in Tachjian, "An Attempt to Recover Armenian Properties in Turkey through the French Authorities in Syria and Lebanon in the 1920s," 352.

162. Tachjian, "An Attempt to Recover Armenian Properties in Turkey through the French Authorities in Syria and Lebanon in the 1920s," 357.

163. T. C. Maliye Vekâleti Milli Emlak Müdürlüğü, *Milli Emlak Muamelelerine Müteallik Mevzuat,* 325–330.

164. Article 32 of the Lausanne Treaty states the right of a person who settled in a state that had separated from Turkey but who was not of the majority composing the people of that state to choose a state in which his or her own people were the majority. For example, an Arab living in Greece could go to Syria or Lebanon, while a Greek living in Syria or Lebanon could go to Greece. Article 34 concerned the right of individuals who are members of the native population of a territory that separated from Turkey (for example, Turks, Greeks, or Arabs) but settled in other countries (for example, the United States, France, or England) to be able to choose the citizenship of the state in which they are part of the native population. Armenians were not included in these categories.

165. T. C. Maliye Vekâleti Milli Emlak Müdürlüğü, *Milli Emlak Muamelelerine Müteallik Mevzuat,* 328–329.

166. T. C. Maliye Vekâleti Milli Emlak Müdürlüğü, *Milli Emlak Muamelelerine Müteallik Mevzuat,* 330.

167. T. C. Maliye Vekâleti Milli Emlak Müdürlüğü, *Milli Emlak Muamelelerine Müteallik Mevzuat,* 330.

Conclusion

1. Tomislav Dulic, *Utopias of Nation: Local Mass Killing in Bosnia and Herzegovina, 1941–42* (Uppsala, Sweden: Uppsala University Library, 2005); Ann Lee Fujii, *Killing Neighbors: Webs of Violence in Rwanda* (Ithaca, NY: Cornell University Press, 2009); Victoria M. Esses and Richard A. Vernon (eds.), *Explaining the Breakdown of Ethnic Relations: Why Neighbors Kill* (Malden, MA:

Blackwell, 2008); Wendy Lower, *Nazi Empire-Building and the Holocaust in Ukraine* (Chapel Hill: University of North Carolina Press, 2005); Scott Straus, *The Order of Genocide: Race, Power, and War in Rwanda* (Ithaca, NY: Cornell University Press, 2006); Alexander L. Hinton, *Why Did They Kill? Cambodia in the Shadow of Genocide* (Berkeley: University of California Press, 2005); Uğur Ü. Üngör, *The Making of Modern Turkey: Nation and State in Eastern Anatolia, 1913–1950* (Oxford: Oxford University Press, 2011), 105.

2. Üngör, *Making of Modern Turkey,* 105.

3. Stephan H. Astourian, "Testing World-System Theory, Cilicia (1830s–1890s): Armenian-Turkish Polarization and the Ideology of Modern Ottoman Historiography" (unpublished PhD diss., University of California, Los Angeles, 1996), 403.

4. Uğur Ü. Üngör, "Explaining Regional Variations in the Armenian Genocide," in *World War I and the End of the Ottomans: From the Balkan Wars to the Armenian Genocide,* ed. Hans-Lukas Kieser, Kerem Öktem, and Maurus Reinkowski (New York: I.B. Tauris, 2015), 241–261.

5. Taner Akçam, *A Shameful Act: The Armenian Genocide and the Question of Turkish Responsibility* (New York: Metropolitan Books, 2006); Vahakn N. Dadrian, *The History of the Armenian Genocide: Ethnic Conflict from the Balkans to Anatolia to the Caucasus* (New York: Berghahn Books, 2004); Taner Akçam, *The Young Turks' Crime Against Humanity: The Armenian Genocide and Ethnic Cleansing in the Ottoman Empire* (Princeton, NJ: Princeton University Press, 2012); Donald Bloxham, *The Great Game of Genocide: Imperialism, Nationalism, and the Destruction of the Ottoman Armenians* (Oxford: Oxford University Press, 2005).

6. Thomas Kühne, "Great Men and Large Numbers: Undertheorising a History of Mass Killing," *Contemporary European History* 21, no. 2 (2012): 139.

7. Thomas Kühne, *Belonging and Genocide: Hitler's Community, 1918–1945* (New Haven, CT: Yale University Press, 2010), 1.

8. Omer Bartov, "Eastern Europe as the Site of Genocide," *Journal of Modern History* 80, no. 3 (2008): 576.

9. Bloxham, "Organized Mass Murder: Structure, Participation, and Motivation in Comparative Perspective," *Holocaust and Genocide Studies* 22, no. 2 (2008): 232.

10. Vahé Tachjian, *La France en Cilicie et en Haute-Mésopotamie: Aux Confins de la Turquie, de la Syrie et de l'Irak* (Paris: Karthala Editions, 2004), 201–216.

11. These include Hüseyin Cemil Göğüş, Hakkı Kozanlı, Taşçızâde Abdullah, Patpatzâde Nuri, Besim Bey, İncooğlu Hasan Agha, Özdemir Mehmet Emin Agha, Çulhalar Şıhıoğlu Mehmet Emin Agha, Mennanzâde Mustafa, Molla Mustafa, Kurd Hacı Ali, Müftüzâde Arif Effendi, Daizâde Ahmed Agha,

Nuri Pazarbaşı, Piafzâde Abdülkadir, Mehmet Hayri, Hacı Ömerzâde, Mehmet Ali, Mahmud Budeyri, Daizâde Ahmed Agha, Sadık Effendi, Kahramanzâde Hacı Mehmed, İncozâde Hüseyin, Timurzâde Rıfat, Kepkepzâde Abdürrezzak, Hacı Hilmi, Hacı Hüseyin Ağazâde, Körükçüzâde Mustafa, Mehmet Hayri, Mutafzâde Abdülkadir, Attarzâde Abdullah, Sait Ağazâde Mustafa, Musa Kazım, and vice mayor of Aintab Refik Bey. Interview with Aykut Tuzcu, 19 November 2014, Gaziantep.

12. Vahé Tachjian, "An Attempt to Recover Armenian Properties in Turkey," *International Criminal Law Review* 14, no. 2 (2014): 345.

13. Some of those families were Ahmet Mazlum (1921) from the Zafiizâde, Ahmet Effendi Kethüzâde, Mustafa Agha (1922) from Kaleağazızâde, Mehmet Ali (1922–1924, 1927–1931) from Hacı Ömerzâde, Şefik Barlas (1924–1927) from Izrapzâde, and Hamdi Kurtlar (1931–1946) from Mısrizâdes. Additionally, those who were the head of the Chamber of Commerce such as Nuri Pazarbaşı (1915–1919), Mahmut Dai (1922–1925), Abdülkadir Söylemezzâde (1925–1926), Asım Kepkep (1926–1929), and Mahmut Ersoy, as well as Ali Bey Mamatağazâde, Bahtiyar Patpatzâde, Mehmet Hayri Bey Müftüzâde, Rıza Cenani, Mahmut Kanevitçizâde, Avni Fazlızâde, Hacı Ahmet Dai, Cemil Alevli, Asım Kepkepzâde, Mahmut Budeyri, and Hacı Kadir Bakkalbey (1929–1944) in the city before 1922 were all from the notables and elites. M. Oğuz Göğüş, "Günümüze Kadar Şehrimizde Ticaret Odası Başkanlıkları Yapanlar," *Gaziantep'i Tanıtıyoruz* 3, no. 2 (1968): 13; "İktisadiyat 1913–1923–1933," *Gaziantep Halkevi Broşürü* (Gaziantep: Gaziantep Halk Fırkası Matbaası, 1935), 301, 308.

14. *Gaziantep Halkevi Broşürü,* 14–15.

15. *Gaziantep Gazetesi,* 11 May 1931, 4; 28 February 1935, 3; 1 August 1935, 3; 8 August 1935, 3; 24 March 1939, 4. *Yeni Gaziantep* 1, no. 1 (18 May 1940): 4; 1, no. 2 (25 May 1940): 4; 1, no. 54 (24 May 1941): 4; 1, no. 55 (31 May 1941): 4; 1, no. 56 (7 June 1941): 4; 2, no. 65 (9 August 1941): 4; 2, no. 68 (30 August 1941): 4. My three interviewees—Aykut Tuzcu, Kamil Gereççi, and Murad Uçaner—attribute the sudden emergence of many rich families in the city to this phenomenon. Interview with Aykut Tuzcu, Kamil Gereççi, and Murad Uçaner, 28 March 2014, Gaziantep.

Bibliography

ARCHIVAL COLLECTIONS

Turkey

Ottoman and Turkish Archives

Başbakanlık Osmanlı Arşivi [Ottoman Prime Ministry Archives] (BOA)
Dahiliye Nezareti İskân-ı Aşâir ve Muhacirin Müdüriyeti (İAMM)
Dahiliye Nezareti Aşâir ve Muhacirin Müdüriyeti Umumiyesi (AMMU)
Dahiliye Nezareti Şifre Kalemi (BOA.DH.ŞFR)
Dahiliye Nezareti Emniyet-i Umumiye Müdürlüğü (BOA.DH.EUM)
Dahiliye Nezareti Emniyet-i Umumiye Asayiş Kalemi (BOA.DH.EUM.AYŞ)
Dahiliye Nezareti Emniyet-i Umumiye İkinci Şube (BOA.DH.EUM.II.Şb.)
Dahiliye Nezareti Emniyet-i Umumiye Üçüncü Şube (BOA.DH.EUM.III.Şb.)
Dahiliye Nezareti Emniyet-i Umumiye Beşinci Şube (BOA.DH.EUM.V.Şb)
Dahiliye Nezareti Hukuk Müşavirliği (BOA.DH.HMŞ)
Dahiliye Nezareti Emniyet-i Umumiye Müdüriyeti Memurin Kalemi (BOA.DH.EUM.MEM)
Dahiliye Nezareti Siyasî Kısım (BOA.DH.SYS)
Dahiliye Nezâreti İdâre-i Umumiye Belgeleri (BOA.DH.İUM)
Dahiliye Kalem-i Mahsus Evrakı (BOA.DH.KMS)
Meclis-i Vükela Mazbataları (BOA.MV)
Hariciye Nezareti Siyasî Kısım (BOA.HR.SYS)
Hariciye Nezareti Hukuk Müşavirliği İstişare Odası (BOA.HR.HMŞ.İŞO)
Bâb-ı Âlî Evrâk Odası (BOA.BEO)

Yıldız Esas Evrakı (BOA.Y.EE)
Başbakanlık Osmanlı Arşivi, Şura-yı Devlet (BOA.ŞD)
İrade Hususi (BOA.İ.HUS)
Bab-ı Ali Sadaret Evrakı, Mektubî Kalemi-Sadaret Mektubî Mühimme Kalemi (BOA.A.MKT.MHM)
Yıldız Perakende Evrakı Dahiliye Nezareti Maruzatı (BOA.Y.PRK.MYD)
Yıldız Dahiliye Nezareti Maruzatı (BOA.Y.PRK.DH)
Yıldız Perakende Evrakı Arzuhal ve Jurnaller (BOA.Y.PRK.AZJ)
Yıldız Mütenevvi Maruzat Evrakı (BOA.Y.MTV)
İrade-Dahiliye (BOA.İ.DH)
Bab-ı Ali Sadaret Evrakı, Mektubî Kalemi (BOA.DH.MKT)
Dahiliye Nezareti Mütenevvia Kısmı (BOA.DH.MTV)
Dahiliye Nezareti Emniyet-i Umumiye Müdüriyeti Kalem-i Hususi (BOA. DH.EUM.KLH)
Dahiliye Nezareti İrade-i Umumiye (BOA.DH.İ.UM)
Dâhiliye Nezareti Emniyet-i Umumiye Müdüriyeti Seyru Sefain Müdüriyeti (BOA.DH.EUM.SSM)
Dâhiliye Nezareti İrade-i Umumîye Müdüriyeti, Ermeniler Kataloğu (BOA. DH.İ.UM.EK)
Dâhiliye Nezareti Tesri-i Muamelat ve Islahat Komisyonu Muamelat Evrakı (BOA.DH.TMIK.M)
Maarif Nezareti Mektubî Kalemi (BOA.MF.MKT)
Hariciye Nezareti Istanbul Murahhaslığı (BOA.HR.İM)
Hariciye Nezareti Harbi Umumi (BOA.HR.HU)
Maliye Nezareti Emval-i Metruke Evrakı (BOA.ML.EEM)
Maliye Nezareti Vezne-i Umumi (BOA.ML.VZN)
Prime Ministry Republican Archives [Başbakanlık Cumhuriyet Arşivi (BCA)]
Başbakanlık Cumhuriyet Arşivi Toprak İskan Genel Müdürlüğü Arşivi (BCA.TİGMA)
Başvekâlet Kalem-i Mahsus Müdüriyeti

Gaziantep

Gaziantep İl Halk Kütüphanesi
Gaziantep Kent Arşivi
Gaziantep Üniversitesi Kütüphanesi Hulusi Yetkin Koleksiyonu
Gaziantep Savaşı Müzesi
Mahmut Oğuz Göğüş Arşivi
Şahinbey Belediyesi Fotoğraf Arşivi

Armenia

Hah'asdani Azkah'in Arxiw [National Archives of Armenia] (NAA)
Catalogue Numbers: 430 / 1 / 844; 430 / 1 / 824; 430 / 1 / 842; 430 / 1 / 838; 340 / 1 / 716
Hah'asdani Azkah'in Krataran [Armenian National Library]

Lebanon

Archives of the Haigazian University Library

France

La Bibliothèque Nubarian:
BNu / Fonds A. Andonian, P.J. 1 / 3, file 4, Aintab, "The Deportation of Armenians in Aintab"
BNu / Fonds "Cilicie: Rapatriement des Arméniens," Cilicie-Adana, 166
BNu / Fonds "Notes Sur La Cilicie"
BNu / Fonds M.S.C. / 1-V, Cilicia-Adana, 227
BNu / M.S.L., 1.v., Cilicia-Adana, 168, "Compte Rendu D'une Tournes Aintab et Marache" Archives of the Ministère des Affaires Étrangères (MAE)
Centre des Archives diplomatiques de Nantes (CADN)
France, Affaires Arméniennes, nos. 116–235
Service Historique de L'Armée de Terre (SHAT)

United Kingdom

National Archives, Public Record Office, Foreign Office Archives (FO)
Cabinet Office Files (CAB)
War Office Records (WO)

United States

US National Archives and Records Administration (NARA), College Park, MD:
Record Group: NA / RG
Record Group 59, General Records of the Department of State
Series 867, Internal Affairs of Turkey, 1910–1929
File 867.4016, Race Problems

American Board of Commissioners for Foreign Missions (ABCFM), Harvard University, Houghton Library, Boston: ABC. 16:9.1.6.1 Central Turkey Mission, Miscellaneous, 1817–1919, Unit 5, vol. 1–2

US Department of State, *Papers Relating to the Foreign Relations of the United States, 1923*, vol. II. Washington, DC: Government Printing Office, 1939, http://digicoll.library.wisc.edu/cgi-bin/FRUS/FRUSidx?type=goto&id=FRUS.FRUS1923v02&isize=M&submit=Go+to+page&page=1045, accessed 10 July 2013

Germany

Politisches Archiv des Auswärtiges Amt (Political Archive of the Foreign Office, DE / PA-AA) cited in Wolfang Gust, http://www.armenocide.net/

Krikor Guerguerian Private Archival Collection

Folder no: 22, file no: 11, 46, 59

PUBLISHED ARCHIVAL DOCUMENTS

1927 Yılı Umumi Nüfus Tahriri, Türkiye Cumhuriyeti Başvekalet İstatistik Umum Müdürlüğü, 28 October 1927, Fascicule 1–2, Ankara, 1929.

Andonian, Aram. *Medz O'jiry*. Boston: Bahag Printing House, 1921.

———. *Documents Officiels Concernant les Massacres Arméniens*. Translated by M. S. David-Beg, Paris: Imprimerie H. Turabian, 1920.

Annuaire Oriéntal: Commerce, Industrie, Administration, Magistraturé de l'Oriént, Edition 1914: Aintab

Antoine, E. *Les Massacres d'Armenie*. Bruxelles: Société belge de librairie, 1897.

The Armenian Genocide: Evidence from the German Foreign Office Archives, 1915–1916, ed. Wolfang Gust. New York: Berghahn Books, 2014.

Armenians in Ottoman Documents (1915–1920). Ankara: Başbakanlık Basımevi, 1995.

Arşiv Belgeleriyle Ermeni Faaliyetleri, 1914–1918, vol. 1. Ankara: Genelkurmay Basımevi, 2005.

Arşiv Belgeleriyle Ermeni Faaliyetleri, vol. 8. Ankara: Genelkurmay ATASE ve Genelkurmay Denetleme Başkanlığı Yayınları, 2008.

Askeri Tarih Belgeleri Dergisi, no. 81, December 1982.

Bardakçı, Murat. *Talat Paşa'nın Evrak-ı Metrukesi: Sadrazam Talat Paşa'nın Özel Arşivinde Bulunan Ermeni Tehciri Konusundaki Belgeler ve Hususi Yazışmalar*. Istanbul: Everest Yayınları, 2008.

Barton, L. James. *Turkish Atrocities: Statements of American Missionaries on the Destruction of Christian Communities in Ottoman Turkey, 1915–1917.* Ann Arbor, MI: Gomidas Institute, 1998.

Bliss, M. Edwin. *Turkey and the Armenian Atrocities.* Philadelphia: Edgewood Publishing Company, 1896.

"British Foreign Office Dossiers on Turkish War Criminals." In *British Foreign Office Dossiers on Turkish War Criminals,* ed. Vartkes Yeghiayan. La Verne, CA: American Armenian International College, 1991.

Bryce, James, and Toynbee, Arnold. *The Treatment of Armenians in the Ottoman Empire, 1915–1916: Document Presented to Viscount Grey of Falloden by Viscount Bryce.* Princeton, NJ: Gomidas Institute: Taderon Press, 2000.

Düstur, series 1, vol. 1. Istanbul: Matbaa-ı Amire, 1289 [1872].

Düstur, series 2, vol. 11. Istanbul: Evkaf Matbaası, 1928.

Eroğlu, Cengiz, et al. (ed.). *Salname-i Vilayet-i Halep, Ayıntab Kazası, 1320/102.* Ankara: Global Strateji Enstitüsü, 2007.

Filian, H. George, Rev. *Armenia and Her People.* Hartford, CT: American Publishing Company, 1896.

Germany. *Grosse Politik,* vol. 10, nos. 2410–76 *passim,* and vol. 12, nos. 2883–2910, 3065–3113 *passim.*

Germany, Turkey and Armenia, A Selection of Documentary Evidence Relating to the Armenian Atrocities from German and Other Sources. London: J. J. Keliher and Co., 1917.

Great Britain, Parliamentary Papers, Cmd. 1556. *Turkey no. 2, Dispatch from His Majesty's Ambassador at Paris, Enclosing the Franco-Turkish Agreement Signed at Angora on October 20, 1921,* London: His Majesty's Stationery Office, 1921, http://www.hri.org/docs/FT1921/Franco-Turkish_Pact_1921.pdf, accessed June 6, 2013.

Great Britain, Sessional Papers, 1896, vol. 95, C. 7927, *Turkey no. 2;* vol. 96, C. 8108, *Turkey no. 6;* C. 8273, *Turkey no. 8;* and 1897, vol. 10, C. 8305, *Turkey no. 3.*

Harris, J. Rendel, and Harris, B. Helen. *Letters from the Scenes of the Recent Massacres in Armenia.* London: James Nisbet & Co., 1897.

Jaeschke, Gotthard. *Kurtuluş Savaşı ile İlgili İngiliz Belgeleri.* Ankara: TTK, 1991.

Kuyumdjian, Lut'fik. *Lkyal Kuykere Hartser* [The Question of Abandoned Property], Surp Prgich Hivantanonts Darekirk (General Year Book of the National Hospital), Istanbul, 1928, 1929, 1931, 1932, 1939.

Lepsius, Johannes (ed.). *Archives du génocide des Arméniens.* Paris: Fayard, 1986.

———. *Armenia and Europe*. London: Hodder and Stoughton, 1897.
———. *Deutschland und Armenien, 1914–1918*. Potsdam, 1919.
———. *Der Todesgang des armenischen Volkes: Bericht über das Schicksal des armenischen Volkes in der Türkei wahrend des Weltkrieges*. Potsdam, 1919.
Mecmua-i Kavanin-i Cedide-i Osmani. İstanbul, Matbaa-i Kütübhane-i Cihan, 1327 (1911).
The Memoirs of Naim Bey, Turkish Official Documents Relating to the Deportations and Massacres of Armenians, compiled by Aram Andonian. London: Hodder and Stoughton, 1920.
The Memoirs of Naim Bey. Newton Square, PA: Armenian Historical Research Association, 1965.
Meray, L. Seha. *Lozan Barış Konferansı, Tutanaklar-Belgeler*, vol. 2, 6, 8. Istanbul: Yapı Kredi Yayınları, 2001.
Osmanlı Belgelerinde Ermenilerin Sevk ve İskânı (1878–1920). Ankara: Devlet Arşivleri Genel Müdürlüğü, 2007.
Osmanlı Belgelerinde Ermeniler (1915–1920). Başbakanlık Devlet Arşivleri Genel Müdürlüğü Yayınları: Ankara, 1995.
Osmanlı Belgelerinde Ermeniler (1915–1920). Ankara: Osmanlı Arşivi Daire Başkanlığı Yayını, 1994.
Paşa, Nazım Hüseyin. *Ermeni Olayları Tarihi*. Ankara: Başbakanlık Basımevi, 1998.
Şimşir, Bilal. *British Documents on Atatürk*, V. I. Ankara: TTK Yayınları, 1973.
———. *Lozan Telgrafları II (Şubat–Ağustos 1923)*. Ankara: TTK, 1994.
Supplément, 1895–1896. Paris: Imprimerie Nationale, no. 1–178, 1897.
Turkish–Armenian Conflict Documents, ed. Hikmet Özdemir and Yusuf Sarınay. Ankara: TBMM Kültür Sanat ve Yayın Kurulu Yayınları, 2007.
United States Official Records on the Armenian Genocide 1915–1917, ed. Ara Sarafian. Princeton, NJ: Gomidas Institute, 2004.
Yeghiayan, Vartkes (ed.). *British Reports on Ethnic Cleansing in Anatolia, 1919–1922: The Armenian-Greek Section*. Glendale, CA: Center for Armenian Remembrance, 2007.

PARLIAMENTARY PROCEEDINGS

Meclis-i Mebusan Zabıt Ceridesi, Period 3, Assembly Year 5, vol. 1. Ankara: TBMM Basımevi, 1992.
T. B. M. M. Gizli Celse Zabıtları, Period 1, Assembly Year 3, vol. 3. Ankara: Türkiye İş Bankası Kültür Yayınları, 1985.

OTHER DOCUMENTS PUBLISHED IN TURKISH

Kardeş, Salâhaddin. *'Tehcir' ve Emval-i Metruke Mevzuatı*. Ankara: T. C. Maliye Bakanlığı Strateji Geliştirme Başkanlığı, 2008.

T. C. Maliye Vekaleti Milli Emlak Müdürlüğü, *Milli Emlak Muamelelerine Müteallik Mevzuat*. Ankara: Başvekalet Matbaası, 1937.

Newspapers (in the 1896–1941 period)

Alemdar
Ati
Chagadamard
Cumhuriyet
Darakir
Gaziantep Gazetesi
Harach
İkdam
İleri
Memleket
New York Times
Resmi Ceride
Resmi Gazete
Takvim-i Vekayi
Tanin
Tarik
Tasvir-i Efkâr
Tercüman-ı Hakikat
Tevhid-i Efkâr
Times
Vakit
Yeni Gaziantep
Yeni Tasvir-i Efkâr

Online Documents and Internet Sites

http://www.armenocide.net/ (accessed 23 March 2015)
http://www.mevzuat.adalet.gov.tr/html/364.html (accessed 3 August 2012)
http://www.gto.org.tr/Eski-Yoneticiler-icerik-7.html (accessed 6 June 2013)
http://ermenistan.de/ermenilerin-ticari-ekonomik-faaliyeti-antep/ (accessed 3 March 2014)

http://wwi.lib.byu.edu/index.php/Treaty_of_Lausanne (accessed 23 March 2012)
http://www.massviolence.org/IMG/article_PDF/The-expulsion-of-non-Turkish-ethnic-and-religious-groups.pdf (accessed 6 June 2013)
http://www.ushmm.org/m/pdfs/Publication_OP_2003-01.pdf (accessed 23 March 2014)
Hürriyet, 19 September 2006, www.hurriyet.com.tr/gundem/5109117_p.asp (accessed 8 May 2014)
Radikal, 20 September 2006, www.radikal.com.tr/haber.php?haberno=199165 (accessed 8 May 2014)
http://bianet.org/bianet/bianet/85432-osmanli-arsivleri-acilirsa-resmitez-zayiflar (accessed 8 May 2014)
http://www.hyeetch.nareg.com.au/genocide/oppres_p4.html (accessed 28 September 2014)
http://www.gkv.k12.tr/kurucumuz.asp (accessed 26 October 2014)
http://www.massviolence.org/The-Extermination-of-Ottoman-Armenians-by-the-Young-Turk-Regime (accessed 14 July 2014)
http://sahinbeysakaryaortaokulu.meb.k12.tr/meb_iys_dosyalar/27/08/716339/icerikler/sakarya-ortaokulu tarihcesi_1568726.html?CHK=88765129affaa4c938af1732dd3f9df8 (accessed 16 December 2014)
http://www.kulturvarliklari.gov.tr/TR,43815/gaziantep—hasan-suzer-etnografya-muzesi.html (accessed 18 March 2015)
http://www.gto.org.tr/Eski-Yoneticiler-icerik-7.html (accessed 12 November 2015)
http://www.gaziantep27.net/guncel-kendirli-kilisesi-kultur-merkezi-oldu-462885.html (accessed 16 July 2015)
http://www.ataturkanimuzesi.org/hakkimizda.html (accessed 18 September 2015)

Unpublished Doctoral and Master's Theses

Astourian, Stephan H. "Testing World-System Theory, Cilicia (1830s–1890s): Armenian-Turkish Polarization and the Ideology of Modern Ottoman Historiography." PhD diss., University of California, Los Angeles, 1996.
Atnur, Ethem İbrahim. "Tehcirden Dönen Rum ve Ermenilerin İskanı." Master's thesis, Erzurum University, Erzurum, 1991.
Canbakal, Hülya. "Aintab at the End of the 17th Century: A Study of Notables and Urban Politics." PhD diss., Harvard University, Cambridge, MA, 1999.

Çetinkaya, Yusuf Doğan. "Muslim Merchants and Working Class in Action: Nationalism, Social Mobilization and Boycott Movement in the Ottoman Empire 1908–1914," PhD. diss., Leiden University, 2010.

Durmaz, Gözel Oya. "A City Transformed: War, Demographic Change and Profiteering in Kayseri (1915–1920)." PhD diss., METU, Ankara, 2014.

Eroğlu, Tayfun. "Tehcirden Milli Mücadeleye Ermeni Malları (1915–1922)." Master's thesis, Dokuz Eylül University, İzmir, 2008.

Günaydın, Adem. "The Return and Resettlement of the Relocated Armenians (1918–1920)." Master's thesis, METU, Ankara, 2007.

Kennedy, W. Judd. "American Missionaries in Turkey & Northern Syria and the Development of Central Turkey and Aleppo Colleges, 1874–1967." Master's thesis, College of William and Mary, Williamsburg, VA, 2008.

Kocaman, Aydın. "Basında Ali Cenani Bey ve Mahmut Muhtar Paşa." Master's thesis, Dokuz Eylül University, İzmir, 2006.

Latham, G. Michelle. "Economic Motives for Total Genocide: A Comparison of the Armenian, the Holocaust and Rwandan Genocides." Master's thesis, Boston College, Boston, 2000.

Matossian, Der Bedross. "Ethnic Politics in Post-Revolutionary Ottoman Empire: Armenians, Arabs, and Jews during the Second Constitutional Period (1908–1909)." PhD diss., Columbia University, New York, 2008.

Miller, Owen. "Sasun 1894: Mountains, Missionaries and Massacres at the End of the Ottoman Empire." PhD diss., Columbia University, New York, 2015.

Taşkın, Faruk. "Amerikan Misyoner Okullarından 'Merkezi Türkiye Koleji' (1876–1924)." PhD diss., Mersin University, Mersin, 2007.

Tiryaki, Kerim. "Gaziantep'teki Ermeniler (1895–1923)." Master's thesis, Gaziantep University, Gaziantep, 2003.

Türkyılmaz, Yektan. "Rethinking Genocide: Violence and Victimhood in Eastern Anatolia, 1913–1915." PhD. diss., Duke University, Durham, NC, 2011.

Periodicals

Aintabi Or
Ayntabiana
Başpınar Aylık Edebiyat ve Kültür Mecmuası
Datev
Gaziantep Halkevi Mecmuası
Gaziantep'i Tanıtıyoruz

Gaziantep Kültür Dergisi
Hah Ah'nt'ab
Hayat Tarih Mecmuası
The Missionary Herald, APS Online
Nor Ah'nt'ab
Türk Yurdu
Yeprad Tert

Interviews

Interview conducted with Alice Kazazian by Richard Hovannisian, 1986, Philadelphia.
Interview conducted with Yevnige Berekjiklian Koundakjian, Zoryan Institute Oral History Project, released online on 7 January 2015.
Interview conducted with an anonymous person, 3 March 2014, Gaziantep.
Interview conducted with Murad Uçaner, Aykut Tuzcu, and Kamil Gereççi, 18 April 2014, Gaziantep.
Interview conducted with Cemil Aslan, 17 November 2014, Gaziantep.
Interviews conducted with İclal İncioglu and Mehmet N. Gültekin, 23 December 2014, Gaziantep.
Interview conducted with Kevork Arslanian, 9 January 2015, Beirut.

Acknowledgments

During the course of my research for this book, I found myself traveling between Boston, London, Paris, Gaziantep, Istanbul, Ankara, Yerevan, and Beirut. Yet, before I extend my gratitude to those I met along the way, I must first thank my family. Without them: Hasan, Hanım, Dilek, Hamit, Figen, Deniz Çağan, Ali Aras, and Dila Zeynep Kurt, I would not have been able to accomplish anything. My family's love and encouragement have made me who I am today.

I have been a beneficiary of outstanding scholars and colleagues at Clark University; California State University, Fresno; Harvard University; and Polonsky Academy at the Van Leer Jerusalem Institute. First and foremost, I offer my gratitude to Taner Akçam. It has been an honor working with and learning from him for the past ten years. His tireless dedication to his students and his never-ending passion for work are utterly inspiring.

Richard G. Hovannisian and Hans-Lukas Kieser remained actively involved in this project. It was Richard Hovannisian who first suggested I apply to Clark University and work with Akçam, and it has been a blessing receiving his advice and wisdom for the past five years. His brilliant and thoughtful comments have enhanced my analysis in ways I did not imagine possible. In addition, Hans-Lukas Kieser has challenged and motivated me to dig deeper into the history and fortify my research. I have valued our conversations over the past six years and am a better historian thanks to the dedication and energy both these scholars have invested in me. Their encouragement and insight guided my project and had a profound impact on the final product.

There are a few people who deserve special thanks here. This book would not have been possible without Murad Uçaner's unprecedented help and support. As a local historian and novelist from Gaziantep, Murad lent his deep knowledge made an enormous contribution to this work. Yektan Türkyılmaz, Donald Bloxham, Margaret Lavinia Anderson, Stefan Ihrig, and Spyros Tsoutsoumpis contributed their valuable time to read various drafts of my book and shared considerations and critiques with me that greatly enriched the work. I will forever be indebted to them. By hiring me as a research associate in the Armenian Studies Program at California State University, Fresno, Barlow Der Mugrdechian and Sergio La Porta provided me with a unique opportunity and comfortable scholarly environment to finish my book. Without their support, this project would never have been accomplished.

I am profoundly grateful to Cemal Kafadar for his support and quiet encouragement, which were critical to my pursuit of an academic career. The Center for Middle Eastern Studies at Harvard University and Polonsky Academy at the Van Leer Jerusalem Institute provided an unsurpassed home for research and writing. I would especially like to thank William Granara, Shai Lavi, and Marc Polonsky for that.

Uğur Z. Peçe, Seçil Yılmaz, Varak Ketsemanian, Marc Mamigonian, Owen Miller, and Edvin Minassian have been wonderful colleagues and friends and sources of inspiration. Yektan Türkyılmaz shared his enthusiasm for the manuscript and his characteristically discerning criticisms and suggestions. Chris McLaren read the manuscript carefully and sharpened it. Ara Sarafian generously gave his time to prepare the maps. They deserve special thanks. I am deeply thankful to Mihran Minassian, a distinctive and humble researcher and archivist, for sharing his priceless photo album with me.

Kathleen McDermott demonstrated enormous patience in editing and improving this book. I want to thank her sincerely, as well as others at Harvard University Press.

I owe a special note of gratitude to my longtime pal Oğuz Alyanak, who could not resist my incessant demands and has always given me incredible encouragement and intellectual stimulation. And the memory of the late Pakrad Kazazian is still between the lines of this book, as his invaluable help made it possible.

I have nothing but thanks and kind words for the librarians and archivists in many places whom I imposed upon over the years. A great deal of the research that went into the creation of this book was made possible by the generous support of the Agnes Manoogian Haurasth Fellowship in Armenian Genocide Studies; the Calouste Gulbenkian Foundation Armenian Studies Scholarship; the National Association for Armenian Studies and Research; the Knights of Vartan Fund for Armenian Studies; the Armenian Studies Program at California State University, Fresno; the Sarah Chitchian Family Foundation; the Nazarian Family Foundation; and the Hrant Dink Foundation.

I would especially like to thank the following people who directly contributed to this book: Alev Er, Raymond Kévorkian, Razmik Panossian, Edhem Eldem, Boghos Levon Zekian, Deborah Dwork, Thomas Kühne, Ali Yaycıoğlu, Christine Philliou, Ehud Toledano, Philip Dwyer, Dror Ze'evi, Eyal Ginio, Ayhan Aktar, Yiğit Akın, Uğur Ümit Üngör, Ryan Gingeras, Hamit Bozarslan, Halil Berktay, Stephan Astourian, Vahram Shemmassian, Levon Marashlian, Vahé Tashjian, Oktay Özel, Janet Klein, Hilmar Kaiser, Nilay Özok Gündoğan, Ayşe Ozil, Khaled Fahmy, Bedross Der Matossian, Yavuz Aykan, Heghnar Watenpaugh, Keith Watenpaugh, Esra Özyürek, Marc Bauer, Olga Litvak, Lerna Ekmekçioğlu, Raz Segal, Amos Goldberg, Dirk Moses, Michael Provence, Eric D. Weitz, Basheer Basheer, Gürer Karagedikli, Fikret Yılmaz, Ahmad Amarra, Sam Dolbee, Lale Can, Murat Yıldız, Chris Gratien, Elvira Di Bona, George Shirinian, George Mavropoulos, Fırat Kurt, Erdal Kaynar, Stefan Ionescu, Mike Phoenix, Oğuz Dilek, Tanıl Bora, Kerem Ünüvar, Ahmet İnsel, Nurhan Becidian, Hırant Gulian, Mark Chenian, Zeynep Türkyılmaz, Antranig Dakessian, Ömer Turan, Güven Gürkan Öztan, Ümit Cizre, Nora Şeni, Henry Shapiro, Güney Çeğin, Ebru Sönmez, Richard Dekmejian, Ömer Türkoğlu, Osman Kavala, Ali Bayramoğlu, Meltem Karadağ, M. Nuri Güntekin, Khatchig Mouradian, Sabri Atman, Natalia Lazar, Anna Aleksanian, Harry and Hripsime Parsekian, Caroline Mugar, Bill Hausrath, Robert A. Kaloosdian, George Aghjayan, Ohannes and Seta Kulag, Shusan Yeni-Komshian

Teager, Varteni and Tatoul Mosditchian, Vicken Assilian, Maggie Goschin, Perla Kotoian, Harold Demirdjian, Harout Ekmanian, Anahid Astoian, Rakel and Delal Dink, Robert Kurkjian, Aykut Tuzcu, Vahram Ter-Matevossian, Ferda Balancar, Michael Rettig, Serdar Korucu, Emre Can Dağlıoğlu, Aris Nalcı, Murat Arslan, Hüseyin Ovayolu, and Uğurcan Arabacıbaşı.

Chapter 1 includes, with minor edits, the text of "Reform and Violence in the Hamidian Era: The Political Context of the 1895 Armenian Massacres in Aintab," *Holocaust and Genocide Studies* 32, no. 3 (2018): 404–423. Chapter 2 builds on ideas first discussed in "The Curious Case of Ahmed Necmeddin Bey: A Look into the Sociopolitical Climate in Aintab on the Eve of 1915," *Middle Eastern Studies* 52, no. 5 (2016): 804–824. Chapters 3, 5, and 6 include portions of text published as "From Aintab to Gaziantep: The Reconstitution of an Elite on the Ottoman Periphery," in *The End of Ottomans: The Genocide of 1915 and the Politics of Turkish Nationalism,* ed. Hans-Lukas Kieser et al. (New York: Bloomsbury / I.B.Tauris, June 2019), 287–319. Chapters 5 and 6 include research first presented in *The Spirit of the Laws: The Plunder of Wealth in the Armenian Genocide* (New York: Berghahn, 2015). All texts are reprinted with kind permission.

More than anything else, the love of my mother, Hanım, and father, Hasan, sustained me through the trying process of writing this book, and to them I dedicate it. All errors are, of course, mine alone.

Index

Page numbers in italics refer to illustrations; page numbers in bold refer to tables.

www.ingramcontent.com/pod-product-compliance
Lightning Source LLC
Chambersburg PA
CBHW022001071225
35624CB00046B/64/J
* 9 7 8 0 6 7 4 2 4 7 9 4 9 *